Street by Str

C000075586

WEST SUSSEX
PLUS BRIGHTON, HASLEMERE, HOVE, PETERSFIELD

Enlarged Areas Bognor Regis, Chichester, Crawley, Horsham, Worthing

1st edition May 2001

© Automobile Association Developments Limited 2001

This product includes map data licensed from Ordnance Survey® with the permission of the Controller of Her Majesty's Stationery Office. © Crown copyright 2000. All rights reserved. Licence No: 399221.

Published by AA Publishing (a trading name of Automobile Association Developments Limited, whose registered office is Norfolk House, Priestley Road, Basingstoke, Hampshire, RG24 9NY. Registered number 1878835).

Mapping produced by the Cartographic Department of The Automobile Association.

A CIP Catalogue record for this book is available from the British Library.

Printed by in Italy by Printer Trento srl

Ref: MD023

Key to map pages   ii-iii

Key to map symbols   iv-1

Enlarged scale pages   2-13

Street by Street   14-265

Index – towns & villages   266-268

Index – streets   269-309

Index – featured places   309-316

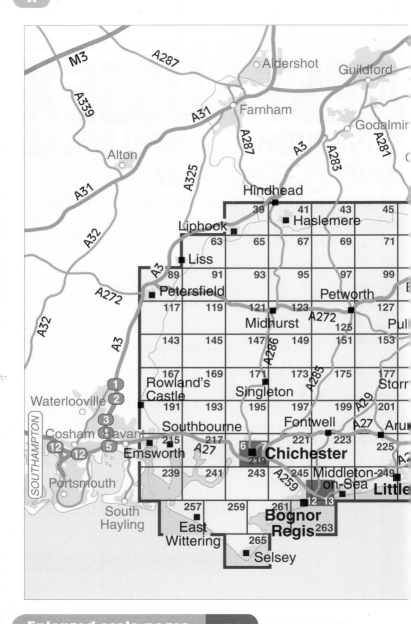

Enlarged scale pages 1:17,500 3.6 inches to 1 mile

0 1/2 miles 1

0 1/2 1 kilometres 1 1/2

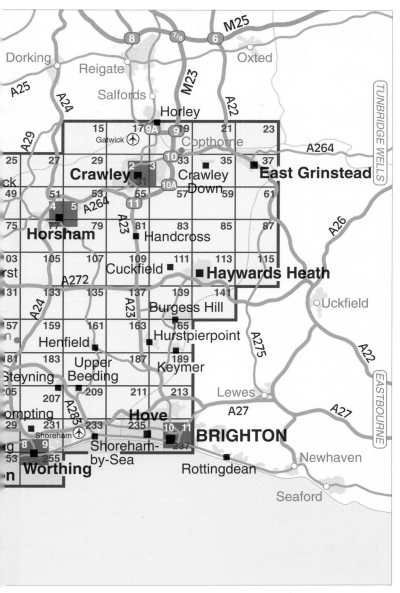

2.5 inches to 1 mile

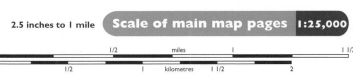

| 0 | 1/2 | miles | 1 | 1 1/2 |

| 0 | 1/2 | 1 | kilometres | 1 1/2 | 2 |

iv

Junction 9	Motorway & junction	P+🚌	Park & Ride
Services	Motorway service area	🚌	Bus/coach station
	Primary road single/dual carriageway		Railway & main railway station
Services	Primary road service area		Railway & minor railway station
	A road single/dual carriageway	⊖	Underground station
	B road single/dual carriageway	⊖	Light railway & station
	Other road single/dual carriageway	++++++++++	Preserved private railway
	Restricted road	LC	Level crossing
	Private road	•—•—•—	Tramway
← ←	One way street	----------	Ferry route
	Pedestrian street	....	Airport runway
==========	Track/ footpath	—·—·—·—	Boundaries- borough/ district
	Road under construction	▼▼▼▼▼▼▼▼	Mounds
⌐ = = = ⌐	Road tunnel	**93**	Page continuation 1:25,000
P	Parking	**7**	Page continuation to enlarged scale 1:17,500

River/canal
lake, pier

♿ Toilet with
disabled facilities

Aqueduct
lock, weir

■ Petrol station

465
▲
Winter Hill

Peak (with
height in
metres)

PH Public house

Beach

PO Post Office

Coniferous
woodland

Public library

Broadleaved
woodland

i Tourist
Information
Centre

Mixed
woodland

⚔ Castle

Park

Historic house/
building

Cemetery

Wakehurst
Place NT

National Trust
property

Built-up
area

M Museum/
art gallery

Featured building

✝ Church/chapel

┤┦┤┦┤ City wall

♘ Country park

A&E Accident &
Emergency
hospital

Theatre/
performing arts

Toilet

Cinema

I grid square represents 500 metres

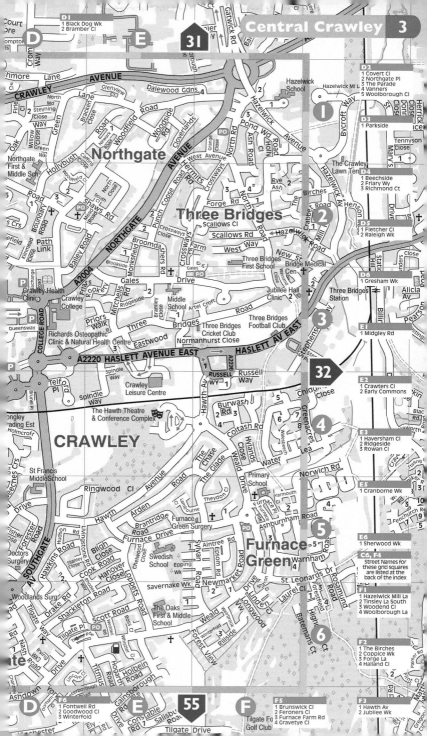

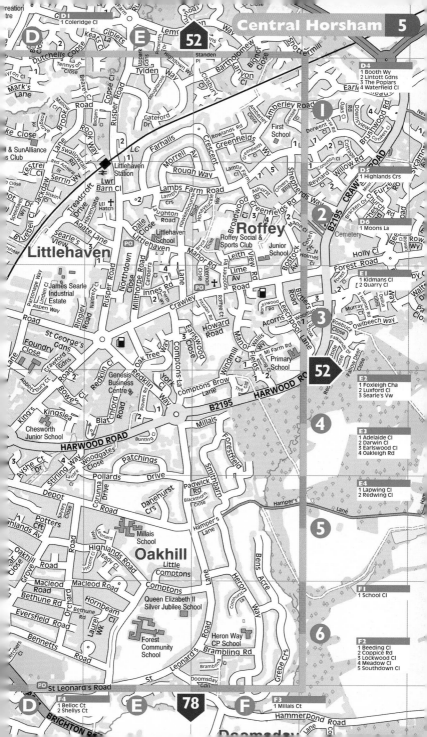

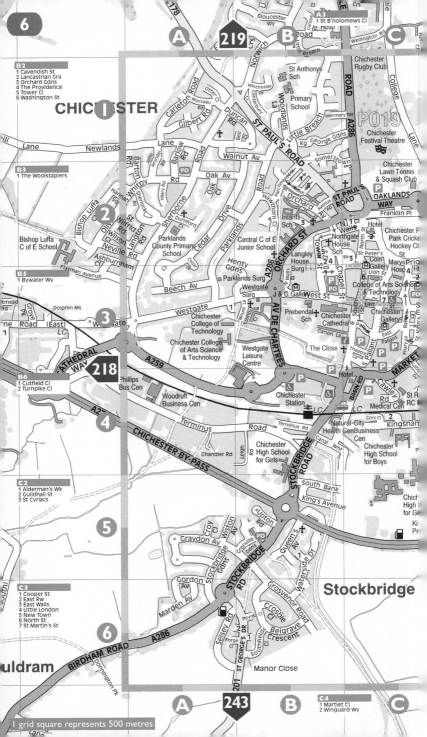

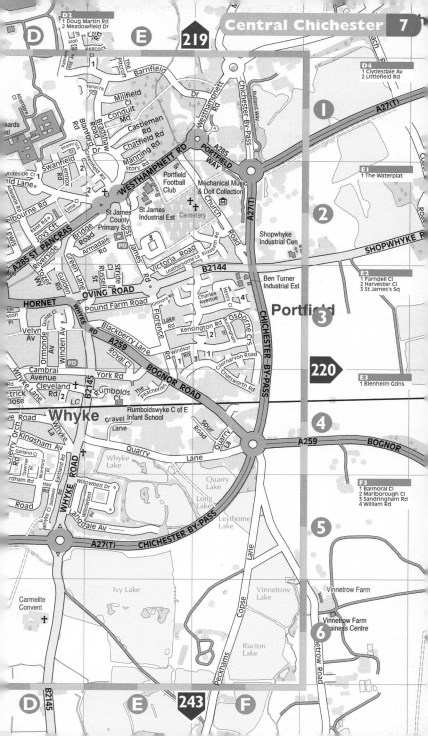

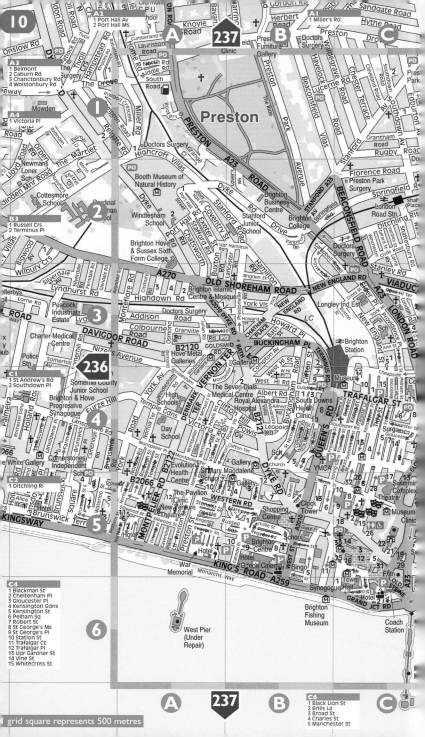

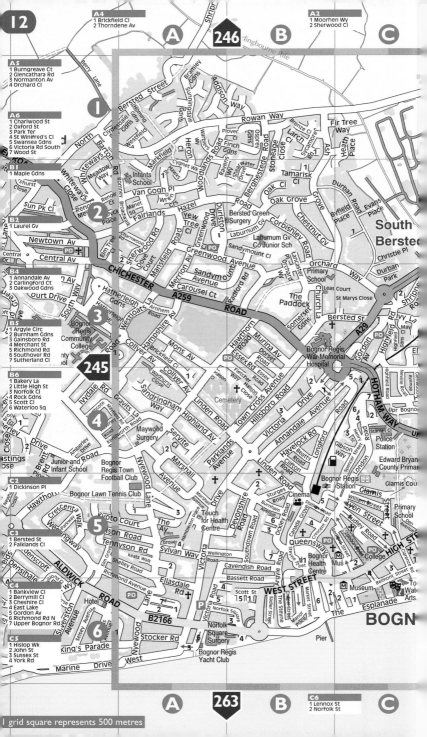

12

A4
1 Brickfield Cl
2 Thorndene Av

A2
1 Moorhen Wy
2 Sherwood Cl

A5
1 Burngreave Ct
2 Glencathara Rd
3 Normanton Av
4 Orchard Cl

A6
1 Charlwood St
2 Oxford St
3 Park Ter
4 St Winifred's Cl
5 Swansea Gdns
6 Victoria Rd South
7 Wood St

B1
1 Maple Gdns

B2
1 Laurel Gv

B4
1 Annandale Av
2 Carlingford Ct
3 Oakwood Gdns

B5
1 Argyle Circ
2 Burnham Gdns
3 Gainsboro Rd
4 Merchant St
5 Richmond Rd
6 Southover Rd
7 Sutherland Cl

B6
1 Bakery La
2 Little High St
3 Norfolk Cl
4 Rock Gdns
5 Scott Cl
6 Waterloo Sq

C2
1 Dickinson Pl

C3
1 Bersted St
2 Falklands Cl

C4
1 Bankview Cl
2 Berrymill Cl
3 Cheshire Cl
4 East Lake
5 Gordon Av
6 Richmond Rd N
7 Upper Bognor Rd

C5
1 Hislop Wk
2 John St
3 Sussex St
4 York Rd

C6
1 Lennox St
2 Norfolk St

246

245

263

South Bersted

BOGN

1 grid square represents 500 metres

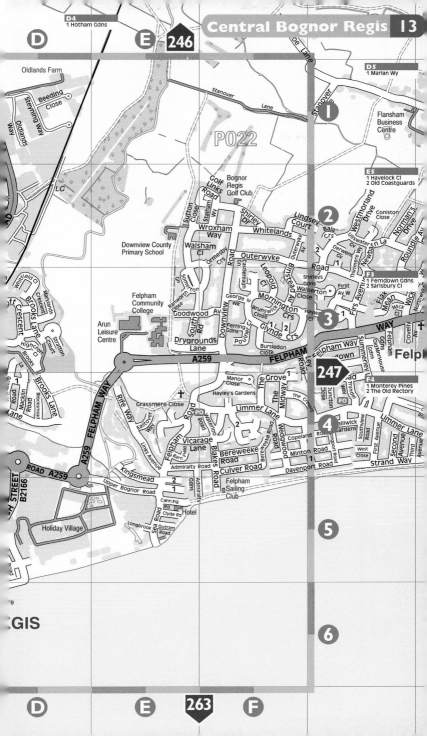

F G H J K

I
2
3
4
16
5
6
7
8

Hales
Bridge

Cidermill Road

Blanks Lane

Red
House

Hatchetts

Sturtwood Farm

Hotel

Beggarshouse Lane

Cudworth Lane

Cudworth

Partridge Lane

The Greenings

Cidermill
Farm

Glover's
Wood

Duke's Drive

**Russ
Hill**

Boothlands
Farm

Charlwood La

Russ Hill

Upper
Prestw
Farm

Ivyhouse
Farm

Sussex Border Path

Oaklands Park

Prestwood Lane

Lower Prestw
Farm

Partridge Lane

Jordans

Orltons

Orlton

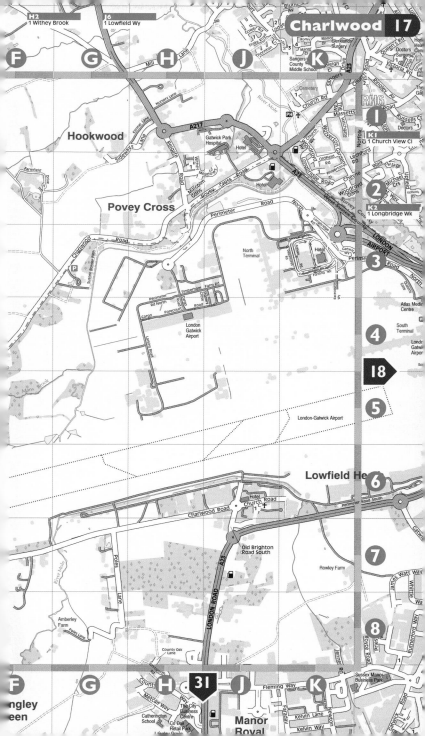

A B C D E

Smalheid

Whitehouse
Farm

Rough
Beech

Byshe
Court

Glen Farm

Downs Lane

1

Chithurst Lane

2

Chithurst
Farm

Kingswood
Farm

Dowlands
Farm

3

Park Lane

4

Keepers
Farm

West
Park

Chithurst

B2028

19

Baker's
Wood

Chithurst Lane

WEST PARK ROAD

5

EFFINGHAM

Dowlands Lane

Perry Farm

East Hill Lane

ROAD

6

Effingham Lane

B2037

Beechfield

Rowland
Close

Heatherley

SNOW HILL

Snowhill Lane

Herons
Lea

Herons Close

Domewood

Snowhill
Business Centre

Herons Lea

7

B2028

WEST PARK ROAD

Hotel

Effingham Park
Golf Club

Chapel Lane

Snowhill
Business Centre

COPTHORNE ROAD

Lake View Road

Furnace Road

COMMON

8

ROAD

Lashmere

Mill Lane

Southland Park

Newlands

HILL ROAD

TURNERS

Green Lane

SNOW HILL

A264

Great Frenches
Park

Falcot Road

Furnace

siness

Sussex Border Path

PO

Newland Green

Southland
View Park

A B C D E

Barn
Court

Shepherd's
Farm

TURNERS HILL ROAD

Cuttinglye

Cuttinglye
Wood

Fu
W

Che

34

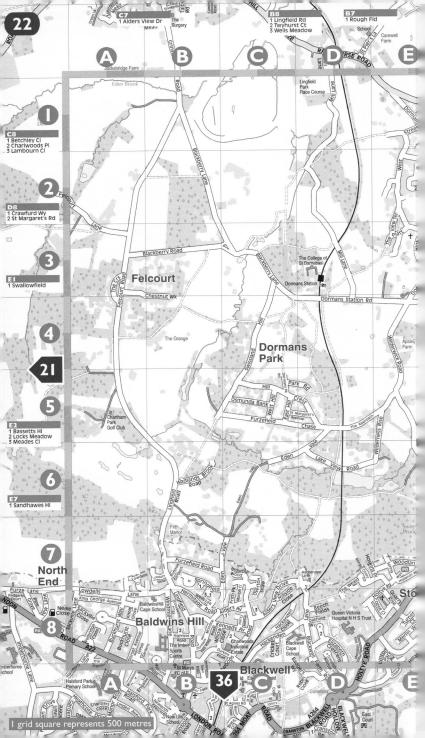

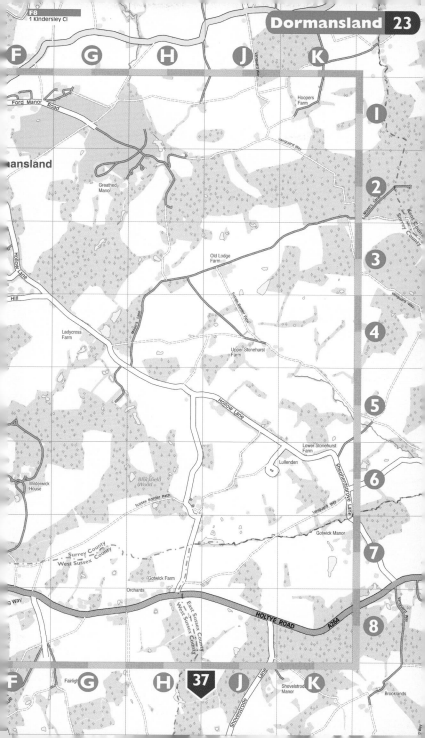

F8
1 Kindersley Cl

F G H J K

1

Hoopers
Farm

Ford Manor Road

ansland

2

Greathed
Manor

Moor's Lane

Kent County
Surrey County

3

Vanguard Way

Old Lodge
Farm

Hollow
Lane

Sussex Border Path

Hill

4

Ladycross
Farm

Upper Stonehurst
Farm

Moor's Lane

5

Hollow Lane

Lower Stonehurst
Farm

Lullenden

Shepherdsgrove Lane

6

Blockfield
Wood

Wilderwick
House

Sussex Border Path

Vanguard Way

Gotwick Manor

7

Surrey County
West Sussex County

Gotwick Farm

g Way

Orchards

East Sussex County
West Sussex County

HOLTYE ROAD A264

8

Vanguard Way

F G H 37 J K

Fairligh

Shovelstrode
Manor

Brooklands

Shovelstrode Lane

Mayes Green

Pond Head Lane

New Ba

Lowerhouse Farm

Hotel

Leith Vale

Standon Lane

Walliswood

Walliswood Farm

Red Junction Lane

Trip Lane

Church Lane

Horsham Road

Froggetts Lane

Lane

PH

Oakfields

Somersbury Wood

Smokejack Farm

Oakwoodhill

26

Honeywood Lane

Broadstone Farm

Honeywood Lane

Monks

hans Farm

Sussex Border Path

Surrey

West Suss

Pinkhurst Farm

Horsham Road

Monks Lane

Sussex Border Path

Monks Lane

Monks Farm

Furzen Lane

Honeywood House

Ridge Farm

Horsham Road

Charmans Farm

en's

49

F G H J K

Vann
Lake

Tiphar

Weare Street

Knoll Farm

HORSHAM ROAD

Clock
House

I Taylors

Holbrook
Farm

Osbrooks

2

Gages
Farms

Ridge Farm

A24

Sussex Border Path

Sussex Border Path

3 Mudberidge's

Sussex Border Path

Surrey County
West Sussex County

ale

Sussex Border Path

Wattlehurst
Farm

Old
Barn

4

Stammert
Business
Centre

Hewells
Farm

28

Kingsfold

DORKING ROAD

Tickfold
Farm

5

Marches Road

THE
Marches

6 Great
Benhams

Friday Street

A24

Green Lan

Langhurst
Close

Bolding Brook

Langhurst

7

Langhurstwood Road

Durfold

8

A24

Geerings

Graylands

A   B   **14**   C   D   E

I

2

3

4

27

5

6

7

8

A   B   **52**   C   D   E

Pleystowe Farm

Rusper Road

Taylors

Clock House

Lyne House

Gages Farms

Ridge Farm

Cowix Farm

Highams

Mightridge's Hill

Sussex Border Path

Capel Road

Surrey County
West Sussex County

New Barn Farm

Sussex

Friday Street

Stammerham Business Centre

Sussex Border Path

Dial Post Farm

Ashmore

Horsham

Friday Street

Great Benhams

The Nunnery

Manns Farm

Wimland Road

Wimland Road

Langhurst Close

Green Lane

Langhurst

Langhurstwood Road

Green Lane

Horsham Road

Old Holbrook

Coorn

Graylands

I grid square represents 500 metres

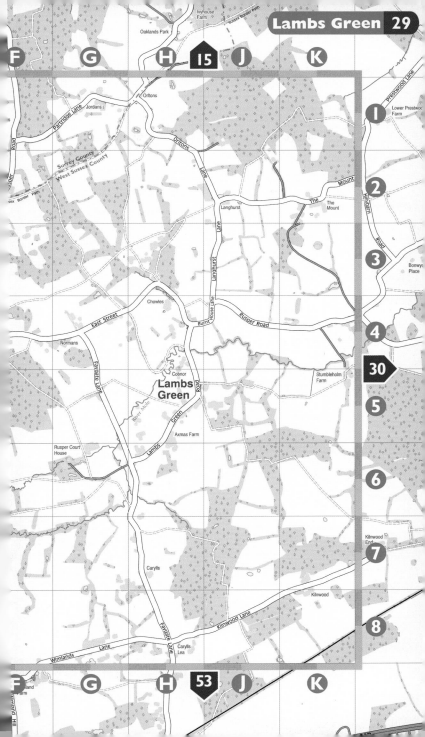

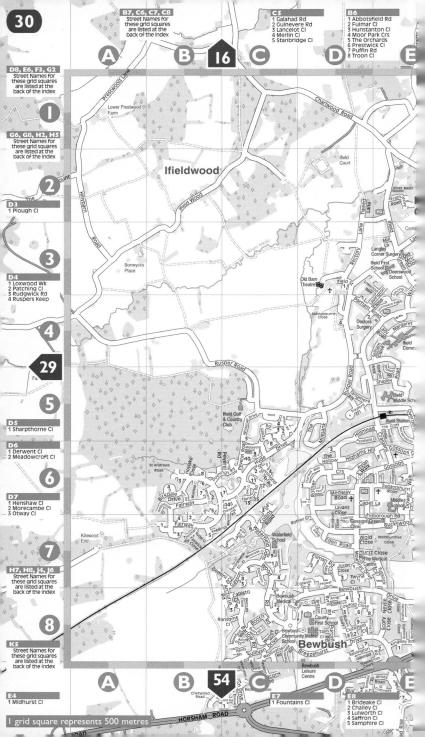

30

I grid square represents 500 metres

A6
1 Beverley Ms
2 Blackfold Rd
3 Brambletye Rd
4 Burwash Rd
5 Dedisham Cl
6 Freshfield Cl
7 Gosden Cl
8 Walesbeech

A5
1 Hawth Av
2 Jubilee Wk

A3
1 Hazelwick Mill La
2 Tinsley La South
3 Woodend Cl
4 Woolborough La

A1
1 Royston Cl

A2
1 Kingfisher Cl

A8
1 Fontwell Rd
2 Goodwood Cl
3 Winterfold

B4
1 Kimberley Rd

B5
1 Maunsell Pk
2 Three Bridges Rd
3 Williams Wy

B6
1 Stanier Cl
2 Stroudley Cl

B7
1 Baxter Cl
2 Hawkhurst Wk
3 Normandy Cl
4 Sheffield Cl
5 Strudgate Cl

B8
1 Charleston Ct
2 Holder Rd
3 Leonardslee Ct
4 Nymans Ct

C3
1 Farmleigh Cl
2 Kipling Cl
3 Milton Mount Av
4 Shelley Cl

C5
1 Sedgewick Cl

D1
1 Horndean Cl
2 Rossmore Cl

D2
1 Balliol Cl
2 Blenheim Cl
3 Blindley Rd
4 Heathfield
5 Lancaster Cl
6 Milton Mount Av

D7
1 Adelphi Cl
2 Benjamin Cl
3 Bray Cl
4 Delfont Cl
5 Drury Cl
6 Strand Cl

D8
1 Bisham Cl
2 Purley Cl
3 Wilson Cl

Three Bridges
Pound Hill
Furnace Green
Maidenbower
Worth

I grid square represents 500 metres

COPTHORNE

A264

F G H 19 J K

THORNE WAY

ROAD

1

2

3

4

34

5

6

7

8

Oak Close
Westway
Bridgelands
Erica Way
Brookside
The Meadow
Erica Way
Caruma Drive
Kitsmead
Brookhill
Church Lane
Fairway
The Copthorne
Business Centre
Church Road
Church Junior
School
Knowle Drive
Arms
New Town
Infro
Bramble Close
Border
Close
Copthorne
Spring
Gardens
Copthorne Golf
Club
Copthorne
Business Park
Road
COMMON ROAD
PO
Fernery Green
Sussex Border Path

Copthorne
Squash Club
Hotel
Copthorne
Squash
Club
Pot Common

Old Hollow

Ley
House

Old
Rowfant

Home
Farm

Rowfant

Wallage

Hundred
Acres

Rowfant
Business
Centre

Hayheath

Worth Way

Compasses
Corner

Turners Hill Road

RH10

Worth
Hall

Majors Hill

Tulleys
Farm

Northlodge
est

Brantridge Lane

Standinghall
Farm

The Grove

Charbour

South Hill

PADDOCKHURST ROAD

Back

F G H 57 J K

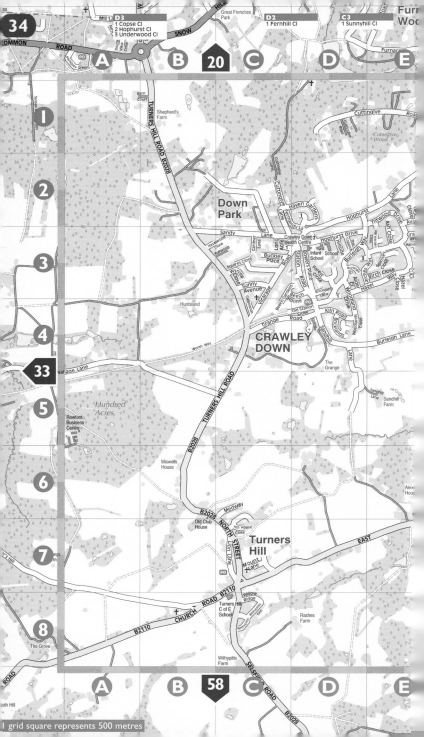

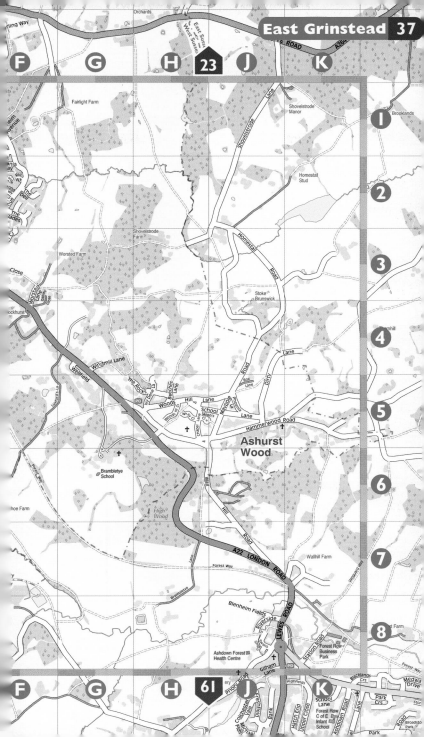

A   B   C   D   E

Coombe Head

The Royal School

...combe

Hazel Gv

1

Amesbury School

2

Hindhead Road A287

Sandy Lane

Farnham Lane

Stoatley Hollow

Bunch Lane

3

Woolmer Hill School

Critchmere

Cherry Tree Avenue

Birdseide

The Avenue

Woodlands Lane

The Paddock

Stoatley Rise

Stoatley River

St Bartholomews C of E School

Middle School

4

Critchmere Hill

Holy Cross Hospital

Chilcrom

Shottermill County Middle School

Underwood

Lion Lane

Dell Close

Weysprings

Bunch Lane

Weydown

Derby Road

Shottermill

Stile Doris

Priors Wd

Haslemere Station

Unicorn Trading Est

Ind Est

LOWER ST

SHEPHE

5

Fir Tree Aven

Oak Tree Lane

HINDHEAD RD

Vicarage Lane Clinic

Victoria Rd

B2131

WEY HILL

Bunch Wy

Longdene Road

Courts Hill Rd

Courts Mt Rd

Sandrock

LIPHOOK RD

Meadow Vale

King's Row

Hasle Dr

6

LINCHMERE ROAD

B2131

The Millstream

New Rd

Camelsdale County First School

Sturt

Sun

Sickle Rd

The Herons Swimming and Fitness Centre

Fountain

Hedgehog Lane

A286

MIDHURST ROAD

Scotland La

Chiltern Cl

Scotlands Close

7

Penwith Drive

CAMELSDALE RD

Marley Combe Road

Camelsdale

Surrey County

Green Lane

Bell Vale Lane

A286

Ferndale

Valewood Rd

Mill Lane

The Old Quarry

Sussex Border Path

Marley Common

8

Marley House

Sussex Border Path

Marley Lane

A286

BELL ROAD

Marley Hanger

Ferndale

Cognor Wood

Whitehanger

A   B   C   D   E

Kingsley Green

1 grid square represents 500 metres

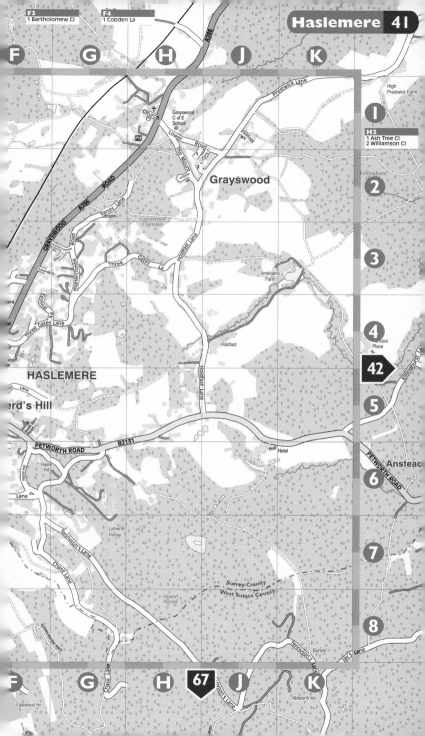

F3 1 Bartholomew Cl
F4 1 Cobden La

I

H2 1 Ash Tree Cl
2 Williamson Cl

F G H J K

High Prestwick Farm

Prestwick Lane

Grayswood C of E School

Church Cl

Lower Road

The Mount

Frillinghurst La

2

Grayswood

Grayswood

Sandy Lane

Grayswood Common

Holdfast Lane

3

Three Cates La

ROAD

A286

GRAYSWOOD

Highercombe Road

Imbhams Farm

Three Cates Lane

4 Furnace Place

Holdfast

Holdfast Lane

42

HASLEMERE

5

...rd's Hill

Lane

Haste Hill

Hotel

PETWORTH ROAD B2131

PETWORTH ROAD

6 Ansteac

Lane

Lythehill House

Tennyson's Lane

7

Chase Lane

Killinghurst La

Home Wood

Surrey County
West Sussex County

8

Barfold

Tennyson's La

ALE Lane

F G H **67** J K

Chase Lane

Tennyson's Lane

Aldworth Ho

Valewood Ho

St Marys
C of E First
School
The Green
PH
Turners Mr
Pickhurst Rd
A283
ROAD
Cherfold
Hazel
Bridge
Pickhurst Road
High Street Green
High Street Green
High Street Green
Cherfold
ingford
Club
Pickhurst
Follies Farm
Tugley
Wood
Fisher Lane
44
Robins Farm
Shillinglee
Park Golf
Club
Fisher Lane
Wood
Plaistow Rd
Shillinglee Road
Shillinglee
Home Farm
Shillinglee Road
Newhouse
Farm
East
End
Deer
Tower
n's Farm
l Farm
69
The
Lake
Haymans Farm
l Farm

F G H J K
I
2
3
4
5
6
7
8

A B C D E

1 Highstreet
Green

High Street Green

Dunsfold
Ryss

2

3 Tugley
Wood

Oaken
Wood

Plaistow Road

Chiddingfold Road Blacknest Farm Chiddingfold Road

Plaistow Road

4 Durfold
Hall Farm

Fisher Lane

5 Fisherlanes
Wood

Durfold
Wood

Dunsfold Road Dungate Farm

Sussex Bord

Sussex Border Path

Durfold

6 Surrey County
West Sussex County

Wood

Shortland
Copse

Durfold Road

7 East
End Farm

Newhouse
Farm

Weald
Barkfold

Durfold Road

8 Haymans Farm

Kingspark
Wood

Lyon's
Farm

Shillinglee Road

Dunsfold

A B   C D E

Birchfold
Copse

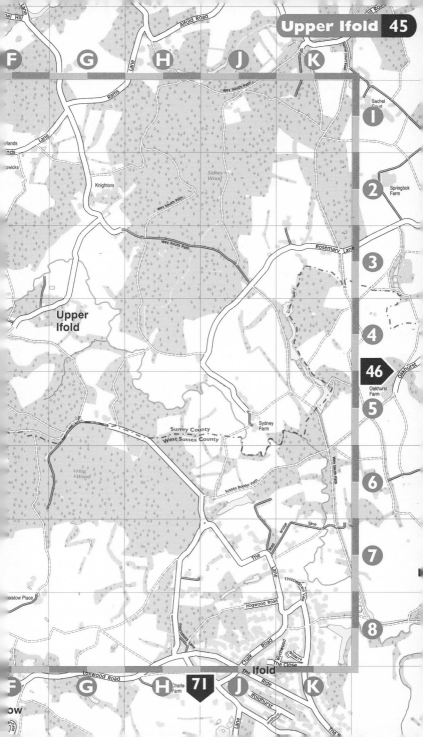

F G H J K

1
Sachel
Court

2
Springbok
Farm

Alfold Road

Pams
Lane

Wey south path

Knightons

Sidney
Wood

Wey south Path

Wey South Path

Rosemary Lane

3

4

**Upper
Ifold**

46 ▶ Oakhurst

5
Oakhurst
Farm

Surrey County
West Sussex County

Sydney
Farm

Wey south Path

Hog
Wood

Sussex Border Path

6

7

The Hollands Lane

Bridge Lane

Thistledown Lane

Maistow Place

Hogwood Road

Foxbridge Lane

Chalk Road

Foxwood
Oakhurst

8

The Close

F G H 71 ◀ J K

Loxwood Road

Charle
Farm

Ifold

The Ridge

Idlehurst

Lane

ow

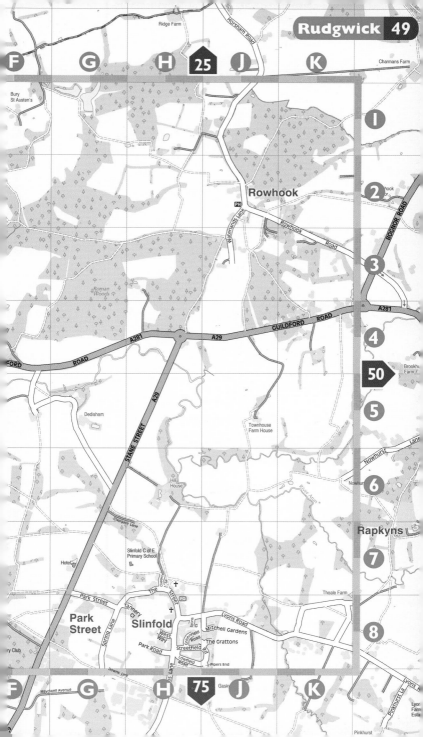

F G H **25** J K

Charmans Farm

Ridge Farm

Horsham Road

Bury St Austen's

I

2

Rowhook

PH

Waterlands Lane

Rowhook Road

BOGNOR ROAD

3

A281

Roman Woods

GUILDFORD ROAD

A281 ROAD A29

4

FORD ROAD

STANE STREET

A29

Dedisham

50

Brookhu Farm

Townhouse Farm House

5

Nowhurst Lane

Nowhur

6

Hill House

River Arun

Rapkyns

Clagate Lane

7

Slinfold C of E Primary School

Hotel

Theale Farm

Park Street

The Street

Lyons Road

Mitchell Gardens

Park Street

Tannery Cl

Spring Lane

Slinfold

West Way

Lyons

Greenfield Road

The Grattons

Lyons Road

8

Park Road

Streetfield

Pipers End

ry Club

Downs Link

Lowfield Road

Lyor Farm Esta

F G **75** H J Gask K

Maydwell Avenue

s Lane

Pinkhurst La

Lyor Farm Esta

Pinkhurst

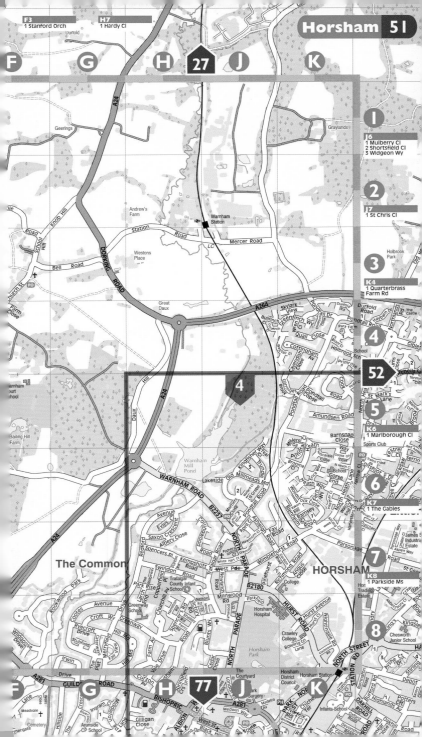

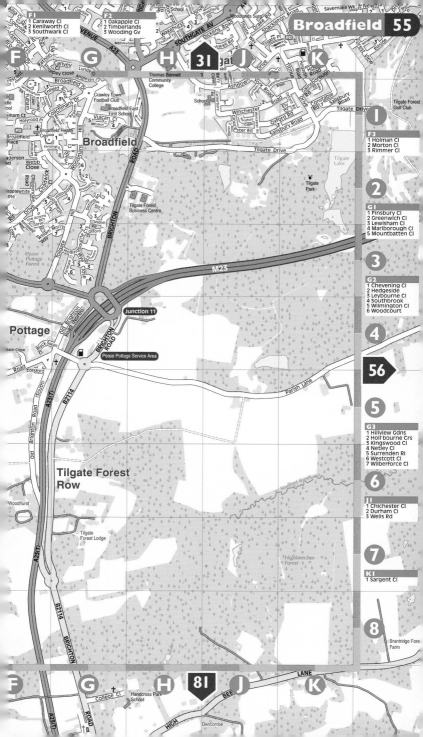

32

C1
1 Dakin Cl
2 Duke Cl
3 Gates Cl
4 Kendale Cl
5 Ritchie Cl

B1
1 Bennett Cl
2 Forbes Cl
3 Phillips Cl
4 Wright Cl

A B C D E

The Oaks
First & Middle
School

Holborn
Road

Salisbury
Road

Road

1

Tilgate Drive

Tilgate Forest
Golf Club

M23

2

Tilgate
Lake

Tilgate
Park

Oldhouse Warren

3

Tilgate Forest

M23

Balcombes
Forest

Cowd
Forest

4

Mount Pleasant
Farm

55

Parish Lane

5

Greentrees
Farm

Crawley Lane

6

Nuthurst Brook

STREET

7

Brantridge
Forest

HIGH

Highbeeches
Forest

Highley
Manor

8

B2110

Brantridge Forest
Farm

Redbridge Lane

Handcross Road

Handcross

LANE

A B C D E

New England

82

Great Cooper's
Comm

West

Branti

1 grid square represents 500 metres

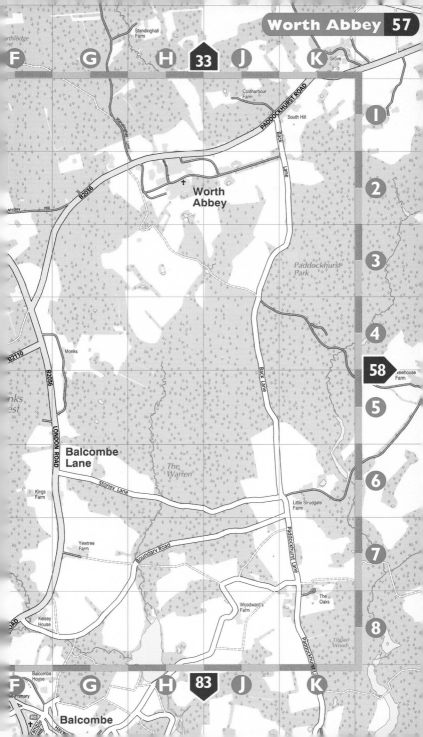

A   West Hoathly Road   B   36   C   D   E

1

Admiral's Bridge Lane

Weir Wood Resevoir

Landscape Trail

2

Charlwood

Neylands Farm

3

Mayes

Blackland Farm

Legsheath Farm

4

w Coombe rm

East Sussex County   West Sussex County

Crisfield Lane

Plaw Wood

Legsheath Lane

59

5

Plawhatch Hall

Coldharbour Manor

Tyes Cross

6

Top Road

Plaw Hatch Lane

Courtlands

7

Horsted Lane

Horncastle Wood

Cripps Manor

Deanlands Farm

Chilling Street

8

Wickenden Farm

A   B   86   C   D   E

Rest   Twyford Lodge

Lane

1 grid square represents 500 metres

Blenheim Fields

Riverside

Blackwall Farm

LEWES

Station

Row Moss

F G H **37** J K

own Forest
h Centre

J

Cemetery

Priory Road

Freshfield

Colchester

Michael Hall Rd

Cave Ridge

Gilham Lane

Bank

Highfields

Hatch End

Upper Close

School Lane

Forest Row
C of E
Infant School

Woodcroft

Road

Blacklands Crs

Ashdown Road

Chapel Lane

PO

Medway Drive

ston

I

Park

Broadstor
Park

Road

FOREST
ROW

Priors
Lane

Michael Hall School

Kidbrooke Park

Dale Road

Shalesbrook Lane

Greenfield School

LEWES ROAD

Chequer
Grange

Highgate Road

Spring Meadow

Bank

imros
Lar

Shalesb
Lane

2

Royal Ashdown Forest Golf Club

Torrs
Lane

Intpen
Lane

Highgate

A22

Balfour Gdns

Tompsetts

**Tompsett
Bank**

3

Kidbrooke
Wood

RH18

4

*Hindleap
Warren*

*Broadstone
Warren*

5

Hindleap Farm

A22

6

Ho

+

**Wych
Cross**

7

Wych Cross Place

Ashdown Forest
Farm

A275

8

own Farm

*Press
Ridge
Warren*

ROAD

F G H **87** J K

Isle of Thorns

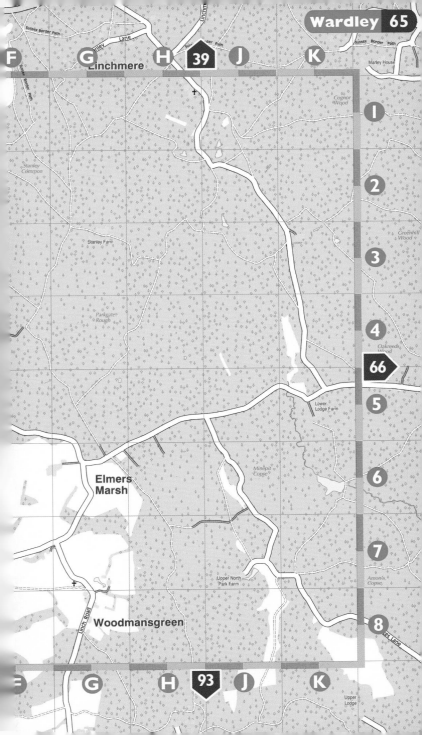

Sussex Border Path

Linchmere Lane

Marley House

F G H **39** J K

Linchmere

Sussex Border Path

Sussex Border Path

Copnor Wood

1

Stanley Common

2

Greenhill Wood

Stanley Farm

3

Parkgate Rough

4

Oakreeds Wood

66

Lower Lodge Farm

5

Elmers Marsh

Minepit Copse

6

7

Arnons Copse

Upper North Park Farm

8

Linch Road

Woodmansgreen

ces Lane

E G H **93** J K

Upper Lodge

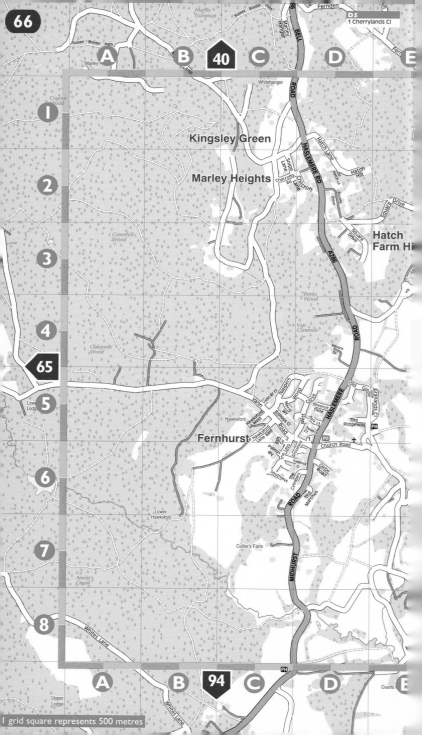

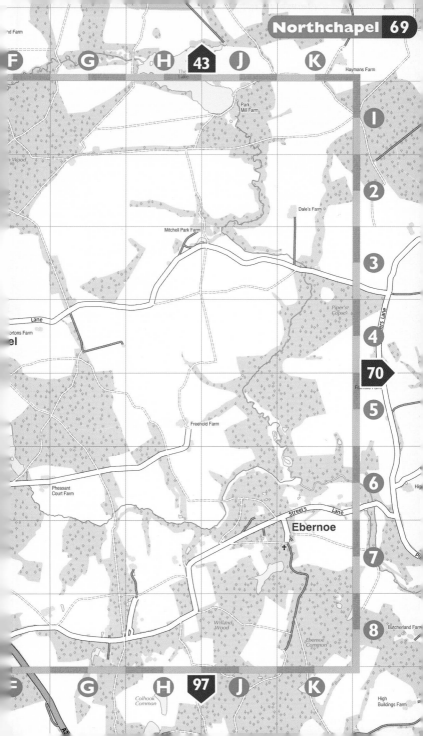

A B 46 C D E

Station Road

Brewhurst Lane

I

The Drive

Plaistow Road

Headfoldswood Farm

2

Wephurst Wood

3

4

Wephurst Park

71

5

Hurst Farm House

Gunshot Common

Roundstreet Common

B2133

Skiff Lane

Durbans Road

Drungewick Lane

6

Burchett's Farm

Dounhurst Farm

Fountain's Farm

7

Naldretts Court

8

Dunhurst Copse

Sparr Farm

Durbans Road

A B 100 C D E

1 grid square represents 500 metres

A B 48 C D E

I

Garlands

The Haven

PH

2

Oxehurst Road

Marles Lane

3

Bignor Farm

4

73

Park Farm

Haven Road

STANE

A29

A29

Buckman Corner

5

Great Wood

Ingfield Manor School

Woodland Close

A29

HORSHA

A264

Five Oaks

Hayes Wood Road

Gra Fa

6

7

Oxehurst Lane

Copped Hall Farm

Menzies Wood Farm

Lannards Gallery

ehurst

8

Wynstrode Farm

STANE STREET

Summers Place

A B 102 C New Road D E

Hilland Farm

Wooddale Farm

The Lane

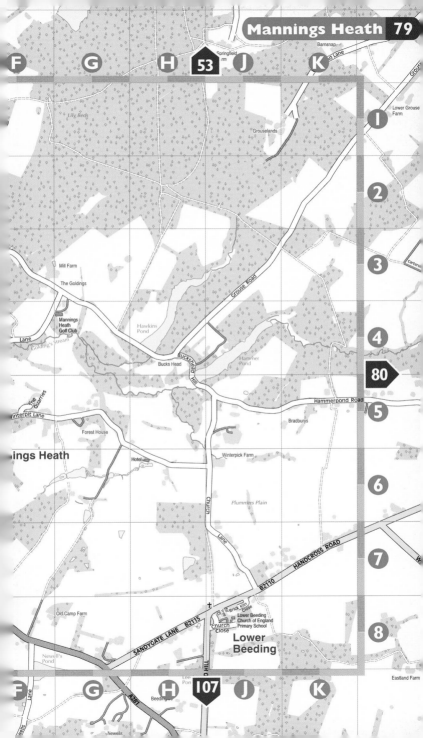

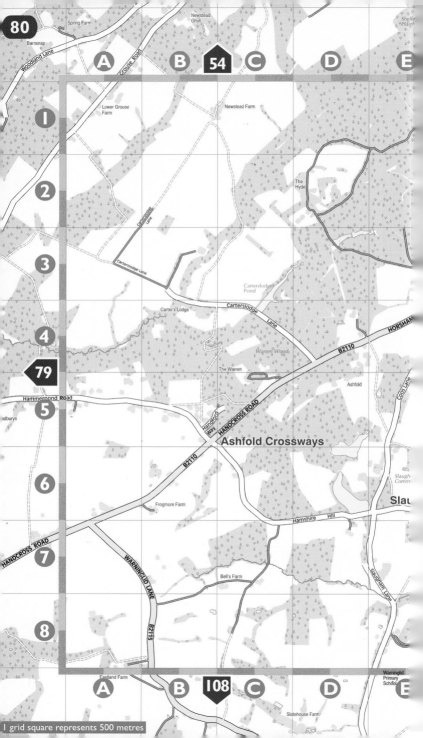

East Liss

90

LISS

B3006

Road

HILL BROW ROAD

Liss County Infant & Junior School

East Hill

Cardew Road

Woodland Drive

A

B

62

C

Hampshire County
West Sussex County

B2070

D

E

Prince's Marsh

1

Stodham Lane

Pruetts Lane

Rake Common

Malvern Road

Hill Brow

Combe Road

2

3

Clayton Court

Knowles Meadow

Sussex Border Path

Durford Wood

Rogate Common

4

89

5

Slade Lane

Slade Farm

6

Sussex Border Path

7

Durleighmarsh Farm

A272

Durford Abbey Farm

Wenham Manor Farm

Durleighmarsh

8

River Rother

A

B

118

C

D

Rival Lodge

West Heath Common

Sussex Border Path

1 grid square represents 500 metres

Goldring

Great Trippetts Farm

Cannhouse Lane

Rake Road

Chorleys Common

I

2

New Barn Farm

Cook's Pond Road

Bobbol Farm

Harting Combe

be

3

Borden Wood

4

Trotten Marsh

Rendle Wood

Borden Lane

92

Borden **5**

Dangstein

Terwick Common

6

on

Fyning

Cumber's Farm

Red House Ct
gate C of E
trolled School

Lane

Carbutts

+

+

Gatehouse Lane

Gatehouse Farm **7**

8

ouse Lane

M72

Wakeham Farm

Fair Oak

G **H** **119** **J** **K**

G **63** **J** **K**

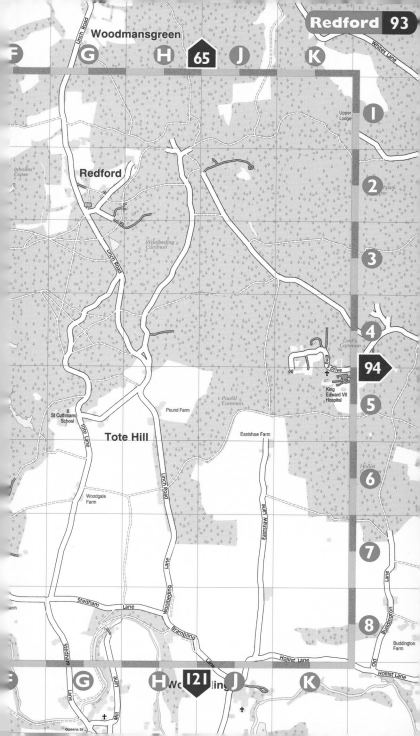

Woodmansgreen

F G H **65** J K

Whites Lane

Upper Lodge

I

Inholms Copse

Redford 2

Linch Road

Woolbeding Common 3

Lord's Common 4

King's Drive

94

King Edward VII Hospital 5

St Cuthmans School

Tote Lane

Tote Hill

Pound Farm

Pound Common

Eastshaw Farm

Hollist 6

Linch Road

Woodgate Farm

Eastshaw Lane 7

Stedham Lane

Woodbeding Lane

Brambling Lane

Hollist Lane

Buddington Lane

Old Buddington

Buddington Farm 8

Stedham Lane

Mill

F G H **121** J K

Woodbeding Lane

Hollist Lane

Queens St

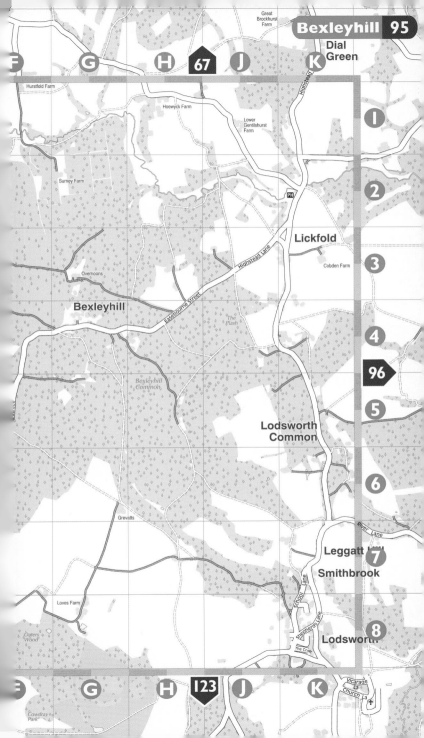

Great Brockhurst Farm

Dial Green

F G H 67 J K

Hurstfold Farm

I

Hoewyck Farm

Lower Gentilshurst Farm

Surney Farm

2

PH

Lickfold

Overnoons

Highstead Lane

Cobden Farm

3

Bexleyhill

Eastbourne Street

The Plash

4

96

Bexleyhill Common

5

Lodsworth Common

6

River Lane

Grevatts

Leggatt Hill 7

Smithbrook

Loves Farm

School Lane

Shepherds Lane

8

Oaters Wood

Lodsworth

The Croft

F G H 123 J K

Vicarage La

Church La

Cowdray Park

Butcherland Farm

F **G** **H** **69** **J** **K**

Willand Wood

I ldings Farm

Colhook Common

A283

2

Redhill House

Palfrey Farm

3

Hoads Common

Farm

4

Osiers Farm

98

Holland Wood

5

A283

Pheasant Copse

Limbo Farm

6

Keyfox Farm

7

Gunter's Bridge

8

Jpperton **G** **H** **125** **J** **K** tery

Petworth Park

Hampers Green

GU28

98

Eberzoe Common

Butcherland Farm

A **B** **70** **C** **D** **E**

1

High Buildings Farm

Allfields Farm

Balls Cross

2

Crawfold Farm

Farm

Langhurst Farm

3

4

Medhone Farm

97

Holland Wood

5

Blackhouse Lane

6

yfox Farm

Blackbrook Farm

Bennyfoi

7

Gunter's Bridge

Moor Farm

Pondtail Copse

8

Blackhouse Lane

Cemetery

A **B** **126** **C** **D** **E**

Hammer Green

ROAD

A272

A2

Hilliers

1 grid square represents 500 metres

Wynstrode Farm

STREET

A3
1 Freemans Cl
2 Platts Meadow

Ⓐ   Ⓑ   **74** Ⓒ   Ⓓ   Ⓔ

Summers Place

Tedfold

New   Road
Hilland Farm

Wooddale Farm
Wooddale Lane

Ⓘ

A29

Roman Way

Coombe Hill
Street

Mill Rd
Mill Wy

The Surgery

②

A29

Ⓐ272   WEST STREET   HIGH STREET   EAST STREET   A272

St Mary's Cl

Dell La

Gratwicke Close

Nightingale Wk

③

ROAD

Newbridge Road

Anvil Cl

St Gabriel

Gorselands

Rowfold Grange

Alan's Hill

Cleve Wy

Willow Dr

Brookfield

④

Forge Way
Ostler's View

Station

Billingshurst County Infant School
Oaklands

Birch Drive

BILLINGSHURST

Weald School

Brooker's Rd
Eagle Estate

Brookers Road
Industrial Estate

Billingshurst Station

Rosier Farm

101

Parbrook

Luxford

Stane Street

Platts

Lwr Station Rd

Chestnut Rd

Brookfield

Daux Road

Daux La

Rosier Way

⑤

Clapham Av

Groomsland Drive

Daux   Avenue

Churchwood Close

A272

CONEYHU

⑥

Kingsfold

Kingslea

STANE STREET

⑦

Hadfold Farm

Oakdene

Marringdean Road

South House Farm

Balls Green

⑧

ADVERSANE LANE

Ⓐ   Ⓑ   **130**   Ⓒ   Ⓓ   Ⓔ

B2133

Highfure

West Chillington Lane

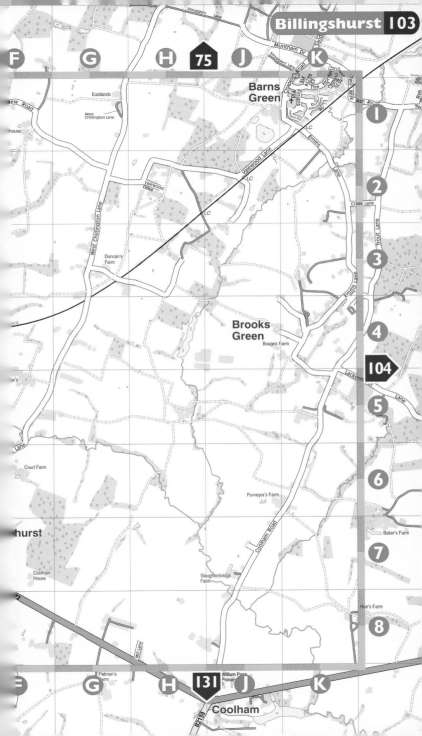

F G H **75** J K

I

Smugglers Lane

Muntham Dr

Sand

Ash Rd

Smugglers Lane

Barns Green

Chapel Wood

Six Acres

C/C

The Hornets

Finans

Two Mile Ash Rd

Eastlands

New Road

West Chiltington Lane

house

Valewood Lane

LC

Emms Lane

2

Cross Lane

Valewood Close

Valewood Lane

West Chiltington Lane

LC

3

Emms Lane

Trout Lane

Duncan's Farm

LC

Brooks Green

Bouges Farm

4

104

Lackenhurst Lane

5

Lane

's Lane

Court Farm

Purveyor's Farm

6

Baker's Farm

hurst

7

Coolham House

Slaughterbridge Farm

Coolham Road

Hoe's Farm

8

Mill Lane

Patman's Farm

William Penn Priman

F G H **131** J K

B2139

Coolham

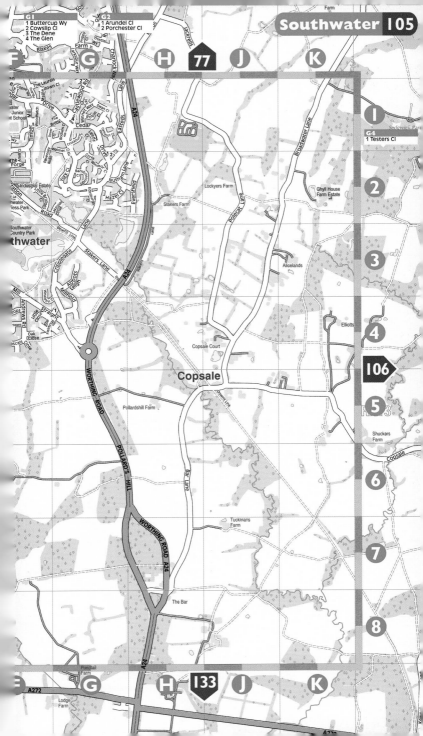

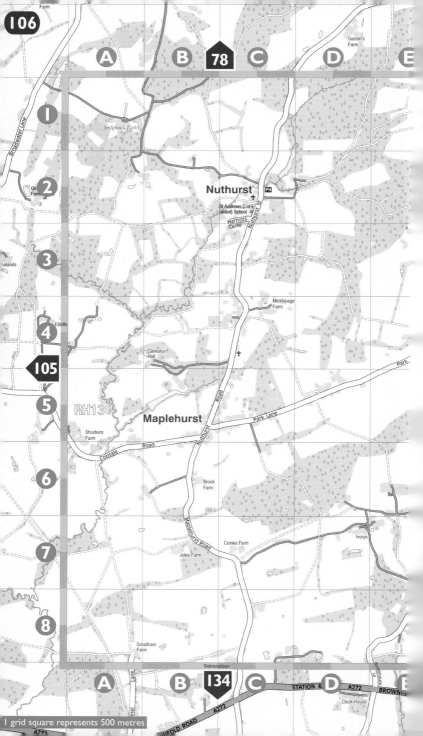

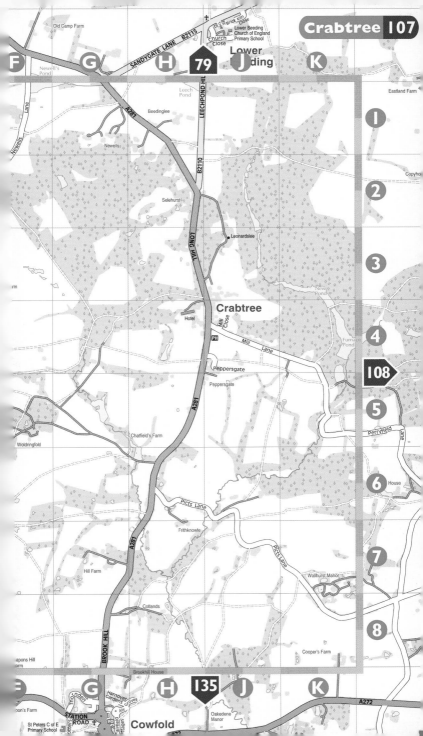

H8
1 Awbrook Cl
2 The Coppice
3 Orchard Cl
4 St Augustine Cl

F G H **85** J K

Woodsland Farm

Key

Park Lane

Plummerden Lane

I

Treemans Road

Paxhill Park

Great Plummerden Farm

2

Montes Hill

Cockhaise Mill Farm

Monteswood Lane

3 Freshfield Crossways

Freshfield

Great Walstead School

4

II**4**

Snowdrop Lane

East Mascalls Road

5

East Mascalls Lane

Henfield Wood

6

Pegden

BEDALES HILL

Bedales

Nash Farm

7 Nash Lane

Awbrook

Vicarage Lane

Church Road

A272

Scaynes Hill

Ham Lane

Hillcrest Lane

Clearwater

Hammond's Farm

8

Sunnycroft Close

G H **141** J K

Tanyard Farm

Brookhouse Bottom

Pennybridge Lane

Wardsland d

F

G

H

87

J

K

Wilmshurst

1

Sheffield Forest

Woolpack Farm

2

Furner's Green

Holmesdale Farm

Searles

Sheffield

Mill

Lane

3

effield
een

4

Moyse's Farm

Spring Farm

5

A275

6

Sheffield Park Farm

Knabbs Farmhouse

Sp Gre

Sheffield Park Garden (NT)

Atherall's Farm

7

PH

Fletching

Fletching C of E School

8

Parsonage Farm

Mill Farm

G

H

J

K

River Ouse

Netherall Farm

A B **88** C D E

PETERSFIELD

Noreuil Rd
Gloucester Close
Barham Rd

1 Nightingale Rd

Bedford Road
A3(T)

Buckingham Road
East Hants
District Council
Petersfield
Community Hosp

York Cl

Swan
Street Surg
The Spain
High St

The Square

Swimming Pool
Town Council

Far Horizons
Gallery
Far Horizons
Gallery

Vauxhall
Way

Industrial
Est

Hylton
Rd

Infant Sch
Petersfield
Turnpike
Gallery
The Avenue

Churchers
College Junior
School

The Bear
Museum

Heath Road West

I

The
Maltings

Grange
Road

Petersfield
School

The Causeway

B2146

Paddock Way
Larcombe Road
Cranford
Road
Borough
Grove

King George
Avenue

The Spain

Orchard
Road

Causeway

2

Weston
Lane

Wyld's Lane

B3010

Hangers Way

Weston

3

THE CAUSEWAY

A3(T)

Nursted House

4

Buriton
Business
Park

Bolinge
Hill Farm

5

Greenway
Lane

Hangers Way

Cowhouse Farm

North
Lane

Pitcroft
Lane

6

Gload Road
Dummer Road
Bones Lane
Pointsfield

Heathfield

PH

North
Lane

Kiln Lane
High Street

Buriton
CP School

Buriton

Kiln La

South La

South Downs Way

7

Hangers Way

Newbarn Road

8

Hangers Way

Coulters
Dean Fm

A B **142** C D

Heath
Down Plantation

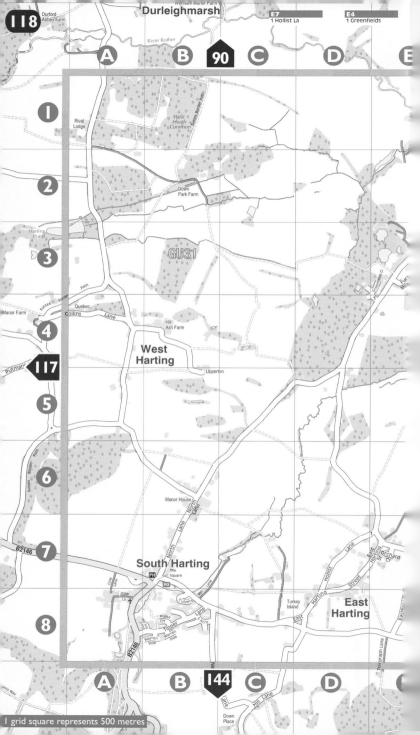

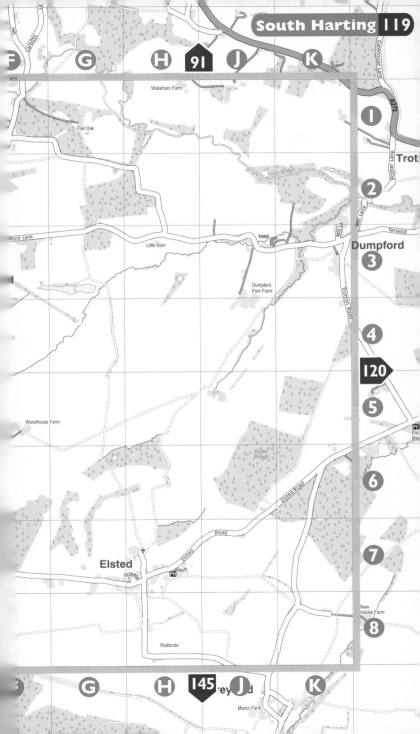

KS
1 Perche Ct
Farm
2 Tufts Fld

Stedham Lane

Woolbeding

Hollist Lane

Buddington
Farm

Woolbeding

Queens St

Common View

PH
School
Stedham
CP School

The Street

Mill Lane

Stedham

A272

Sandy Lane

June Mdw

June Lane

PETERSFIELD ROAD

Heatherwood

Quags
Corner

Severals Road

Severals

Midhurst
Common

Midh
Gramm
Sch

Guildings Oak

Carron

Cemetery

Heathfield

Lane

BELTON ROAD

Station Rd

Victoria Avenue

Cavalier

GU29

122

Mead

Bourne

ROAD

Beeton Road

Meadow

The Fairway

Falconhurst

Heathlands Farm

Pitsham
Lane

Fairfield

Beeton Road

Pitsham Lane

Pitsham Farm

Cuc
Cau

A286

Cocking
Park

Paddock W

147

Bex

Lan

Park Ho
(Hotel)

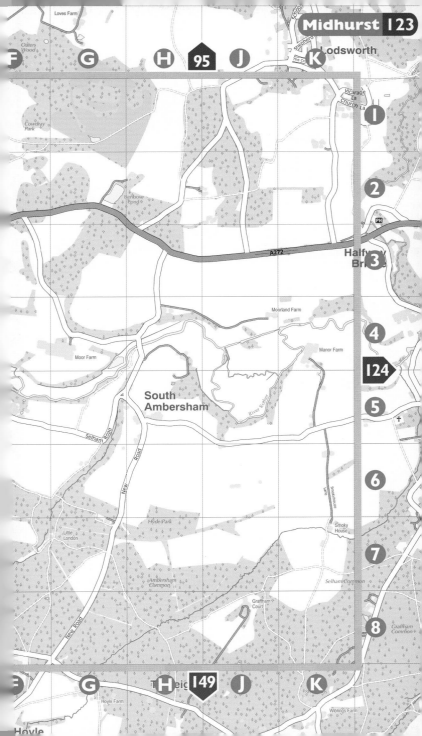

Loves Farm

School

Shepherd

the Cl

Lodsworth

F

G

H

95

J

K

Oaters
Wood

Vicarage
La

Church La

I

Cowdray
Park

2

Benbow
Pond

PH

A272

Halfway
Bridge

3

Moorland Farm

4

Manor Farm

124

Moor Farm

River Rother

5

+

**South
Ambersham**

Selham Road

New Road

6

Line

Smokehouse

Hyde Park

Smoky
House

Little
London

7

Ambersham
Common

Selham Common

Graffham
Court

8

Graffham
Common

New Road

G

H

149

J

K

Hoyle Farm

Wiblings Farm

Hoyle

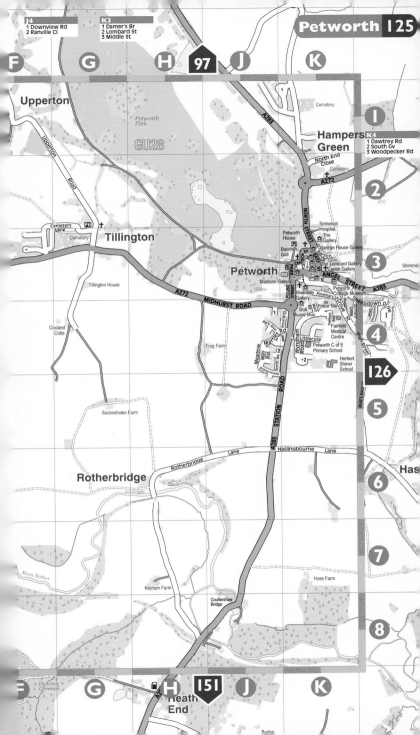

F **G** **H** **97** **J** **K**

I

J4
1 Downview Rd
2 Ranville Cl

K3
1 Damer's Br
2 Lombard St
3 Middle St

K4
1 Dawtrey Rd
2 South Gv
3 Woodpecker Rd

Upperton

Petworth Park

GU28

2

Hampers Green

North End
Close

Cemetery

A272

Cemetery Lane

PH

Cemetery

Tillington

Petworth House

Somerset Hospital
The Gallery

Bacchus Gall

George House Gallery

3

Petworth

The Lombard Gallery
Canon Gallery

NORTH STREET

ANGEL STREET

Madison Gallery

Petworth Cottage Museum

A285

A272 MIDHURST ROAD

Tillington House

Riverside Gallery

Rosemary Lane

Sheepdown Drive

Coxland Cotts

Police Stn

Doll House Mus

Fairfield Medical Centre

Park Rise

Meadow Way

Frog Farm

North West

Rothermead

Wyndham Road

Littlecote

Petworth C of E Primary School

Herbert Shiner School

High Street

4

126

5

Sockenholes Farm

STATION ROAD

A283

Haslingbourne Lane

Rotherbridge Lane

Rotherbridge

Has

6

River Rother

Kilsham Farm

Hoes Farm

7

Coultershaw Bridge

8

River Rother

Dencton Common

F **G** **H** **151** **J** **K**

Heath End

Burton

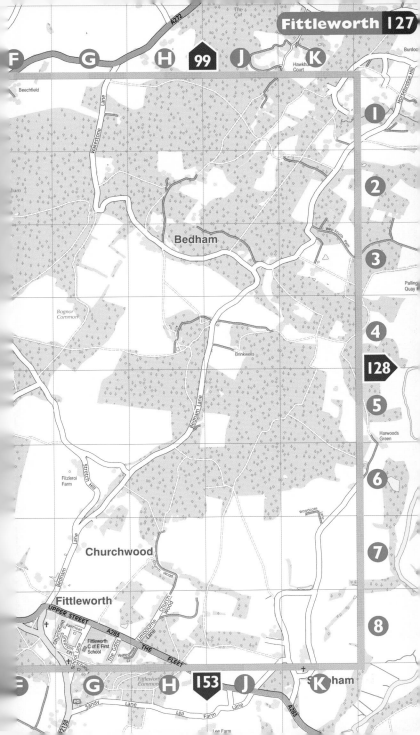

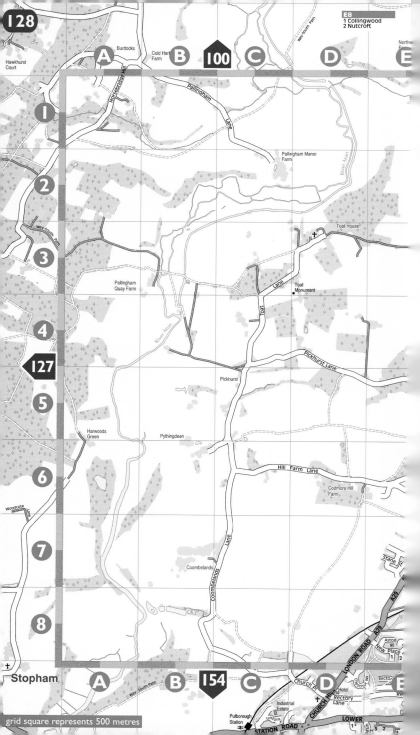

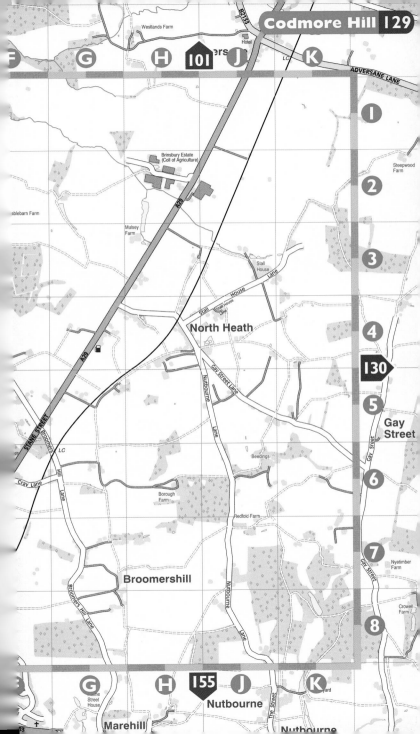

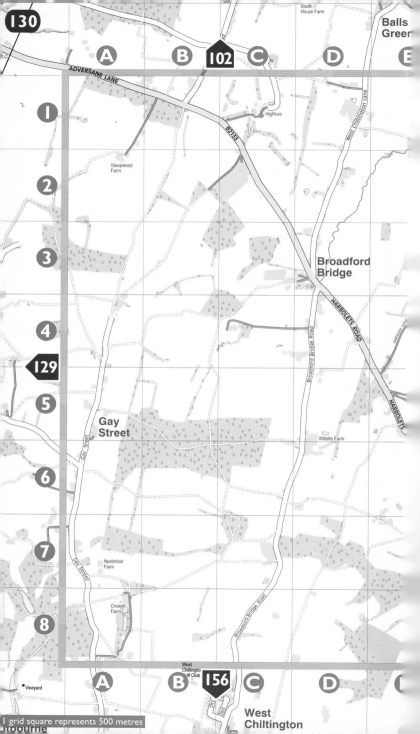

F　G　Mill Lane　H　**103**　J　K

Patman's Farm

William Penn Primary School

A272

I

Coolham

B2139

2

Bridgehill Farm

Goringlee

3

Sproutes

Jendens Farm

Sproutes Lane

COOLHAM ROAD

Barnhouse Farm

Saucelands Farm

Saucelands

4

Smoke House F

Road

Broomer's Corner **132**

Sincox Lane

Falconers

5

...th ...inglee Farm

Hungerhill Farm

6

Redlands

B2139

Palace Land Farm

Brookhouse Farm

7

Apsley Farm

Danhill Farm

ROAD

Blonks Farm

8

COOLHAM

B2133

...icketty Cotts

GOOSEGREEN

G　H　**157**　J　K

Goffsland House

Laybrook Farm

Goose Green

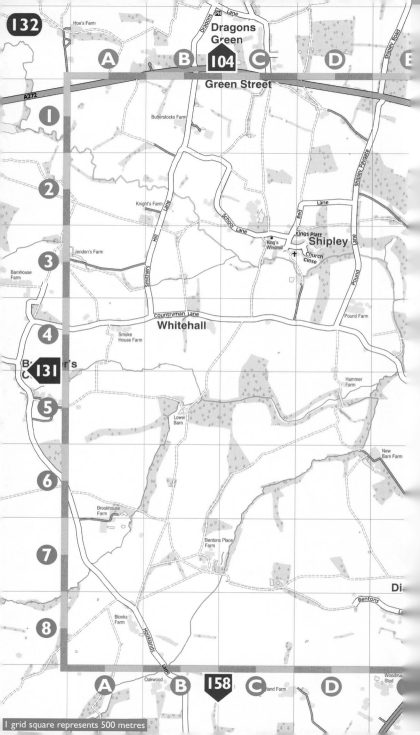

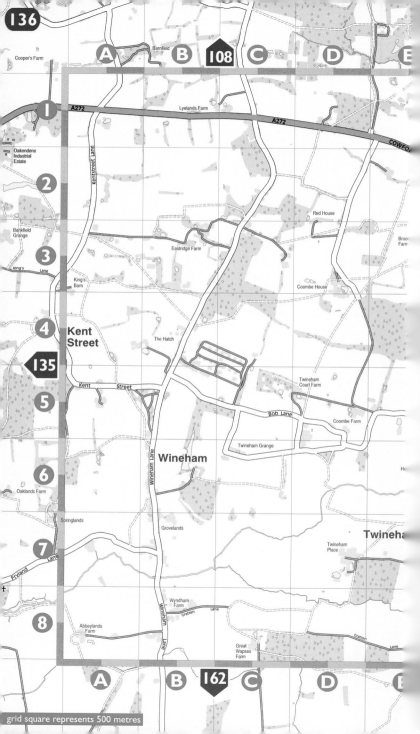

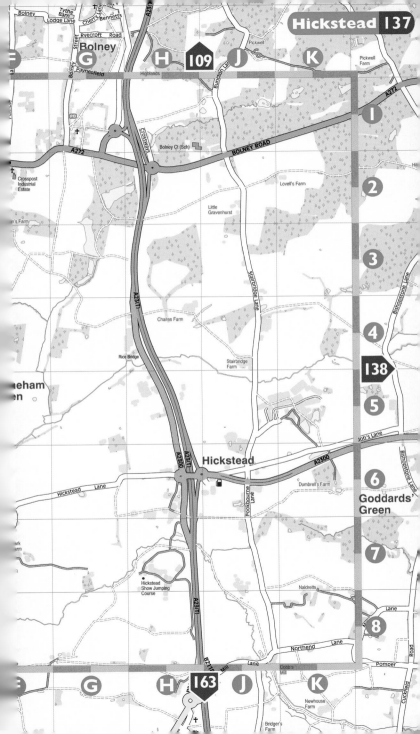

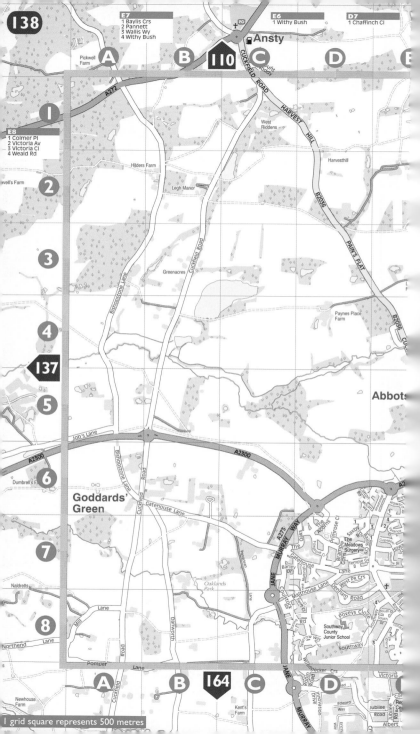

F6
1 Chillington Cl
2 Spicers Cl
3 Tate Crs
4 Woodcroft

F7
1 Packham Wy
2 Shepherds Mead
3 South Lodge Cl
4 Tudor Gdns
5 Turners Wy

F8
1 Commercial Rd
2 London Rd
3 Orchard Wy

G6
1 Gander Cl
2 The Hawthorns

G7
1 Marle Av
2 Sheddingdean Cl

H6
1 Bedelands Cl

140

H7
1 Midfields Cl
2 Midfields Wk
3 The Ridgeway
4 The Twitten

H8
1 Crescent Cl
2 Turkey La

J5
1 Valebridge Cl

J6
1 Ladymead
2 Valebridge Dr

165

K8
1 St Andrews Rd
2 Tilers Cl
3 Tindal Cl

K6
1 Hawthorn Cl
2 Laurel Cl

K1
1 Pinewood Wy

J7
1 Woodland Cl

BURGESS HILL

World's End

1 grid square represents 500 metres

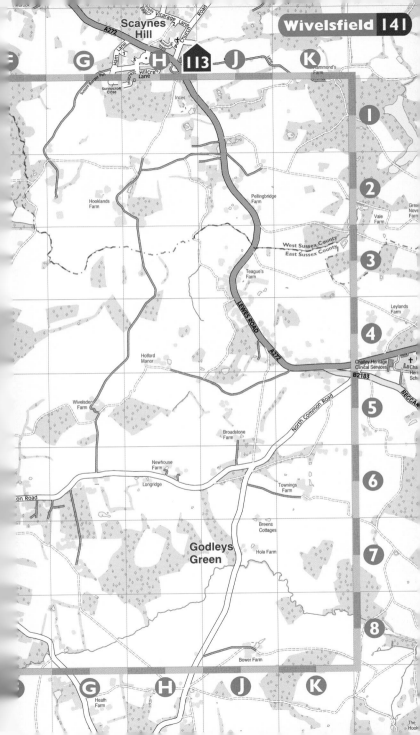

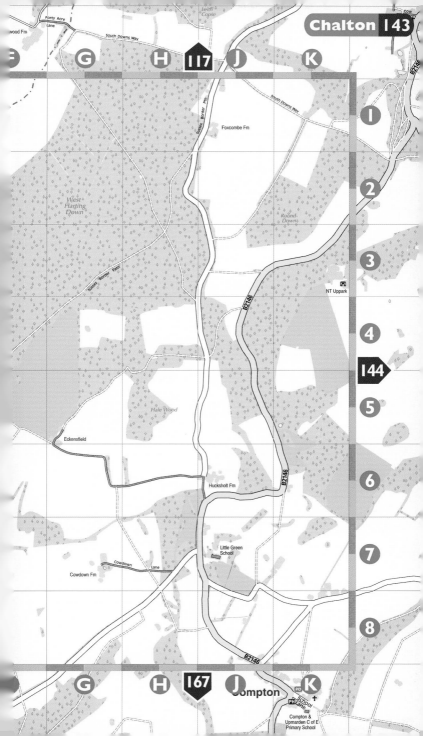

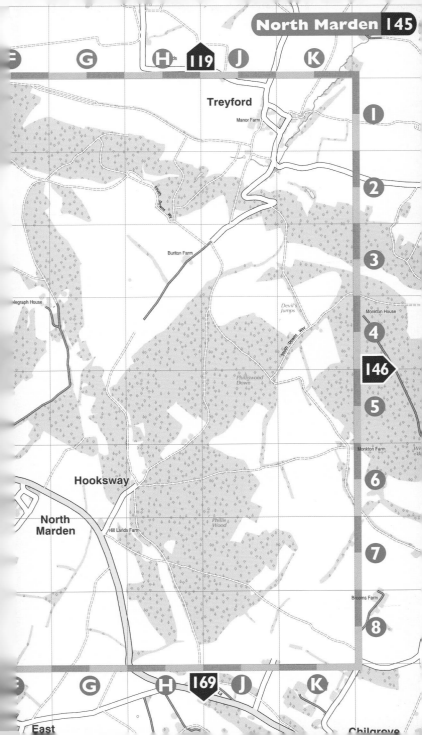

Treyford

Manor Farm

South Downs Way

Buriton Farm

Telegraph House

Devil's Jumps

South Downs Way

Monkton House

146

Philliswood Down

Monkton Farm

Hooksway

North Marden

Hill Lands Farm

Phillis Wood

Brooms Farm

119

169

East

Chilgrove

G H J K

E G H J K

I 2 3 4 5 6 7 8

146

New
House Farm

Piper's Farm

Ⓐ   Ⓑ   120 Ⓒ   Ⓓ   Ⓔ

Ⓘ

Didling

Linch Farm

Bugshill Lane

2

†

3

249
Linch
Down

Monkton House

Devil's
Jumps

4

bourne Way

145

5

Monkton Farm

Winden
Wood

Linchball
Wood

6

7

Westdell
Woods

Brooms Farm

8

Staple
Ash Farm

Manor
Place

Colworth
Down

Ⓐ   Ⓑ   170 Ⓒ   Ⓓ   Ⓒ

1 grid square represents 500 metres

Chilgrove

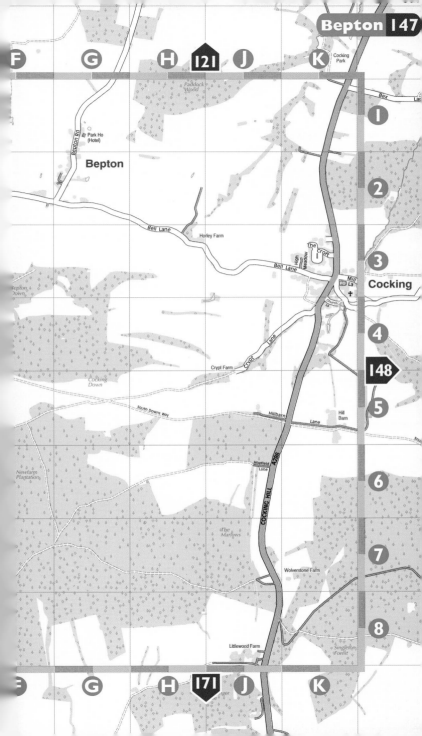

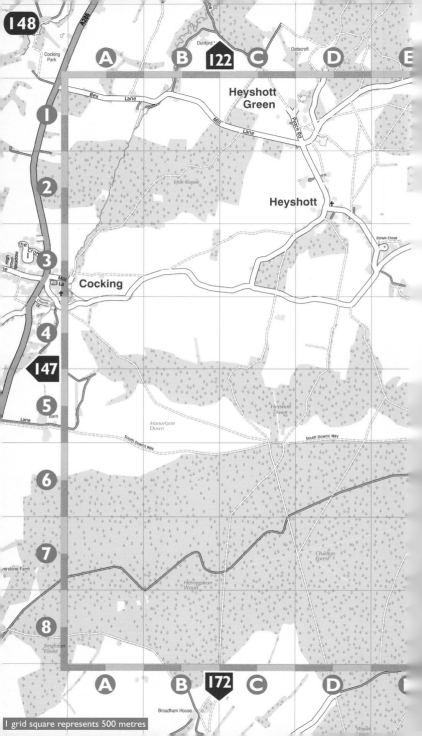

A986

148

A · B · 122 · C · Oatscroft · D · E

Cocking
Park

Bex Lane

Heyshott
Green

Mill Lane

Pease Rd

I

Hue Copse

2

Heyshott

The Croft

High Meadow

3

Mill La
PO
Cocking
Church La

Down Close

4

147

5

Lane
Barn

Manorfarm
Down

Heyshott
Down

South Downs Way · South Downs Way

6

7

erstone Farm

Herringdean
Wood

Charlton
Forest

8

Singleton
Forest

A · B · 172 · C · D

Broadham House

Wood

I grid square represents 500 metres

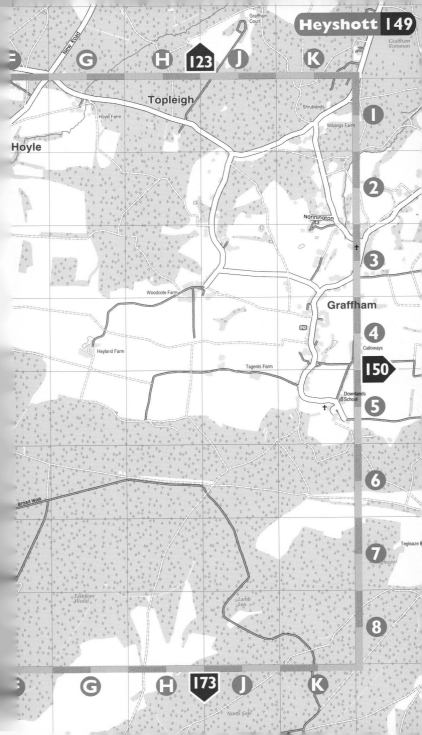

Graffham Court

New Road

Graffham Common

E **G** **H** 123 **J** **K**

1

Topleigh

Shrublands

Wiblings Farm

Hoyle Farm

Hoyle

2

Nonnington La

✝

3

Woodcote Farm

Graffham

PO

4

Calloways

Hayland Farm

150

Tagents Farm

Downlands
School

✝

5

6

Broad Walk

7

Tegleaze

Tegleaze

Eastdean
Wood

Lamb
Lea

8

G **H** 173 **J** **K**

North Side

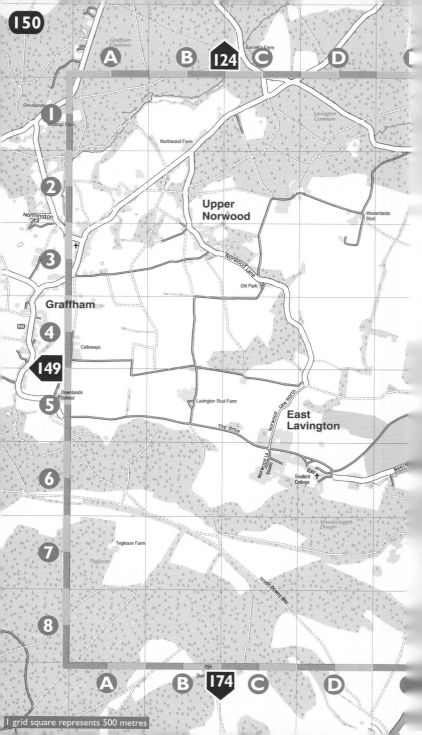

A B 124 C D

Graffham Common

Shrublands

1 Frimings Farm

2 Nonnington La

3 +

Graffham

4

149

5 Downlands School

Northwood Farm

Upper Norwood

Calloways

Lavington Stud Farm

The Drive

6

7 Tegleaze Farm

Tegleaze

8

Barnett's Farm

Lavington Common

Westerlands Stud

Old Park

Norwood Lane

Norwood Lane North

East Lavington

Norwood La South

Seaford College

Beec

Woolavington Down

South Downs Way

1 grid square represents 500 metres

152

A   B   **126**   C   D   E

1

Rother Width

Shopham Bridge   Bignor Farm

2

Burton Park Road

Burton Mill Pond

3   Coates

Coates Lane

Coates Castle

Crouch Farm

4   Broad Halfpenny

151

5   Bignor Park Cott

Sutton End

6

7   Bignor Park Road   Bignor

School Lane

Sutton

Bignorpark

8

PH

Greenfield   A   B   **176**   C   D

Bignor

Bignor

Hadworth Farm

Sutton

I grid square represents 500 metres

127

177

154

F8
1 Bury Rd
K6
1 Piers Secombe Cl

Stopham

Stopham
House

Lower
Horncroft

Lee Farm

Lea Farm Lane

Sandy Lane

Fittleworth
Common

Wey South Path

Kings Lane

Old London Rd

Coldwaltham

Ashurst

Waltham Park Road

Coldwaltham
Farm

St James
C of E
School

Greatham
Bridge

Church Lane

Silverdale

Arun Cl

London Road

Brookdale

Arun
Vale

Brook

Brookland
Way

Sandy Lane

Colebrook Lane

River Lane

Watersfield

Beacon Hill

A29

Quell Farm
Industrial
Estate

River Arun

Bury
Mill Farm

A29

BURY

Wey South Path

E   G   H   J   K

I

2

3

4

5

6

7

8

G   H   J   K

C2
1 Wheelwrights
Farm

B4
1 Haglands Copse

A4
1 Kingswood

A   B   130   C   D   E

C6
1 High Spinney

Nutbourne
Common

1

2

D8
1 Brook Cl
2 Rainbow Wy
3 Snapes Rd

3

4

155

5

6

7

8

West
Chiltington

West Chiltington
Golf Club

West Chiltington
School

Smock
Alley

Southlands
Farm

Town Ho
Farm

Hardbarrow
Woods

Linfield
Copse

Furze Common
Road

High Bar Lane

Champions
Farm

Crossways
Park

Crossways

Garden Wood
Close

Fir Tree Lane

Badgers
Wood

Silver
Glade

Threals
Copse

Rambledown

Monkmead Lane

Westward Lane

Sunset

Spinney

Hotel

Perrett's Farm

West Chiltington Road

Greenhurst   Lane

Northlands Lane

West
Wantley Farm

Fryern

Fryern
Hall

Melton
Drive
1 Melton
Av

Bognor Way

Storrington

Storrington
Road

B2139

B2139

The Rydon
Community Sch

Hillside Road

A   B   180   C   D

THAKE

Champions
Farm

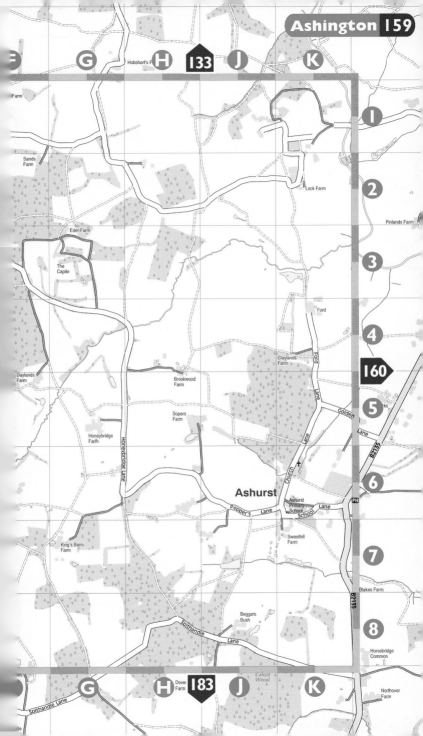

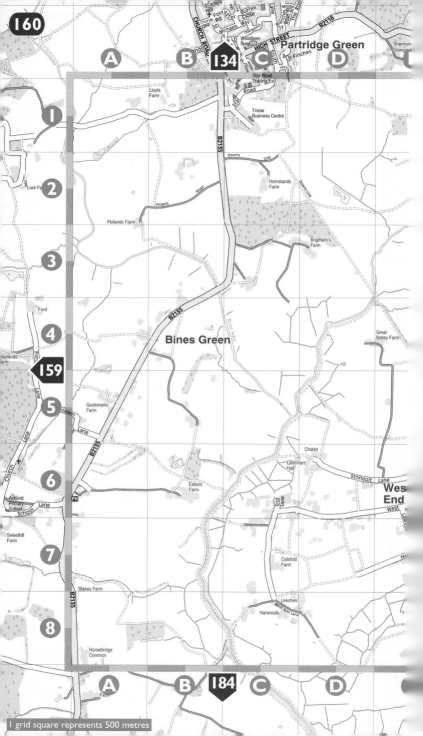

A   B   136   C   D

Wyndham Farm
Wineham Lane
Gratten Lane
Gratten Lane

Abbeylands Farm

Green Wapses Farm

1

Fieldlands Farm

Rice Lane
Lane

2

Lanehurst

Firsland Farm

Firsland Park Estate

3

Heatenthorn Farm

Morley Farm

B2116

4

Park Farm

Blackstone Gate Farm

High Cross

161

Trusler's Hill

5

Kingsfold

Woodhouse

Trusler's Hill Farm

6

Bylsborough Farm

Lane

Blackstone Lane

7

Blackstone St

Blackstone

Wick Farm

8

Woodmancote Place

A   B   186   C   D

Blackstone Lane

Woodmancote

Terry's Cross

A2

1 grid square represents 500 metres

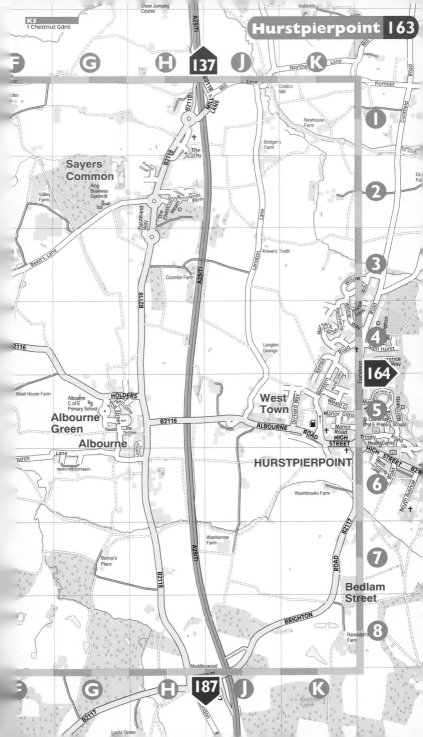

Keymer 165

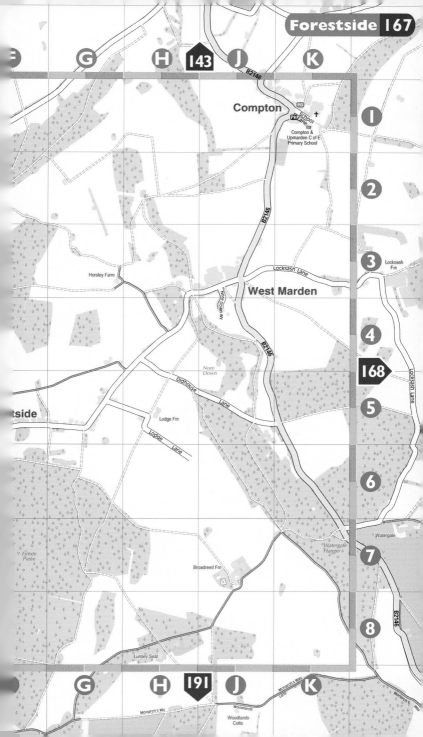

168

A **B** **144** **C** **D** **E**

1
PO
School Lane
PH
Compton & Upmarden C of E
Primary School

2

3 Locksash Lane Locksash Fm

Grevitts Copse

Up Marden

4
167 Locksash Lane

Lowerfarm Copse

5

6 Haslett Copse

Pitlands Fm

7 Watergate Watergate

Monarch's Way Church Fm

8
B2146

Monarch's Way

A **B** **192** **C** **D**

Monarch's Way Lane Cooks Ln Monarch's Way

Walderton

Bevis's Thumb

Long Lane Long

1 grid square represents 500 metres

F
G
H 145
J
K

I

East Marden

B2141

Phillswood La

Manor Place

Chilgrove

East Marden Down

2

Hillbarn

3

4

Wildhams Wood

170 Monarch's Way

5

6

Stoughton Down

Monarch's Way

7

Monarch's Way

8

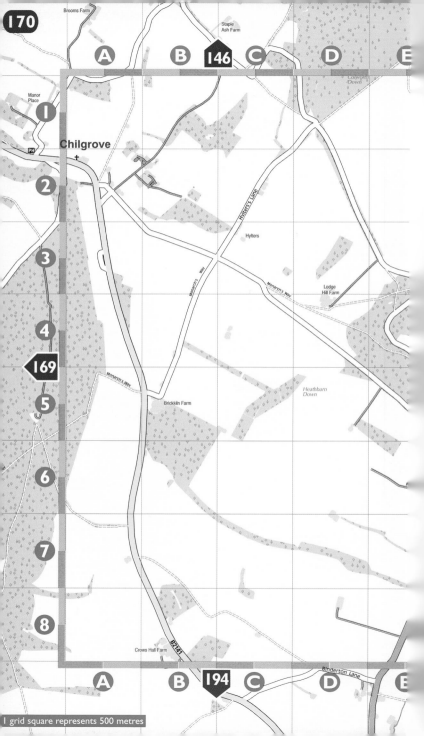

Brooms Farm

Staple
Ash Farm

A   **B**   **146**   **C**   **D**   **E**

Colworth
Down

Manor
Place

1

Chilgrove

PH

2

3

Rylter's Lane

Hylters

Monarch's Way

Monarch's Way

Lodge
Hill Farm

4

169

5

Monarch's Way

Brickkiln Farm

Heathbarn
Down

6

7

8

B2141

Crows Hall Farm

Binderton Lane

A   **B**   **194**   **C**   **D**   **E**

1 grid square represents 500 metres

Singleton Forest

I

Wellhanger Copse

Downley Cottage

Drovers

Canada Cotts

Cucumber Farm

Singleton

Singleton C Primary S

Church Wy

172

Cha

West Dean Gardens

West Dean College

West Dean

Waald & Downland Open Air Museum

Town Lane

Monarch's Way

Monarch's Way

195

G
H 149
J
K

I
2
3
4
174
5
6
7
8

Eastdean Wood

Lamb Lea

North Side

Waltham Down

New Road

Malecomb

Oxen Down

se Farm

New Road

Droke Lane

Ide's Barn

Droke

Selhurstpark Road

Selhurst Park

ark Road

Monarch's Way

Selhurst Park Farm

Monarch's Way

G
H 197
J
K

Red Copse

Middle

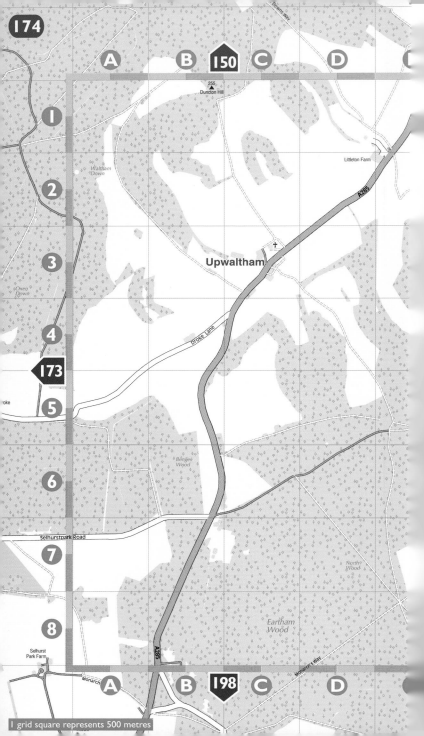

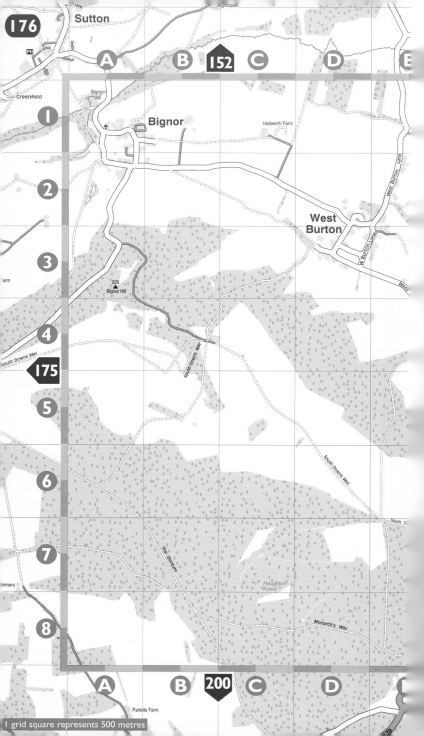

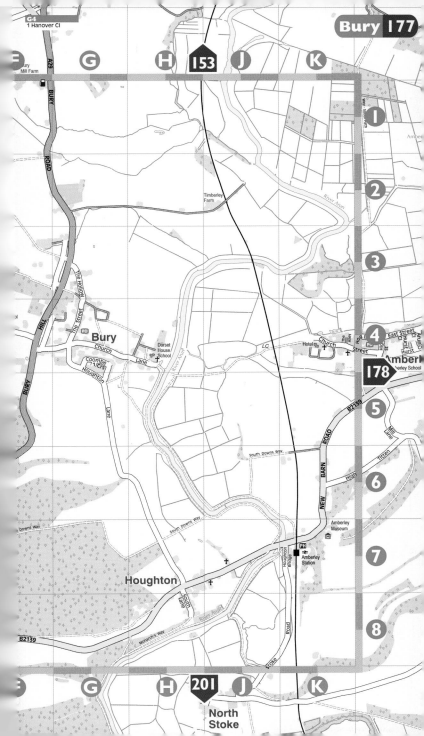

K1
1 Hormare Crs

K2
1 Greenacre Cl

G   H   155   J   K

Fryern
Hall

Dean
Way

Farmham
Crs

Hormare

I

Splerbrid

Chanctonbury
Leisure Centre

Cootham
Green

A283

PULBOROUGH   ROAD

Cootham

Warren
Croft

The Plantation

Amberley Cl

Cassidy Pl

FOX
Dell

Fox Ct

Plantatio
Way

B

Monastery

The G
Surge

2

Parham
Historic
House

Clay Lane

Link   Hi

ROAD

Kithurst Park

Kithurst Lane

Cemetery

school

Storrin
Lawn T
Club

Kithurst

AMBERLEY

Kithurst
Farm

Kithurst
Road

Gerston Business
Park

STORRIN

3

Springhead
Farm

4

180

5

212
Kithurst
Hill

South Downs Way

south dow

6

7

8

G   H   203   J   K

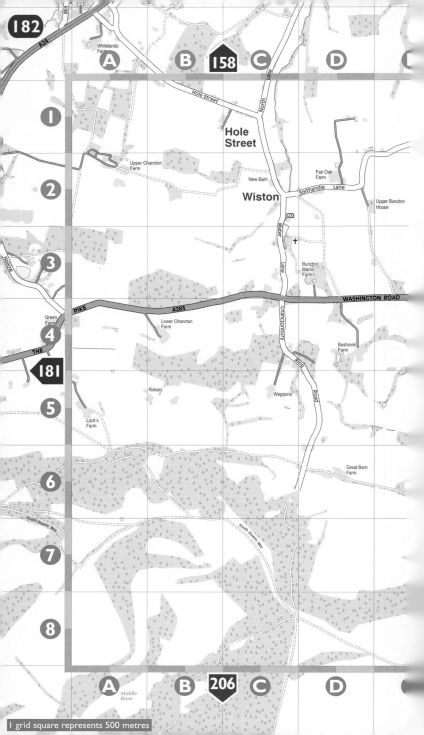

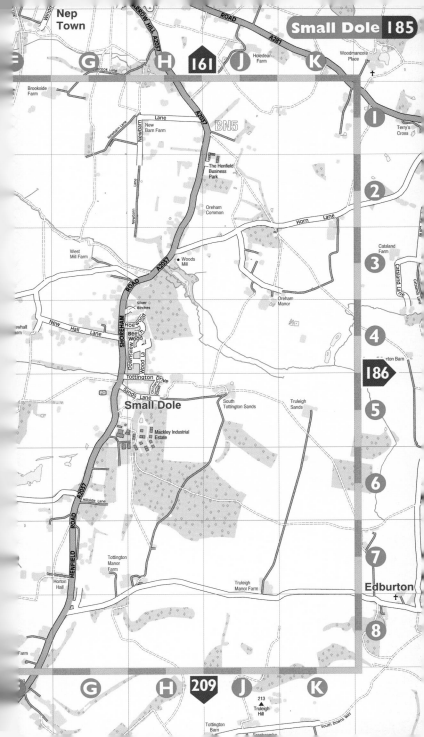

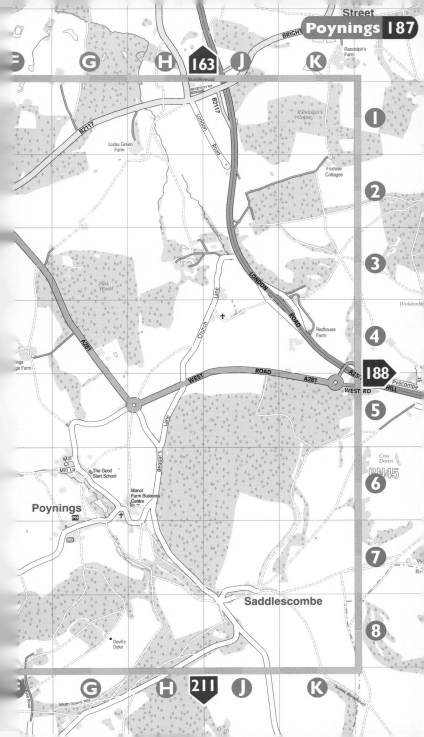

I grid square represents 500 metres

F6
1 Byerley Cl

F8
1 Church Vw
2 Old Rectory Cl
3 The Square

167

Lumley Seat

Monarch's Way Lane

Woodlands
Cotts

Monarch's Wy

Woodlands

Stanstead House

Newbarn Lane

Park Lane

Park Lane

Sindle's Fm

Monument La

B2146

Racton
Park Fm

192

B2147

Aldsworth

Ractonpark
Wood

Common Road

Marriott Lane

Commonside

Orchard
Mill Road

Westbourne
County Primary School

FOXBURY LANE

B2147

Woodmancote Lane

Woodmancote

Woodmancote Lane

Woodmanco

Westbourne

Edgell Rd

Cemetery Lane

Cemetery

Westbourne Surg

Duffield Lane

Walnut

South La

Old Farm Lane

A27(T)

Devils Copse

8

A27(T)

215

Lauder Cl

Hither
Gn

Fraser
Gdns

Breach Avenue

Bourne
Vw Cl

Haslemere
Road

East

Ham

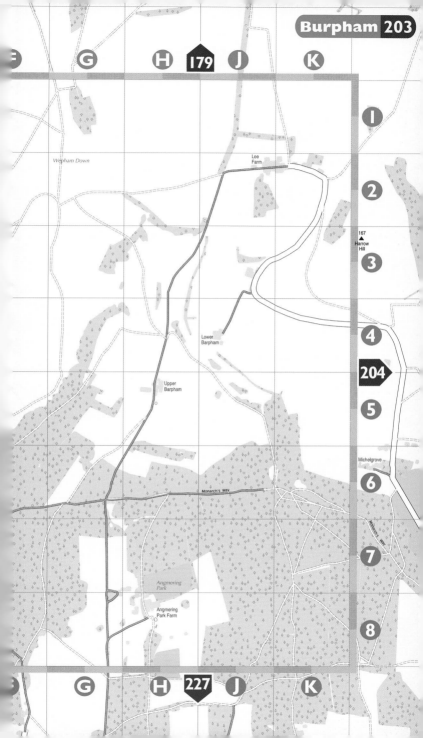

E G H 179 J K

I

Wepham Down

Lee Farm

2

167 ▲ Harrow Hill

3

Lower Barpham

4

204 ▶

Upper Barpham

5

Michelgrove

6

Monarch's Way

7

Angmering Park

Angmering Park Farm

8

Ⓐ Ⓑ 180 Ⓒ Ⓓ

Cobden
Farm

1

2

167
▲
Harrow
Hill

3

New
Barn

4

203

5

Monarch's Way

Myrtle Grove
Farm

Michelgrove

Monarch's Way

6

BN13

Longfurlong Lane

7

Longfurlong
Barn

LONG FURLONG A280

8

Ⓐ Ⓑ 228 Ⓒ Ⓓ

The Street

✝ Patching

206

182

205

230

A B C D

1

2 Pest House

3 Gallops Farm

4

5

6 **Nepcote**

7

8

Middle Brow

Findon Park Farm

No Man's Land

Monarch's Way

Canada Bottom

Cissbury Ring

Mount Carvey

BN14

Findon Valley

Storrington Rise
Sullington Gardens
May Tree Avenue
Findon Road
Central Avenue
Lime Tree Avenue
Cissbury Drive
Shepherds Mead
Hollinbury
Marshall Av
A24
Vale Avenue
Vale Drive

1 grid square represents 500 metres

KI
1 Coombe Dro

E

G

H

183

J

K

STEYNING

I

Peppercoombe

George's
Mill Road
Tanyard Lane
Charlton St
Steyning
Health
Centre
Steyning
Athletic
Club
Grammar
School
Holland Rd
Av
Rosemary
Road

Newham
Lane
Charltons
Way
Hill
Perrots
Penfold
Way
Coomb
De Braose Way
Castle La
Roman
Road

Jarvis
Chantil
The Coppice

Ingram
Portway
Penlands
Rise
Bramber Rd
Clays

Coombe Rd
Penlands
The Coombes

Maudlyn
Park
Maudlyn
Close
Monarchs
Way
Annington
Road

Newham
Lane
Limes Road
Bostal Road
Sopers
Lane
Maudlyn
Parkway
Lane
Kingsmead
Close

Bostal Road

Monarch's Way

2

Upper Maudlin
Farm

3

Annington

New Hill
Barn

*Steyning
Bowl*

Sopers Lane

South Downs Way

4

South Downs Way

South Downs Way

208

Annington
Hill Barn

5

6

7

*Steep
Down*

Valley
Barn

ggars
sh

8

E

G

H

231

J

K

Titch Hill

Titch Hill Farm

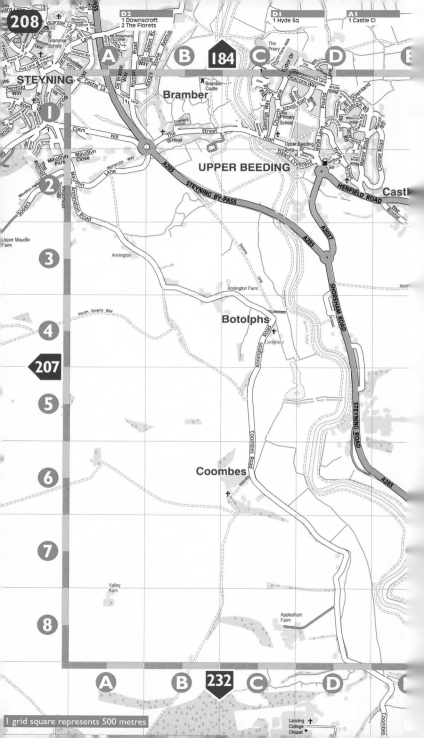

G   **H**   **185**   **J**   **K**

1

213
Truleigh
Hill

Tottington
Barn

Freshcombe
Farm

south Downs Way

2

The
Warren

Bushy
Bottom

3

Monarchs Way

4

210

5

Mill Hill

New Erringham
Farm

6

7

BN43

Old Erringham
Farm

8

G   **H** kingha   **233**   **J**   **K**
Barn

Slonk Hill
Farm

Ⓐ　　　Ⓑ　**186**　Ⓒ　　　Ⓓ　　Ⓔ

E7
1 Ridge Cl

Perching
Manor Farm
D8
1 Foxhunters Rd

C7
1 Nursery Cl
2 Westway Cl

South Downs Way

❶

South Downs Way

❷

West Sussex County
Brighton and Hove

Sussex

Border

❸

Bus
Bott

209

❹

West Sussex County
East Sussex County

Sussex Border Path

❺

❻

Mile Oak
Farm

BN41

A2701

❼

Overdown

Gorse Cl

Thornhill
Rise

Graham
Av

Granham

Oakdene

Oakdene
Wy

Denehurst Rd

Stanley

Healthfield

North England

Broomfield

❽

A2701

Margeurits Way

Mile Oak
Road

Stonery

Mile
Oak

Mile Oak Clinic

Chalky
Rd

Junior
School

Portslade
Community
College

Wickhurst

Ⓐ　　　Ⓑ　**234**　Ⓒ　　　Ⓓ

Slonk Hill
Farm

Portslade
Community
College

Holmbush
Cl

Hawkins
Crs

Hill Farm Way

White

Cromleigh
Way

I grid square represents 500 metres

D6
1 Deneside
2 Downside

C8
1 Barrowfield Cl

A8
1 Elizabeth Cl
2 Qu Caroline Cl
3 Sandringham Cl

A B 188 C D E

West Sussex
Brighton

1

D8
1 Blackthorn Cl

2

E5
1 Highview Rd

South
Hill Farm

Sussex Border Path

3

E6
1 Grangeways

Sussex Border Path

Sussex Border Path

4

211

Waterhall
Golf Course

Waterhall

A23(T)

LONDON ROAD

Braypool Lane

A23 (T)

LONDON ROAD

Court
Close

Church Hill

Old Patcham
Mews

5

Will's Dyke Road

Waterhall   Road

Brighton
Rugby Club

Mill Road

Windmill   Drive

Fernwood Rise

Branwyn
Crescent

Branwyn Av

PATCHAM BY-PASS

Patcham
House
School

A25

NORTON ROAD

6

A27(T)

Green   Ridge

Glen Rise

Bramble

Highbank

Bankside

Westdene
Primary
School

Cooke Hill

Barn Rise

Eldred

Ridge

Oving

Hill Top

Glen Rd

Westdene
Rise

Millcroft

Redhill

Dene Vale

Westdene

Glenham Drive

Hillcrest

Fairview

Avenue

Colbourne
Road

Dockers
Surgery

The
Deneway

W

7

A2038

Valley   Drive

Redhill   Drive

Hillbrow
Road

Tongdean

Withins   Lane

DYKE ROAD AVENUE

Woodland   Drive

Shepherds   Ctr

Tongean
Lane

Tongdean
Court

Cedars Gardens

8

Downland   Rd

Dornford

Steyning Av

Clarke   Av

KING GEORGE VI AVENUE

Sandringham Dr

Windlesham

George   Rd

Woodland

Victoria

Queen

Edward   Ct

Copton Drive

Elizabeth Av

Mary Av

Shepherds
Brow

Downside

Deanway

Tongdean

Road

Woodland drive

Tongdean   Drive

Dyke   Rd

The Spinney

DYKE ROAD AVENUE

Waverley   Rd

The Beeches

Cedars Gardens

Cuckmere Way

ROAD   Downland   Pk

Court Farm

St Peter's

NEVIL ROAD

A2023

Goldstone

Chartfield

Shirley

Hedcroft

A B 236 C D

Drive

Woodruff

Woodruff   Av

Mallory   Rd

Maldon   Rd

Preston
Park Stn

Clermont Road

Clermont

CPU
School

Leahurst

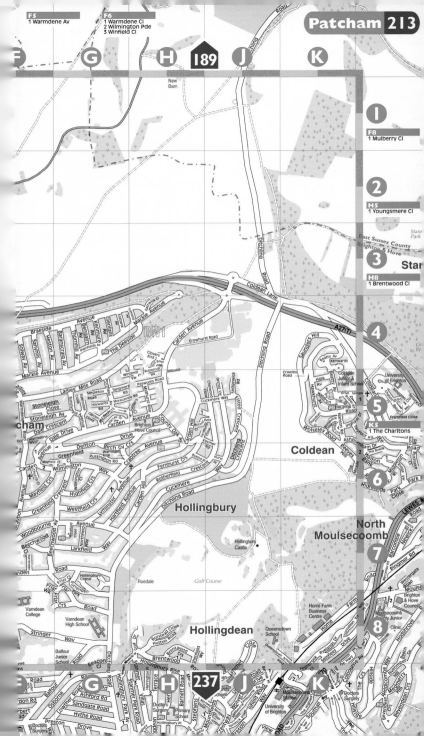

F5
1 Warmdene Av

F6
1 Warmdene Cl
2 Wilmington Pde
3 Winfield Cl

F **G** **H** **189** **J** **K**

I

F8
1 Mulberry Cl

2

H5
1 Youngsmere Cl

3 Star

Stanr
Park

East Sussex County
Brighton & Hove

H8
1 Brentwood Cl

New
Barn

Ditchling Road

Coldean Lane

Coldean Lane

A27(T)

Saunders Hill

Crawley
Road

4

Cr

5

K5
1 The Charltons

University
of Brighton

Coldean Junior
Infant School

Framfield Close

Braeside

Mackie Avenue

Carden Avenue

Crowhurst Road

BN1

Clovers
End

Windmill

Singleton
Road

Tangmere

Morecambe Rd

Petworth Road

Haywards
Rd

Stoneleigh
Close

Stoneleigh Av

Dale Crescent

cham

Carden
Avenue

Brighton &
Hove Council

County Oak

Carden Hill

Cuckmere Way

Sedgewick Rd

Sedgewick Rd

Beatty Av

Kenwards

Coldean
Junior
Infant School

Selham Drive

Haig
Av

Coldean Lane

Ingram Cres

Ashburnham Dr

Wolseley Road

Coldean

Denton

Greenfield

Birch Gv Crs

Warnham
Rustington Rd

Crabtree Avenue

Mayfield

Mayfield Crs

Highfield Crs

Greenfield Crescent

Fernhurst Crs

Rotherfield

Cuckmere Crescent

Ditchling Crescent

Reeves Hill

Walton Bank

Ashburnham Dr

The Rivene

Highclere

Park
Close

6

Park
Road

Wilmington

Way

Westfield Crs

Lyminster Avenue

Hartfield Avenue

Carden Hill

Ditchling Crescent

Cuckmere Way

Hollingbury

Woodbourne

Beechwood

Northfield
Close

Larkfield

Avenue

Way

**North
Moulsecoomb**

LEWES
Road

7

Frant
Wk

Hollingbury
Copse

Hollingbury
Castle

Roedale

Golf Course

Home Farm
Business
Centre

Farm
Road

Barcombe Road

Newick Road

Mouse

Brighton
& Hove
Council

8

Varndean
College

Varndean
High School

Stringer
Way

Balfour
Junior
School

Ditchling
Road

Beacon Cl

Hollingdean

Hurstwood Close

Hutton Road

Brentwood

Stanmer Road

237

Queensdown
School

Moulsecoomb
Station

University
of Brighton

Doctors
Surgery

Clinic

Hillside

ens

Road

Balfour
Osborne

Lowther
Rd

Ashford Rd

Sandgate Road

Hythe Rd

Hollingbury Rise

Stanmer Villas

Hollingbury Park Av

Barnett Road

Stephens
Terrace

Doctors
Surgery

Primary
School

Hollingbury Pl

G **H** **237** **J** **K**

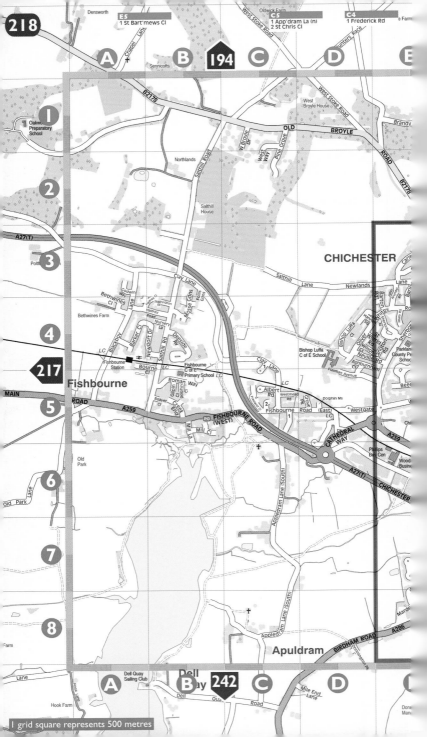

F2
1 Hereford Cl
2 Salisbury Wy

F4
1 Cavendish St
2 Lancastrian Gra
3 Orchard Gdns
4 The Providence
5 Tower Cl
6 Washington St

195

F5
1 The Woolstaplers

F7
1 Bywater Wy

F8
1 Cutfield Cl
2 Turnpike Cl

G4
1 Alderman's Wk
2 Guildhall St
3 St Cyriacs

220

G5
1 Cooper St
2 East Rw
3 East Walls
4 Little London
5 New Town
6 North St
7 St Martin's St

G6
1 Martlet Cl
2 Winguard Wy

H4
1 Doug Martin Rd
2 Meadowfield Dr

H6
1 Clydesdale Av
2 Littlefield Rd

J3
1 The Waterplat

Summersdale

Whyke

Stockbridge

243

K5
1 Balmoral Cl
2 Marlborough Cl
3 Sandringham Rd
4 William Rd

J5
1 Blenheim Gdns

J4
1 Farndell Cl
2 Harvester Cl
3 St James's Sq

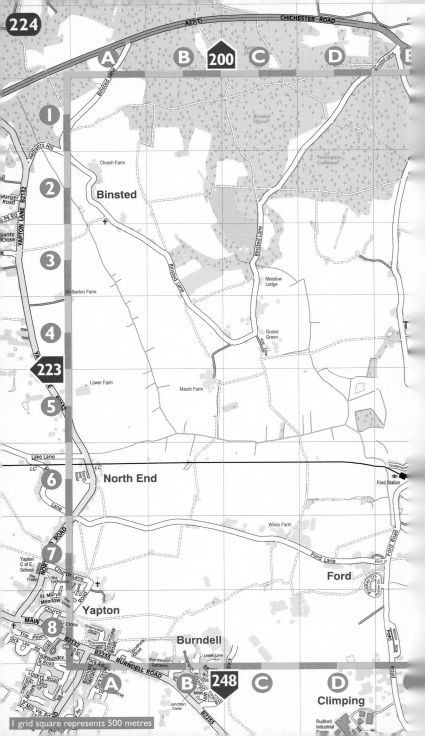

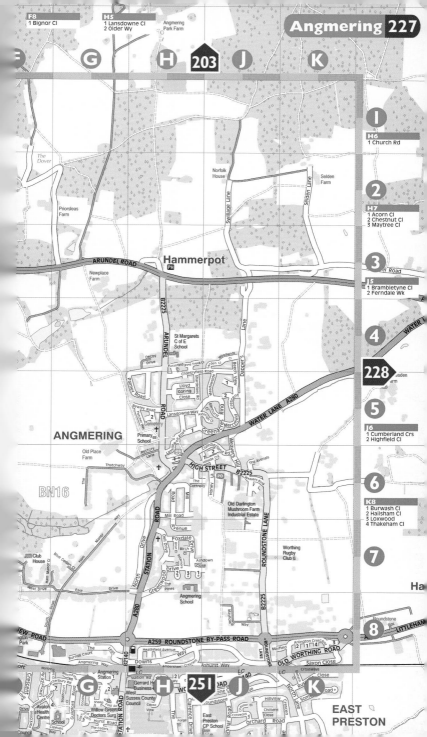

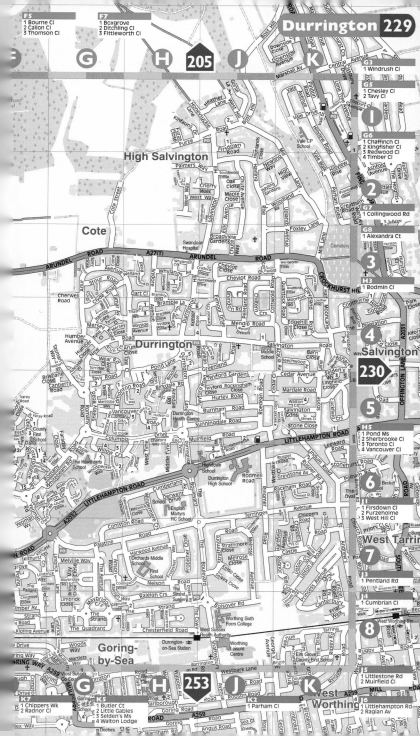

F6
1 Fishermans Wk
2 Mariners Cl
3 Seahaven Gdns

G4
1 Buckingham St
2 Little High St

G **H** **209** **J** **K**

Buckingham Barn

Slonk Hill Farm

I

H2
1 Amberley Cl
2 Annington Gdns
3 Buckingham Ms
4 Mill Av
5 Newtimber Gdns
6 Ravensbourne Cl

2

H3
1 The Cygnets
2 Northbourne Cl

3

H4
1 St Mary's Cl

Old Shoreham

Saxons

Slonk Hill Road

Downside

Greenways Crescent

Shoreham

Adur Avenue

Upper Shoreham Road

St Nicolas La

Greenacres

Cemetery

Shoreham County First School

Windlesham Rd

Northbourne Medical Centre

Worthing & Southlands Hospitals N H S Trust

St Nicholas & St Mary School

St Peters R C School

Buckingham Middle School

Nicolson Drive

Park Rd

Park Avenue

Kingston Buci School

West Sussex County Council

Middle Road

Kingston by Sea

4

Riverbank Business Centre

Rosslyn Road

Worthing District Health Authority

Shoreham-by-Sea Station

Police Stn

Civic Centre

The Cyril Richings Business Centre 202-210

Dolphin Way

BRIGHTON

234

HIGH STREET A259

Marlipins Museum

Adur District Council

Riverside Business Centre

Lower Beach Road

Riverside Road

Anchor Cl

Harbour Way

H5
1 Collingwood Ct
2 Hardy Cl

5

Cheal Cl

First Sch The Marlinspike

Winterton Way

Fowey Close

Feversham Close

The Burrells

Falcon

Kingston Bay Road

River Cl

Beach Green

The Meadway

Old Fort Road

Nature Reserve

Kings Walk

Woodards View

Havenside

Beach Road

SHOREHAM-BY-SEA

Shoreham Beach

6

J3
1 Buckingham Cl

7

K2
1 Berberis Ct
2 Marjoram Pl
3 New Barn Cl
4 Tottington Wy

8

G **H** **J** **K**

K3
1 Glebelands Cl

238

A North Hayli **B** **214** **C** **D** **E**

St Peter's Av

I
HAYLING ISLAND

St Peter's Road

Chichester Road

Tye

Woodgaston Lane

Cutner Lane

2

3

4

Emsworth Channel

Marker Point

Mill Rithe

5

6

Eastwood

Beech Grove

Laburnum Grove

7

Mengham Salterns

8
Mengham

Simmons

Salterns Cl

Salterns Lane

Marine

Seaview Road

Walk

Black Po

Blackthorn Dr

Delsmore Avenue

North Cres

Norman Rd

Brackle Rd

A **B** Saltsmore **C** **D**

Fisher

Harold Road

Foreland Ct

St Andrew's Road

St Hermans Rd

Eastoke

Bowin Close

Avenue

Eastoke

Bosmere

Thorney Island

West Thorney

Thorney Island Airfield

Smith Lane

Church

Pleasant Lane

Victor Rd

Beverley Rd

Vulcan Road

Valiant Road

Varsity Road

Valetta Road

Thorney Channel

Stanbury Point

Longmere Point

Pilsey Island

Pilsey Sand

Chichester Harbour

's Lake

East Head

Ellanore

Roman Landing

Roman Landing

Roman Landing

Lockbash

Summerfield Road

Elmstead Pk Rd

Cunliffe Close

Rookwood Lane

Rookwood Lane

Summerfield Rd

Summerfield Road

ROOKWOOD RD

G   H   215   J   K

I

2

3

4

240

5

6

7

8

G   H   256   J   K

A B **216** C D E

E4
1 Chandlers Reach
2 Waterstone Cl

1

New Barn

Cobnor Fm

Bosham
Channel

Gerald Daniel
Sailing Club

Cobnor Ho

Low

Hone

Lower

Lower Lane

2

3

Cobnor
Point

Chichester Channel

Itchenor
Sailing Club

4

West Itchenor

The Street

Orchard Orchard
Lane

Itchenor Road

Spinney

5

Itchenor Ho

Ole

Itchenor Road

6

Chalkdock
Lane

Itchenor Road

7

Rookwood
Lane

Sheepwash Lane

Redlands Fm

Redlands Lane

Sheepwash Lane

Rookwood Lane

Ellanore Lane

Summerfield
Rd

8

B2179

B2179

Acre Street

an Landing

A B **257** C D

Rookwood Rd

Summerfield Road
Elmstead
Park Road
Cunliffe

Channel Lane

Hall Lane

Holmes Fm

Nunnington Farm

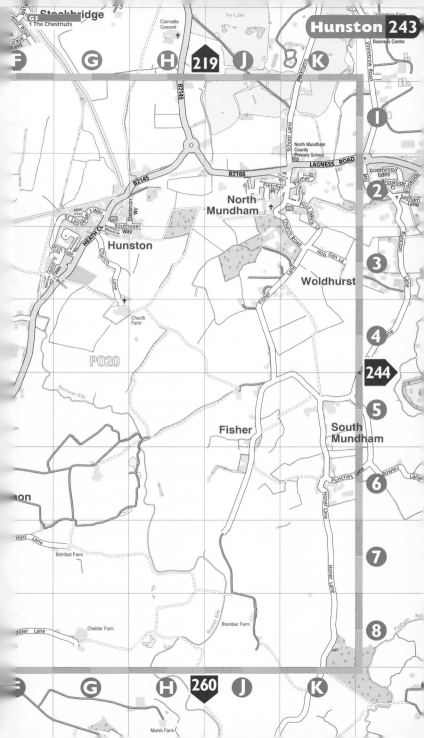

Stockbridge
G3
1 The Chestnuts

Carmelite Convent

Ivy Lake

Business Centre

F

G

H

219

J

K

Vinnetrow Road

I

B2145

Peckhams

School Lane

North Mundham County Primary School

LAGNESS ROAD

Goodwood Gdns

Brookside Cl

Saltham Lane

2

B2145

B2166

Palmer

Fletcher Pl

Mill Lane

Brookside

High trees

St Leod

Cedar's Way

Southover Way

Meadow

Blackman Wy

Post Office La

Church Road

Runcton Lane

North Mundham

3

HEATH CL

Orch Side

Hilton Way

Hunston

Church Lane

Hop Gdn La

Woldhurst

Church Farm

Fisher Lane

4

PO20

244

Bremere Rife

Fisher

South Mundham

5

Punches Lane

Bowley Lane

6

fast Lane

Brimfast Farm

Honer Lane

7

alder Lane

Chalder Farm

Bremere Rife

Bramber Farm

Honer Lane

Pagham Rife

8

on

G

H

260

J

K

Marsh Farm

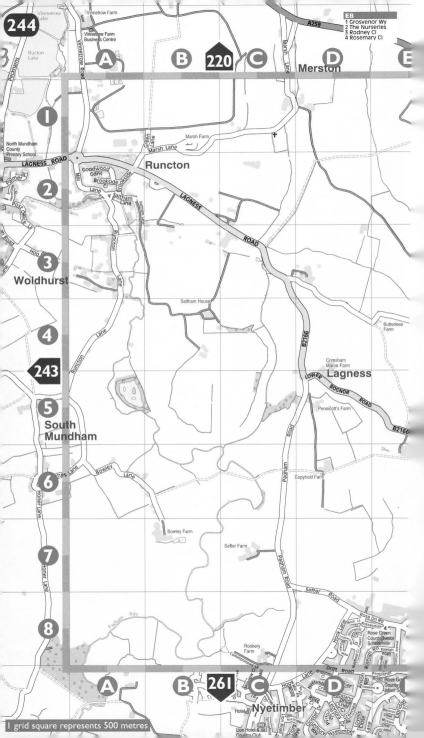

H1
1 Broad Piece

J1
1 Chapel Cl

River Arun

A259

F

G

H

225

J

K

I

Greenfields
Wheatcroft
Joyce Close
Furlong
Courtwick
The
Crossways
Grand Avenue
West Way
Wickbourne
Whitelea
Road
Flora Mcdonald
County Junior School
Wick Farm Road
Roman Acre
Harwood Road

WICK STREET
North Street
St Catherines RC
Primary
School
Littlehampton
Community
School

Littlehampton
County
Junior School

ARUNDEL ROAD

A284

Elm Grove
County
Infants School

LITTLEHAMPTO

Cornwall
Parham
Blackhurst Wy

BRIDGE ROAD

Riverside
Industrial Estate
Quayside

BRIDGE ROAD
Gloucester
East Ham
Howard
Road

TERMINUS RD

FRANCISCAN WAY

Police
Station

East Street
Medical
Centre

EAST STR

St Mary's

Littlehampton
Station

Rope Walk

Ferry Road

A259

BN17

Brookpits

Golf
Course

The Mill

ngton

NEW ROAD

Pier Road

Arun Road

South Terrace

Irvine

Clifton Road

St Catherines Rd

Bayford Road

BEACH ROAD

Littlehampton
Town Council

Maltravers Rd

Arun
District
Council

Littlehampton
Health Centre

Selborne

3

Coastguard
Road

250

5

6

7

8

F

G

H

J

K

WICK STREET

WORTHING ROAD

WORTHING ROAD

B2187

WORTHING

A **B** **C** **D** **E**

B2
1 St Flora's Cl
2 St Mary's Wy

B1
1 Bellscroft Cl
2 Esmonde Cl

A2
1 Church Ap
2 P'son Wilson Rd
3 St Mary's Gdns

B3
1 The Cloisters
2 Norfolk Pl

1

LITTLEHAMPTON

C1
1 Barque Cl
2 Compass Cl
3 Derwent Cl
4 Portland Cl
5 Rydal Cl

2

3

D1
1 Staffords Cl

SOUTH TERRACE

4

5

D2
1 Highfield Gdns
2 Milton Cl
3 Sutherland Cl

6

D3
1 Green Bushes Cl
2 Hardham Cl
3 Knightscroft Cl
4 Parham Cl
5 Rudgwick Cl

7

D4
1 Aldwick Cl
2 The Gilberts
3 Howards Wy
4 Rackham Rd

8

A **B** **C** **D**

E1
1 Fairlawn
2 Holmfield Cl
3 Shopfield Cl
4 Sussex Gdns

E3
1 Abbotswood Wk
2 Normanhurst Cl

1 grid square represents 500 metres

Goring-by-Sea

229

West Worthing

254

G · 1 Aldsworth Ct

G1
1 Barrington Cl
2 Goring Rd
3 Mersham Gdns
4 Mulberry Gdns
5 Ryecroft Gdns

H2
1 Warnham Cl

H1
1 Marlborough Wy

K1
1 St Raphael's Rd

K2
1 Anscombe Cl

WORTHING

TARRING ROAD

COWPER ROAD

RICHMOND ROAD

B1
1 Highgrove Gdns

A1
1 Hastings Rd

A1
1 Dorchester Gdns
2 Lansdowne Ct
3 The Rowans
4 West Av

B2
1 Boundary Cl

C1
1 Elizabeth Rd
2 Park Crs
3 Richmond Ct
4 Treveor Cl

C2
1 Brunswick Rd
2 Milton St
3 Western Rw

D1
1 Chapel Rd
2 Grafton Pl
3 Grosvenor Rd
4 Humphrys Rd
5 Stoke Abbott Rd

D2
1 Montague Pl
2 New St
3 Prospect Pl

E1
1 Alfred Pl
2 Warwick Pl

1 grid square represents 500 metres

East Head

239

ck Point

Bracklesham Rd

West Sussex County
Hampshire County

Eastoke Point

Roman Landing

Roman Landing

West Wittering
Parochial School

Coastguard Lane

West Strand

1 grid square represents 500 metres

A B 241 C D E

1

Somerley

Hale Farm

2

Church Farm Lane

3

Stubcroft Farm

4

257

Downview

STOCKS

5

257

6

Bracklesham

7

8

A B C D

Holt Place

B2179

Pinks Lane

B2198

Hundredsteddle La

Somerley Lane

Carthagena Farm

Tile Barn Lane

Mill House

B2198

Bookers Lane

Second Avenue

Third Avenue

Earnley Road

Earnley Grange

Stubcroft Lane

Clayton Lane

Holden's Farm

BRACKLESHAM LANE

Earnley Mnr Close

Earnley

Barton Wy

Middleton Close

Clappers Lane

Graywood Av

Elm Close

Hale Close

Beech Av

Cormorant

Landingham

Harmony Dr

Elcombe Acre

Drove Lane

Marsh Farm

Sussex Beach Holiday Village

Stoney Lane

Seafield Drive

East Bracklesham Drive

West Bracklesham Drive

Witterings

Hilton Park

Bracklesham Bay

I grid square represents 500 metres

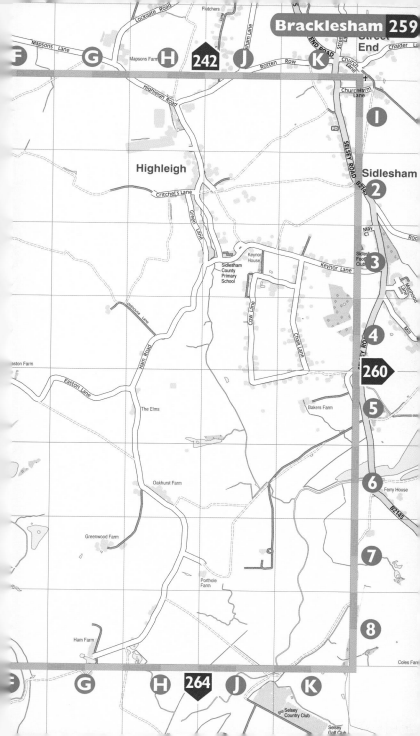

Rose Green

B1
1 C'mare Coppice
2 Cheveley Gdns
3 Edinburgh Cl
4 Little Babbsham
5 Ludlow Cl
6 Redwood Pl
7 Stanmore Gdns

A2
1 Coastguard Pde
2 Fisherman's Wk
3 Seacourt Cl

A1
1 Alborough Wy
2 Grangewood Dr
3 Hamilton Gdns
4 Old Farm Cl
5 Tangmere Gdns

Aldwick

I

B2
1 Aldwick Hundred
2 Strange Gdn

2

C1
1 Mauldmare Cl
2 Raycroft Cl
3 Shipfield
4 Thrusloes
5 Wallfield
6 Woodstock Gdns

3

D1
1 Wessex Av

4

5

E1
1 Charlwood St
2 Oxford St
3 Park Ter
4 St Winifred's Cl
5 Swansea Gdns
6 Victoria Rd South
7 Wood St

6

7

8

A   B   C   D   E

1 grid square represents 500 metres

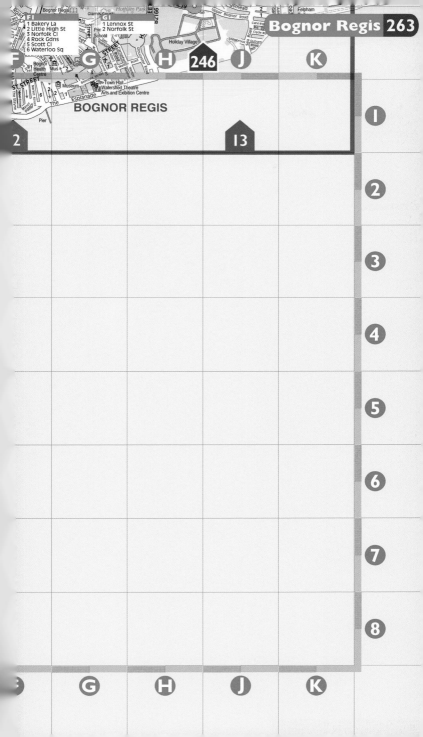

F1
1 Bakery La
2 Little High St
3 Norfolk Cl
4 Rock Gdns
5 Scott Cl
6 Waterloo Sq

G1
1 Lennox St
2 Norfolk St

BOGNOR REGIS

E4
1 Grant Cl

D3
1 Broadway

C3
1 Cross Eels
2 Mayridge

A

B

259

C

D

E

1

E5
1 Ursula Av North

2

E6
1 Beaufield Cl

3

4

5

6

7

8

Selsey
Country Club

Chainbridge
Duck
Lane
Seagull
Teal Lane
Tower
La
Webster
Lobster
Prawn Cl
Peter's
Pl
Mackerel La
Round
Piece
Warner's
Rd
Warner's La
Warner's La
Spinney
Deer
Pk
Coppice La
Meomerry
Cranary La
Chair
Montain Crs
Freeways
1 The
Wadeway
Dirk Lane
Hornet
Horse
West Sands
Leisure Centre
Mill Lane
Birches Esplanade
The Horse
Shoe
Large
Hersee Way
Thorney
Dr
West Street
Coxes
Rd
Murray
Rd
Vincent
Bonmar
Cl
Bonmar
HILLFIELD ROAD
Pear
Road
B2145
Clayton
Warner
Rd
The
Bridge
Dainfield
Road
Seal
Marine
Loto

A

B

C

D

Abbotsford 138 E5
Abingworth 156 E5
Adversane 101 H8
Albourne 163 G5
Albourne Green 163 F5
Aldingbourne 221 H4
Aldrington 235 J4
Aldwick 262 B1
Alfold 46 B2
Alfold Bars 46 B4
Almodington 258 E3
Amberley 178 A4
Ancton 247 K5
Angmering 227 G5
Ansteadbrook 42 A6
Ansty 110 C8
Apuldram 218 C8
Ardingly 84 D3
Arundel 201 H8
Ashfold Crossways 80 C5
Ashington 157 K7
Ashurst 159 J6
Ashurst Wood 37 J5
Atherington 249 F5
Balcombe 83 G1
Balcombe Lane 57 G6
Baldwins Hill 22 A8
Balls Cross 98 B2
Balls Green 102 E8
Barlavington 151 J6
Barnham 223 G6
Barns Green 103 J1
Beare Green 14 A1
Bedham 127 H3
Bedlam Street 163 K7
Beggars Bush 207 F8
Bell Hill 88 C6
Bepton 147 G2
Bewbush 30 D8
Bexleyhill 95 G4
Bignor 176 B1
Billingshurst 102 C4
Bilsham 247 K2
Bines Green 160 B4
Binsted 224 A2
Birchgrove 86 E2
Birdham 241 J5
Black Corner 18 D7
Blackstone 162 C6
Blackwell 36 C1
Bognor Regis 12 C6
Bolney 109 G8
Borden 91 K5
Bosham 217 G6
Bosham Hoe 241 F3
Botolphs 208 B4
Boxgrove 196 E8
Bracklesham 258 B6
Bramber 208 B1
Bramshott 38 C5
Breach 215 H2
Brighton 11 D6
Broadbridge 217 H4
Broadbridge Heath 50 B7
Broadfield 55 G1
Broadford Bridge 130 D3
Broadwater 230 D5
Brookpits 249 F3
Brooks Green 103 J4
Brook Street 111 F1
Broomer's Corner 131 K4
Broomershill 129 G7
Buchan Hill 54 E3
Bucks Green 47 K5
Burgess Hill 139 G8
Buriton 116 C6
Burndell 224 B8
Burpham 202 C5
Burstow 19 G4
Bury 177 G4
Byworth 126 B5
Camelsdale 40 C6
Castle Town 208 E2
Causeway 116 C1
Charlton 172 A5
Charlwood 16 D4
Charlwood 60 C2
Chelwood Common 87 H5
Chelwood Gate 87 G2
Chichester 218 D3
Chidham 216 C7
Chilgrove 169 K1
Chithurst 92 C8
Church Norton 260 C7
Churchwood 127 G7
Cinder Hill 85 J3
Clapham 228 D2

Clayton 188 E3
Climping 248 D1
Coates 152 C3
Cocking 148 A3
Cocking Causeway 122 A7
Codmore Hill 128 E6
Cold Ash Hill 38 E6
Coldean 213 K6
Coldwaltham 153 J5
Colgate 54 A5
Colworth 245 G1
The Common 51 G7
Compton 167 J1
Coneyhurst 103 F7
Coolham 131 J1
Coombes 208 B6
Cootham 179 J2
Copsale 105 H5
Copthorne 19 H8
Cote 229 G3
Cowfold 135 H1
Cox Green 48 C1
Crabtree 107 J4
Crawley 3 D4
Crawley Down 34 C4
Critchmere 40 A4
Crockerhill 197 J8
Crossbush 226 A2
Cross Gate 178 C4
Crosspost 136 E2
Crouchers 242 B2
Cuckfield 111 F6
Cudworth 15 G3
Danehill 86 E7
Deanlane End 166 B6
Dell Quay 242 B1
Denne Park 77 J4
Denvilles 214 A1
Dial Green 67 K8
Dial Post 132 E7
Didling 146 B1
Ditchling 165 K8
Domewood 20 D6
Donnington 242 E2
Doomsday Green 78 C3
Dormansland 23 F2
Dormans Park 22 C4
Down Park 34 C2
Dragons Green 104 B8
Dumpford 120 A3
Duncton 151 F4
Durleighmarsh 90 A8
Durrington 229 H4
Earnley 258 B5
Eartham 198 B3
Easebourne 122 A1
East Ashling 193 J7
East Beach 265 H2
East Dean 172 E5
Eastergate 222 D4
East Grinstead 36 C2
East Hampnett 221 G1
East Harting 118 D8
East Kingston 252 A2
East Lavant 195 G6
East Lavington 150 C5
East Liss 62 B8
East Marden 169 F1
East Preston 251 K1
East Wittering 257 K5
East Worthing 231 H8
Ebernoe 69 K7
Edburton 186 A7
Egdean 126 D6
Elbridge 245 G2
Ellen's Green 24 C7
Elmer 248 B6
Elmers Marsh 65 G6
Elsted 119 G7
Emsworth 214 C4
Faygate 53 G2
Felbridge 21 H7
Felcourt 22 A3
Felpham 247 F6
Fernhill 18 E4
Fernhurst 66 B5
Ferring 252 D1
Finchdean 166 B5
Findon 205 J4
Findon Valley 230 B1
Fishbourne 217 K5
Fisher 243 J5
Fishersgate 234 D4
Fisherstreet 42 D8
Fittleworth 127 G8
Five Oaks 74 C6
Flansham 247 G4

Flathurst 1
Fontwell 2
Ford 2
Forest Row 1
Forestside 1
Fulking 1
Funtington 1
Furnace Green 1
Furnace Wood 1
Furner's Green 1
Fyning 1
Gay Street 1
Goddards' Green 1
Godleys Green 1
Goose Green 1
Gorehill 1
Goring-by-Sea 1
Gossops Green 1
Graffham 1
Grayswood 1
Great Common 1
Greatham 1
Green Street 1
Gunter's Bridge 1
Habin 1
Halecommon 1
Halfway Bridge 1
Halnaker 2
Hambrook 2
Hammer 1
Hammer Bottom 1
Hammerpot 1
Hampers Green 1
Handcross 1
Hangleton 2
Hangleton 1
Hardham 1
Haslemere 1
Haslingbourne 1
Hassocks 1
Hatch Farm Hill 1
The Haven 1
Haywards Heath 1
Heath Common 1
Heath End 1
Henfield 1
Henley 1
Henley Common 1
Hermitage 2
Heyshott 1
Heyshott Green 1
Hickstead 1
Highbrook 1
High Cross 1
Highgate 1
Highleigh 1
High Salvington 1
Highstreet Green 1
Hill Brow 1
Hillgrove 1
Hill Side 1
Hill Top 1
Hole Street 1
Hollingbury 1
Hollingdean 1
Hooksway 1
Hookwood 1
Horsemere Green 1
Horsham 1
Horsted Keynes 1
Houghton 1
Hove 1
Hoyle 1
Hunston 1
Hurstpierpoint 1
Hurst Wickham 1
Ifield 1
Ifield Green 1
Ifieldwood 1
Ifold 1
Ingrams Green 1
Iping 1
Itchingfield 1
Kemp Town 1
Kent Street 1
Keymer 1
Kingsfold 1
Kingsley Green 1
Kingston by Sea 1
Kingston Gorse 1
Kirdford 1
Lagness 2
Lambs Green 1
Lancing 1
Langley 1
Langley Green 1
Leggatt Hill 1

...ld	95 K3	Preston	10 A1	Tangmere	220 E1

Entry	Ref
...ld	95 K3
......	222 B8
...nere	39 G8
...eld	112 D3
...k	38 A8
......	62 A8
...Bognor	126 E5
...Common	124 D3
...ampton	249 K1
...aven	5 D2
...vorth	134 C6
...orth	95 K8
...orth Common	95 J5
... Beeding	79 J8
...Fittleworth	153 F2
...Horncroft	153 F3
...ld Heath	17 K6
...ood	46 A7
...y	214 E2
...hall	96 B1
...ster	225 K5
...rel's Common	71 G6
...urst	200 B2
...abower	32 C7
...gs Heath	79 F6
... Royal	31 J1
...urst	106 A5
...ill	155 G1
... Heights	66 B2
...n	220 A1
...n	220 D8
...ton-on-Sea	247 J6
...st	122 B5
...avant	194 E5
...ak	210 D8
...l	92 A1
...d	120 E5
...nt	62 A6
... Gate	78 E7
...c Hill	68 B6
...te	205 K6
...wn	161 G8
...righton	190 E8
...apel	21 G2
...gate	14 C2
...und Common	73 G8
...wn	77 K3
...wn	64 B1
...Bersted	245 J4
...hapel	68 E4
...End	21 K7
...End	205 H3
...End	224 A6
...ate	3 E1
...Hayling	214 A8
...Heath	129 H4
...Lancing	232 B3
...Marden	145 F7
...Moulsecoomb	213 K7
...Mundham	243 J2
...ey	214 A7
...Stoke	201 J1
......	221 K1
......	260 B8
...d	117 G4
...rne	155 J1
...rne	215 K4
...rne Common	155 K1
...nbe	39 K1
...st	106 B2
...ber	261 H1
...od	118 E3
......	222 A3
......	5 E5
...odhill	25 K4
......	201 K5
...reham	233 G2
......	220 E4
...n	261 F3
...ok	101 K4
...reet	49 G8
...ge Green	134 C8
...n	213 F5
...g	228 B1
...Green	26 C3
...ottage	54 E4
...ield	88 B8
...th	125 J3
...w	71 F1
......	226 D5
...Corner	226 C3
...d	7 F3
...de-by-Sea	235 F5
...de Village	234 E1
...Hill	32 C3
...Cross	17 G2
...gs	187 F6

Entry	Ref
Preston	10 A1
Prince's Marsh	89 K1
Prinsted	215 G4
Pulborough	154 D2
Pyecombe	188 B5
Quags Corner	121 G4
Queen's Corner	92 E3
Rackham	178 E3
Rake	62 E7
Ramsnest Common	42 C5
Rapkyns	50 A7
Redford	93 G2
Ridge Common	88 A6
River	124 C1
Robins	92 C4
Rock	181 H2
Roffey	5 F2
Rogate	90 E8
Rose Green	244 E8
Rotherbridge	125 G6
Roundstreet Common	72 D5
Rowhook	49 J2
Rowland's Castle	190 B1
Rudgwick	48 A4
Runcton	244 B2
Rusper	28 E4
Russ Hill	16 A6
Rustington	251 F2
Saddlescombe	187 J8
Salvington	230 A4
Saxby	223 J6
Sayers Common	163 G2
Scayne's Hill	113 G8
Selham	124 B5
Selsey	265 G5
Selsfield Common	58 D2
Sharpthorne	59 J5
Sheet	89 F6
Sheffield Green	115 F4
Shepherd's Hill	40 E5
Shermanbury	135 F8
Shipley	132 D3
Shipley Bridge	19 F5
Shipton Green	240 E7
Shopp Hill	68 A5
Shopwyke	220 B4
Shoreham Beach	233 K6
Shoreham-by-Sea	233 H6
Shottermill	40 A5
Shripney	246 B2
Sidlesham	260 A2
Sidlesham Common	242 E6
Singleton	171 J4
Slaugham	80 E6
Slindon	199 H6
Slinfold	49 H8
Slough Green	110 B2
Small Dole	185 G5
Smallfield	19 G1
Smithbrook	95 K7
Smock Alley	156 B4
Somerley	258 B1
Sompting	231 H5
Sompting Abbotts	231 G3
South Ambersham	123 H5
South Bersted	12 C2
Southbourne	215 J3
Southern Cross	234 E3
Southgate	2 C5
South Harting	118 A7
South Lancing	232 A6
South Mundham	243 K5
South Stoke	201 K3
Southwater	105 F3
Southwater Street	76 C8
Southwick	234 C3
Staplefield	81 K6
Staples Hill	70 E8
Stedham	121 G2
Steep	88 C4
Steep Marsh	88 E2
Steyning	207 K1
Stockbridge	6 B6
Stonequarry	22 E8
Stopham	153 K1
Storrington	180 A3
Stoughton	168 E8
Street End	243 F8
Strettington	196 C7
Strood Green	50 B5
Stubbermere	190 E3
Sullington	180 D4
Sullington Warren	180 D2
Summersdale	219 G1
Sunnyside	36 C5
Sutton	152 A8
Sutton End	151 K5

Entry	Ref
Tangmere	220 E1
Temple Bar	196 C8
Terwick Common	91 H6
Thakeham	157 F4
Thorney Island	215 G8
Three Bridges	3 E2
Tilgate	2 C6
Tilgate Forest Row	55 G6
Tillington	125 G3
Tinsley Green	18 C7
Tisman's Common	47 J6
Titty Hill	92 E3
Toddington	226 B7
Tompset's Bank	61 K3
Topleigh	149 H1
Tortington	224 E4
Tote Hill	93 G6
Tower Hill	77 F3
Treyford	145 J1
Trotten Marsh	91 J4
Trotton	120 A2
Tullecombe	90 E3
Turners Hill	34 C7
Twineham	136 D7
Twineham Green	137 F5
Two Mile Ash	76 D8
Tye	238 A2
Up Marden	168 D3
Upper Beeding	208 B2
Upper Ifold	45 G4
Upper Norwood	150 B2
Upperton	125 F1
Upper Wardley	64 C6
Upwaltham	174 B3
Walberton	223 H3
Walderton	192 C1
Walliswood	25 J2
Wardley	64 C7
Warminghurst	157 G5
Warnham	50 E3
Warningcamp	202 B8
Warninglid	108 E2
Washington	181 J5
Waterbeach	196 C6
Watersfield	153 G7
Wepham	202 C5
West Ashling	193 G8
West Blatchington	235 K2
Westbourne	191 F7
West Burton	176 D2
West Chiltington	156 C1
West Chiltington Common	155 J4
West Dean	171 G5
Westdene	212 B6
West End	160 E6
Westergate	222 A4
Westerton	196 B8
West Green	2 B2
West Grinstead	133 K4
Westhampnett	220 A2
West Harting	118 A4
West Hill	83 J2
West Hoathly	59 G5
West Itchenor	240 C4
West Kingston	252 A2
West Lavington	122 C5
West Marden	167 J3
West Stoke	194 A5
West Tarring	8 A2
West Thorney	239 H1
West Town	163 J5
West Wittering	257 G3
West Worthing	253 K1
Whitehall	132 B4
Whitemans Green	110 E3
White's Green	96 C3
Whyke	7 D4
Wick	225 J7
Wiggonholt	155 F5
Wineham	136 B6
Wisborough Green	100 D3
Wiston	182 C2
Withdean	212 E7
Wivelsfield	140 C6
Woldhurst	243 K3
Woodgate	222 B6
Woodmancote	186 B1
Woodmancote	191 K7
Woodmansgreen	65 G8
Woolbeding	121 H1
Woolmer Hill	39 J4
World's End	139 K7
Worth	32 E6
Worth Abbey	57 H2
Worthing	8 B2
Wych Cross	61 J7
Yapton	224 A8

USING THE STREET INDEX

Street names are listed alphabetically. Each street name is followed by its postal town or area locality, the Postcode District, the page number, and the reference to the square in which the name is found.

Example: **Abbotsfield Rd** *CRAWW* RH11................. **30** B6 🔲

Some entries are followed by a number in a blue box. This number indicates the location of the street within the referenced grid square. The full street name is listed at the side of the map page.

GENERAL ABBREVIATIONS

ACC	ACCESS	GA	GATE	PL	
ALY	ALLEY	GAL	GALLERY	PLN	
AP	APPROACH	GDN	GARDEN	PLNS	
AR	ARCADE	GDNS	GARDENS	PLZ	
ASS	ASSOCIATION	GLD	GLADE	POL	POLICE S
AV	AVENUE	GLN	GLEN	PR	
BCH	BEACH	GN	GREEN	PREC	PR
BLDS	BUILDINGS	GND	GROUND	PREP	PREPA
BND	BEND	GRA	GRANGE	PRIM	P
BNK	BANK	GRG	GARAGE	PROM	PROM
BR	BRIDGE	GT	GREAT	PRS	P
BRK	BROOK	GTWY	GATEWAY	PRT	
BTM	BOTTOM	GV	GROVE	PT	
BUS	BUSINESS	HGR	HIGHER	PTH	
BVD	BOULEVARD	HL	HILL	PZ	
BY	BYPASS	HLS	HILLS	QD	QUA
CATH	CATHEDRAL	HO	HOUSE	QU	
CEM	CEMETERY	HOL	HOLLOW	QY	
CEN	CENTRE	HOSP	HOSPITAL	R	
CFT	CROFT	HRB	HARBOUR	RBT	ROUNE
CH	CHURCH	HTH	HEATH	RD	
CHA	CHASE	HTS	HEIGHTS	RDG	
CHYD	CHURCHYARD	HVN	HAVEN	REP	RE
CIR	CIRCLE	HWY	HIGHWAY	RES	RES
CIRC	CIRCUS	IMP	IMPERIAL	RFC	RUGBY FOOTBA
CL	CLOSE	IN	INLET	RI	
CLFS	CLIFFS	IND EST	INDUSTRIAL ESTATE	RP	
CMP	CAMP	INF	INFIRMARY	RW	
CNR	CORNER	INFO	INFORMATION	S	
CO	COUNTY	INT	INTERCHANGE	SCH	
COLL	COLLEGE	IS	ISLAND	SE	SOU
COM	COMMON	JCT	JUNCTION	SER	SERVIC
COMM	COMMISSION	JTY	JETTY	SH	
CON	CONVENT	KG	KING	SHOP	SH
COT	COTTAGE	KNL	KNOLL	SKWY	
COTS	COTTAGES	L	LAKE	SMT	
CP	CAPE	LA	LANE	SOC	
CPS	COPSE	LDG	LODGE	SP	
CR	CREEK	LGT	LIGHT	SPR	
CREM	CREMATORIUM	LK	LOCK	SQ	
CRS	CRESCENT	LKS	LAKES	ST	
CSWY	CAUSEWAY	LNDG	LANDING	STN	
CT	COURT	LTL	LITTLE	STR	
CTRL	CENTRAL	LWR	LOWER	STRD	
CTS	COURTS	MAG	MAGISTRATE	SW	SOU
CTYD	COURTYARD	MAN	MANSIONS	TDG	T
CUTT	CUTTINGS	MD	MEAD	TER	T
CV	COVE	MDW	MEADOWS	THWY	THROL
CYN	CANYON	MEM	MEMORIAL	TNL	
DEPT	DEPARTMENT	MKT	MARKET	TOLL	
DL	DALE	MKTS	MARKETS	TPK	TL
DM	DAM	ML	MALL	TR	
DR	DRIVE	ML	MILL	TRL	
DRO	DROVE	MNR	MANOR	TWR	
DRY	DRIVEWAY	MS	MEWS	U/P	UNE
DWGS	DWELLINGS	MSN	MISSION	UNI	UNI
E	EAST	MT	MOUNT	UPR	
EMB	EMBANKMENT	MTN	MOUNTAIN	V	
EMBY	EMBASSY	MTS	MOUNTAINS	VA	
ESP	ESPLANADE	MUS	MUSEUM	VIAD	\
EST	ESTATE	MWY	MOTORWAY	VIL	
EX	EXCHANGE	N	NORTH	VIS	
EXPY	EXPRESSWAY	NE	NORTH EAST	VLG	
EXT	EXTENSION	NW	NORTH WEST	VLS	
F/O	FLYOVER	O/P	OVERPASS	VW	
FC	FOOTBALL CLUB	OFF	OFFICE	W	
FK	FORK	ORCH	ORCHARD	WD	
FLD	FIELD	OV	OVAL	WHF	
FLDS	FIELDS	PAL	PALACE	WK	
FLS	FALLS	PAS	PASSAGE	WKS	
FLS	FLATS	PAV	PAVILION	WLS	
FM	FARM	PDE	PARADE	WY	
FT	FORT	PH	PUBLIC HOUSE	YD	
FWY	FREEWAY	PK	PARK	YHA	YOUTH
FY	FERRY	PKWY	PARKWAY		

STCODE TOWNS AND AREA ABBREVIATIONS

...........................Angmering/East Preston	
....Arundel	
....Battle	
....Bexhill	
v ....Bexhill west	
...................................Billingshurst	
.............................Bognor Regis	
....Brighton	
CH ......Burwash/Etchingham	
..............................Burgess Hill	
......................................Chichester	
....Cranleigh	
...................................Crawley east	
.................................Crawley west	
....Cranbrook	
...................................Crowborough	
...................................Eastbourne	
....Edenbridge	
STW ......East Dean/Eastbourne west	
...................................East Grinstead	
......................................Emsworth	
...........................Petersfield east	

| FERR...Ferring |
| FIN/BW.............Findon/Broadwater |
| FROW...............................Forest Row |
| GSHT.....................................Grayshott |
| HAIL.......................................Hallsham |
| HAS...Hastings |
| HASM...............................Haslemere |
| HAV...Havant |
| HAWK...............................Hawkhurst |
| HFD...Henfield |
| HISD.........................Hayling Island |
| HORL...Horley |
| HORN...............................Horndean |
| HORS.....................................Horsham |
| HOVE...Hove |
| HPPT/KEY...........Hurstpierpoint/Keymer |
| HWH...............................Haywards Heath |
| LAN/SOMP..............Lancing/Sompting |
| LHPTN...............................Littlehampton |
| LING...Lingfield |
| LIPH...Liphook |
| LISS...Liss |

| MIDH...............................Midhurst |
| MIDOS................Middleton-on-Sea |
| PETW...............................Petworth |
| POY/PYE...........Poynings/Pyecombe |
| PSF...............................Petersfield |
| PTSD...............................Portslade |
| PUL/STOR...........Pulborough/Storrington |
| RCCH...............................Rural Chichester |
| RDKG...............................Rural Dorking |
| RGODL...............................Rural Godalming |
| RHWH...........Rural Haywards Heath |
| RING/NEW...........Ringmer/Newick |
| ROTT...............................Rottingdean |
| SALV...............................Salvington |
| SELS...............................Selsey |
| SHOR...............................Shoreham |
| STEY/UB...........Steyning/Upper Beeding |
| STHW...............................Southwick |
| SWTR...............................Southwater |
| UCK...............................Uckfield |
| WTHG...............................Worthing |

Abb - Anc

Index - streets

A

on Fld HPPT/KEY BN6 .... 164 B6	
Cl LAN/SOMP BN15 .... 232 D5	
Rd LAN/SOMP BN15 .... 231 J4	
BN2 .... 11 F6	
UB BN44 .... 184 A7	
BN11 .... 8 B5	
bury Ct SWTR RH13 .... 5 D4	
Cl HPPT/KEY BN6 .... 164 E7	
field Rd CRAWW RH11 .... 30 D6	
Leigh SWTR RH13 .... 105 C3	
wood Wk ANG/EP BN16 .... 250 E3	
sbury BOGR PO21 .... 261 H3	
s Cl WTHG BN11 .... 8 C4	
s Vw LAN/SOMP BN15 .... 231 J3	
s Wy LAN/SOMP BN15 .... 232 B5	
t Gdns SALV BN13 .... 229 K5	
t's Av BOGR PO21 .... 261 J1	
re Cl CCH PO19 .... 7 D1	
en Rd ROTT BN2 .... 11 D2	
Rd PTSD BN41 .... 235 F3	
ms Rd CRAWW RH11 .... 54 E2	
Av HOVE BN3 .... 235 K2	
N13 .... 229 K4	
v SWTR RH13 .... 135 G2	
ANG/EP BN16 .... 227 H7	
RH19 .... 36 C3	
O20 .... 264 D4	
nd BOGR PO21 .... 262 A1	
SWTR RH13 .... 5 F3	
rns CRAWW RH11 .... 55 F2	
KEY BN6 .... 138 D7	
KEY BN6 .... 163 H1	
ANG/EP BN16 .... 250 D1	
RH16 .... 139 K1	
e Cl WTHG BN11 .... 8 B4	
SELS PO20 .... 265 C5	
Cl BRI BN1 .... 257 J1	
Rd CRAWW RH11 .... 30 E8	
ury Av EMRTH PO10 .... 190 D7	
Cl LAN/SOMP BN15 .... 232 A5	
Rd HOVE BN3 .... 10 A3	
Wy MIDOS PO22 .... 12 A1	
e Cl CRAWW RH11 .... 31 H2	
RH12 .... 5 E3	
N13 .... 229 C5	
e Crs HOVE BN3 .... 236 C6	
e Rd CCH PO19 .... 7 D2	
e Sq SHOR BN43 .... 233 K4	
Cl CRAWE RH10 .... 32 D7	
Crs LIPH GU30 .... 64 C1	
Rd CRAWW RH11 .... 30 E8	
s Bridge La EGRIN RH19 .... 60 A1	
s Wk ANG/EP BN16 .... 250 C1	
PO18 .... 192 E6	
ty Gdns MIDOS PO22 .... 13 E5	
ty Rd MIDOS PO22 .... 13 E4	
SALV BN13 .... 229 G3	
BN43 .... 233 G2	
LAN/SOMP BN15 .... 232 E6	
SHOR BN43 .... 233 J4	
Burh RH15 .... 139 J7	
BN43 .... 233 G3	
ne La BIL RH14 .... 101 K8	
ne Rd FIN/BW BN14 .... 8 B1	
HORS RH12 .... 5 D2	
d WTHG BN11 .... 253 K2	

Agnes St ROTT BN2	11	E3
Aigburth Av BOGR PO21	245	F8
Ailsa Cl CRAWW RH11	2	A6
Ainsdale Cl SALV BN13	229	H5
Ainsdale Rd SALV BN13	229	H5
Airport Wy HORL RH6	18	A3
Ajax Pl MIDOS PO22	247	G6
Akehurst Cl CRAWE RH10	19	G8
Alandale Rd LAN/SOMP BN15	231	J3
SELS PO20	241	K7
Albany Cl WTHG BN11	8	A5
Albany Ms HOVE BN3	236	B5
Albany Rd CRAWW RH11	2	B5
Albany Vls HOVE BN3	236	B6
Alberta Rd SALV BN13	229	H5
Albert Cl HWH RH16	112	C7
Albert Dr BURH RH15	164	E1
Albert Ms HOVE BN3	236	B5
Albert Rd ANG/EP BN16	250	E1
BOGR PO21	12	C5
BRI BN1	10	B4
CCH PO19	218	C5
LHPTN BN17	249	K2
STHW BN42	234	B4
Albery Cl HORS RH12	4	A3
Albion Cl CRAWE RH10	32	D6
Albion Ct BURH RH15	165	F1
Albion Hl ROTT BN2	11	D4
Albion Rd SELS PO20	265	C5
Albion St PTSD BN41	234	B5
PTSD BN41	235	F4
ROTT BN2	11	D4
STHW BN42	234	E4
Albion Wy HORS RH12	4	A5
SWTR RH13	4	C6
Alborough Wy BOGR PO21	262	A1
Albourne Rd HFD BN5	161	H4
HPPT/KEY BN6	163	J5
Aldbourne Dr BOGR PO21	262	A1
Alder Cl CRAWE RH10	34	D3
SALV BN13	229	G6
Alderfield Rd PSF GU32	88	C8
Alderman's Wk CCH PO19	6	C2
Aldermoor Rd PUL/STOR RH20	180	C1
Alderney Rd FERR BN12	252	D3
Alders Av EGRIN RH19	22	B8
Alders View Dr EGRIN RH19	22	C7
Alder Wy MIDOS PO22	247	J5
Aldingbourne Cl CRAWW RH11	30	D4
Aldingbourne Dr RCCH PO18	197	J8
SELS PO20	197	K8
Aldrington Av HOVE BN3	236	A3
Aldrington Cl HOVE BN3	235	H4
Aldsworth Av FERR BN12	253	F1
Aldsworth Ct FERR BN12	253	F1
Aldwick Av BOGR PO21	262	C2
Aldwick Cl ANG/EP BN16	250	D4
Aldwick Crs FIN/BW BN14	230	A2
Aldwick Felds BOGR PO21	262	C1
Aldwick Gdns BOGR PO21	245	H8
Aldwick Hundred BOGR PO21	262	B2
Aldwick Pl BOGR PO21	262	C1
Aldwick Rd BOGR PO21	245	H8
Aldwick St BOGR PO21	262	B1
Alexander Cl BOGR PO21	262	B1
Alexandra Ct FERR BN12	229	G8
Alexandra Rd BURH RH15	165	J1
CCH PO19	7	D2
LAN/SOMP BN15	232	B6

WTHG BN11	9	F4
Alexandra Vls BRI BN1	10	B4
Alford Cl FIN/BW BN14	230	A4
Alfred Cl CRAWE RH10	32	E6
MIDOS PO22	247	K6
Alfred Pl WTHG BN11	9	E4
Alfred Rd BRI BN1	10	B4
Alfrey Cl EMRTH PO10	215	G3
Alfriston Cl FIN/BW BN14	8	B1
MIDOS PO22	247	G5
Alfriston Rd FIN/BW BN14	8	B1
Alice St HOVE BN3	236	D6
Alice Av CRAWE RH10	32	B5
PUL/STOR RH20	158	A6
Alicks Hl BIL RH14	102	B3
Alinora Av FERR BN12	253	H1
Alinora Cl FERR BN12	253	H1
Alinora Crs FERR BN12	253	G3
Alinora Dr FERR BN12	253	G2
Allandale Cl SELS PO20	265	F3
Allangate Dr ANG/EP BN16	251	F1
Allcard Cl HORS RH12	4	C2
Allcot Cl CRAWW RH11	30	C8
Allee Dr LIPH GU30	38	B6
Allendale SWTR RH13	77	F8
Allendale Av EMRTH PO10	190	C8
FIN/BW BN14	230	A2
Allen Rd HWH RH16	112	C6
Allen's Cl EGRIN RH19	37	H5
Alley Groves SWTR RH13	135	G1
Alleyne Wy MIDOS PO22	248	B6
The Alley ARUN BN18	177	K4
MIDH GU29	121	G2
Allfreys Whf PUL/STOR RH20	154	D1
Allington Rd FIN/BW BN14	230	E4
Allwood Crs RHWH RH17	140	E7
Allyington Wy CRAWE RH10	32	D6
Alma Rd HWH RH16	112	D3
Alma St LAN/SOMP BN15	232	A7
Almodington La SELS PO20	258	C5
Almond Cl CRAWW RH11	30	E6
Alpha Rd CRAWW RH11	2	K3
Alpine Rd HOVE BN3	235	K3
Alverstone Rd WTHG BN11	9	F3
Amber Gld SWTR RH13	105	F2
Amberley Cl BURH RH15	139	G7
CRAWE RH10	32	C5
HORS RH12	5	D4
HWH RH16	111	K7
LHPTN BN17	250	A1
PUL/STOR RH20	180	A2
SHOR BN43	233	J2
Amberley Dr BOGR PO21	245	H7
FERR BN12	253	F2
FIN/BW BN14	211	J8
HOVE BN3	236	B6
Amberley Ga PUL/STOR RH20	179	K2
Amberley Rd ANG/EP BN16	250	E3
HORS RH12	5	F1
PUL/STOR RH20	179	J3
Ambersham Crs ANG/EP BN16	251	H1
Ambleside Cl CRAWW RH11	30	B6
MIDOS PO22	247	F5
Ambleside Rd LAN/SOMP BN15	231	J6
Ambrose Pl WTHG BN11	9	D4
Amelia Rd WTHG BN11	8	C4
America La HWH RH16	112	C6
Amesbury Crs HOVE BN3	235	J4
Amherst Crs HOVE BN3	235	K3
Amundsen Rd CRAWW RH11	4	C1
Anchor Cl SHOR BN43	233	J5

Anchor Springs *LHPTN* BN17 ..... 249 K2
Ancren Cl *FERR* BN12 ..... 228 D7
Ancton Cl *MIDOS* PO22 ..... 247 K6
Ancton Dr *MIDOS* PO22 ..... 248 A5
Ancton La *MIDOS* PO22 ..... 247 K5
Ancton Lodge La *MIDOS* PO22 ..... 248 A6
Ancton Wy *MIDOS* PO22 ..... 248 B6
Andlers Ash Rd *LISS* GU33 ..... 89 J1
Andrew Av *MIDOS* PO22 ..... 247 G6
Andrew Cl *ANG/EP* BN16 ..... 250 D1
  STEY/UB BN44 ..... 207 K1
Andrews La *MIDH* GU29 ..... 120 E4
  SWTR RH13 ..... 105 F2
Andrews Rd *SWTR* RH13 ..... 105 F4
Andromeda Cl *CRAWW* RH11 ..... 30 C7
Angel St *PETW* GU28 ..... 125 K3
Anglesea St *WTHG* BN11 ..... 8 C5
Anglesey Cl *CRAWW* RH11 ..... 9 D4
Angmering La *ANG/EP* BN16 ..... 251 G3
Angmering Wy *ANG/EP* BN16 ..... 227 G8
Angola Rd *FIN/BW* BN14 ..... 9 F2
Angus Rd *SWTR* RH12 ..... 4 C3
Angus Rd *FERR* BN12 ..... 253 J1
Annandale Rd *BOGR* PO21 ..... 12 B4 ⬛
Ann Cl *HPPT/KEY* BN6 ..... 165 G6
Anne Howard Gdns *ARUN* BN18 .. 201 G8 ⬛
Annington Gdns *SHOR* BN43 ..... 233 H2 ⬛
Annington Rd *LAN/SOMP* BN15 ..... 208 C5
  STEY/UB BN44 ..... 208 A2
Ann St *BRI* BN1 ..... 10 C3
  WTHG BN11 ..... 9 D5
Annweir Av *LAN/SOMP* BN15 ..... 232 A5
Anscombe Cl *WTHG* BN11 ..... 253 K2 ⬛
Anscombe Rd *WTHG* BN11 ..... 253 K2
Ansisters Rd *FERR* BN12 ..... 252 C2
Anson Rd *BOGR* PO21 ..... 261 J4
  FERR BN12 ..... 229 G2
Antlands La *HORL* RH6 ..... 19 F6
Antlands La East *HORL* RH6 ..... 18 E6
Antlands La West *HORL* RH6 ..... 18 E5
Anvil Cl *BIL* RH14 ..... 102 A3
  PTSD BN41 ..... 235 F1
  SWTR RH13 ..... 105 F2
Appledore Gdns *HWH* RH16 ..... 112 B5
Appledram La (North)
  CCH PO19 ..... 218 C5 ⬛
Appledram La (South) *SELS* PO20 .. 218 C8
Applefield *CRAWE* RH10 ..... 3 D2
Apple Gv *BOGR* PO21 ..... 261 J2
  EMRTH PO10 ..... 215 F3
Applesham Av *HOVE* BN3 ..... 235 J1
Applesham Wy *PTSD* BN41 ..... 234 E2
Appletree Dr *MIDOS* PO22 ..... 223 F5
Appletrees *ANG/EP* BN16 ..... 251 K3 ⬛
Apple Tree Wk *LHPTN* BN17 ..... 248 D2
The Approach *BRI* BN1 ..... 212 E8
  EGRIN RH19 ..... 22 D5
April Cl *FERR* BN12 ..... 252 C3 ⬛
  HORS RH12 ..... 4 B3
Apsley Wy *SALV* BN13 ..... 228 E6
Arcade Rd *LHPTN* BN17 ..... 249 K2
Archibald Rd *WTHG* BN11 ..... 231 G8
Arcturus Rd *CRAWW* RH11 ..... 30 C7
Ardale Cl *WTHG* BN11 ..... 253 K1
Arden Cl *CRAWE* RH10 ..... 3 E5
Ardingly Cl *CRAWW* RH11 ..... 2 A1
Ardingly Dr *FERR* BN12 ..... 229 F8
Ardingly Rd *HWH* RH16 ..... 112 E1
  RHWH RH17 ..... 111 F4
Ardingly St *ROTT* BN2 ..... 11 D5
Ardings Cl *RHWH* RH17 ..... 84 D1
Ardsheal Cl *FIN/BW* BN14 ..... 8 C1
Ardsheal Rd *FIN/BW* BN14 ..... 230 C5
Argus Wk *CRAWW* RH11 ..... 30 B8
Argyle Circ *BOGR* PO21 ..... 12 B5 ⬛
Argyle Rd *BOGR* PO21 ..... 12 B6
  BRI BN1 ..... 10 B2
Ariadne Rd *WTHG* BN11 ..... 8 B5
Arlington Av *FERR* BN12 ..... 253 F3
Arlington Cl *FERR* BN12 ..... 253 F2
Arlington Crs *ANG/EP* BN16 ..... 227 K8
Armadale Rd *CCH* PO19 ..... 7 D2
Armada Wy *ANG/EP* BN16 ..... 250 C1
Arndale Rd *LHPTN* BN17 ..... 249 H1
Arne Cl *CRAWW* RH11 ..... 30 D8
Arnell Av *SELS* PO20 ..... 265 K9
Arnfield Cl *CRAWW* RH11 ..... 30 C6 ⬛
Arnhem Rd *BOGR* PO21 ..... 12 A3
Arnold St *ROTT* BN2 ..... 11 E3
Arnold Wy *RCCH* PO18 ..... 217 G4
Arnside Cl *LAN/SOMP* BN15 ..... 231 J6
Aron Cl *PSF* GU32 ..... 116 C1
Arran Cl *CRAWW* RH11 ..... 2 A6
Artel Cft *CRAWE* RH10 ..... 3 E5
Artex Av *ANG/EP* BN16 ..... 226 E8
Arthur Rd *CRAWW* RH11 ..... 30 C5
  SWTR RH13 ..... 4 C6
Arthur St *HOVE* BN3 ..... 236 A3
Arun Cl *ANG/EP* BN16 ..... 250 E1
  ARUN BN18 ..... 178 A4
  EPSF GU31 ..... 116 C1
  LAN/SOMP BN15 ..... 231 J4
  SALV BN13 ..... 229 H4
Arun Ct *PUL/STOR* RH20 ..... 154 E1
Arun Crs *SALV* BN13 ..... 229 G4

Arundel By-pass *ARUN* BN18 ..... 201 G8
  ARUN BN18 ..... 225 H1
Arundel Cl *BOGR* PO21 ..... 245 J7 ⬛
  CRAWE RH10 ..... 32 C5
  SHOR BN43 ..... 234 A3
  SWTR RH13 ..... 105 G2 ⬛
Arundel Dr *LHPTN* BN17 ..... 225 J6
Arundel Rd *ANG/EP* BN16 ..... 227 H4
  ARUN BN18 ..... 198 C8
  LHPTN BN17 ..... 249 K2
  SWTR RH13 ..... 229 H3
Arundel Wy *MIDOS* PO22 ..... 248 B6
Arun Pde *LHPTN* BN17 ..... 249 K3
Arun Rd *BIL* RH14 ..... 102 A2
  BOGR PO21 ..... 245 J7
Arunside *HORS* RH12 ..... 77 G2
Arun St *ARUN* BN18 ..... 225 H1
Arun V *PUL/STOR* RH20 ..... 153 J6
Arun Wy *BOGR* PO21 ..... 261 J3
  SWTR RH13 ..... 5 D6
Ascot Cl *SELS* PO20 ..... 257 J3
Ascot Wy *ANG/EP* BN16 ..... 251 C1
Ashacre La *SALV* BN13 ..... 229 K4
Ashacre Ms *SALV* BN13 ..... 229 K4
Ashacre Wy *SALV* BN13 ..... 229 K4
Ashburnham Cl *CCH* PO19 ..... 218 D4
  SALV BN13 ..... 229 F6 ⬛
Ashburnham Dr *BRI* BN1 ..... 213 K5
Ashburnham Rd *CRAWE* RH10 ..... 3 F5
Ash Cl *CRAWE* RH10 ..... 34 E2
  FIN/BW BN14 ..... 205 J5
  HOVE BN3 ..... 212 C8
Ashcroft Cl *SHOR* BN43 ..... 234 B4
Ashcroft La *HORN* PO8 ..... 166 B5
Ashcroft Wy *BOGR* PO21 ..... 261 H4
Ashdown Cl *ANG/EP* BN16 ..... 227 H7
  HWH RH16 ..... 112 D7
Ashdown Dr *CRAWE* RH10 ..... 55 J1
Ashdown Rd *FROW* RH18 ..... 61 K1
  ROTT BN2 ..... 11 H2
  WTHG BN11 ..... 9 D3
Ashdown Vw *EGRIN* RH19 ..... 36 C4
Ashenground Cl *HWH* RH16 ..... 112 A8 ⬛
Ashenground Rd *HWH* RH16 ..... 111 K8
Ashfield Cl *MIDH* GU29 ..... 122 A3
Ashfield Rd *MIDH* GU29 ..... 122 A4
Ashfold Av *FIN/BW* BN14 ..... 230 A2
Ashford Rd *BRI* BN1 ..... 237 G1
Ash Gv *HASM* GU27 ..... 66 C6
  HWH RH16 ..... 139 K1
  LIPH GU30 ..... 38 D8
  MIDOS PO22 ..... 12 B1
  WTHG BN11 ..... 9 F2
Ash Keys *CRAWE* RH10 ..... 3 D4
Ash La *ANG/EP* BN16 ..... 250 E2
Ashleigh Cl *ANG/EP* BN16 ..... 227 H5
Ashleigh Rd *HORS* RH12 ..... 4 B2
Ashley Cl *BRI* BN1 ..... 212 E4
Ashlings Wy *HOVE* BN3 ..... 235 J1 ⬛
  SHOR BN43 ..... 233 G4
Ashmere Gdns *MIDOS* PO22 ..... 247 H6
Ashmere La *MIDOS* PO22 ..... 247 H6
Ashmore La *HORS* RH12 ..... 28 E5
Ash Rd *CRAWE* RH10 ..... 3 F1
  SWTR RH13 ..... 104 E2
Ashton Gdns *ANG/EP* BN16 ..... 250 E3
Ashton Ri *ROTT* BN2 ..... 11 D4 ⬛
Ash Tree Cl *HASM* GU27 ..... 66 C7
Ashurst Cl *BOGR* PO21 ..... 245 J5
  FERR BN12 ..... 253 F2
  HORS RH12 ..... 5 F2
Ashurst Dr *CRAWE* RH10 ..... 32 D5
  FERR BN12 ..... 253 F2
Ashurst Wy *ANG/EP* BN16 ..... 251 H1
Ashway *BURH* RH15 ..... 165 G1 ⬛
Ashwood Cl *WTHG* BN11 ..... 9 F2
Ashwood Dr *ANG/EP* BN16 ..... 250 E2
Aspen Cl *HWH* RH16 ..... 112 D7
Aspen Wy *HORS* RH12 ..... 5 D7
  MIDOS PO22 ..... 247 J5 ⬛
Aston Rd *PUL/STOR* RH20 ..... 128 E8
Astra Cl *RCCH* PO18 ..... 217 G6
Astrid Cl *HISD* PO11 ..... 238 A8
Athelstan Cl *CRAWE* RH10 ..... 32 E5
Athelstan Rd *SALV* BN13 ..... 8 A2
Atkinson Rd *CRAWE* RH10 ..... 32 C7 ⬛
Atlingworth St *ROTT* BN2 ..... 11 D6
Attree Dr *ROTT* BN2 ..... 11 E4
Auckland Cl *CRAWW* RH11 ..... 31 H2 ⬛
Audrey Cl *BRI* BN1 ..... 212 E6
Augusta Pl *WTHG* BN11 ..... 9 D5
Augustines Wy *HWH* RH16 ..... 112 A7
Aurum Cl *HORL* RH6 ..... 18 B1 ⬛
Austen Cl *EGRIN* RH19 ..... 35 K2
Avalon Wy *SALV* BN13 ..... 229 H5
Avebury Cl *HORS* RH12 ..... 5 D3
  SELS PO20 ..... 258 B6
Aveling Cl *CRAWE* RH10 ..... 32 C7 ⬛
The Avenals *ANG/EP* BN16 ..... 227 J6
Avenue Ap *CCH* PO19 ..... 6 B2
Avenue Cl *LIPH* GU30 ..... 38 B2
Avenue De Chartres *CCH* PO19..... 6 B3
Avenue Gdns *HORL* RH6 ..... 18 C1
The Avenue *BOGR* PO21 ..... 12 A5
  CCH PO19 ..... 219 F1

Egrin RH19 .....
EPSF GU31 .....
FERR BN12 .....
HASM GU27 .....
HORL RH6 .....
LIPH GU30 .....
RCCH PO18 .....
RCCH PO18 .....
ROTT BN2 .....
SHOR BN43 .....
SWTR RH13 .....
Avery Cl *PTSD* BN41 .....
Avian Gdns *BOGR* PO21 2
Aviary Wy *CRAWE* RH10 .....
Avisford Park Rd *ARUN* BN18 .....
Avocet Quay *EMRTH* PO10 .....
Avon Cl *LAN/SOMP* BN15 .....
  MIDOS PO22 .....
  PSF GU32 .....
Avondale Cl *FERR* BN12 2
Avondale Rd *HOVE* BN3 .....
Avonhurst *BURH* RH15 .....
Avon Rd *LHPTN* BN17 .....
Avon Wk *CRAWW* RH11 .....
Awbrook Cl *RHWH* RH17 1
Aylwin Pl *SELS* PO20 .....
Aymer Rd *HOVE* BN3 .....
Ayshe Court Dr *SWTR* RH13.....
Azalea Cl *HAV* PO9 .....
Azalea Dr *HASM* GU27 .....

Babsham La *BOGR* PO21 .....
Back La *BIL* RH14 .....
  CRAWE RH10 .....
  RHWH RH17 .....
Backwoods Cl *HWH* RH16 .....
Backwoods La *HWH* RH16 .....
Baden Powell Rd *LISS* GU33 .....
Baden Rd *ROTT* BN2 .....
Badger Cl *PTSD* BN41 .....
Badger Dr *RHWH* RH17 .....
Badgers Cl *HORS* RH12 .....
Badgers Holt *PUL/STOR* RH20.....
Badgers Wk *BURH* RH15 .....
Badgers Wy *BIL* RH14 .....
  EGRIN RH19 .....
Badgers Wd *PUL/STOR* RH20 .....
Baffin's La *CCH* PO19 .....
Bailey Cl *ANG/EP* BN16 2
  HORS RH12 .....
Bailing Hl *HORS* RH12 .....
Baird Cl *CRAWE* RH10 .....
Bakehouse Barn Cl *HORS* RH12 .....
Baker Cl *CRAWE* RH10 .....
Bakers Arms Hl *ARUN* BN18 2
Baker's La *SWTR* RH13 .....
Baker St *BRI* BN1.....
Bakery La *BOGR* PO21 .....
Bala Crs *MIDOS* PO22 .....
Balchins Cl *BIL* RH14 .....
Balcombe Av *FIN/BW* BN14.....
Balcombe Gdns *HORL* RH6 .....
Balcombe La *RHWH* RH17 .....
  RHWH RH17 .....
Balcombe Rd *CRAWE* RH10 .....
  CRAWE RH10 .....
  HWH RH16 .....
Baldwin Cl *CRAWE* RH10 .....
  MIDOS PO22 .....
Balfour Gdns *FROW* RH18 .....
Balfour Rd *BRI* BN1 .....
Balliol Cl *BOGR* PO21.....
  CRAWE RH10 .....
Balmoral Cl *BOGR* PO21 .....
  CCH PO19 .....
Balmoral Wy *PSF* GU32 .....
Bamborough Cl *SWTR* RH13 .....
Bampfield St *PTSD* BN41 .....
Bancroft Rd *CRAWE* RH10 .....
Banjo Rd *LHPTN* BN17 .....
Bank La *CRAWE* RH10 .....
Bank Pas *STEY/UB* BN44 .....
Banks Cft *PUL/STOR* RH20.....
Bankside *BRI* BN1 .....
  HPPT/KEY BN6 .....
Banks Rd *CRAWE* RH10.....
Bankview Cl *BOGR* PO21 .....
Bannerman Rd *PSF* GU32 .....
Bannister Gdns *PUL/STOR* RH20.....
Bannister Wy *HWH* RH16 .....
Banstead Cl *FERR* BN12 .....
Baranscraig Av *BRI* BN1 .....
Barbary La *FERR* BN12 .....
Barber Cl *CRAWE* RH10.....
Barfield Pk *LAN/SOMP* BN15.....
Barford Rd *CCH* PO19.....
Barham Rd *PSF* GU32.....
Barkdale *BURH* RH15 .....
Barker Cl *RCCH* PO18 .....
Barkworth Wy *PUL/STOR* RH20 2
Bar La *SWTR* RH13.....

ington Wy *MIDH* GU29 .... 122 A6
 Cl BOGR PO21 .... 261 G1
WW RH11 .... 2 C4
croft Cl SWTR RH13 .... 135 G2
Dr BURH RH15 .... 138 C7
y Rd CCH PO19 .... 6 A2
WW RH11 .... 30 C8
d Ga HWH RH11 .... 112 A4
l CRAWW RH11 .... 19 H2
TH PO10 .... 214 B3
T/KEY BN6 .... 163 G5
'N BN17 .... 226 A7
*BN13 .... 229 K4
ottage La HWH RH16 .... 112 C6
t CRAWE RH10 .... 34 A1
oft Cl SELS PO20 .... 220 E2
nd HFD BN5 .... 161 H6
t Cl SELS PO20 .... 222 C3
t Rd BRI BN1 .... 237 H1
t's Fld SELS PO20 .... 222 B4
Wy HOVE BN3 .... 211 J8
d MIDOS PO22 .... 13 E4
eld Cl EMRTH PO10 .... 215 J1
eld Dr CCH PO19 .... 7 E1
ield Gdns ROTT BN2 .... 11 E4
eld Rd CRAWE RH10 .... 2 C2
GU31 .... 89 G8
m La PUL/STOR RH20 .... 223 G8
m Rd SELS PO20 .... 222 D4
use Cl PUL/STOR RH20 .... 154 E1
ouse La PUL/STOR RH20 .... 154 E1
d MIDOS PO22 .... 246 B2
ead HWH RH16 .... 111 K4
eadow RHWH RH17 .... 83 C2
BRI BN1 .... 212 D6
S PO22 .... 223 G5
d SELS PO20 .... 257 J4
arm La PUL/STOR RH20 ..... 181 F4
old La HORS RH12 .... 47 C5
le RCCH PO18 .... 217 H4
te Av BURH RH15 .... 165 J2
te Gdns ANG/EP BN16 .... 250 D1
ap Cl HORS RH12 .... 4 C1
lk SELS PO20 .... 257 J5
ood Cl CRAWE RH10 .... 32 C4
Cl SELS PO20 .... 222 B4
Ct BURH RH15 .... 165 H1
Md BOGR PO21 .... 261 H3
Cl ANG/EP BN16 .... 250 C1
k La BOGR PO21 .... 262 A1
Av BRI BN1 .... 213 F4
ton Cl FERR BN12 .... 253 D
RH16 .... 112 C3
ton Rd CRAWE RH10 .... 2 C5
*BN12 .... 253 C1
*RH13 .... 5 D5
ton Wd HWH RH16 .... 112 B3
Cl BRI BN1 .... 237 J1
field RHWH RH17 .... 111 F4
field Cl HOVE BN3 .... 212 C8
field Dr HOVE BN3 .... 236 C1
HI BRI BN1 .... 237 J1
*BN5 .... 161 H7
l CRAWW RH11 .... 3 D6
k ROTT BN2 .... 11 E3
omew Cl HASM GU27 .... 41 F3
omews BRI BN1 .... 10 C5
omew Wy HORS RH12 .... 5 F1
Cl BOGR PO21 .... 261 J3
*BN13 .... 8 A1
Crs EGRIN RH19 .... 36 E3
La PETW GU28 .... 125 K3
Rd CCH PO19 .... 6 A1
S PO22 .... 245 J4
s Rd HAV PO9 .... 190 A7
Wy SELS PO20 .... 258 A5
ot Rd HORS RH12 .... 4 A6
Gv EMRTH PO10 .... 190 C8
Cl ANG/EP BN16 .... 226 D8
rds La FIN/BW BN14 .... 9 D2
d Wy CRAWE RH10 .... 32 D3
st Copse SWTR RH13 .... 75 K3
st HI SWTR RH13 .... 75 H7
n Wy CRAWW RH11 .... 30 C8
HI PUL/STOR RH20 .... 158 C4
d CCH PO19 .... 6 C4
d South PTSD BN41 .... 234 D3
La SWTR RH13 .... 133 G5
Rd BOGR PO21 .... 12 B6
E RH10 .... 32 D8
s HI LING RH7 .... 22 E2
ere Rd SELS PO20 .... 258 E1
ns Cl SALV BN13 .... 229 F6
ns Ct CRAWE RH10 .... 3 F6
d BRI BN1 .... 237 F1
WTHG BN11 .... 9 D5
EMRTH PO10 .... 214 D3
*BN11 .... 8 A5
BRI BN1 .... 10 B3
HFD BN5 .... 161 H6
PUL/STOR RH20 .... 155 H2
Rd BRI BN1 .... 236 E1
Cl CRAWE RH10 .... 32 B7
La RHWH RH17 .... 87 G5

Baxter St *ROTT* BN2 .... 11 E3
Bay Br *SWTR* RH13 .... 133 G5
Baycombe La *ARUN* BN18 .... 199 H5
Bayford Rd *LHPTN* BN17 .... 249 K3
Bayhams Fld *EGRIN* RH19 .... 59 H5
Bayhorne La *HORL* RH6 .... 9 F1
Bayley Rd *SELS* PO20 .... 220 E2
Bayley Rd *BURH* RH15 .... 138 E7
Baynards Rd *HORS* RH12 .... 47 J1
Baythorn La *HORL* RH6 .... 18 C2
Baytree Cl *BURH* RH15 .... 219 F1
Bay Tree Gdn *ANG/EP* BN16 .... 251 H2
Bay Wk *BOGR* PO21 .... 261 K3
Beach Cl *BOGR* PO21 .... 261 K2
Beach Crs *LHPTN* BN17 .... 250 A4
Beachcroft Pl *LAN/SOMP* BN15 .. 232 A7
Beach Gdns *SELS* PO20 .... 264 C6
Beach Gn *SHOR* BN43 .... 233 F5
Beach Pde *WTHG* BN11 .... 9 E5
Beach Rd *BOGR* PO21 .... 261 H4
   EMRTH PO10 .... 214 C3
   LHPTN BN17 .... 250 A3
   SELS PO20 .... 265 C3
   SHOR BN43 .... 233 G6
Beachside Cl *FERR* BN12 .... 253 J2
Beachy Rd *CRAWW* RH11 .... 54 E2
Beacon Cl *BRI* BN1 .... 237 G1
   PUL/STOR RH20 .... 153 G7
Beacon Hurst *HPPT/KEY* BN6 .. 165 H8
Beacon HI *LING* RH7 .... 23 F3
Beaconsfield Rd *MIDOS* PO22 .. 247 J6
Beaconsfield Rd *BRI* BN1 .... 10 C2
   LHPTN BN17 .... 225 K8
   PTSD BN41 .... 235 F3
   RHWH RH17 .... 87 H3
Beaconsfield Vls *BRI* BN1 .... 10 B3
Beacon Sq *EMRTH* PO10 .... 214 C4
Beacon Wy *LHPTN* BN17 .... 250 C1
Beagle Dr *ARUN* BN18 .... 248 B1
Beal Crs *BRI* BN1 .... 213 K1
Beale St *BURH* RH15 .... 164 E2
Bear Rd *ROTT* BN2 .... 11 E2
Bearsden Wy *HORS* RH12 .... 50 D8
Beatty Av *BRI* BN1 .... 213 K4
Beatty Rd *BOGR* PO21 .... 12 B4
Beaufield Cl *SELS* PO20 .... 264 E6
Beaufort Ter *CRAWW* RH11 ...... 11 E4
Beaumont Cl *CRAWW* RH11 .... 30 C6
Beaumont Pk *LHPTN* BN17 ...... 250 C3
Beaumont Rd *FIN/BW* BN14 .... 9 D1
Beaver Cl *CCH* PO19 .... 218 D5
   HORS RH12 .... 5 D1
Beccles Rd *WTHG* BN11 .... 8 B4
Becket Rd *FIN/BW* BN14 .... 8 A3
Beckett La *CRAWW* RH11 .... 31 H2
Beckett Wy *EGRIN* RH19 .... 36 D5
Beckford Wy *CRAWE* RH10 .... 56 B2
Beckham La *PSF* GU32 .... 88 B7
Beckworth Cl *HWH* RH16 .... 112 C5
   SALV BN13 .... 229 F6
Beckworth La *HWH* RH16 .... 112 C5
Bedale Cl *CRAWW* RH11 .... 2 B5
Bedales HI *HWH* RH16 .... 113 F6
Bedelands Cl *BURH* RH15 .... 139 H6
Bedenscroft *BOGR* PO21 .... 245 J8
Bedford Av *BOGR* PO21 .... 245 J5
Bedford Pl *BRI* BN1 .... 10 A5
Bedford Rd *PSF* GU32 .... 88 B8
   SWTR RH13 .... 4 C6
Bedford Wy *WTHG* BN11 .... 9 E4
Bedford Sq *BRI* BN1 .... 10 A5
Bedford St *BOGR* PO21 .... 12 B5
   ROTT BN2 .... 11 E6
Bedham La *PUL/STOR* RH20 .... 127 G7
Beech Av *CCH* PO19 .... 6 A3
   SELS PO20 .... 258 A5
Beech Cl *FIN/BW* BN14 .... 205 J4
   PTSD BN41 .... 210 D8
   SELS PO20 .... 222 B4
Beechers Rd *PTSD* BN41 .... 210 D8
Beeches Av *FIN/BW* BN14 .... 230 D4
Beeches Crs *CRAWE* RH10 .... 3 D5
Beeches La *EGRIN* RH19 .... 37 H5
The Beeches *BRI* BN1 .... 212 D8
Beechey Cl *CRAWE* RH10 .... 19 H8
Beechey Wy *CRAWE* RH10 .... 19 H8
Beech Flds *EGRIN* RH19 .... 22 D8
Beech Gdns *CRAWE* RH10 .... 34 C4
Beech Gv *MIDH* GU29 .... 122 A5
   PUL/STOR RH20 .... 156 D8
Beech HI *HWH* RH16 .... 112 D8
Beech Holme *CRAWE* RH10 .... 34 C3
Beech Hurst Cl *HWH* RH16 .... 111 J7
Beechings *HFD* BN5 .... 161 F6
Beeching Wy *EGRIN* RH19 .... 36 C2
Beechlands Cl *ANG/EP* BN16 .... 251 J2
Beech Rd *FIN/BW* BN14 .... 205 J5
   HASM GU27 .... 41 F4
   HORS RH12 .... 52 D6
Beechside *CRAWE* RH10 .... 3 D4
Beech Tree Cl *CRAWW* RH11 .... 2 C2
Beech Vw *ANG/EP* BN16 .... 227 J4

Beech Wd *HFD* BN5 .... 185 H4
Beechwood Ct *LISS* GU33 .... 104 E3
Beechwood Av *BRI* BN1 .... 213 F7
   SALV BN13 .... 229 K4
Beechwood Cl *BRI* BN1 .... 213 F7
Beechwood Ct *LISS* GU33 .... 62 A5
Beechwood La *PETW* GU28 ...... 150 E6
Beechwoods *BURH* RH15 .... 165 G2
Beeding Av *HOVE* BN3 .... 211 K8
Beeding Cl *HORS* RH12 .... 5 F2
   LAN/SOMP BN15 .... 231 K3
Beedingwood Dr *HORS* RH12 ..... 53 G5
Beehive Cl *FERR* BN12 .... 252 D2
Beehive La *FERR* BN12 .... 252 C1
Beehive Ring Rd *CRAWE* RH10 .... 18 B7
Beggarshouse La *HORL* RH6 ...... 16 A3
Beggar's La *POY/PYE* BN45 .... 187 H6
Behenna Cl *CRAWW* RH11 .... 30 C6
Belfast St *HOVE* BN3 .... 236 B5
Belgrave Crs *CCH* PO19 .... 6 B6
Belgrave Pl *ROTT* BN2 .... 11 F6
Belgrave St *ROTT* BN2 .... 11 D4
Belinus Dr *BIL* RH14 .... 102 A3
Bellamy Rd *CRAWE* RH10 .... 56 C1
Bell Cl *CCH* PO19 .... 6 B1
Bell Ct *BOGR* PO21 .... 261 K1
Bell Davies Rd *LHPTN* BN17 .... 250 B1
Belle Meade Cl *SELS* PO20 ...... 222 B6
Bellevue Gdns *ROTT* BN2 .... 11 E5
Bellevue La *EMRTH* PO10 .... 214 D1
Bell Hammer *EGRIN* RH19 .... 36 C3
Bell HI *PSF* GU32 .... 88 B6
Bell Hill Rdg *PSF* GU32 .... 88 C6
Bellingham Crs *HOVE* BN3 .... 235 H3
Bell La *MIDH* GU29 .... 147 H3
   SELS PO20 .... 258 C1
Belloc Cl *CRAWE* RH10 .... 32 B4
Belloc Ct *SWTR* RH13 .... 5 F4
Belloc Rd *LHPTN* BN17 .... 225 J8
Bell Rd *HASM* GU27 .... 40 C8
   HORS RH12 .... 51 G3
Bellscroft Ct *LHPTN* BN17 .... 250 B1
Bell Vale La *HASM* GU27 .... 40 D7
Bellview Rd *SALV* BN13 .... 8 A1
Belmont *BRI* BN1 .... 10 A3
Belmont Cl *HPPT/KEY* BN6 ...... 164 E6
Belmont La *HPPT/KEY* BN6 ...... 164 C7
Belmont St *BOGR* PO21 .... 12 C6
   BRI BN1 .... 10 C3
Belmont Ter *ARUN* BN18 .... 248 A1
Belsize Cl *WTHG* BN11 .... 8 A3
Belsize Rd *WTHG* BN11 .... 8 B3
Belton Rd *ROTT* BN2 .... 11 D2
Belvedere Av *LAN/SOMP* BN15 .. 231 K5
Belverdere Cl *PSF* GU32 .... 88 D7
Belyngham Crs *LHPTN* BN17 .... 249 J1
Bembridge St *ROTT* BN2 .... 11 D2
Benbow Cl *CRAWW* RH11 .... 30 C6
Benchfield Cl *EGRIN* RH19 .... 36 E3
Benedict Cl *WTHG* BN11 .... 231 H8
Benedict Dr *WTHG* BN11 .... 231 G8
Benett Av *HOVE* BN3 .... 236 B1
Benett Dr *HOVE* BN3 .... 236 B1
Benfield Crs *PTSD* BN41 .... 235 G2
Benfield Wy *PTSD* BN41 .... 235 G3
Bengairn Av *BRI* BN1 .... 213 G4
Benjamin Cl *CRAWE* RH10 .... 32 D7
Bennett Cl *CRAWE* RH10 .... 56 B1
Bennetts *RHWH* RH17 .... 109 G8
Bennetts Cl *SELS* PO20 .... 257 J4
Bennetts Rd *SWTR* RH13 .... 5 D6
Bens Acre *SWTR* RH13 .... 5 F5
Benson Rd *HFD* BN5 .... 161 H6
Benson's La *HORS* RH12 .... 52 E2
Bentham Rd *ROTT* BN2 .... 11 E3
Bentons La *SWTR* RH13 .... 132 C8
Bentswood Crs *HWH* RH16 ...... 112 C6
Bentswood Rd *HWH* RH16 .... 112 B6
Bepton Cl *MIDH* GU29 .... 121 K5
Bepton Down *EPSF* GU31 .... 88 E8
Bepton Rd *MIDH* GU29 .... 121 H6
Berberis Ct *SHOR* BN43 .... 234 A2
Beresford Rd *ROTT* BN2 .... 11 F5
Bereweeke Rd *MIDOS* PO22 .... 13 F4
Bergamot Crs *SHOR* BN43 .... 234 A2
Berghestede Rd *MIDOS* PO22 ..... 12 B2
Berkeley Cl *CRAWW* RH11 .... 54 C1
Berkeley Sq *WTHG* BN11 .... 8 A4
Bernard Pl *ROTT* BN2 .... 11 E3
Bernard Rd *ARUN* BN18 .... 225 F1
   ROTT BN2 .... 11 E3
   WTHG BN11 .... 253 K2
Berriedale Av *HOVE* BN3 .... 235 J5
Berriedale Cl *LAN/SOMP* BN15 .. 231 J4
Berriedale Dr *LAN/SOMP* BN15 .. 231 J4
Berryban La *SELS* PO20 .... 256 E3
Berry Cl *BURH* RH15 .... 139 G6
Berrylands *LISS* GU33 .... 62 A4
Berrylands Farm *HPPT/KEY* BN6 .. 161 H2
Berry La *LHPTN* BN17 .... 250 B3
   MIDOS PO22 .... 245 J4
   RHWH RH17 .... 84 E4
Berrymill Cl *BOGR* PO21 .... 12 C4
Bersted St *MIDOS* PO22 .... 12 C3

Bessborough Ter
LAN/SOMP BN15 .... 231 K7 🔟
Betchley Cl *EGRIN* RH19 .... 22 C8 🔟
Bethune Cl *CRAWE* RH10 .... 32 D6 🔟
Bethune Rd *SWTR* RH13 .... 5 D6
Bethwines Rd *RCCH* PO18 .... 218 A3
Betts Wy *CRAWW* RH11 .... 31 H1
Bevendean Rd *ROTT* BN2 .... 11 F2
Beverley Cl *CRAWE* RH10 .... 265 G4 🔟
Beverley Gdns *ANG/EP* BN16 .... 250 D1
Beverley Ms *CRAWE* RH10 .... 3 F4 🔟
Bewbush Dr *CRAWW* RH11 .... 30 D8
Bewley Rd *ANG/EP* BN16 .... 227 H5
Bex La *MIDH* GU29 .... 148 A1
Biggin Cl *CRAWW* RH11 .... 2 B5 🔟
Bignor Cl *ANG/EP* BN16 .... 227 F8 🔟
HORS RH12 .... 5 F1
Bignor Park Rd *PUL/STOR* RH20 .... 152 D7
Bigwood Av *HOVE* BN3 .... 236 D4
Bilberry Cl *CRAWW* RH11 .... 2 A6 🔟
Billingshurst La *PUL/STOR* RH20 .. 157 J3
Billingshurst Rd *HORS* RH12 .... 50 C8
Billinton Dr *CRAWE* RH10 .... 32 B5
Bilsham La *ARUN* BN18 .... 247 J2
Bilsham Rd *ARUN* BN18 .... 247 K2
Binderton La *RCCH* PO18 .... 194 D1
Binney Ct *CRAWE* RH10 .... 32 E2 🔟
Binstead Av *SELS* PO20 .... 5 F1
Binstead Cl *CRAWW* RH11 .... 2 A1 🔟
Binsted Cl *ANG/EP* BN16 .... 250 D5
ARUN BN18 .... 224 A1
Birch Av *HWH* RH16 .... 112 C8
Birch Cl *ANG/EP* BN16 .... 227 H7
ARUN BN18 .... 224 E2
BOGR PO21 .... 245 F8
CRAWE RH10 .... 34 E3
HWH RH16 .... 112 D8
LAN/SOMP BN15 .... 231 K7 🔟
LISS GU33 .... 62 A7
Birch Dr *BIL* RH14 .... 102 B4
Birch End *PUL/STOR* RH20 .... 156 B4
Birchen La *HWH* RH16 .... 112 A3
Birches Cl *SALV* BN13 .... 229 G6
SELS PO20 .... 264 D4
Birches Rd *HORS* RH12 .... 52 D6
The Birches *CRAWE* RH10 .... 3 F2 🔟
SWTR RH13 .... 78 E4
Birch Gv *PUL/STOR* RH20 .... 156 B6
Birch Grove Crs *BRI* BN1 .... 213 C6
Birchgrove Rd *RHWH* RH17 .... 86 D2
Birchgrove Rd *RHWH* RH17 .... 86 B6
Birch Lea *CRAWE* RH10 .... 32 A2
Birch Tree Cl *EMRTH* PO10 .... 190 D7
Birch Tree Dr *EMRTH* PO10 .... 190 D7
Birch Tree La *PUL/STOR* RH20 .... 156 B5
Birch Wy *HWH* RH16 .... 140 C1
PUL/STOR RH20 .... 181 F1
Birchwood Cl *CRAWE* RH10 .... 32 C8 🔟
Birchwood Grove Rd *BURH* RH15 .. 165 H2
Birdham Ct *BOGR* PO21 .... 245 H6
CRAWW RH11 .... 2 A1 🔟
Birdham Rd *SELS* PO20 .... 242 B5
Birkdale Cl *SALV* BN13 .... 229 H5
Birkdale Dr *CRAWW* RH11 .... 30 B6
Birkdale Rd *SALV* BN13 .... 229 H5
Birling Cl *ROTT* BN2 .... 11 F1
Biscay Cl *ANG/EP* BN16 .... 250 D1
Bisham Cl *CRAWE* RH10 .... 32 D8 🔟
Bishop Luffa Cl *CCH* PO19 .... 218 D4
Bishopric *HORS* RH12 .... 4 A5
Bishops Cl *BOGR* PO21 .... 261 H3
HASM GU27 .... 66 C5
HFD BN5 .... 161 G6
SALV BN13 .... 8 A2 🔟
Bishopsgate Wk *CCH* PO19 .... 6 C2
Bishops Rd *HOVE* BN3 .... 236 C2
SELS PO20 .... 221 F1
Bishopstone La *HPPT/KEY* BN6 .. 138 A6
RHWH RH17 .... 138 A4
Bitmead Cl *CRAWW* RH11 .... 30 C6 🔟
Bittern Cl *CRAWW* RH11 .... 30 B6
Blackberry La *CCH* PO19 .... 7 E5
LING RH7 .... 22 B1
Blackboy La *EGRIN* RH19 .... 22 A3
Blackboy La *RCCH* PO18 .... 218 A4
Blackbridge La *HORS* RH12 .... 77 G2
Blackcap Cl *CRAWW* RH11 .... 2 B5 🔟
Black Dog Wk *CRAWE* RH10 .... 3 D1 🔟
Blackdown Rd *SALV* BN13 .... 229 K4 🔟
Blackett Rd *CRAWE* RH10 .... 32 C6
Blackfold Rd *CRAWE* RH10 .... 3 F4 🔟
Blackgate La *HFD* BN5 .... 161 G7
Black Gate La *PUL/STOR* RH20 .... 128 E2
Blackheath *CRAWE* RH10 .... 32 D3
Black Hl *HWH* RH16 .... 112 C4
Black Horse Wy *HORS* RH12 .... 4 A5
Blackhouse La *BURH* RH15 .... 139 H7
PETW GU28 .... 98 D5
Blackhouse Rd *SWTR* RH13 .... 54 A5
Blacklands Crs *FROW* RH18 .... 61 K1
Black Lion St *BRI* BN1 .... 10 C6 🔟
Blackman St *BRI* BN1 .... 10 C4 🔟
Blackman Wy *SELS* PO20 .... 243 H2
Blackmill La *RCCH* PO18 .... 198 A8

Blacksmiths Cl *PUL/STOR* RH20 .. 158 A7 🔟
Blacksmiths Crs *LAN/SOMP* BN15 .. 231 H5
Blackstone La *HFD* BN5 .... 162 C6
Blackstone St *HFD* BN5 .... 162 B6
Blackstone Wy *BURH* RH15 .... 139 G6
Black Swan Cl *CRAWW* RH11 .... 55 F4
Blackthorn Cl *BRI* BN1 .... 212 D8 🔟
CRAWW RH11 .... 2 B1
PTSD BN41 .... 235 F1 🔟
SWTR RH13 .... 5 E5
Blackthorn Dr *HISD* PO11 .... 238 A8
Blackthorn Rd *HISD* PO11 .... 238 A8
Blackthorns *HPPT/KEY* BN6 .... 163 K4
HWH RH16 .... 112 C4
Blackthorns Cl *HWH* RH16 .... 112 C4
The Blackthorns *BURH* RH15 .... 139 H6
Blackwater La *CRAWE* RH10 .... 32 C6
Blackwell Farm Rd *EGRIN* RH19 .. 22 D8
Blackwell Hollow *EGRIN* RH19 .... 36 D1
Blackwell Rd *EGRIN* RH19 .... 36 D1
Bladon Dr *HAV* PO9 .... 190 A8 🔟
Blake Cl *CRAWE* RH10 .... 55 K1
Blakehurst La *ARUN* BN18 .... 226 C1
Blakehurst Wy *LHPTN* BN17 .... 249 K1
Blakemyle *BOGR* PO21 .... 262 C1
Blaker St *ROTT* BN2 .... 11 D5
Blakes Farm Rd *SWTR* RH13 .... 77 F8
Blakes Rd *MIDS* PO22 .... 13 F4
Blanches Rd *SWTR* RH13 .... 134 C8
Blanches Wk *SWTR* RH13 .... 134 C8 🔟
Blanford Rd *CCH* PO19 .... 7 D1
The Blatchen *LHPTN* BN17 .... 250 B3
Blatchford Rd *SWTR* RH13. .... 5 E4
Blatchington Rd *HOVE* BN3 .... 236 B4
Blenheim Cl *SALV* BN13 .... 229 J5
Blenheim Cl *ANG/EP* BN16 .... 226 D8 🔟
CRAWE RH10 .... 32 D2 🔟
EGRIN RH19 .... 22 E8
Blenheim Ct *BOGR* PO21 .... 245 G7
Blenheim Dr *ANG/EP* BN16 .... 226 D8
Blenheim Flds *FROW* RH18 .... 37 J8
Blenheim Gdns *CCH* PO19 .... 7 E3 🔟
Blenheim Rd *ARUN* BN18 .... 247 K1
HORS RH12 .... 4 C2
LAN/SOMP BN15 .... 231 K7 🔟
Bligh Cl *CRAWE* RH10 .... 32 B7
Blindley Rd *CRAWE* RH10 .... 32 D2 🔟
Blomfield Dr *CCH* PO19 .... 219 C2
Blondell Dr *BOGR* PO21 .... 245 F8
Bloomsbury Pl *ROTT* BN2 .... 11 E6 🔟
Bloomsbury St *ROTT* BN2 .... 11 E6 🔟
Bloor Cl *HORS* RH12 .... 51 K4
Blount Av *EGRIN* RH19 .... 36 A2
Bluebell Cl *CRAWW* RH11 .... 2 A6 🔟
EGRIN RH19 .... 35 K2
HORS RH12 .... 5 D2
HWH RH16 .... 112 B7 🔟
Bluebell Dr *ANG/EP* BN16 .... 226 D8
Blueberry Hl *PUL/STOR* RH20 .... 181 F2
Blue Cedars Cl *ANG/EP* BN16 .... 227 G7
Bluecoat Pond *SWTR* RH13 .... 76 D5
Blunden Dr *RHWH* RH17 .... 111 F3
Blunts Wy *HORS* RH12 .... 4 B4
Blunts Wood Crs *RHWH* RH17 .... 111 H5
Blunts Wood Rd *RHWH* RH17 .... 111 H5
The Blytons *EGRIN* RH19 .... 35 K2
Bob La *RHWH* RH17 .... 136 C5
Boddingtons La *HPPT/KEY* BN6 .. 165 K8 🔟
Bodiam Av *FERR* BN12 .... 252 E1
Bodiam Cl *CRAWE* RH10 .... 32 C5
SWTR RH13 .... 105 C1
Bodmin Cl *SALV* BN13 .... 229 H3 🔟
Bodmin Rd *SALV* BN13 .... 229 H3
Bognor Rd *RDKG* RH5. .... 26 C4
CCH PO19 .... 7 E3
HORS RH12 .... 50 A3
SELS PO20 .... 7 F4
Bolding Wy *HWH* RH16 .... 139 K1
Boleyn Cl *CRAWE* RH10. .... 32 D8
Boleyn Dr *BOGR* PO21 .... 261 J2
Bolney Chapel Rd *RHWH* RH17 .... 137 F3
Bolney Ct *CRAWW* RH11 .... 30 D8
Bolney Lodge La *RHWH* RH17 .... 109 F8
Bolney Rd *RHWH* RH17 .... 137 J2
Bolney St *RHWH* RH17 .... 109 G8
Bolnore Rd *HWH* RH16 .... 111 J7
Bolsover Rd *HOVE* BN3 .... 235 J4
SALV BN13 .... 229 J8
Bolton Rd *CRAWE* RH10 .... 56 B2
Boltro Rd *HWH* RH16 .... 111 K6
Bonchurch Rd *ROTT* BN2 .... 11 E2
Bond St *ARUN* BN18 .... 201 G8
BRI BN1 .... 10 C5 🔟
Bones La *EPSF* GU31 .... 100 D6
Bonfire La *RHWH* RH17 .... 86 A7
Bonnar Cl *SELS* PO20 .... 264 D5
Bonnar Rd *SELS* PO20 .... 264 D5
Bonnetts La *CRAWW* RH11 .... 16 E8
Bonny Wood Rd *HPPT/KEY* BN6 .. 164 E8
Bookers La *SELS* PO20 .... 258 B3
Booth Rd *CRAWW* RH11 .... 30 C8
Booth Wy *SWTR* RH13 .... 54 E1 🔟
Borage La *CRAWW* RH11 .... 2 B5 🔟
Bordehill La *HWH* RH16 .... 83 K7
Borden La *LIPH* GU30 .... 91 K5

Border Cha *CRAWE* RH10. ....
Border Ct *EGRIN* RH19 ....
Border Rd *HASM* GU27 ....
Borers Arms Rd *CRAWE* RH10 ....
Borough Gv *PSF* GU32 ....
Borough Hl *PSF* GU32 ....
Borough Rd *PSF* GU32 ....
Borough St *BRI* BN1 ....
Borrowdale Cl *CRAWW* RH11 ....
Bosham La *RCCH* PO18. ....
Bosham Rd *CRAWE* RH10 ....
Bosmere Gdns *EMRTH* PO10 ....
Bostal Rd *STEY/UB* BN44 ....
The Bostal *STEY/UB* BN44 ....
Bost Hl *FIN/BW* BN14 ....
SALV BN13 ....
Bostock Av *HORS* RH12 ....
Boston Rd *HWH* RH16 ....
Boston St *BRI* BN1 ....
Boswell Rd *CRAWE* RH10 ....
Botany Cl *ANG/EP* BN16. ....
Bough Beeches *BURH* RH15 ....
The Boulevard *CRAWE* RH10 ....
FERR BN12 ....
SALV BN13 ....
Boundary & Station Roads
PTSD BN41 ....
Boundary Cl *WTHG* BN11 ....
Boundary Rd *CRAWE* RH10 ....
LAN/SOMP BN15 ....
RHWH RH17 ....
WTHG BN11 ....
Boundary Wy *ANG/EP* BN16 ....
Boundstone Cl *LAN/SOMP* BN15 ....
Boundstone La
LAN/SOMP BN15 ....
Bourg-de-peage Av *EGRIN* RH19 ....
Bourne Cl *CCH* PO19 ....
SALV BN13 ....
The Bourne *HPPT/KEY* BN6. ....
Bourne View Cl *EMRTH* PO10 ....
Bourne Wy *MIDH* GU29 ....
Bowater Rd *CRAWE* RH10 ....
Bower La *PUL/STOR* RH20 ....
Bowers Pl *CRAWE* RH10 ....
The Bower *HWH* RH16 ....
Bowes Cl *SWTR* RH13 ....
Bowes Hl *HAV* PO9 ....
Bowhill La *RCCH* PO18 ....
Bowley La *SELS* PO20 ....
Bowling Green La *HORS* RH12 ....
Bowmans Cl *STEY/UB* BN44 ....
Bowness Av *LAN/SOMP* BN15 ....
Bowring Wy *ROTT* BN2 ....
Boxall Wk *SWTR* RH13 ....
Box Cl *CRAWW* RH11 ....
Boxes La *RHWH* RH17 ....
Boxgrove *FERR* BN12 ....
Boxgrove Cl *LAN/SOMP* BN15. ....
Boxgrove Gdns *BOGR* PO21 ....
Boxham La *SELS* PO20 ....
Box La *EGRIN* RH19 ....
Box's La *RHWH* RH17 ....
Box Tree Av *ANG/EP* BN16. ....
Boyce's St *BRI* BN1 ....
Brackenbury Cl *PTSD* BN41 ....
Bracken Cl *CRAWE* RH10 ....
CRAWE RH10 ....
PUL/STOR RH20 ....
Bracken Gv *HORS* RH12 ....
Bracken La *PUL/STOR* RH20 ....
Bracken Rd *EPSF* GU31 ....
Bracklesham Cl *SELS* PO20 ....
Bracklesham La *SELS* PO20 ....
Bradbury Rd *CRAWE* RH10 ....
Brading Rd *ROTT* BN2 ....
Bradlond Cl *BOGR* PO21 ....
Bradshaw Rd *CCH* PO19. ....
Braemar Wy *BOGR* PO21 ....
Braemore Rd *HOVE* BN3 ....
Braeside Av *BRI* BN1. ....
Braeside Cl *HASM* GU27 ....
Brainsmead *RHWH* RH17 ....
Brainsmead Cl *RHWH* RH17 ....
Bramber Av *HOVE* BN3. ....
PUL/STOR RH20 ....
Bramber Cl *BOGR* PO21 ....
CRAWE RH10 ....
HWH RH16 ....
LAN/SOMP BN15 ....
Bramber Rd *CCH* PO19 ....
FIN/BW BN14 ....
STEY/UB BN44 ....
Bramber Wy *BURH* RH15 ....
Bramble Cl *CRAWE* RH10 ....
HAV PO9 ....
SALV BN13 ....
Bramble Crs *SALV* BN13 ....
Brambledean Rd *PTSD* BN41 ....
Bramble Gdns *BURH* RH15 ....
Bramble Hl *RHWH* RH17 ....
Bramble La *SALV* BN13 ....
Bramble Md *RHWH* RH17 ....
Bramble Ri *BRI* BN1 ....

le Rd *EPSF* GU31 .... 89 G8
les *HPPT/KEY* BN6 .... 165 F6 🔲
rambles *RHWH* RH17 .... 111 G5
letye La *FROW* RH18 .... 37 H8
letye Rd *CRAWE* RH10 .... 3 F4 🔲
letyne Cl *ANG/EP* BN16 ...... 227 J5 🔲
ling Cl *SWTR* RH13 .... 5 F6
ling La *MIDH* GU29 .... 93 H8
ling Rd *SWTR* RH13 .... 5 F6
ramblings *ANG/EP* BN16 ..... 251 F2
field Rd *MIDOS* PO22 .... 247 G7
ands La *HFD* BN5 .... 186 A2
ey Cl *CRAWE* RH10 .... 3 E5
BW BN14 .... 230 D5 🔲
ey Gdns *EMRTH* PO10 .... 215 F3
OS PO22 .... 12 A1
ey Rd *FIN/BW* BN14 .... 230 D5
ton Cl *SELS* PO20 .... 264 E4
on Cl *CRAWE* RH10 .... 32 D7
y Hole La *CCH* PO19 .... 218 E1
wyn Av *BRI* BN1 .... 212 E5
wyn Crs *BRI* BN1 .... 212 E5
wyn Dr *BRI* BN1 .... 212 D5
wyn Wy *BRI* BN1 .... 212 E6
idge La *RHWH* RH17 .... 81 K6
idge Rd *CRAWE* RH10 .... 3 E5
ands Dr *PTSD* BN41 .... 234 D2
on Av *BRI* BN1 .... 213 F7
CRAWE RH10 .... 32 D7 🔲
ool La *BRI* BN1 .... 212 D3
ck Av *BOGR* PO21 .... 245 H4
Av *EMRTH* PO10 .... 215 H1
Cl *LHPTN* BN17 .... 249 F5
St *BRI* BN1 7
La *SALV* BN13 .... 229 K4
Cl *SALV* BN13 .... 229 K4
hurst Dr *CRAWW* RH11 .... 30 D8
n Rd *SALV* BN13 .... 229 J3
n Wy *ANG/EP* BN16 .... 250 J3
ct *EMRTH* PO10 .... 214 C3
Rd *BOGR* PO21 .... 245 J7
ood Cl *BRI* BN1 .... 213 H8 🔲
ood Crs *BRI* BN1 .... 213 H8
ood Rd *BRI* BN1 .... 213 H8
gham Cl *CRAWW* RH11 .... 30 C8 🔲
n *BURH* RH15 .... 138 E6
Is La *LISS* GU33 .... 62 E5
Rd *CRAWE* RH10 .... 2 C5
St *ROTT* BN2 .... 11 D3
rs Yd *PUL/STOR* RH20 .... 180 B2 🔲
ry Hl *ARUN* BN18 .... 225 H1 🔲
urst La *BIL* RH14 .... 72 C1
y *SELS* PO20 .... 257 J2
ANG/EP BN16 .... 227 H7
*BN18 .... 223 K8
W RH11 .... 31 G2
PO20 .... 220 E5
ood Cl *CRAWE* RH10 .... 32 D3
d *LISS* GU33 .... 64 A4
eld Cl *BOGR* PO21 .... 12 A4 🔲
lin Cl *SWTR* RH13 .... 79 J8
nds *CRAWE* RH10 .... 34 D4
rd La *CRAWE* RH10 .... 34 D3
ke Cl *CRAWW* RH11 .... 30 E8 🔲
Cl *BURH* RH15 .... 139 F7
BN12 .... 229 G8
SOMP BN15 .... 232 A6
Field Cl *MIDH* GU29 .... 122 A5 🔲
Foot Pth *EMRTH* PO10 .... 214 D3
ham Wy *HORL* RH6 .... 19 H1
ands *CRAWE* RH10 .... 19 F8
Rd *CCH* PO19 .... 7 D2
H PO19 .... 214 D2
W BN14 .... 9 D5
GU27 .... 40 E4
H12 .... 48 B4
RH16 .... 112 B4
W BN17 .... 249 H2
smill *HWH* RH16 .... 111 K4
dgeway *SELS* PO20 .... 264 D5
orth Cl *SALV* BN13 .... 229 F6
Cl *STEY/UB* BN44 .... 208 D1
d *ARUN* BN18 .... 199 H7
Vy *CRAWE* RH10 .... 32 D4
dle Wy *SELS* PO20 .... 264 E4
ey Cl *BOGR* PO21 .... 261 J1
y Gdns *LAN/SOMP* BN15 ... 232 B5 🔲
St *BRI* BN1 .... 10 B3
n Pl *MIDOS* PO22 .... 247 H7 🔲
n Pl *BRI* BN1 .... 10 C5 🔲
n Rd *CRAWE* RH10 .... 55 C4
W RH11 .... 30 D4
W RH11 .... 55 C3
N5 .... 161 H7
KEY BN6 .... 163 K8
KEY BN6 .... 187 H1
KEY BN6 .... 188 D1
SOMP BN15 .... 232 B7
d RH17 .... 81 G4
BN43 .... 233 F5
RH13 .... 78 C4
BN11 .... 9 F4
BN11 .... 231 J8

Brighton Road Hornbrook Hl
SWTR RH13 .... 78 B3
Brills La *BRI* BN1 .... 10 C6 🔲
Brimfast La *SELS* PO20 .... 242 E6
Brisbane Cl *CRAWW* RH11 ..... 31 H2 🔲
SALV BN13 .... 229 F5
Bristol Av *LAN/SOMP* BN15 . 232 D6
Bristol Cl *CRAWE* RH10 .... 32 D2
Bristol Gdns *CCH* PO19 .... 219 F1
Bristol Ga *ROTT* BN2 .... 11 F6
Bristol Rd *ROTT* BN2 .... 11 F6
Britany Rd *FIN/BW* BN14 .... 8 C2
HOVE BN3 .... 235 H5
Britten Cl *CRAWW* RH11 .... 30 D8
Britten's La *ARUN* BN18 ...... 198 C6
Broadbridge Ct *RCCH* PO18 . 217 G4
Broadbridge Heath Rd *HORS* RH12 .. 50 D7
Broadbridge La *HORL* RH6 ..... 19 G1
Broad Cft *HAV* PO9 .... 190 A1
Broadfield *EGRIN* RH19 .... 59 G4
Broadfield Dr *CRAWW* RH11 .... 2 A6
Broadfield Pl *CRAWW* RH11 .. 55 F1
Bradford Bridge Rd *BIL* RH14.. 130 D5
PUL/STOR RH20 .... 130 D8
Broad Green Av *BURH* RH15 .. 165 J1
Broadlands *BURH* RH15 .... 165 H5
Broadmark Av *ANG/EP* BN16 250 E5
Broadmark La *ANG/EP* BN16 250 E3
Broadmark Wy *ANG/EP* BN16. 250 E5
Broad Piece *LHPTN* BN17 ..... 249 H1 🔲
Broad Rig *HOVE* BN3 .... 211 H7
Broad Rd *RCCH* PO18 .... 216 B3
Broad Strd *ANG/EP* BN16 ..... 251 F4
Broad St *RHWH* RH17 .... 10 C6 🔲
ROTT BN2 .... 10 C6 🔲
Broad Vw *SELS* PO20 .... 265 C4
Broadview Gdns *SALV* BN13 . 229 J3
Broad Wk *RCCH* PO18 .... 149 F6
The Broad Wk *RCCH* PO18 ... 193 C5
Broadwater La *SWTR* RH13 .. 105 K2
Broadwater St East *FIN/BW* BN14 .. 9 D2
Broadwater St West *FIN/BW* BN14 .. 9 D1
Broadwater Wy *FIN/BW* BN14 230 D5
Broadway *SELS* PO20 .... 264 D5 🔲
The Broadway *CCH* PO19 ..... 219 G1
CRAWE RH10 .... 2 C3
HWH RH16 .... 111 K6
LAN/SOMP BN15 .... 232 D6
Broadwood Cl *HORS* RH12 ... 54 E2
Brock End *RHWH* RH17 .... 110 E3
Brockhurst Dr *HORS* RH12 .... 77 F3 🔲
Brockley Cl *FIN/BW* BN14 .... 8 C2
Brock Rd *CRAWW* RH11 .... 31 F2
Bromley Cl *HPPT/KEY* BN6 .. 165 G7
Bromley Rd *ROTT* BN2 .... 11 D3
Brompton Cl *BRI* BN1 .... 212 E5
The Brontes *EGRIN* RH19 ...... 36 B2 🔲
Bronze Cl *MIDOS* PO22 .... 12 B1
Brook Av *HPPT/KEY* BN6 ..... 165 F8
RCCH PO18 .... 217 F6
Brook Barn Wy *FERR* BN12 .. 253 J2
Brook Cl *BOGR* PO21 .... 245 H7
EGRIN RH19 .... 37 F2
PUL/STOR RH20 .... 156 D8 🔲
WTHG BN11 .... 231 C7
Brookdean Rd *WTHG* BN11 .. 231 H8
Brookenbee Cl *ANG/EP* BN16 226 D8 🔲
Brooker Pl *HOVE* BN3 .... 236 A4
Brooker's Rd *BIL* RH14 .... 102 B4
Brooker St *HOVE* BN3 .... 236 A4
Brookfield La *PETW* GU28 .... 124 D1
Brookfield Wy *BIL* RH14 .... 102 B5
Brook Gdns *EMRTH* PO10 ... 214 B3
Brook Gn *RHWH* RH17 .... 110 E2
Brook Hl *SWTR* RH13 .... 107 G8
Brookhill Cl *CRAWE* RH10 ..... 19 G8
Brookhill Rd *CRAWE* RH10 .... 33 G1
Brookhouse Bottom *RHWH* RH17 .. 87 G8
Brooklands *BOGR* PO21 .... 261 H2
Brooklands Rd *CRAWW* RH11 . 55 G2
Brooklands Wy *EGRIN* RH19 .. 36 B3
Brookland Wy *PUL/STOR* RH20 . 153 J6
Brook La *ANG/EP* BN16 .... 226 E8
FERR BN12 .... 252 C2
HORS RH12 .... 53 F4
HWH RH16 .... 112 B3
PUL/STOR RH20 .... 153 J6
Brooklyn Av *WTHG* BN11 ..... 253 K1
Brookpits La *LHPTN* BN17 ... 248 E3
Brook Rd *HORS* RH12 .... 5 D1
Brookside *CRAWE* RH10 .... 3 E2
CRAWE RH10 .... 19 G8
PUL/STOR RH20 .... 158 A7 🔲
SELS PO20 .... 244 A2
Brookside Av *ANG/EP* BN16 . 226 E8
Brookside Cl *FERR* BN12 ...... 228 C8 🔲
SELS PO20 .... 244 A2
Brookside Rd *ANG/EP* BN16 . 252 B3
Brooks La *MIDOS* PO22 .... 13 D3
RCCH PO18 .... 217 H3
Brooks La West *MIDOS* PO22 . 12 C3
Brooksmead *MIDOS* PO22 ..... 13 D4
The Brooks *BURH* RH15 .... 138 E6

Brook St *RHWH* RH17 .... 110 E2
Brooks Wy *PUL/STOR* RH20 .. 154 E1
The Brook *SWTR* RH13 .... 105 G1
Brookview *CRAWE* RH10 .... 19 G8
PUL/STOR RH20 .... 153 J6
Brookway *BURH* RH15 .... 139 J8
HWH RH16 .... 112 C3
Brook Wy *LAN/SOMP* BN15 . 232 B6
Broomcroft Rd *MIDOS* PO22 . 247 G7
Broomdashers Rd *CRAWE* RH10 ..... 3 E2
Broome Cl *HORS* RH12 .... 4 C2
Bromers Hill La *PUL/STOR* RH20 . 129 G7
Broomers La *SELS* PO20 .... 241 K6
Broomfield Av *FIN/BW* BN14 ... 8 B1
Broomfield Dr *BIL* RH14 ...... 102 C4
PTSD BN41 .... 210 E7
Broomfield Rd *HFD* BN5 .... 161 F6
SELS PO20 .... 265 C3
Broom Rd *EPSF* GU31 .... 117 G1
Brou Cl *ANG/EP* BN16 .... 251 K2
Brougham Rd *WTHG* BN11 ... 231 G8
Brow Cl *PUL/STOR* RH20 ..... 179 K2
Browning Cl *CRAWE* RH10 .... 32 C4
Browning Rd *LAN/SOMP* BN15 . 232 A3
WTHG BN11 .... 8 B5
Browning's Hl *SWTR* RH13 .. 134 E1
The Brownings *EGRIN* RH19 . 36 A2 🔲
Brown's La *PUL/STOR* RH20 . 180 B2
Browns Wd *EGRIN* RH19 .... 22 C7
The Brow *BURH* RH15 .... 165 G1
Broxmead La *RHWH* RH17 ... 109 J6
Broyle Cl *CCH* PO19 .... 219 F2
Broyle Rd *CCH* PO19 .... 219 F2
Bruce Av *WTHG* BN11 .... 253 K1
Bruce Cl *HWH* RH16 .... 112 A8
Bruce Wy *WTHG* BN11 .... 229 K8
Brunel Dr *CRAWE* RH10 .... 3 D4
Brunswick Cl *CRAWE* RH10 ... 3 F5 🔲
MIDOS PO22 .... 13 F3
Brunswick Ms *HOVE* BN3 .... 236 D6 🔲
Brunswick Pl *HOVE* BN3 ...... 236 D5
SHOR BN43 .... 233 H4
WTHG BN11 .... 8 C5 🔲
Brunswick Sq *HOVE* BN3 ..... 236 D6
Brunswick St East *HOVE* BN3 236 D6
Brunswick St West *HOVE* BN3 236 D6 🔲
SHOR BN43 .... 233 H4
Brunswick St West *HOVE* BN3 236 D6
Brushes La *HWH* RH16 .... 112 D5
Bryce Cl *HORS* RH12 .... 5 F2
Buchans Lawn *CRAWW* RH11 . 55 F1
Buci Crs *SHOR* BN43 .... 234 A3
Buckhurst Cl *EGRIN* RH19 .... 22 A8
Buckhurst Wy *EGRIN* RH19 ... 22 A8
Buckingham Av *SHOR* BN43 . 233 G2
Buckingham Cl *SHOR* BN43 . 233 J3 🔲
Buckingham Dr *CCH* PO19 ...... 7 F3
EGRIN RH19 .... 36 E4
Buckingham Ga *HORL* RH6 ... 18 C3
Buckingham Ms *SHOR* BN43 233 H2 🔲
Buckingham Pl *BRI* BN1 .... 10 B3
Buckingham Rd *BRI* BN1 .... 10 B4
PSF GU32 .... 88 B8
SHOR BN43 .... 233 H4
WTHG BN11 .... 9 D4
Buckingham St *BRI* BN1 .... 10 B4 🔲
SHOR BN43 .... 233 G4 🔲
Buckland Dr *BOGR* PO21 ..... 261 J1
Buckler St *PTSD* BN41 .... 235 F3 🔲
Buckley Cl *HOVE* BN3 .... 211 J7
Buckley Pl *CRAWE* RH10 .... 34 C3
Buckmans Rd *CRAWW* RH11 ... 2 C3
Buckmore Av *PSF* GU32 .... 88 B7
Bucknor Cl *BOGR* PO21 .... 261 K1
Bucksham Av *BOGR* PO21 .... 245 H4
Buckshead Hl *SWTR* RH13 .... 79 H4
Buckswood Dr *CRAWW* RH11 . 2 B5
Buckwish La *HFD* BN5 .... 160 E7
Buddington La *MIDH* GU29 ... 94 B8
Budgen Cl *CRAWE* RH10 .... 32 D2
Buffbeards La *HASM* GU27 ... 40 A4
Bugshill La *MIDH* GU29 .... 146 C2
Bulbeck Cl *BURH* RH15 .... 164 E2
Bulkington Av *FIN/BW* BN14 ... 8 B2
Bulldogs Bank *EGRIN* RH19 ... 59 H6
Buller Rd *ROTT* BN2 .... 11 F1
Bullfinch Cl *HORS* RH12 .... 51 J4
Bull Hl *LISS* GU33 .... 62 E7
Bull's La *SWTR* RH13 .... 108 B7
Bunbury Cl *PUL/STOR* RH20 . 181 F7
Bunch La *HASM* GU27 .... 40 C1
Bunch Wy *HASM* GU27 .... 40 C5
Buncton La *RHWH* RH17 ...... 137 J1
Bunting Cl *SWTR* RH13 .... 5 E4
Bunyan Cl *CRAWW* RH11 ...... 30 C8
Burbeach Cl *CRAWW* RH11 ..... 2 A6 🔲
Burchetts Cl *HWH* RH16 ...... 139 K1
Burchett Wk *BOGR* PO21 ..... 245 H6
Burch Gv *ARUN* BN18 .... 223 H2
Burdale Dr *HISD* PO11 .... 238 B8
Burdett Cl *CRAWE* RH10 .... 32 D6 🔲
Burdock Cl *CRAWW* RH11 ..... 54 E1 🔲
Burdocks Dr *BURH* RH15 ..... 165 J2
Burford Cl *SALV* BN13 .... 230 A4

Burford Rd *SWTR* RH13 .... 5 D5
Burgh Cl *CRAWE* RH10 .... 32 D2
Burlands *CRAWW* RH11 .... 30 E2
Burleigh Cl *CRAWE* RH10 .... 34 D3
Burleigh La *CRAWE* RH10 .... 34 E4
Burleigh Wy *CRAWE* RH10 .... 34 D3
Burley Cl *BIL* RH14 .... 46 C7 🔟
  LAN/SOMP BN15 .... 232 A5 🔟
Burley Rd *MIDOS* PO22 .... 247 H7
Burleys Rd *CRAWE* RH10 .... 32 D5
Burlington Gdns *PTSD* BN41 ...... 235 G2
Burlington Rd *FERR* BN12 .... 229 H8
Burlington St *ROTT* BN2 .... 11 E6
Burlow Cl *SELS* PO20 .... 241 H7
Burma Cl *HWH* RH16 .... 112 E7
Burmill Ct *ANG/EP* BN16 .... 227 G8
Burndell Rd *ARUN* BN18 .... 224 A8
Burners Cl *BURH* RH15 .... 165 K2
Burngreave Ct *BOGR* PO21 .... 12 A5 🔟
Burnham Av *BOGR* PO21 .... 12 B5
Burnham Gdns *BOGR* PO21 .... 12 B5 🔟
Burnham Rd *SALV* BN13 .... 229 J5
Burns Cl *HORS* RH12 .... 52 A4
Burns Gdns *MIDOS* PO22 .... 247 H6
Burnside Crs *LAN/SOMP* BN15 .... 231 J6
Burns Rd *CRAWE* RH10 .... 32 C3
Burns Wy *EGRIN* RH19 .... 36 A2
  HORS RH12 .... 54 A2

Burnthouse Bostall
  HPPT/KEY BN6 .... 189 J4
Burnt House La *HORS* RH12 .... 29 H4
Burnthouse La *SWTR* RH13 .... 106 E8
Burrell Av *LAN/SOMP* BN15 .... 231 K6
Burrell Cl *SWTR* RH13 .... 34 C8
Burrell Gn *RHWH* RH17 .... 111 F3
Burrell Rd *HWH* RH16 .... 111 K5
The Burrells *SHOR* BN43 .... 233 K5
Bursledon Cl *MIDOS* PO22 .... 13 F3
Burstead Cl *BRI* BN1 .... 213 H8
Burston Gdns *EGRIN* RH19 .... 22 B7
Burstowhill La *RHWH* RH17 .... 85 F5
Burton Cl *HORL* RH6 .... 18 A1 🔟
Burton Park Rd *PETW* GU28 .... 151 H1
Burton Vls *HOVE* BN3 .... 236 D3 🔟
Burwash Cl *ANG/EP* BN16 .... 227 K8 🔟
Burwash Rd *CRAWE* RH10 .... 5 F4 🔟
  HOVE BN3 .... 211 J8
Bury Dr *FERR* BN12 .... 253 F1
Bury Hl *PUL/STOR* RH20 .... 177 F5
Bury Rd *PUL/STOR* RH20 .... 153 F8 🔟
Bushby Av *ANG/EP* BN16 .... 251 F2
Bushby Cl *LAN/SOMP* BN15 .... 231 J6
Bush Farm Dr *PTSD* BN41 .... 235 F1
Bushfield *BIL* RH14 .... 71 F1
Busticle La *LAN/SOMP* BN15 .... 231 J4
Bute St *ROTT* BN2 .... 11 F5
Butler Ct *SALV* BN13 .... 229 K5 🔟
Butler's Green Rd *HWH* RH16 ...... 111 J7
Butlers Rd *SWTR* RH13 .... 5 F3
Butterbox La *RHWH* RH17 .... 114 B7
Buttercup Wk *BRI* BN1 .... 213 H6
Buttercup Wy *SWTR* RH13 .... 105 G1 🔟
Butterfield *EGRIN* RH19 .... 21 K8
Buttermere Cl *HORS* RH12 .... 52 D5 🔟
Buttermere Wy *ANG/EP* BN16 .... 226 C8 🔟
Butt La *ARUN* BN18 .... 199 G5
Butts Cl *CRAWW* RH11 .... 2 A2
Butts Meadow *BIL* RH14 .... 100 D2
Butts Rd *STHW* BN42 .... 234 C4
Buxshalls Hl *HWH* RH16 .... 112 E2
Buxted Ri *BRI* BN1 .... 213 H6
Buxton Rd *BRI* BN1 .... 10 A3
Bycroft Wy *CRAWE* RH10 .... 32 B3
Byerley Cl *EMRTH* PO10 .... 191 F6 🔟
Byerley Wy *CRAWE* RH10 .... 32 E4
The Bye Wy *BOGR* PO21 .... 261 K3
The Byeway *SELS* PO20 .... 257 F2
Byfleets La *HORS* RH12 .... 50 D1
Bylanes Cl *RHWH* RH17 .... 111 F4
Bylanes Crs *RHWH* RH17 .... 111 F4
Byne Cl *PUL/STOR* RH20 .... 180 C2
Byrd Rd *CRAWW* RH11 .... 30 D8
Byron Cl *CRAWE* RH10 .... 32 B4
  HORS RH12 .... 5 D1
  MIDOS PO22 .... 247 H5
Byron Cv *EGRIN* RH19 .... 36 A3
Byron Rd *ANG/EP* BN16 .... 250 C2
  WTHG BN11 .... 8 C4
Byron St *HOVE* BN3 .... 236 A4
By Sunte *HWH* RH16 .... 112 B3
Bywater Wy *CCH* PO19 .... 6 B5 🔟
Byways *SELS* PO20 .... 264 E6
The Byway *MIDOS* PO22 .... 247 J6

C

Caburn Hts *CRAWW* RH11 .... 2 B5
Caburn Rd *HOVE* BN3 .... 10 A3 🔟
The Cackstones *CRAWE* RH10 .... 32 D4 🔟
Caedwalla Dr *SELS* PO20 .... 220 E2 🔟
Caernarvon Rd *CCH* PO19 .... 7 F4

Caffins Cl *CRAWE* RH10 .... 3 D1
Cagefoot La *HFD* BN5 .... 161 G7
Caister's Cl *HOVE* BN3 .... 236 C3
Cakeham Rd *SELS* PO20 .... 257 F3
Cakeham Wy *SELS* PO20 .... 257 H4
Calbourne *HWH* RH16 .... 111 K6 🔟
Caledon Av *MIDOS* PO22 .... 247 H6
Caledonian Rd *CCH* PO19 .... 6 C5
  ROTT BN2 .... 11 D2 🔟
Caledonian Wy *HORL* RH6 .... 18 B4 🔟
Callisto Cl *CRAWW* RH11 .... 30 C8
Calluna Dr *CRAWE* RH10 .... 33 G1
Callon Cl *SALV* BN13 .... 229 F5 🔟
Calvecroft *LIPH* GU30 .... 38 C7
Camber Cl *CRAWE* RH10 .... 32 C5
Cambrai Av *CCH* PO19 .... 7 D4
Cambria Cl *RCCH* PO18 .... 217 G6
Cambridge Av *SELS* PO20 .... 257 H5
Cambridge Dr *BOGR* PO21 .... 245 H7
Cambridge Gv *HOVE* BN3 .... 236 C4
Cambridge Rd *HOVE* BN3 .... 236 D5
  SWTR RH13 .... 4 C5
  WTHG BN11 .... 8 C3
Camden St *PTSD* BN41 .... 235 G5 🔟
Camelford St *ROTT* BN2 .... 11 D6 🔟
Camelia Cl *ANG/EP* BN16 .... 226 C8
Camelot Cl *SWTR* RH13 .... 105 G1
Camelsdale Rd *HASM* GU27 .... 40 B6
Campbell Crs *EGRIN* RH19 .... 35 K2
Campbell Dr *ANG/EP* BN16 .... 250 D1
Campbell Rd *BOGR* PO21 .... 12 C5
  BRI BN1 .... 10 B2
  CRAWE RH10 .... 32 C7
  SELS PO20 .... 220 D1
Canada Gv *BOGR* PO21 .... 12 B5
Canada Rd *ARUN* BN18 .... 201 F8
Canal Rd *ARUN* BN18 .... 247 K1
Canal Whf *CCH* PO19 .... 6 B4
Canberra Cl *CRAWW* RH11 .... 31 H2 🔟
  HORS RH12 .... 5 E3
Canberra Pl *SELS* PO20 .... 221 F1
Canberra Rd *EMRTH* PO10 .... 214 E8
  SALV BN13 .... 229 G5
Canfield Cl *ROTT* BN2 .... 11 F1
Canfield Rd *ROTT* BN2 .... 11 F1 🔟
Canhouse La *LISS* GU33 .... 63 F8
Canning Rd *MIDOS* PO22 .... 13 E5
Canning St *ROTT* BN2 .... 11 E5
Cannon Pl *BRI* BN1 .... 10 B5 🔟
Canon La *CCH* PO19 .... 6 B3
Canon's Cl *BOGR* PO21 .... 262 A2
Canons Cl *STEY/UB* BN44 .... 183 K7
Cantelupe Rd *EGRIN* RH19 .... 36 D2
Canterbury Cl *BOGR* PO21 .... 261 H2 🔟
  CCH PO19 .... 6 B1
Canterbury Ct *SALV* BN13 .... 229 K8 🔟
Canterbury Dr *ROTT* BN2 .... 11 D3
Canterbury Rd *ANG/EP* BN16 .... 251 F1
  CRAWE RH10 .... 55 J1
  SALV BN13 .... 229 K8
The Canter *CRAWE* RH10 .... 32 E4
Cants Cl *BURH* RH15 .... 139 J8
Cants La *BURH* RH15 .... 139 J7
Canute Rd *RCCH* PO18 .... 217 F6
Canvey Cl *CRAWW* RH11 .... 2 B6
Cape Copse *HORS* RH12 .... 48 B4
Capel La *CRAWW* RH11 .... 30 D6
Capel Rd *HORS* RH12 .... 28 D5
Capenors *BURH* RH15 .... 165 F2
The Cape *LHPTN* BN17 .... 250 C2
Capricorn Cl *CRAWW* RH11 .... 30 C7
Capsey Rd *CRAWW* RH11 .... 30 C6
Capstan Dr *ANG/EP* BN16 .... 250 C1
Caraway Cl *CRAWW* RH11 .... 55 F1 🔟
Carden Av *BRI* BN1 .... 212 E7
Carden Cl *BRI* BN1 .... 213 G5
Carden Crs *BRI* BN1 .... 213 G5
Carden Hl *BRI* BN1 .... 213 H6
Cardinal's Dr *BOGR* PO21 .... 261 H2
Cardonnel Rd *HORL* RH6 .... 17 H4
Cargo Rd *HORL* RH6 .... 17 H5
Carisbrooke Cl
  LAN/SOMP BN15 .... 232 A3 🔟
Carisbrooke Dr *SALV* BN13 .... 229 F6
Carisbrooke Rd *ROTT* BN2 .... 11 F3
Carleton Rd *CCH* PO19 .... 6 A1
Carlingford Cl *BOGR* PO21 .... 12 B4 🔟
Carlisle Gdns *CCH* PO19 .... 219 F2
Carlisle Rd *HOVE* BN3 .... 235 K5
Carlton Av *BOGR* PO21 .... 244 E8
Carlton Hl *ROTT* BN2 .... 11 D5
Carlton Ms *WTHG* BN11 .... 8 A4
Carlton Pl *ROTT* BN2 .... 11 D5 🔟
Carlton Ter *HOVE* BN3 .... 235 G3
Carlyle Av *ROTT* BN2 .... 11 F1
Carlyle St *ROTT* BN2 .... 11 E3
Carnegie Cl *FIN/BW* BN14 .... 8 C1
Carnegie Gdns *FIN/BW* BN14 .... 8 C1
Carnegie Rd *FIN/BW* BN14 .... 8 C1
Carnforth Rd *LAN/SOMP* BN15 .. 231 H6

Carol Cl *BRI* BN1
Caron Cl *LAN/SOMP* BN15
Carousel Ct *BOGR* PO21
Carpenters *BIL* RH14
Carpenters Meadow
  PUL/STOR RH20 1
Carron La *MIDH* GU29
Carse Rd *CCH* PO19
Carter Rd *CRAWE* RH10
Cartersland La *LIPH* GU30
Carterslodge La *RHWH* RH17
Carters Wy *BIL* RH14
Carvel Wy *LHPTN* BN17
Carylls Meadow *SWTR* RH13
Casher Rd *CRAWE* RH10
Cassells Rd *CCH* PO19
Cassidy Pl *PUL/STOR* RH20
Castle Cl *SALV* BN13 2
  STEY/UB BN44
Castle Dr *HORL* RH6
Castlegate *PUL/STOR* RH20
Castle La *STEY/UB* BN44
  SWTR RH13
Castleman Rd *CCH* PO19
Castlereagh Gn *MIDOS* PO22
Castle Rd *HORS* RH12
  SALV BN13
Castle St *BRI* BN1
The Castle *HORS* RH12
Castle Wy *SALV* BN13
  STEY/UB BN44
Castlewood Rd *SWTR* RH13
Caterways *HORS* RH12
Cathedral Wy *CCH* PO19
Catkin Wy *HWH* RH16 1
Catsland La *HFD* BN5
Catslands La *HFD* BN5
The Causeway *ARUN* BN18
  BOGR PO21
  EPSF GU31
  FERR BN12
  HORS RH12
  SELS PO20
  SELS PO20
Cavalier Cl *MIDH* GU29
Cavalier Wy *EGRIN* RH19
Cavell Wy *CRAWE* RH10
Cavendish Cl *FERR* BN12
  HORS RH12
Cavendish Pl *BRI* BN1
Cavendish Rd *BOGR* PO21
  ROTT BN2
Cawley Rd *CCH* PO19
Caxton Cl *CRAWE* RH10
Caxton Wy *HWH* RH16
Cecilian Av *FIN/BW* BN14
Cecil Rd *LAN/SOMP* BN15
Cedar Av *SALV* BN13
Cedar Cl *BOGR* PO21
  BURH RH15
  CRAWW RH11
  FERR BN12
  HORS RH12
  LAN/SOMP BN15
  SALV BN13
Cedar Cl East *BOGR* PO21
Cedar Ct *HASM* GU27
Cedar Dr *CCH* PO19
  SWTR RH13
Cedars Farm Cl *BIL* RH14
Cedars Gdns *BRI* BN1
The Cedars *ANG/EP* BN16
  HWH RH16
Cedar Wy *HFD* BN5
  HWH RH16
Celandine Cl *CRAWW* RH11
Cemetery La *EMRTH* PO10
  PETW GU28
Central Av *ANG/EP* BN16
  BOGR PO21
  FIN/BW BN14
Central Dr *BOGR* PO21
  MIDOS PO22
Centrecourt Cl *FIN/BW* BN14
Centrecourt Rd *FIN/BW* BN14
Centurion Rd *BRI* BN1
Ceres Pl *MIDOS* PO22
Chadborn Cl *ROTT* BN2
Chadwick Cl *CRAWW* RH11
Chaffer La *SELS* PO20
Chaffinch Cl *BURH* RH15 1
  CRAWW RH11
  HORS RH12
  SALV BN13
Chailey Cl *CRAWW* RH11
Chainbridge La *SELS* PO20
Chalcraft Cl *LIPH* GU30
Chalcraft La *BOGR* PO21
Chalder La *SELS* PO20
Chaldon Rd *CRAWW* RH11
Chalet Cl *FERR* BN12
Chalet Gdns *FERR* BN12
Chalet Rd *FERR* BN12

nt Cl MIDOS PO22 247 J6
nt Dr HOVE BN3 212 C8
nt Wy SALV BN13 229 H5
'ock La SELS PO20 240 E6
rs La HPPT/KEY BN6 164 B3
.a SELS PO20 259 K4
Rd BIL RH14 45 J8
PO18 172 C7
Rd PTSD BN41 210 D8
Cl SELS PO20 220 E4
ners RHWH RH17 86 A7
v Cl HPPT/KEY BN6 164 E7 1
ers Ct HORL RH6 16 C5
er Cl HWH RH16 112 D4
er Rd HWH RH16 112 D4
ellors Pk HPPT/KEY BN6 165 F7
onbury PUL/STOR RH20 158 A7 3
onbury Cl PUL/STOR RH20 181 J5
onbury Dr SHOR BN43 233 G2
onbury Ring Rd
/UB BN44 182 C4
onbury Rd ANG/EP BN16 250 D3
RH15 165 F2
BN3 10 A3 3
onbury Vw HFD BN5 161 F7
onbury Wk
STOR RH20 180 B2 2
onbury Wy CRAWW RH11 2 B5
on Cl PUL/STOR RH20 157 F8
BN11 229 K8
on View Rd WTHG BN11 229 K8 2
er Cl CRAWW RH11 2 C5
ers Reach SELS PO20 240 E4 1
ers Wy STEY/UB BN44 183 J8
s Rd WTHG BN11 9 D5
el Vw BOGR PO21 261 H3 1
ers Cl EGRIN RH19 36 A1
ey Rd CRAWE RH10 3 D6
y Cl HFD BN5 161 G5
STOR RH20 180 C2 1
yfield Rd ANG/EP BN16 227 H5
y La SALV BN13 180 B6
y Rd SALV BN13 230 A5
Cl BURH RH15 139 F6
V BN17 249 J1 1
fields RHWH RH17 111 F3
La CRAWE RH10 20 B7
RH19 37 H5
RH18 61 K2
STOR RH20 179 J2
PO18 194 A8
RH17 86 A6
PO20 257 J1
Ms HOVE BN3 236 D6 3
Pl PTSD BN41 235 F4
Rd HORL RH6 16 C4
BN41 234 E4 1
RH13 103 K1
BN11 9 D4 1
Rw EGRIN RH19 59 G4
PO18 172 E5
St BOGR PO21 12 B6
O19 6 B3
J32 88 D7
BN2 11 D5
Ter ROTT BN2 11 F6 2
an Rd CRAWE RH10 56 B1
an's La EGRIN RH19 35 K2
RH19 36 B2 2
ll Cl LIPH GU30 38 C7
ote Rd WTHG BN11 9 E4
Av BURH RH15 164 E1
O19 7 F3
Cl HOVE BN3 212 A8
St PSF GU32 88 C8
BN2 10 C6 4
ton Ct CRAWE RH10 32 B8 1
worth Pk HWH RH16 112 E7
ead SELS PO20 257 J5
k Cl CRAWW RH11 54 E1 4
k Wy SWTR RH13 77 G8
te St ROTT BN2 11 D6 3
n Mill Wy RCCH PO18 172 B5
n Rd RCCH PO18 172 A4
rltons BRI BN1 213 K5 1
n St STEY/UB BN44 183 J8
ood Gdns BURH RH15 139 J6
ood La RDKG RH5 15 J6
ood Rd BURH RH15 139 J6
W RH11 30 D1
RH6 17 G3
oods Business Centre
RH19 36 B1 1
oods Pl EGRIN RH19 22 C8 2
oods Rd EGRIN RH19 36 B1
ood St BOGR PO21 12 A6 1
ood Wk CRAWW RH11 31 F2 1
ndean La FIN/BW BN14 230 D3
ndean Rd FIN/BW BN14 230 D5
ood Rd MIDOS PO22 12 A2
gton Wy HORS RH12 50 C8
ld HOVE BN3 236 A1
ell Dr HAV PO9 190 A8
ell Rd LAN/SOMP BN15 231 K6
LISS GU33 62 A7

Chase La HASM GU27 41 G7
Chase Rd LISS GU33 62 A7
The Chase CRAWE RH10 3 F4
FIN/BW BN14 205 J6
Chatfield Rd CCH PO19 7 E1
RHWH RH17 111 G5
Chatfields CRAWW RH11 2 A5
Chatham Pl BRI BN1 10 B3
Chatham Rd WTHG BN11 231 G8
Chatsmore Crs FERR BN12 228 E8
Chatsworth Av HASM GU27 40 E3
Chatsworth Cl ANG/EP BN16 226 D8 3
Chatsworth Dr ANG/EP BN16 226 D8 4
Chatsworth Rd BRI BN1 10 A2
CCH PO19 7 F4
WTHG BN11 9 D4
Chaucer Av EGRIN RH19 36 A3
Chaucer Rd CRAWE RH10 32 B3
WTHG BN11 8 B3
Chaucer Wy MIDOS PO22 247 G5
Chaucher Av ANG/EP BN16 250 D2
Chawkmare Coppice
BOGR PO21 262 B1 1
Cheal Cl SHOR BN43 233 J5
Cheam Rd ANG/EP BN16 251 F3
Cheapside BRI BN1 10 C4
Cheeleys RHWH RH17 86 A6
Cheesemans La RCCH PO18 192 C7
Chelston Av HOVE BN3 235 H4
Cheltenham Pl BRI BN1 10 C4 2
Chelwood Av FERR BN12 253 G2
Chelwood Cl BRI BN1 213 J5
CRAWE RH10 3 E5
Chelwood Gate Rd UCK TN22 87 K5
Chennells Wy HORS RH12 4 C2
Chepstow Cl CRAWE RH10 32 E5
Chequer Gra FROW RH18 61 J2
Chequer La RCCH PO18 217 H5
Chequer Rd EGRIN RH19 36 D2 1
Cherington Cl HPPT/KEY BN6 164 B6 1
Cherrimans Orch HASM GU27 40 B5 1
Cherry Av ARUN BN18 247 K1
Cherry Cl BOGR PO21 262 A1
BURH RH15 138 E8
Cherry Ct SWTR RH13 4 C6
Cherry Cft LHPTN BN17 225 K8
Cherry Gdns SALV BN13 229 J2 1
Cherrylands Cl HASM GU27 66 D5 1
Cherry La CRAWW RH11 31 G2
RHWH RH17 83 F6
RHWH RH17 109 G8
SELS PO20 241 K6
Cherry Orchard Rd CCH PO19 7 D4
Cherry Tree Av HASM GU27 40 B4
Cherry Tree Cl BIL RH14 102 A2
CRAWE RH10 32 D3 1
SALV BN13 229 H2
Cherry Tree Dr SELS PO20 222 D3
Cherry Wk SALV BN13 229 J2
Cherwell Rd SALV BN13 229 G3
Cherwell Wk CRAWW RH11 30 D6
Chesham Cl FERR BN12 253 J1
Chesham Pl ROTT BN2 11 F6 3
Chesham Rd ROTT BN2 11 F6
Chesham St ROTT BN2 11 F6
Cheshire Cl BOGR PO21 12 C4 3
Cheshire Crs SELS PO20 220 E2
Cheshire Wy EMRTH PO10 215 J1
Chesholt Cl HASM GU27 66 D5
Chesley Cl SALV BN13 229 G5 1
Chess Brook Gn HFD BN5 161 H5
Chesswood Av MIDOS PO22 247 G5
Chesswood Cl WTHG BN11 9 F2
Chesswood Rd WTHG BN11 9 E3
Chester Av LAN/SOMP BN15 232 A7
WTHG BN11 231 G8
Chesterfield Cl CRAWE RH10 20 E7
Chesterfield Rd FERR BN12 229 H8
Chester Ter BRI BN1 10 C1
Chesterton Cl EGRIN RH19 36 D4
Chestnut Av CCH PO19 195 F8
HASM GU27 40 E4
Chestnut Cl ANG/EP BN16 227 H7 2
BURH RH15 139 H6
EGRIN RH19 36 E2
LIPH GU30 38 D8
MIDH GU29 121 K6
PUL/STOR RH20 157 F8
Chestnut Ct ANG/EP BN16 251 J2
Chestnut Gdns HORS RH12 4 B2
HPPT/KEY BN6 163 K5 1
Chestnut Gv MIDOS PO22 12 B2
Chestnut Rdg PUL/STOR RH20 156 A4
Chestnut Rd BIL RH14 102 B4
Chestnuts Cl HWH RH16 112 C4
The Chestnuts HPPT/KEY BN6 163 H2
HWH RH16 112 B4
SELS PO20 243 G3 1
Chestnut Wk CRAWW RH11 31 G2
EGRIN RH19 22 A4
FERR BN12 229 F7
PUL/STOR RH20 154 D1
SELS PO20 220 E2
Chestnut Wy HFD BN5 161 G6
Chesworth Cl SWTR RH13 77 J3

Chesworth Crs SWTR RH13 4 B6
Chesworth Gdns SWTR RH13 4 B6
Chesworth La SWTR RH13 4 B6
Chetwood Rd HORS RH12 54 B1
Cheveley Gdns BOGR PO21 262 B1 2
Chevening Cl CRAWW RH11 55 G2 1
Cheviot Cl ANG/EP BN16 251 J1
SALV BN13 229 J3
Cheviot Rd SALV BN13 229 J3
Cheyne Wk HORL RH6 17 K2
Chichester By-pass CCH PO19 7 F1
SELS PO20 6 A4
Chichester Cl CRAWE RH10 55 J1 1
HOVE BN3 211 J7
Chichester Dr SELS PO20 220 E2
Chichester Pl ROTT BN2 11 F6 4
Chichester Rd ARUN BN18 200 C8
BOGR PO21 245 H4
HISD PO11 238 A2
MIDH GU29 122 B5
SELS PO20 242 D6
SELS PO20 265 F2
Chichester Ter HORS RH12 4 C5
ROTT BN2 11 F6
Chichester Wy BURH RH15 139 J6
SELS PO20 265 H3
Chiddingly Cl CRAWE RH10 3 F4
Chidham La RCCH PO18 216 C4
Chilcomb BURH RH15 165 J2
Chilcroft La HASM GU27 66 D2
Chilcroft Rd HASM GU27 40 B4
Chilcrofts Rd HASM GU27 66 C2
Childerstone Cl LIPH GU30 38 B7 1
Chilgrove Cl FERR BN12 229 F8
Chilling St EGRIN RH19 60 B7
EGRIN RH19 85 K3
Chillis Wood Rd HWH RH16 111 J6
Chiltern Cl ANG/EP BN16 251 J1
CRAWW RH11 2 A3
HASM GU27 40 D6
SHOR BN43 234 A3
Chiltern Crs SALV BN13 229 J3
Chiltington Cl BURH RH15 139 F6 1
PUL/STOR RH20 156 A5
Chiltlee Cl LIPH GU30 38 C8
Chiltlee Mnr LIPH GU30 38 C7
Chiltley La LIPH GU30 64 D1
Chiltley Wy LIPH GU30 64 C1
Chilton Cl CRAN GU6 46 B1
The Chine LHPTN BN17 250 C3
Chippendale Rd CRAWW RH11 55 F2
Chippers Cl SALV BN13 229 K7
Chippers Rd SALV BN13 229 K6
Chippers Wk SALV BN13 229 K7 1
Chithurst La HORL RH6 20 A4
LIPH GU30 92 B5
Chownes Mead La RHWH RH17 111 H7
Chrisdory Rd PTSD BN41 210 C8
Christchurch Crs BOGR PO21 245 G8
Christchurch Rd WTHG BN11 9 D3
Christies EGRIN RH19 36 B3 1
Christopher Rd EGRIN RH19 36 C2
Christopher Wy EMRTH PO10 214 D1
Christ's Hospital Rd SWTR RH13 76 B5
Church Ap LHPTN BN17 250 A2 1
Church Av HWH RH16 112 A5
Church Cl BOGR PO21 261 F3
BRI BN1 213 F6
BURH RH15 139 G8
HASM GU27 41 H1
LAN/SOMP BN15 232 A3
SALV BN13 228 D2
STEY/UB BN44 184 C8 1
SWTR RH13 79 J8
SWTR RH13 132 D3
Churcher Rd EMRTH PO10 191 F7
Church Farm La SELS PO20 257 J3
Churchfarm La SELS PO20 259 K1
Church Farm Wk STEY/UB BN44 184 C8
Churchfield PUL/STOR RH20 127 G8
Churchfield Rd EPSF GU31 89 F7
Church Gn SHOR BN43 234 A4
Church Gv PUL/STOR RH20 156 B2
Church Hl ARUN BN18 199 G6
BRI BN1 212 E5
MIDH GU29 122 B3
POY/PYE BN45 188 C5
PUL/STOR RH20 154 D1
Church House Cl STHW BN42 234 C2
Churchill Av BOGR PO21 245 G7
HORS RH12 4 A4
Churchill Ct CRAWE RH10 31 K2
Churchill Dr EMRTH PO10 190 D7
Churchill Wy BURH RH15 165 J1
Church La RDKG RH5 25 K2
ARUN BN18 223 J3
BOGR PO21 260 E3
CRAWE RH10 33 G1
EGRIN RH19 36 D2
FERR BN12 252 C1
HASM GU27 40 E4
HFD BN5 161 G6
HISD PO11 214 A8
HORL RH6 18 E5
HORS RH12 50 D8

HPPT/KEY BN6 ..... 163 F6
HPPT/KEY BN6 ..... J8
HWH RH16 ..... 140 D5
LAN/SOMP BN15 ..... 231 G3
LHPTN BN17 ..... 248 E2
LIPH GU50 ..... 38 B5
MIDH GU29 ..... 147 K4
MIDOS PO22 ..... 12 B3
MIDOS PO22 ..... 223 F7
PETW GU28 ..... 123 K1
POY/PYE BN45 ..... 187 H4
PUL/STOR RH20 ..... 153 J5
PUL/STOR RH20 ..... 157 K7
PUL/STOR RH20 ..... 177 G4
RCCH PO18 ..... 171 F6
RCCH PO18 ..... 192 E6
RCCH PO18 ..... 197 F8
RHWH RH17 ..... 84 B3
RHWH RH17 ..... 86 A5
RHWH RH17 ..... 86 B8
SELS PO20 ..... 220 E2
SELS PO20 ..... 220 E4
SELS PO20 ..... 222 C4
SELS PO20 ..... 241 J6
SELS PO20 ..... 242 E8
SELS PO20 ..... 243 G3
STEY/UB BN44 ..... 159 K6
STEY/UB BN44 ..... 183 K7
STEY/UB BN44 ..... 208 C1
STHW BN42 ..... 234 B4
SWTR RH13 ..... 79 J6
SWTR RH13 ..... 104 D2
SWTR RH13 ..... 134 B8
Church Md HPPT/KEY BN6 ..... 165 G8
STEY/UB BN44 ..... 183 K7
Churchmead Cl RCCH PO18 ..... 195 F5
Church Meadow RCCH PO18 ..... 217 F6
RCCH PO18 ..... 168 E7
Church Pl PUL/STOR RH20 ..... 154 D1
Church Platt RHWH RH17 ..... 110 E6
Church Rd ANG/EP BN16 ..... 227 H6
ANG/EP BN16 ..... 250 D2
ARUN BN18 ..... 223 K8
BURH RH15 ..... 139 G8
BURH RH15 ..... 165 G1
CCH PO19 ..... 7 F2
CRAWE RH10 ..... 19 H8
CRAWE RH10 ..... 32 E5
CRAWE RH10 ..... 34 B8
EGRIN RH19 ..... 59 G5
EMRTH PO10 ..... 191 F8
EMRTH PO10 ..... 215 H4
EMRTH PO10 ..... 239 H2
HASM GU27 ..... 40 E4
HASM GU27 ..... 66 D6
HORL RH6 ..... 17 K1
HORL RH6 ..... 17 J6
HORL RH6 ..... 19 G4
HORS RH12 ..... 50 D8
HORS RH12 ..... 52 D6
HOVE BN3 ..... 236 B5
HWH RH16 ..... 112 A7
LHPTN BN17 ..... 225 J3
LIPH GU30 ..... 38 C5
MIDH GU29 ..... 122 C5
PSF GU32 ..... 88 C4
PTSD BN41 ..... 235 F4
RHWH RH17 ..... 113 H8
SALV BN13 ..... 8 A1
SELS PO20 ..... 221 J3
SELS PO20 ..... 243 J2
SELS PO20 ..... 257 J4
SELS PO20 ..... 265 F3
SWTR RH13 ..... 78 E6
SWTR RH13 ..... 134 B8
Church St ARUN BN18 ..... 177 K4
BRI BN1 ..... 10 B5
CRAWW RH11 ..... 2 E5
HFD BN5 ..... 161 C6
HORS RH12 ..... 48 C3
HORS RH12 ..... 51 F4
LHPTN BN17 ..... 250 A2
PETW GU28 ..... 125 K3
PTSD BN41 ..... 235 F4
PUL/STOR RH20 ..... 156 C2
PUL/STOR RH20 ..... 180 B2
RHWH RH17 ..... 110 E5
SHOR BN43 ..... 233 H4
STEY/UB BN44 ..... 183 K8
Church Vw EMRTH PO10 ..... 191 F8
Church View Cl HORL RH6 ..... 17 K1
Church Wk HORL RH6 ..... 17 K1
WTHG BN11 ..... 9 F4
Church Wy BOGR PO21 ..... 261 H4
RCCH PO18 ..... 171 K4
SALV BN13 ..... 8 A1
Church Way SALV BN13 ..... 8 A1
Church Wd PUL/STOR RH20 ..... 127 H8
Churchwood Dr SELS PO20 ..... 221 F2
Chute Av SALV BN13 ..... 229 J2
Chute Wy SALV BN13 ..... 229 J3
Cinder Hl EGRIN RH19 ..... 85 K2
The Circle ANG/EP BN16 ..... 251 J3
Circus St ROTT BN2 ..... 10 C5

Cissbury Av FIN/BW BN14 ..... 229 K1
Cissbury Cl HORS RH12 ..... 5 F1
Cissbury Dr FIN/BW BN14 ..... 205 K8
Cissbury Gdns FIN/BW BN14 ..... 206 A8
Cissbury Hl CRAWW RH11 ..... 2 B5
Cissbury Rd BURH RH15 ..... 138 E7
FERR BN12 ..... 228 C8
FIN/BW BN14 ..... 230 C5
HOVE BN3 ..... 10 A3
City Fields Wy SELS PO20 ..... 221 F1
Civic Wy BURH RH15 ..... 139 C8
Claigmar Rd ANG/EP BN16 ..... 250 E2
Clair Rd HWH RH16 ..... 112 A6
Clapgate La SWTR RH13 ..... 49 H7
Clapham Cl SALV BN13 ..... 228 D2
Clapham Common SALV BN13 ..... 228 C3
Clappers Ga CRAWE RH10 ..... 2 C2
Clappers La HFD BN5 ..... 186 D4
SELS PO20 ..... 258 A5
Clappers Meadow CRAN GU6 ..... 46 C1
Clare Cl CRAWE RH10 ..... 32 C2
Clare Gdns EPSF GU31 ..... 89 C8
Claremont Wy MIDH GU29 ..... 122 A4
Clarence Av LHPTN BN17 ..... 225 J8
Clarence Dr ANG/EP BN16 ..... 251 H1
EGRIN RH19 ..... 36 D4
Clarence Rd BOGR PO21 ..... 12 C5
SWTR RH13 ..... 4 C6
Clarence Sq BRI BN1 ..... 10 B5
Clarendon Pl PTSD BN41 ..... 235 G5
HOVE BN3 ..... 236 B4
Clarendon Rd FIN/BW BN14 ..... 230 E5
HOVE BN3 ..... 236 B4
SHOR BN43 ..... 234 A3
Clarendon Ter ROTT BN2 ..... 11 F6
Clarendon Vls HOVE BN3 ..... 236 A4
Claridge Gdns LING RH7 ..... 22 E1
Claridges Md LING RH7 ..... 22 E1
Clarke Av HOVE BN3 ..... 211 K8
Clay Hall La CRAWE RH10 ..... 19 J7
Clay La ARUN BN18 ..... 226 B2
LING RH7 ..... 21 F1
PUL/STOR RH20 ..... 179 J2
RCCH PO18 ..... 217 H2
Claypit La RCCH PO18 ..... 195 K8
Clays Cl EGRIN RH19 ..... 36 C3
Clays Hl STEY/UB BN44 ..... 208 A1
Clayton Av HPPT/KEY BN6 ..... 164 E8
Clayton Dr BURH RH15 ..... 165 F2
Clayton Hl CRAWW RH11 ..... 211 K8
POY/PYE BN45 ..... 188 D4
Clayton La SELS PO20 ..... 258 A4
Clayton Rd HPPT/KEY BN6 ..... 189 J1
ROTT BN2 ..... 11 F3
SELS PO20 ..... 264 D5
Claytons Cnr SELS PO20 ..... 241 J6
Clayton Wy HOVE BN3 ..... 211 K8
Clearwater La RHWH RH17 ..... 113 J8
Clearwaters La BURH RH15 ..... 139 K3
Cleaver's La RHWH RH17 ..... 110 B1
Cleeves Wy ANG/EP BN16 ..... 251 H1
Clerks Acre HPPT/KEY BN6 ..... 165 G7
Clermont Rd BRI BN1 ..... 236 D1
Clermont Ter BRI BN1 ..... 236 E1
Cleveland Cl SALV BN13 ..... 229 K3
Cleveland Gdns BURH RH15 ..... 165 H1
Cleveland Rd BRI BN1 ..... 10 C1
CCH PO19 ..... 7 D4
SALV BN13 ..... 229 K3
Cleve Wy BIL RH14 ..... 102 B3
Clifton Hl BRI BN1 ..... 10 A4
Clifton Pl BRI BN1 ..... 10 A4
Clifton Rd BOGR PO21 ..... 12 B4
BRI BN1 ..... 10 B4
BURH RH15 ..... 138 D6
CRAWE RH10 ..... 32 C6
LHPTN BN17 ..... 249 K3
WTHG BN11 ..... 8 C3
Clifton St BRI BN1 ..... 10 B4
Clifton Ter BRI BN1 ..... 10 B4
Climping Cl HWH RH16 ..... 111 K8
Climping Rd CRAWW RH11 ..... 2 A1
Climping St LHPTN BN17 ..... 248 D3
Clinton Hl LING RH7 ..... 22 E2
Clitherow Gdns CRAWE RH10 ..... 3 D4
Clive Av FERR BN12 ..... 253 H1
Clivedale Gdns STEY/UB BN44 ..... 183 K8
Clive Wy CRAWE RH10 ..... 32 C5
The Cloisters LHPTN BN17 ..... 250 B3
The Close ANG/EP BN16 ..... 251 F5
BIL RH14 ..... 45 J8
BOGR PO21 ..... 261 K2
BRI BN1 ..... 212 D6
BURH RH15 ..... 139 J7
EGRIN RH19 ..... 36 B3
HORL RH6 ..... 18 C2
HPPT/KEY BN6 ..... 165 F7
LAN/SOMP BN15 ..... 232 B7
MIDOS PO22 ..... 248 A6
PUL/STOR RH20 ..... 158 A6
RCCH PO18 ..... 197 F8
RHWH RH17 ..... 84 D4
SELS PO20 ..... 265 H3
SHOR BN43 ..... 233 H3

Closewalks MIDH GU29
Clothalls La SWTR RH13
Clovelly Av MIDOS PO22
Clovelly Rd EMRTH PO10
EMRTH PO10
HISD PO11
Cloverlands CRAWE RH10
Clover La FERR BN12
Clovers End BRI BN1
HORS RH12
Clovers Wy HORS RH12
Clover Wy PTSD BN41
Club Wk ANG/EP BN16
Clun Rd LHPTN BN17 2
Clyde Cl SALV BN13
Clyde Rd BRI BN1
MIDOS PO22
SALV BN13
Clydesdale Av CCH PO19
Clydesdale Gdns MIDOS PO22
Coach & Horses La RHWH RH17
Coach House Cl SELS PO20
Coach La RHWH RH17
Coachmans Dr CRAWW RH11
Coach Rd RCCH PO18
SELS PO20
Coastal Rd ANG/EP BN16
Coastguard La SELS PO20
Coastguard Pde BOGR PO21
Coastguard Rd LHPTN BN17
Coates La PUL/STOR RH20
Cobbett Cl CRAWE RH10
Cobbetts Md HWH RH16
Cobbles Crs CRAWE RH10
Cobblewood EMRTH PO10
Cob Cl CRAWE RH10
Cobden La HASM GU27
Cobden Rd MIDH GU29 1
ROTT BN2
WTHG BN11
Cobham Cl ARUN BN18
Cobham Wy CRAWE RH10
Cob La RHWH RH17
Cobnor Cl CRAWW RH11
Cobton Dr HOVE BN3
Cob Wk CRAWW RH11
Cocking Hl RCCH PO18
Cockshott La PSF GU32
Cohen Cl SELS PO20
Cokeham Gdns LAN/SOMP BN15
Cokeham La LAN/SOMP BN15
Cokeham Rd LAN/SOMP BN15
Colbourne Av ROTT BN2
Colbourne Rd HOVE BN3
Colchester V FROW RH18
Colchins BURH RH15
Coldean La BRI BN1
Coldharbour Farm Rd
EMRTH PO10
Coldharbour La SALV BN13
Coldwaltham La BURH RH15
Colebrook Cl WTHG BN11
Colebrook La PUL/STOR RH20
Colebrook Rd BRI BN1
LHPTN BN17
STHW BN42
Cole Cl CRAWW RH11
Coleman Av HOVE BN3
Coleman St ROTT BN2
Coleridge Cl FERR BN12
HORS RH12
Coleridge Crs CRAWE RH10
Coleridge Rd FERR BN12
Coleridge St HOVE BN3
Colet Rd CRAWE RH10
Colgate Cl CRAWW RH11
Colindale Rd FERR BN12
Colindale Rd North FERR BN12
Collards La HASM GU27
College Cl BOGR PO21
EGRIN RH19
HAV PO9
PTSD BN41
RHWH RH17
College Gdns ROTT BN2
WTHG BN11
College Hl HASM GU27
STEY/UB BN44
College Hill Ter HASM GU27
College La CCH PO19
EGRIN RH19
HPPT/KEY BN6
College Pl HPPT/KEY BN6
ROTT BN2
College Rd CRAWE RH10
HWH RH16
HWH RH16
ROTT BN2
STEY/UB BN44
SWTR RH13
College St EPSF GU31
ROTT BN2
College Ter ROTT BN2
College Wy CRAWE RH10
Collier Rw CRAWE RH10
Collingford La RHWH RH17

...wood PUL/STOR RH20 ..... 128 E8
...wood Cl EGRIN RH19 ..... 36 D4
...wood Rd SHOR BN43 ..... 233 H5
...wood Rd CRAWE RH10 ..... 32 D6
... BN12 ..... 229 C7
...s RH12 ..... 4 A2
...La EPSF GU31 ..... 117 K4
...Rd CRAWW RH11 ..... 30 C7
...Av BOGR PO21 ..... 12 A3
...s Crs LIPH GU30 ..... 38 E7
...Ct BURH RH15 ..... 138 E8
...Pl BURH RH15 ..... 138 E8
...Cl SALV BN13 ..... 229 G3
...ay Rd CRAWW RH11 ..... 2 A6
...n Rd CRAWE RH10 ..... 3 F4
...Bay BOGR PO21 ..... 261 K2
...ot Dr HORS RH12 ..... 5 D2
...ple La SWTR RH13 ..... 77 J7
... SELS PO20 ..... 264 D3
...oia La SALV BN13 ..... 229 G5
...Av SHOR BN43 ..... 233 F3
...Cl HWH RH16 ..... 112 B8
...Gdns HWH RH16 ..... 112 B8
...La HWH RH16 ..... 112 D8
... RH17 ..... 140 B2
...Rd HWH RH16 ..... 140 B1
...el La RHWH RH17 ..... 109 C5
...Cl CRAWW RH11 ..... 30 C7
...Dr STEY/UB BN44 ..... 207 K2
...Rd LISS GU33 ..... 90 B2
...Wi HAV PO9 ..... 190 A4
...erce Wy LAN/SOMP BN15 ..... 231 J6
...ercial Rd BURH RH15 ..... 139 F8
...n Hl PUL/STOR RH20 ..... 156 A4
...on La HPPT/KEY BN6 ..... 165 K6
...onmead La BOGR PO21 ..... 244 D3
...n Rd EMRTH PO10 ..... 191 K6
...onside EMRTH PO10 ..... 191 F6
...mmon PUL/STOR RH20 ..... 156 A3
...n Vw MIDH GU29 ..... 121 F2
...ss Cl LHPTN BN17 ..... 225 J8
...ssion Cl CRAWW RH11 ..... 30 C6
...r Cl CRAWW RH11 ..... 30 C7
...on Av BRI BN1 ..... 10 B4
... BN12 ..... 253 F1
...on Cl CCH PO19 ..... 195 G8
...on Dr MIDOS PO22 ..... 247 H5
...on Rd BRI BN1 ..... 236 D2
... RH16 ..... 112 D3
...ons Brow La SWTR RH13 ..... 5 E4
...ons La SWTR RH13 ..... 5 E6
...Av ANG/EP BN16 ..... 250 E1
...le Cl PUL/STOR RH20 ..... 156 D8
...Wy BURH RH15 ..... 138 E8
...Md CCH PO19 ..... 7 E1
...Cl CRAWW RH11 ..... 2 A1
... PO20 ..... 257 J5
...ft HORS RH12 ..... 52 D6
...urst Rd BIL RH14 ..... 102 E6
...d SELS PO20 ..... 257 J5
...ix SELS PO20 ..... 257 J5
...ve Dr RCCH PO18 ..... 216 C1
...s Cl HORS RH12 ..... 52 D5
...Rd EMRTH PO10 ..... 190 D8
...n CRAWW RH11 ..... 30 B7
... RH12 ..... 52 D6
...OMP BN15 ..... 231 J5
... PO22 ..... 247 F5
...n Rd EMRTH PO10 ..... 229 C7
...n Wy ANG/EP BN16 ..... 226 C8
...ght Av SHOR BN43 ..... 233 G3
...ght Gdns CRAWW RH11 ..... 2 C1
...ght Rd HOVE BN3 ..... 236 A5
... BN17 ..... 249 K2
...ght Ter HOVE BN3 ..... 236 B4
...Wy BURH RH15 ..... 164 E1
...Wy East RH6 ..... 18 B1
...le Dr SELS PO20 ..... 265 G4
...Rd CRAWE RH10 ..... 55 K1
...La RHWH PO10 ..... 214 D3
...Dr BOGR PO21 ..... 261 H3
...Pl HORS RH12 ..... 52 D5
...St HOVE BN3 ..... 236 B3
...CRAWE RH10 ..... 3 D5
... RH12 ..... 4 C1
...HORS RH12 ..... 47 H2
...a EMRTH PO10 ..... 215 J1
... PO18 ..... 192 B1
...d HORS RH12 ..... 29 F4
...Pond Rd LIPH GU30 ..... 92 A3
...RU PUL/STOR RH20 ..... 157 F1
... RH13 ..... 103 J7
...st La SWTR RH13 ..... 5 F6
...Cl BIL RH14 ..... 101 J2
...N RH11 ..... 30 C2
...Crs PUL/STOR RH20 ..... 177 G4
...Dro STEY/UB BN44 ..... 207 K1
...Hl BIL RH14 ..... 102 B2
...Hill Rd EGRIN RH19 ..... 36 A5
...lands La PUL/STOR RH20 ..... 128 C8
...La ARUN BN18 ..... 202 E4
...Ri FIN/BW BN14 ..... 230 C1
...Rd ROTT BN2 ..... 11 F1
...UB BN44 ..... 207 J1

Coombers RHWH RH17 ..... 83 G2
Coombers La RHWH RH16 ..... 112 D6
Coombes Rd LAN/SOMP BN15 ..... 208 C5
Coomes Wy LHPTN BN17 ..... 225 K7
Cooper Rw CRAWE RH10 ..... 2 C6
Coopers Cl BURH RH15 ..... 139 H6
The Coopers SWTR RH13 ..... 75 H7
Cooper St CCH PO19 ..... 18 C3
Coopers Wy HFD BN5 ..... 161 H6
Coos La RHWH RH17 ..... 80 E5
Cootes Av HORS RH12 ..... 51 G8
Cootes La MIDOS PO22 ..... 247 K6
Cootham Gn PUL/STOR RH20 ..... 179 K1
Copeland Rd MIDOS PO22 ..... 13 F4
Copestake Dr BURH RH15 ..... 139 K8
Copnall Wy HORS RH12 ..... 4 B5
Coppards Cl RHWH RH17 ..... 140 E7
Copper Beech Dr SELS PO20 ..... 220 E2
Copperfield Pl HORS RH12 ..... 4 A4
Copperfields SWTR RH13 ..... 78 D3
Copper Hall Cl ANG/EP BN16 ..... 251 G1
Coppice La SELS PO20 ..... 264 E3
Coppice Rd HORS RH12 ..... 5 F2
The Coppice CRAWE RH10 ..... 34 D3
RHWH RH17 ..... 113 H8
Coppice Wk CRAWE RH10 ..... 3 F2
Coppice Wy HWH RH16 ..... 111 K8
Copsale Rd SWTR RH13 ..... 106 A6
Copse Cl CRAWE RH10 ..... 34 D3
EGRIN RH19 ..... 22 D8
EPSF GU31 ..... 89 G7
HORS RH12 ..... 5 E1
LISS GU33 ..... 62 A7
Copse Crs CRAWW RH11 ..... 2 B2
Copse Hl BRI BN1 ..... 212 D6
Copse La ARUN BN18 ..... 223 C1
Copse Rd HASM GU27 ..... 39 K6
The Copse CCH PO19 ..... 219 G1
HWH RH16 ..... 112 D6
SWTR RH13 ..... 105 F1
Copse Vw ANG/EP BN16 ..... 251 H1
Copthorne Bank CRAWE RH10 ..... 19 H8
HORL RH6 ..... 19 J5
Copthorne Cl SALV BN13 ..... 230 A3
Copthorne Common Rd
CRAWE RH10 ..... 19 J8
Copthorne Hl SALV BN13 ..... 229 K4
Copthorne Rd CRAWE RH10 ..... 20 D7
CRAWE RH10 ..... 32 D3
EGRIN RH19 ..... 21 G7
Copthorne Wy BOGR PO21 ..... 245 F7
CRAWE RH10 ..... 33 F1
Copyhold Hl HASM GU27 ..... 66 E3
Copyhold La RHWH RH16 ..... 111 K1
RHWH RH17 ..... 111 F7
Copyhold Rd EGRIN RH19 ..... 36 B8
Corbishley Rd MIDOS PO22 ..... 12 B2
Corbyn Crs SHOR BN43 ..... 233 J4
Cordal Cl ANG/EP BN16 ..... 250 D4
Corfe Cl SALV BN13 ..... 229 F6
SWTR RH13 ..... 105 G2
Cormorant Wy SELS PO20 ..... 257 K5
Corner Garth FERR BN12 ..... 252 D2
Cornfield Cl LHPTN BN17 ..... 226 A8
Cornflower Wy SWTR RH13 ..... 77 G8
Cornford Cl BURH RH15 ..... 138 E6
PTSD BN41 ..... 235 F1
Cornwall Gdns BRI BN1 ..... 212 E6
EGRIN RH19 ..... 36 D3
LHPTN BN17 ..... 226 A8
Cornwall Rd LHPTN BN17 ..... 249 K1
Coronation Av EGRIN RH19 ..... 36 C4
Coronation St ROTT BN2 ..... 11 E3
The Coronet HORL RH6 ..... 18 C2
Corsletts Av HORS RH12 ..... 50 D8
Cortis Av FIN/BW BN14 ..... 8 C1
Corunna Dr SWTR RH13 ..... 5 E5
Cory Cl CCH PO19 ..... 6 C4
Costells Edge RHWH RH17 ..... 113 H7
Cote St SALV BN13 ..... 229 G2
Cotland Rd SELS PO20 ..... 265 G5
Cot La RCCH PO18 ..... 216 B6
Cotsford CRAWW RH11 ..... 55 F5
Cotswold Cl CRAWW RH11 ..... 2 A3
SALV BN13 ..... 229 J3
Cotswold Rd SALV BN13 ..... 229 K4
The Cotswolds STHW BN42 ..... 234 C4
Cotswold Wy ANG/EP BN16 ..... 251 J1
Cottage Bush Cl PTSD BN41 ..... 235 G1
Cottage Cl BOGR PO21 ..... 261 K1
HORS RH12 ..... 52 D5
Cottage Pl CRAWE RH10 ..... 20 A8
Cottenham Rd WTHG BN11 ..... 9 F3
Cottingham Av HORS RH12 ..... 51 K4
Cotton Dr EMRTH PO10 ..... 190 C8
The Cottrells ANG/EP BN16 ..... 227 H6
Coulstock Rd HPPT/KEY BN6 ..... 138 C7
Coultershaw Br PETW GU28 ..... 125 J8
Countisbury Cl BOGR PO21 ..... 245 H8
Countryman La SWTR RH13 ..... 132 B4
County Oak Av BRI BN1 ..... 213 H5
County Oak La CRAWW RH11 ..... 17 H8
County Oak Wy CRAWW RH11 ..... 31 H1
Court Barn La SELS PO20 ..... 241 J5
Court Cl BRI BN1 ..... 212 E4

EGRIN RH19 ..... 36 D2
LIPH GU30 ..... 38 B8
Court Crs EGRIN RH19 ..... 36 E2
Court Farm Rd HOVE BN3 ..... 235 K1
Courtlands HWH RH16 ..... 112 A8
Courtlands Cl FERR BN12 ..... 253 J2
Courtlands Wy FERR BN12 ..... 253 J2
MIDOS PO22 ..... 247 G5
Courtmead Rd RHWH RH17 ..... 111 F5
Courts Hill Rd HASM GU27 ..... 40 D5
Courts Mount Rd HASM GU27 ..... 40 D5
The Court BOGR PO21 ..... 261 H2
Courtwick La LHPTN BN17 ..... 225 J7
Courtwick Rd LHPTN BN17 ..... 225 J8
The Courtyard EGRIN RH19 ..... 37 F2
EPSF GU31 ..... 88 D8
Cousins Wy PUL/STOR RH20 ..... 128 E8
Coventry Cl BOGR PO21 ..... 245 E7
Coventry St BRI BN1 ..... 10 A2
Cove Rd ANG/EP BN16 ..... 250 D3
Covert Cl CRAWE RH10 ..... 3 D2
Covert Md PUL/STOR RH20 ..... 157 K6
RHWH RH17 ..... 81 F4
The Covey HORS RH12 ..... 32 D5
Covington Rd EMRTH PO10 ..... 191 H6
Cowdens Cl HOVE BN3 ..... 211 H7
Cowdown La RCCH PO18 ..... 143 C7
Cowdray Cl ANG/EP BN16 ..... 226 D8
CRAWE RH10 ..... 32 C6
FERR BN12 ..... 253 H2
Cowdray Ct MIDH GU29 ..... 122 D3
Cowdray Dr ANG/EP BN16 ..... 226 D8
FERR BN12 ..... 253 H2
Cowdray Rd MIDH GU29 ..... 122 C2
Cowfold Cl CRAWW RH11 ..... 30 D8
Cowfold Rd RHWH RH17 ..... 136 E1
SWTR RH13 ..... 134 B2
Cow La EPSF GU31 ..... 118 A8
SELS PO20 ..... 259 J4
Cowley Dr LAN/SOMP BN15 ..... 232 B6
Cowper Rd WTHG BN11 ..... 8 B4
Cowper St HOVE BN3 ..... 236 A4
Cowslip Cl SWTR RH13 ..... 105 C1
Coxes Meadow PSF GU32 ..... 88 C6
Coxes Rd SELS PO20 ..... 264 D5
Cox Green Rd HORS RH12 ..... 47 K1
Cox Gv BURH RH15 ..... 138 E6
Coxham La STEY/UB BN44 ..... 183 J7
Coxswain Wy SELS PO20 ..... 265 F6
Crabbet Rd CRAWE RH10 ..... 32 B4
Crablands SELS PO20 ..... 264 D4
Crablands Cl SELS PO20 ..... 264 D4
Cradock Pl SALV BN13 ..... 229 H3
Craggits La HFD BN5 ..... 161 G6
Cragans CRAWW RH11 ..... 30 E5
Craignair Av BRI BN1 ..... 213 F4
Craigweil La BOGR PO21 ..... 262 B2
Craigwell Mnr BOGR PO21 ..... 262 A2
Cranborne Wk CRAWE RH10 ..... 3 E5
Cranford Rd PSF GU32 ..... 116 C1
Cranham Av BIL RH14 ..... 102 A5
Cranleigh Rd FIN/BW BN14 ..... 8 B1
Cranmer Av HOVE BN3 ..... 235 K2
Cranmer Cl SALV BN13 ..... 8 A3
Cranston Cl EGRIN RH19 ..... 36 D1
Cranworth Rd WTHG BN11 ..... 9 F3
Craven Rd CRAWE RH10 ..... 32 B6
ROTT BN2 ..... 11 F4
Crawford Gdns SWTR RH13 ..... 5 D4
Crawfurd Wy EGRIN RH19 ..... 22 D8
Crawley Av CRAWE RH10 ..... 1 D6
CRAWE RH10 ..... 32 C1
CRAWW RH11 ..... 2 A6
Crawley Down Rd EGRIN RH19 ..... 21 G8
Crawley La CRAWE RH10 ..... 32 C4
RHWH RH17 ..... 56 D6
Crawley Rd BRI BN1 ..... 213 K5
HORS RH12 ..... 5 E3
HORS RH12 ..... 52 E8
Crawters Cl CRAWE RH10 ..... 3 E2
Crayford Rd ROTT BN2 ..... 11 F1
Cray La PUL/STOR RH20 ..... 129 F6
Cray's La PUL/STOR RH20 ..... 115 G4
Creasys Dr CRAWW RH11 ..... 55 F3
Crede La RCCH PO18 ..... 217 G5
Creek End CCH PO19 ..... 218 B5
EMRTH PO10 ..... 214 D4
Crescenta Wk BOGR PO21 ..... 245 J8
Crescent Cl BURH RH15 ..... 139 H8
Crescent Pl ROTT BN2 ..... 11 E6
Crescent Ri PUL/STOR RH20 ..... 156 E8
Crescent Rd BOGR PO21 ..... 12 B5
BURH RH15 ..... 139 G8
EGRIN RH19 ..... 36 B2
ROTT BN2 ..... 11 D2
WTHG BN11 ..... 8 C4
The Crescent ANG/EP BN16 ..... 250 C3
BOGR PO21 ..... 261 H3
EGRIN RH19 ..... 22 A3
EMRTH PO10 ..... 215 H3
HORL RH6 ..... 18 A2
HORS RH12 ..... 77 G1

HPPT/KEY BN6	165	H8
LAN/SOMP BN15	232	K2
MIDOS PO22	13	F4
PUL/STOR RH20	179	J2
SELS PO20	257	H4
STEY/UB BN44	207	K1
STHW BN42	234	D3
Crescent Wy BURH RH15	139	G8
HORL RH6	18	A2
Crespin Wy BRI BN1	11	E1
Crest Wy PTSD BN41	211	F8
The Crestway BRI BN1	11	E1
Cricket Ct EGRIN RH19	22	C8
Cricket Field Rd HORS RH12	4	A6
Crimbourne La BIL RH14	99	J7
Cripland Cl HWH RH16	112	D5
Cripplecrutch Hl MFD/CHID GU8	42	D5
Cripplegate La SWTR RH13	105	G3
Cripps La STEY/UB BN44	184	A8
Critchel's La SELS PO20	259	H2
Critchfield Rd RCCH PO18	217	F6
Critchmere Dr SELS PO20	222	D4
Critchmere Hl HASM GU27	40	A4
Critchmere La HASM GU27	40	A5
Critchmere V HASM GU27	39	K1
Crockford Rd EMRTH PO10	191	F7
Crockhurst Cl CRAWW RH11	2	B5
Crockhurst La SALV BN13	105	G1
Crockhurst Hl SALV BN13	229	K3
Croft Av STHW BN42	234	C4
Croft Dr PTSD BN41	210	E8
Croft La HFD BN5	161	F7
Croft Rd BRI BN1	219	G1
SELS PO20	264	E5
The Croft ANG/EP BN16	251	J2
ARUN BN18	223	K7
BOGR PO21	245	H6
CRAWW RH11	30	E5
HPPT/KEY BN6	165	H8
MIDH GU29	147	K3
PETW GU28	95	K8
Croft Wy HORS RH12	51	G8
MIDOS PO22	247	G5
SELS PO20	264	E4
Cromleigh Wy STHW BN42	234	C1
Crompton Flds CRAWE RH10	31	J2
Crompton Wy CRAWE RH10	3	D1
Cromwell Pl EGRIN RH19	36	D3
HOVE BN3	236	C4
Cromwell Rd BURH RH15	139	F8
HOVE BN3	236	C4
Cromwell St ROTT BN2	11	E3
Crooked La SELS PO20	241	J6
Crookthorn La LHPTN BN17	248	D3
Crosbie Cl CCH PO19	6	B6
Crosby Cl SALV BN13	229	H5
Croshaw Cl LAN/SOMP BN15	231	K6
Crossbush La ARUN BN18	226	A2
Crossbush Rd MIDOS PO22	247	G7
Cross Colwood La RHWH RH17	108	F7
Crossfield HASM GU27	66	C6
Cross Keys CRAWW RH11	2	C3
Cross La FIN/BW BN14	205	J3
HORL RH6	19	J3
SWTR RH13	103	K2
Cross Rd ANG/EP BN16	251	G2
STHW BN42	234	B3
Crossroad Cl STHW BN42	234	B3
Cross St BRI BN1	10	D3
HOVE BN3	236	D6
WTHG BN11	8	C3
Crossways ANG/EP BN16	251	K1
CRAWE RH10	3	E1
MIDH GU29	122	D1
MIDOS PO22	247	K6
PUL/STOR RH20	156	B5
RHWH RH17	137	H1
Crossways Av EGRIN RH19	36	A2
FERR BN12	228	D3
Crossways Pk PUL/STOR RH20	156	B4
The Crossways LHPTN BN17	225	J8
The Crossway BRI BN1	237	H1
PTSD BN41	234	E1
Crouch La RCCH PO18	196	E8
Crouch Hl HFD BN5	161	H1
Crouchlands Farm RHWH RH17	110	E3
Crowberry La CRAWW RH11	54	E1
Crowborough Dr FERR BN12	253	F1
Crowhurst Cl CRAWE RH10	32	C1
Crown Rd PTSD BN41	234	E1
SHOR BN43	233	K3
Crown St BRI BN1	10	D5
Crowsbury Cl EMRTH PO10	190	C8
Croxton La HWH RH16	112	D5
Croy Cl CCH PO19	6	A5
Crundens Cnr ANG/EP BN16	251	G1
Crundles EPSF GU31	88	E8
Crypt La MIDH GU29	147	J4
Cuckfield Cl CRAWW RH11	30	D8
Cuckfield Crs SALV BN13	229	H5
Cuckfield La RHWH RH17	109	F2
Cuckfield Rd BURH RH15	138	E4

HPPT/KEY BN6	164	A5
RHWH RH17	110	B2
RHWH RH17	138	B3
Cuckmere Crs CRAWW RH11	30	D6
Cuckmere Wy BRI BN1	213	H6
Cudlow Av ANG/EP BN16	250	E3
Cudlow Gdn ANG/EP BN16	250	E3
Cudworth La RDKG RH5	15	F3
Cuffs Hl CRAWE RH10	56	E1
Culimore Cl SELS PO20	257	H4
Culimore Rd SELS PO20	257	H4
Culpepper Cl BURH RH15	138	E7
Culpepper Cl ROTT BN2	237	K1
Culross Av HWH RH16	111	K6
Culver Rd LAN/SOMP BN15	232	A5
MIDOS PO22	13	F4
Culvers EPSF GU31	118	B8
Cumberland Av EMRTH PO10	190	C7
FERR BN12	229	H5
Cumberland Crs ANG/EP BN16	227	J6
Cumberland Dr BRI BN1	236	E1
Cumberland Rd ANG/EP BN16	227	J6
BRI BN1	236	E1
Cumbrian Cl SALV BN13	229	J4
Cunliffe Cl SELS PO20	257	F1
Cunningham Gdns MIDOS PO22	247	G6
Curbey Cl PUL/STOR RH20	156	B2
Curlescroft BOGR PO21	262	C1
Curlew Cl EMRTH PO10	214	C3
The Curlews SHOR BN43	233	J3
Curvins Wy LAN/SOMP BN15	232	B4
Curwen Pl BRI BN1	212	E8
Curzon Av HORS RH12	4	A5
Curzon Cl SALV BN13	229	K5
Cutfield Cl CCH PO19	6	B6
Cuthbert Rd ROTT BN2	11	E4
Cuttinglye La CRAWE RH10	34	C2
Cuttinglye Rd CRAWE RH10	34	D1
The Cygnets SHOR BN43	233	H3
Cygnet Wk MIDOS PO22	13	A2
The Cylinders HASM GU27	66	C6
Cypress Av SALV BN13	229	G6
Cypress Cl SHOR BN43	233	H4
Cypress Wy BOGR PO21	261	K1
GSHT GU26	39	K1
Cyprus Rd BURH RH15	139	G8

D

Dagbrook La HFD BN5	161	G8
Dagmar St WTHG BN11	9	D3
Dairyfields CRAWW RH11	30	E6
RCCH PO18	220	B2
Dairy La ARUN BN18	223	H3
Dakin Cl CRAWE RH10	56	C1
The Dakins EGRIN RH19	36	C3
Dale Av BRI BN1	213	F6
HPPT/KEY BN6	165	F8
Dale Cl HORS RH12	5	E2
Dale Crs BRI BN1	213	F5
Dale Dr BRI BN1	213	F5
Dale Rd POY/PYE BN45	188	A3
Dale Rd FROW RH18	61	K2
WTHG BN11	231	H7
Dale Vw HASM GU27	40	B6
HOVE BN3	235	H1
Dale View Gdns HOVE BN3	235	H1
Dalewood Gdns BURH RH15	165	J1
CRAWE RH10	3	E1
Dallaway Gdns EGRIN RH19	36	C2
Dallaway Rd CCH PO19	7	D5
Dallington Rd HOVE BN3	235	J5
Dalloway Rd ARUN BN18	224	E2
Dalton Cl CRAWW RH11	54	E1
Daltons Pl ARUN BN18	225	G1
Damer's Br PETW GU28	125	K3
Damian Wy HPPT/KEY BN6	165	H7
Danbury Rd SELS PO20	264	D6
Danefield Rd SELS PO20	264	D6
Danehill La RHWH RH17	86	C6
Danehurst Crs SWTR RH13	5	E5
Daniel Cl LAN/SOMP BN15	232	A4
Dankton Gdns LAN/SOMP BN15	231	H4
Dankton La LAN/SOMP BN15	231	H5
Danley La HASM GU27	39	G8
Danworth La HPPT/KEY BN6	138	B8
Dapper's La ANG/EP BN16	227	J5
Darcey Dr BRI BN1	213	G5
Dark La BOGR PO21	262	D1
Darleydale CRAWW RH11	2	B6
Darlington Cl CRAWW RH11	229	H3
Darwin Cl HORS RH12	5	E3
Daux Av BIL RH14	102	B4
Daux Hl HORS RH12	4	A1
Daux Rd BIL RH14	102	B4
Daux Wy BIL RH14	102	B5
Dauxwood Cl BIL RH14	102	B5
Davenport Rd MIDOS PO22	13	F4
Davey Dr BRI BN1	11	D1
Davids Cl BOGR PO21	245	H6
Davigdor Rd HOVE BN3	236	D4

Davis Cl CRAWW RH11		
Davits Dr LHPTN BN17		
Dawes Av WTHG BN11		
Dawes Cl WTHG BN11		
Dawn Cl STEY/UB BN44		
Dawn Crs STEY/UB BN44		
Dawson Ter ROTT BN2		
Dawtrey Cl ANG/EP BN16		2
Dawtrey Rd PETW GU28		1
Daynes Wy BURH RH15		
Days La ARUN BN18		
Deacons Dr PTSD BN41		
Deacons Wy STEY/UB BN44		
Deacon Wy FIN/BW BN14		
Deak's La RHWH RH17		
Dean Cl LHPTN BN17		
PTSD BN41		
Dean Gdns PTSD BN41		
Deanland Rd RHWH RH17		
Dean La HORN PO8		
PETW GU28		
Dean St BRI BN1		
Deanway HOVE BN3		
Dean Wy HASM GU27		
De Braose Wy STEY/UB BN44		
Decoy Dr ANG/EP BN16		
Decoy Rd FIN/BW BN14		
Dedisham Cl CRAWE RH10		
Deep Dene HASM GU27		
Deepdene Cl MIDOS PO22		
Deer Pk HFD BN5		
Deer Park La SELS PO20		
Deerswood Cl CRAWW RH11		
SALV BN13		2
Deerswood Rd CRAWW RH11		
Deeside Av CCH PO19		
The Deeside BRI BN1		
Defiance Pl MIDOS PO22		2
De la Warr Rd EGRIN RH19		
Delfont Cl CRAWE RH10		
Delius Gdns SWTR RH13		
Dell Cl HASM GU27		
Dell Dr ANG/EP BN16		
Delling Cl RCCH PO18		
Delling Rd RCCH PO18		
Dell La BIL RH14		
Dellney Av HWH RH16		
Dell Quay Rd SELS PO20		
The Dell EGRIN RH19		
HWH RH16		
Delta Dr HORL RH6		
De Montfort Rd ROTT BN2		
Dempsey Rd CCH PO19		
Den Av BOGR PO21		
Denbigh Rd HASM GU27		
Denchers Plat CRAWW RH11		
Dene Cl HASM GU27		
Deneside BRI BN1		
The Dene HOVE BN3		
SWTR RH13		
Dene Tye CRAWE RH10		
Dene V BRI BN1		
The Deneway BRI BN1		
LAN/SOMP BN15		
Denham Cl MIDOS PO22		
Denham Rd BURH RH15		
Denmans CRAWE RH10		
Denman's Cl HWH RH16		
Denman's La HWH RH16		
SELS PO20		
Denmark Rd PTSD BN41		
Denmark Ter BRI BN1		
Denmark Vls HOVE BN3		
Denne Pde HORS RH12		
Denne Rd CRAWW RH11		
HORS RH12		
Dennis Wy LISS GU33		
Denny's Cl SELS PO20		
Denshare Rd SELS PO20		
Denshire Dr PUL/STOR RH20		
Densihale BOGR PO21		
Denton Cl FERR BN12		
Denton Dr BRI BN1		
Depot Rd CRAWW RH11		
SWTR RH13		
Derby Rd HASM GU27		
Derek Av HOVE BN3		
Derek Rd LAN/SOMP BN15		
Derwent Cl ANG/EP BN16		
CRAWW RH11		
HORS RH12		
LAN/SOMP BN15		
SELS PO20		
Derwent Dr FERR BN12		
Derwent Gv MIDOS PO22		
Detling Rd CRAWW RH11		
Devil's Dyke Rd HOVE BN3		
POY/PYE BN45		
PTSD BN41		
Devils La LIPH GU30		
Devonport Pl WTHG BN11		
Devonport Rd WTHG BN11		
Devonshire Pl ROTT BN2		
Devonshire Rd BOGR PO21		
SWTR RH13		

...r Cl *CRAWW* RH11 .... 30 C6 🆔
...Rd *ROTT* BN2 .... 11 E1
...r Dr *EGRIN* RH19 .... 36 C5
...*MIDOS* PO22 .... 223 C6 🆔
...s Cl *EMRTH* PO10 .... 190 C7
...ns Rd *CRAWE* RH10 .... 2 C6
...son Pl *MIDOS* PO22 .... 12 C2 🆔
...ingle *CRAWW* RH11 .... 2 A5
...ey Rd *ANG/EP* BN16 .... 250 D2
...ale Gdns *ANG/EP* BN16 .... 250 E1
...La *EGRIN* RH19 .... 37 J5
...ield Cl *MIDOS* PO22 .... 247 H5
...ing Bostall *HPPT/KEY* BN6 .. 189 K4
...ing Ct *BRI* BN12 .... 229 F7 🆔
...ing Crs *BRI* BN1 .... 213 J6
...ng Gdns *BRI* BN1 .... 10 C1
...ng Hl *CRAWW* RH11 .... 2 B6
...ing Ri *BRI* BN1 .... 10 C2 🆔
...ing Rd *BRI* BN1 .... 213 J5
...r BN2 .... 10 C4
...ns Pl *CRAWW* RH11 .... 30 C6 🆔
...n Rd *CRAWW* RH11 .... 31 H1
...ey *MIDH* GU29 .... 122 C1
...ey La *MIDH* GU29 .... 122 C1
... *STEY/UB* BN44 .... 183 K8
...Cl *CRAWE* RH10 .... 32 C6 🆔
...in Cl *CCH* PO19 .... 218 B5
...U GU27 .... 40 A5
...n Ms *CCH* PO19 .... 218 C5
...in Rd *SHOR* BN43 .... 233 K4
...n Wy *ANG/EP* BN16 .... 251 F5
...R BN45 .... 233 K4
...house Cl *SELS* PO20 .... 265 F6 🆔
...ion Cl *FIN/BW* BN14 .... 9 E2
...ion Rd *FIN/BW* BN14 .... 9 E1
...ion Wy *ANG/EP* BN16 .... 226 E8
...BW BN14 .... 9 F1
...ion Wy West *FIN/BW* BN14 .... 9 F1
...l Hall Rd *ROTT* BN2 .... 11 F5
...y La *HORL* RH6 .... 18 D4 🆔
...y Ms *HOVE* BN3 .... 236 D6 🆔
... Cl *CRAWW* RH11 .... 32 B5
...ngton Ct *CRAWW* RH11 .... 30 D8 🆔
...gton Pk *SELS* PO20 .... 218 D8
...nsday Gdn *SWTR* RH13 .... 5 E6
... End *FERR* BN12 .... 252 D8 🆔
...ester Gdn *WTHG* BN11 .... 8 A4 🆔
...g Rd *HORS* RH12 .... 51 G3
...ns *CRAWW* RH11 .... 30 E6
...ns Av *LING* RH7 .... 22 E1
...n's Cl *LING* RH7 .... 22 E3
...ns High St *LING* RH7 .... 22 E4
...ns Park Rd *EGRIN* RH19 ...... 22 B8
...ns Rd *LING* RH7 .... 22 E1
...ns Station Rd *LING* RH7 ...... 22 D4
...ry Rd *HOVE* BN3 .... 235 H3
... Av *EGRIN* RH19 .... 22 A8
...Cl *LHPTN* BN17 .... 250 A2
...Gdns *EGRIN* RH19 .... 22 A8
...' BN2 .... 11 D5
...Pl *ROTT* BN2 .... 11 D5 🆔
...Rd *BOGR* PO21 .... 12 B3
...St *ROTT* BN2 .... 10 C5 🆔
...days *BURH* RH15 .... 165 H1
...s Av *WTHG* BN11 .... 253 K1
...s Cl *ARUN* BN18 .... 248 B1
...S PO22 .... 247 K6
...'s BN11 .... 253 K1
...s Martin Rd *CCH* PO19 .... 7 D2 🆔
...l *CRAWW* RH11 .... 2 C1
...ote Ms *LAN/SOMP* BN15 ...... 231 J3
...t *MIDOS* PO22 .... 12 A3
...ale Crs *CRAWW* RH11 .... 2 A5
...Cl *SWTR* RH13 .... 105 F1
...Rd *BRI* BN1 .... 237 C1
...' BN11 .... 8 A5
...Wk *CRAWW* RH11 .... 30 E6
...nds La *HORL* RH6 .... 19 K1
...Cl *MIDH* GU29 .... 148 E3
...g Cl *BOGR* PO21 .... 245 G7
...and Av *STHW* BN42 .... 234 B2
...and Cl *PUL/STOR* RH20 .... 205 J5
...*UB* BN44 .... 208 D1
...*/ BN42 .... 234 B2
...and Crs *HOVE* BN3 .... 211 K8
...and Dr *CRAWW* RH11 .... 2 B5
...' BN3 .... 211 K8
...and Pl *CRAWW* RH11 .... 2 B5
...and Rd *STEY/UB* BN44 .... 208 D1
...ands *PUL/STOR* RH20 .... 155 F1
...' RH13 .... 134 B8
...ands La *FIN/BW* BN14 .... 230 D4
...ands Cl *BOGR* PO21 .... 261 H1
...SOMP BN15 .... 231 J4
...ands Gdns *FIN/BW* BN14 .... 230 E4 🆔
...Cl *LAN/SOMP* BN15 .... 232 D5
...croft *BURH* RH15 .... 139 K6
...*/UB* BN44 .... 208 D2 🆔
...de *BRI* BN1 .... 212 D6 🆔
... BN3 .... 212 B8
...' BN43 .... 233 J2
...de Av *FIN/BW* BN14 .... 205 K8 🆔
...de Cl *FIN/BW* BN14 .... 205 J8
...BN43 .... 233 H2

Downs Link *HFD* BN5 .... 184 E3
HORS RH12 .... 48 A3
STEY/UB BN44 .... 208 C3
SWTR RH13 .... 48 E7
SWTR RH13 .... 76 B3
SWTR RH13 .... 134 A7
SWTR RH13 .... 160 C2
Downs Md *LAN/SOMP* BN15 .. 231 J3 🆔
Downs Rd *BURH* RH15 .... 138 E7
RCCH PO18 .... 193 F5
Down St *RCCH* PO18 .... 193 F5
Downsview *HFD* BN5 .... 185 H4
HOVE BN3 .... 211 H8
Downsview Av *PUL/STOR* RH20 .. 180 C1
Downsview Dr *MIDH* GU29 .... 122 A6
RHWH RH17 .... 140 E7
Downsview Rd *ANG/EP* BN16.. 252 B5
HORS RH12 .... 52 D5
Downs View Rd *HPPT/KEY* BN6 .. 165 F8
Downs Wy *ANG/EP* BN16........ 227 H8
Downs Wy *MIDH* GU29 .... 122 A6
Downsway *SHOR* BN43 .... 233 H2
STHW BN42 .... 234 D1
Down Ter *ROTT* BN2 .... 11 E4
The Down *HOVE* BN3 .... 211 G7
Downview Av *FERR* BN12 ...... 228 C8
Downview Rd *ARUN* BN18 ...... 224 A8
RCCH PO18 .... 194 E5 🆔
SELS PO20 .... 257 K5
Downview Rd *ARUN* BN18 ...... 224 A8
FERR BN12 .... 228 C8
FIN/BW BN14 .... 205 J4
MIDOS PO22 .... 13 F5
MIDOS PO22 .... 222 E4
PETW GU28 .... 125 J4 🆔
Down View Rd *WTHG* BN11 ...... 8 A3
Downview Wy *ARUN* BN18 ...... 224 A8
Dragons Green Rd *SWTR* RH13.. 104 C5
Dragons La *SWTR* RH13 .... 104 B8
SWTR RH13 .... 135 G4
Dragon St *EPSF* GU31 .... 116 D1
Drake Av *FERR* BN12 .... 229 H7
Drake Cl *HORS* RH12 .... 5 D1
Drake Gv *ARUN* BN18 .... 248 B1
Drake Pk *MIDOS* PO22 .... 247 G7
Drake Rd *CRAWE* RH10 .... 3 D6
Drakes Cl *LAN/SOMP* BN15 .... 232 D5
Draxmont Wy *BRI* BN1 .... 213 F8
Draycliff Cl *FERR* BN12.......... 252 C2
Drayton Cl *SELS* PO20 .... 220 B5
Drewetts Cl *ANG/EP* BN16 .... 226 D8
Drewetts Ms *SELS* PO20 .... 220 D4
Drift La *RCCH* PO18 .... 216 C4
SELS PO20 .... 264 D4
Drift Rd *BOGR* PO21 .... 261 J1
SELS PO20 .... 265 H3
The Driftway *ANG/EP* BN16 .... 184 D8
STEY/UB BN44 .... 184 D8
The Drive *ANG/EP* BN16 .... 251 K3
BIL RH14 .... 71 K1
BOGR PO21 .... 262 A2
BURH RH15 .... 139 H7
CCH PO19 .... 195 G8
CRAWE RH10 .... 19 J8
EMRTH PO10 .... 215 H3
HORL RH6 .... 18 B1
HOVE BN3 .... 236 C4
LAN/SOMP BN15 .... 231 K7
LAN/SOMP BN15 .... 232 D2
PETW GU28 .... 150 B5
RCCH PO18 .... 217 F6
SHOR BN43 .... 233 H3
STHW BN42 .... 234 D1
WTHG BN11 .... 229 K8
The Driveway *SHOR* BN43 ...... 233 H3
Droke La *RCCH* PO18 .... 173 G5
Dropping Holms *BN5* 161 F7
Drove Crs *PTSD* BN41 .... 234 E1
Drove La *ARUN* BN18 .... 247 H1
SELS PO20 .... 258 C5
Drove Rd *PTSD* BN41 .... 234 E2
Drovers Cl *PTSD* BN41 .... 235 C1
Drovers Wy *BURH* RH15 .... 165 J1
The Drove *BRI* BN1 .... 236 D2
The Droveway *HOVE* BN3 ...... 236 C2
RHWH RH17 .... 111 J5
Drum Md *PSF* GU32 .... 88 C8
Drummond Cl *HWH* RH16 ...... 111 K7
Drummond Rd *CRAWW* RH11 .. 30 C6
FERR BN12 .... 253 J2
Drungewick La *BIL* RH14 ...... 72 E5
Drury Cl *CRAWE* RH10 .... 32 D7 🆔
Dryad Wk *MIDOS* PO22 .... 247 H7 🆔
Dryad Wy *MIDOS* PO22 .... 247 H7
Dryden Wy *LIPH* GU30 .... 38 A6
Drygrounds La *MIDOS* PO22 .. 13 E3
Duck La *MIDH* GU29 .... 122 B3
SELS PO20 .... 264 C2
Duckmead La *LISS* GU33 .... 62 B5
Dudley Rd *BRI* BN1 .... 11 D7
Duffield La *EMRTH* PO10 ...... 191 H8
Duke Cl *CRAWE* RH10 .... 56 C1 🆔
Dukes Cl *ARUN* BN18 .... 201 F8
PSF GU32 .... 88 B7

Duke's Dr *RDKG* RH5................ 15 F5
Duke's Hl *PUL/STOR* RH20 .... 156 E3
Dukes Meadow *BOGR* PO21 .. 244 D8
RCCH PO18 .... 192 E6
Duke's Mound *ROTT* BN2 ...... 11 F6
Dukes Rd *ARUN* BN18 .... 198 C2
HWH RH16 .... 112 D3
Duke St *BRI* BN1 .... 10 B5
LHPTN BN17 .... 249 K2
Dukes Vd *STEY/UB* BN44 ...... 183 K8
Dumbrells Court Rd
HPPT/KEY BN6 .... 165 K7
Dumbrills Cl *BURH* RH15 ...... 139 G6
Dumpford La *EPSF* GU31 ...... 119 F3
Duncan Rd *CCH* PO19 .... 6 A1
Duncton Cl *HWH* RH16 .... 111 K7
MIDOS PO22 .... 247 F7
Duncton High St *PETW* GU28.. 151 F5
Duncton Rd *ANG/EP* BN16 .... 226 E8 🆔
The Dunes *BOGR* PO21 .... 261 J3
Dunford Hollow *MIDH* GU29 .. 122 B7
Dunlop Cl *HPPT/KEY* BN6 ...... 165 H2
Dunning's Rd *EGRIN* RH19 ...... 36 C4
EGRIN RH19 .... 36 C5
Dunsfold Cl *CRAWW* RH11 .... 30 E6
Dunsfold Rd *BIL* RH14 .... 44 D7
MFD/CHID GU8 .... 44 C4
Dunstall Av *BURH* RH15 .... 138 E7
Dunstall Farm Rd *BURH* RH15.. 139 F7
Dunstan Cl *CCH* PO19 .... 195 G8 🆔
Dunster Cl *BRI* BN1 .... 11 D1
Durbans Rd *BIL* RH14 .... 100 D2
Durfold Rd *HORS* RH12 .... 51 K4
Durfold Wd *BIL* RH14 .... 44 C5
Durford Rd *EPSF* GU31 .... 119 G8
Durham Cl *BOGR* PO21 .... 261 H3
CRAWE RH10 .... 55 J1 🆔
Durham Gdns *CCH* PO19 ...... 219 F2
Durkins Rd *EGRIN* RH19 .... 22 B8
Durlston Dr *MIDOS* PO22 ...... 12 A2
Durnford Cl *CCH* PO19 .... 6 A2
Durrington Hl *SALV* BN13 ...... 229 H4
Durrington La *SALV* BN13 ...... 229 H4
Dutchells Copse *HORS* RH12 .. 5 D1
Dyall Cl *BURH* RH15.............. 138 E7
Dyers La *ARUN* BN18 .... 199 G6
Dyke Cl *HOVE* BN3.................. 212 B7
Dyke Rd *BRI* BN1 .... 10 A4
HOVE BN3 .... 10 A3
Dyke Road Av *HOVE* BN3...... 212 B7
Dyke Road Dr *BRI* BN1 .... 10 B3
Dyke Road Pl *HOVE* BN3 ...... 212 C8
The Dymock's *HPPT/KEY* BN6 .. 165 K8 🆔
Dymoke St *EMRTH* PO10 ...... 190 C7

E

Eady Cl *SWTR* RH13.................. 5 E5
Eagles Cha *LHPTN* BN17........ 225 J7
Earles Meadow *HORS* RH12 .... 52 D5
Earlswood Cl *SWTR* RH13 ...... 5 E3 🆔
Early Commons *CRAWE* RH10 .. 3 E2 🆔
CRAWE RH10 .... 3 E2 🆔
Earnley Manor Cl *SELS* PO20 .. 258 C4
Earnley Rd *SELS* PO20 .... 258 C4
Earwig La *RHWH* RH17 .... 108 C5
Easebourne La *MIDH* GU29 .. 122 C2
Easebourne St *MIDH* GU29 .... 94 E8
MIDH GU29 .... 122 D1
PETW GU28 .... 95 H4
East Av *FERR* BN12 .... 253 K2
MIDOS PO22 .... 247 K5
East Bank *SELS* PO20 .... 265 G4
Eastbank *STHW* BN42 .... 234 D3
East Beach Rd *SELS* PO20 .... 265 H4
Eastbourne Rd *EGRIN* RH19 .... 21 H5
ROTT BN2 .... 11 F1
East Bracklesham Dr *SELS* PO20 .. 258 A6
Eastbrook Rd *PTSD* BN41 ...... 235 F4
Eastbrook Wy *STHW* BN42 .... 234 E4
East Cl *MIDOS* PO22 .... 247 J6
Eastcourt Rd *FIN/BW* BN14 ...... 8 C2
East Court Wy *ANG/EP* BN16 .. 251 G1
Eastdale Rd *BURH* RH15 .... 139 J7
Eastdean Hl *RCCH* PO18 .... 172 E6
East Dr *ANG/EP* BN16............ 227 C7
MIDOS PO22 .... 248 A6
ROTT BN2 .... 11 E5
Easteds La *SWTR* RH13 .... 105 G1
East End La *HPPT/KEY* BN6 .. 165 K8
Eastergate Rd *FERR* BN12 .... 252 D1
Eastergate La *ARUN* BN18 .... 223 F2
SELS PO20 .... 222 D2
Eastern Av *SHOR* BN43.......... 233 J4
Eastern Cl *ANG/EP* BN16 ...... 251 K1
SHOR BN43 .... 233 J4
Eastern Rd *HWH* RH16 .... 112 B8
ROTT BN2 .... 11 E6
Eastern Ter *ROTT* BN2 .... 11 F6 🆔
Eastern Terrace Ms *ROTT* BN2.. 11 F6 🆔
East Field Cl *EMRTH* PO10 .... 215 J1
Eastfield La *EPSF* GU31 .... 118 E8
East Front Rd *BOGR* PO21 .... 261 H4

East Gdns *HPPT/KEY* BN6 .... 165 K8
East Hampnett La *SELS* P020 .... 221 G1
East Ham Rd *LHPTN* BN17 .... 249 J2
East Harting St *EPSF* GU31 .... 118 D8
East Hill Dr *LISS* GU33 .... 62 A8
East Hill La *CRAWE* RH10 .... 19 K5
Easthill Dr *PTSD* BN41 .... 235 F2
Easthill La *CRAWE* RH10 .... 19 K5
Easthill Wy *PTSD* BN41 .... 235 F2
East Lake *BOGR* P021 .... 12 C4 🔢
Eastlake Cl *EPSF* GU31 .... 89 G8
Eastland Rd *CCH* P019 .... 7 D5
East Leigh Rd *HAV* P09 .... 190 A8
East Mascalls Rd *HWH* RH16 .... 113 F5
East Md *P021* 261 H3
   FERR BN12 .... 252 D2
East Meadway *SHOR* BN43 .... 233 J5
Easton Crs *BIL* RH14 .... 102 C3
Easton La *SELS* P020 .... 259 G5
East Onslow Cl *FERR* BN12 .... 252 C1 🔢
Eastover Wy *MIDOS* P022 .... 13 E4
East Pallant *CCH* P019 .... 6 C3
East Pk *CRAWE* RH11 .... 2 C4
East Park La *LING* RH7 .... 20 E2
East Rw *CCH* P019 .... 6 C3 🔢
Eastshaw La *MIDH* GU29 .... 93 J7
East St *ARUN* BN18 .... 178 A4
   BIL RH14 .... 102 B3
   BRI BN1 .... 10 C5 🔢
   CCH P019 .... 6 C3
   CRAWE RH10 .... 34 D7
   EMRTH P010 .... 191 H8
   HORS RH12 .... 4 B6
   HORS RH12 .... 29 G4
   LAN/SOMP BN15 .... 232 A7
   LHPTN BN17 .... 250 A2
   PETW GU28 .... 125 K3
   PTSD BN41 .... 235 G5
   PUL/STOR RH20 .... 156 C2
   SELS P020 .... 265 F4
   SHOR BN43 .... 233 H4
East Tyne *SALV* BN13 .... 229 H5
East View Cl *RCCH* P018 .... 195 F4
East Walls *CCH* P019 .... 6 C3 🔢
East Wick *HWH* RH16 .... 112 C4
Eastwick Cl *BRI* BN1 .... 213 H4
Eastwood *CRAWE* RH10 .... 3 E3
Eaton Gdns *HOVE* BN3 .... 236 C4
Eaton Gv *HOVE* BN3 .... 236 C4 🔢
Eaton Pl *ROTT* BN2 .... 11 F6
Eaton Rd *HOVE* BN3 .... 236 C5
Eaton Vls *HOVE* BN3 .... 236 B4
Edburton Av *BRI* BN1 .... 10 C1
Edburton Dr *HFD* BN5 .... 186 B4
Edburton Gdns *SHOR* BN43 .... 233 H2
Eddington Hl *CRAWW* RH11 .... 54 E2
Eden Rd *CRAWW* RH11 .... 54 E2
Eden V *EGRIN* RH19 .... 22 D7
Edgar Cl *CRAWE* RH10 .... 32 E6
Edgehill Cl *SALV* BN13 .... 229 K4
Edgehill Wy *PTSD* BN41 .... 234 D1
Edgell Rd *EMRTH* P010 .... 191 F7
Edinburgh Cl *BOGR* P021 .... 262 B1 🔢
   SWTR RH13 .... 105 G2
Edinburgh Rd *ROTT* BN2 .... 11 D2 🔢
Edinburgh Sq *MIDH* GU29 .... 122 B4 🔢
Edinburgh Wy *EGRIN* RH19 .... 36 D4
Edmonton Rd *SALV* BN13 .... 229 G5
Edrich Rd *CRAWW* RH11 .... 54 E2
Edward Av *BRI* BN1 .... 212 A8
Edward Cl *HOVE* BN3 .... 212 A8
Edward Rd *HWH* RH16 .... 112 A8
Edwards Av *SELS* P020 .... 220 E1
Edward St *ROTT* BN2 .... 11 D3
Edwards St *LHPTN* BN17 .... 225 J7 🔢
Edwen Cl *BOGR* P021 .... 244 D8
Edwin Cl *LAN/SOMP* BN15 .... 231 J5
Effingham La *CRAWE* RH10 .... 20 A6
Effingham Rd *HORL* RH6 .... 19 J5
Egmont Rd *HOVE* BN3 .... 235 H2
   MIDH GU29 .... 122 C1
Egremont Pl *ROTT* BN2 .... 11 D5 🔢
Eighth Av *LAN/SOMP* BN15 .... 232 A4 🔢
Eirene Av *FERR* BN12 .... 253 K2
Eirene Rd *FERR* BN12 .... 253 J2
Elbridge Crs *BOGR* P021 .... 261 K1
Elcombe Cl *SELS* P020 .... 258 A4
Elder Cl *PTSD* BN41 .... 235 F1
Elderfield Cl *EMRTH* P010 .... 190 E8
Elder Pl *BRI* BN1 .... 10 C5
Eldon Rd *WTHG* BN11 .... 9 F3
Eldon Wy *LHPTN* BN17 .... 225 H8
   LHPTN BN17 .... 249 H1
Eldred Av *BRI* BN1 .... 212 D6
Eleanor Gdns *MIDOS* P022 .... 247 H6
Elfin Gv *BOGR* P021 .... 12 A5
Elgar Wy *HORS* RH12 .... 52 D7
Elger Wy *CRAWE* RH10 .... 19 G7
Elgin Rd *FERR* BN12 .... 253 H1
Eliot Dr *HASM* GU27 .... 19 J5
Elizabethan Wy *CRAWE* RH10 ..... 32 C6
Elizabeth Av *BOGR* P021 .... 244 E7
   HOVE BN3 .... 212 A8

Elizabeth Cl *BOGR* P021 .... 244 E8
   HOVE BN3 .... 212 A8 🔢
Elizabeth Crs *EGRIN* RH19 .... 22 D8
Elizabeth Pl *LAN/SOMP* BN15 ...... 231 J6
Elizabeth Sq *CCH* P019 .... 7 F2
   SHOR BN43 .... 234 A3
   WTHG BN11 .... 8 C4
Ella Cl *SELS* P020 .... 257 H4
Ellanore La *SELS* P020 .... 259 K8
Ellastale Rd *BOGR* P021 .... 12 A6
Ellen St *HOVE* BN3 .... 236 B4
   PTSD BN41 .... 235 G4
Ellesmere Orch *EMRTH* P010 ...... 191 F7
Elliot Cl *CRAWE* RH10 .... 32 C6 🔢
Ellis Av *SALV* BN13 .... 229 J3
Ellis Cl *ARUN* BN18 .... 225 F1
Ellis Wy *BOGR* P021 .... 261 H3
Ellman Rd *CRAWW* RH11 .... 30 D7
Elson Cl *CRAWE* RH10 .... 32 C7 🔢
Elm Av *ANG/EP* BN16 .... 187 J4
Elm Cl *BOGR* P021 .... 261 H2
   HOVE BN3 .... 236 C1
   SELS P020 .... 258 A5
   SHOR BN43 .... 233 H2
Elmcroft Pl *SELS* P020 .... 222 B5
Elm Dr *EGRIN* RH19 .... 36 E2
   HOVE BN3 .... 235 J2
   MIDOS P022 .... 248 B6
Elmer Cl *MIDOS* P022 .... 248 B6
Elmer Ct *MIDOS* P022 .... 248 C6
Elmer Rd *MIDOS* P022 .... 247 K6
Elm Gv *BOGR* P021 .... 245 J8
   LAN/SOMP BN15 .... 231 K6
   MIDOS P022 .... 222 C4
   ROTT BN2 .... 11 E3
   SELS P020 .... 264 E4
   SWTR RH13 .... 5 D6
   WTHG BN11 .... 229 K8
Elm Grove La *STEY/UB* BN44 ...... 183 K8
Elmgrove Rd *LHPTN* BN17 .... 250 A1
Elm Gv South *MIDOS* P022 .... 222 E5
Elmhurst Cl *ANG/EP* BN16 .... 227 J5
Elmhurst La *SWTR* RH13 .... 75 F5
Elmleigh *MIDH* GU29 .... 122 A4
Elmore Rd *ROTT* BN2 .... 11 D4
Elm Pk *FERR* BN12 .... 228 D8
   RCCH P018 .... 217 G5
Elm Ri *ANG/EP* BN16 .... 251 F2
Elm Ri *FIN/BW* BN14 .... 205 K2
Elm Rd *PTSD* BN41 .... 235 F3
   SELS P020 .... 222 C4
   WTHG BN11 .... 9 E4
Elms Dr *LAN/SOMP* BN15 .... 231 K5
Elmsfield *SELS* P020 .... 265 F4 🔢
Elms La *SELS* P020 .... 257 F2
Elms Lea Av *BRI* BN1 .... 212 E8
Elms Ride *SELS* P020 .... 257 F2
Elmstead Gdns *SELS* P020 .... 257 F1
Elmstead Park Rd *SELS* P020 ...... 257 F1
Elmstone Cl *LAN/SOMP* BN15 ...... 231 K5
Elm Tree Close. *BOGR* P021 .... 245 J5
Elm Tree Cl *SELS* P020 .... 265 F3
Elmwood Av *MIDOS* P022 .... 12 C3
Elrington Rd *HOVE* BN3 .... 236 C2
Elsie Rd *WTHG* BN11 .... 8 B5
Elsted Cl *CRAWW* RH11 .... 2 A1
Elsted Crs *BRI* BN1 .... 213 J5
Elsted Rd *MIDH* GU29 .... 119 H7
Elverlands Cl *FERR* BN12 .... 252 D2
Ely Cl *CRAWE* RH10 .... 55 K1
   SALV BN13 .... 229 K7
   SELS P020 .... 257 J3
Ely Gdns *BOGR* P021 .... 245 F8 🔢
Ely Rd *SALV* BN13 .... 229 K7
Emerald Quay *SHOR* BN43 .... 233 J5
Emms La *SWTR* RH13 .... 103 K1
Emsbrook Dr *EMRTH* P010 .... 214 D1 🔢
Emsworth Cl *CRAWE* RH10 .... 32 C8 🔢
Emsworth Common Rd
   EMRTH P010 .... 190 B6
Emsworth Rd *EMRTH* P010 .... 215 F7
End La *HFD* BN5 .... 160 C5
Enfield Cl *LIPH* GU30 .... 38 D8 🔢
Enfield Rd *CRAWW* RH11 .... 55 F1
Engalee *EGRIN* RH19 .... 22 B3
Englefield *HORS* RH12 .... 77 F1
English Cl *HOVE* BN3 .... 235 J3
Ennerdale Cl *CRAWW* RH11 .... 2 A5 🔢
Ennerdale Dr *LAN/SOMP* BN15 .... 231 H6
Ensign Wy *ANG/EP* BN16 .... 250 C1
Epping Wk *CRAWE* RH10 .... 3 E5
Epsom Rd *CRAWE* RH10 .... 3 F5
Erica Wy *CRAWE* RH10 .... 19 F8
   HORS RH12 .... 4 C2
Eridge Cl *CRAWE* RH10 .... 32 C5
Eridge Rd *HOVE* BN3 .... 236 A1
Erin Wy *BURH* RH15 .... 138 E8
Eriskay Ct *SALV* BN13 .... 229 F5
Eriswell Rd *WTHG* BN11 .... 8 C4
Erles Rd *LIPH* GU30 .... 38 C7 🔢
Ernest Cl *EMRTH* P010 .... 214 D2
Erringham Rd *SHOR* BN43 .... 233 G2

Erroll Rd *HOVE* BN3 .... [ ]
Erskine Cl *CRAWW* RH11 .... [ ]
Esher Cl *BOGR* P021 .... [ ]
Esher Dr *LHPTN* BN17 .... [ ]
Eskbank Av *BRI* BN1 .... [ ]
Esmond Cl *EMRTH* P010 .... [ ]
Esmonde Cl *LHPTN* BN17 .... 25[ ]
The Esplanade *BOGR* P021 .... [ ]
   WTHG BN11 .... [ ]
Essenhigh Dr *SALV* BN13 .... [ ]
Essex Rd *BOGR* P021 .... [ ]
Essex St *ROTT* BN2 .... [ ]
Estcots Dr *EGRIN* RH19 .... [ ]
The Estuary *LHPTN* BN17 .... [ ]
Ethelred Rd *SALV* BN13 .... [ ]
Ethel St *HOVE* BN3 .... [ ]
Ethelwulf Rd *SALV* BN13 .... [ ]
Eton Cl *BOGR* P021 .... [ ]
Eton Dr *SELS* P020 .... [ ]
Eton Rd *WTHG* BN11 .... [ ]
Ettrick Cl *CCH* P019 .... [ ]
Ettrick Rd *CCH* P019 .... [ ]
Evans Cl *CRAWE* RH10 .... [ ]
Evelyn Av *ANG/EP* BN16 .... [ ]
Evelyn Rd *FIN/BW* BN14 .... [ ]
Evelyn Ter *ROTT* BN2 .... [ ]
Eversfield *SWTR* RH13 .... [ ]
Eversfield Rd *SWTR* RH13 .... [ ]
Ewart St *ROTT* BN2 .... [ ]
Ewens Gdns *MIDOS* P022 .... [ ]
Ewhurst Cl *CRAWW* RH11 .... [ ]
Ewhurst Rd *CRAWW* RH11 .... [ ]
   ROTT BN2 .... [ ]
Excalibur Cl *CRAWW* RH11 .... [ ]
Exchange Rd *CRAWE* RH10 .... [ ]
Exeter Cl *BOGR* P021 .... 24[ ]
   CRAWE RH10 .... [ ]
   EMRTH P010 .... [ ]
Exeter Rd *CCH* P019 .... [ ]
Exeter St *BRI* BN1 .... [ ]
Exmoor Cl *SALV* BN13 .... [ ]
Exmoor Dr *SALV* BN13 .... [ ]
Exmoor Dr *SALV* BN13 .... [ ]
Exton Rd *CCH* P019 .... [ ]
Eyles Cl *HORS* RH12 .... [ ]

F

Fabians Wy *HFD* BN5 .... [ ]
Fairbanks *HWH* RH16 .... [ ]
Fairbridge Wy *BURH* RH15 .... [ ]
Faircox La *HFD* BN5 .... [ ]
Fairdene *STHW* BN42 .... [ ]
Fairfield Av *HORL* RH6 .... [ ]
Fairfield Cl *BURH* RH15 .... [ ]
   EMRTH P010 .... [ ]
   RCCH P018 .... [ ]
   RHWH RH17 .... [ ]
   SHOR BN43 .... [ ]
Fairfield Cottages *SWTR* RH13 .... [ ]
Fairfield Crs *HPPT/KEY* BN6 .... [ ]
Fairfield Gdns *PTSD* BN41 .... [ ]
Fairfield Ri *PETW* GU28 .... [ ]
Fairfield Rd *BURH* RH15............. [ ]
   EGRIN RH19 .... [ ]
   PUL/STOR RH20 .... [ ]
   RCCH P018 .... [ ]
Fairfield Wy *HWH* RH16 .... [ ]
   PUL/STOR RH20 .... [ ]
Fairford Cl *HWH* RH16 .... [ ]
Fairholme Dr *ARUN* BN18 .... [ ]
Fairlands *ANG/EP* BN16 .... [ ]
   MIDOS P022 .... [ ]
Fairlawn *ANG/EP* BN16 .... 2[ ]
Fairlawn Crs *EGRIN* RH19 .... [ ]
Fairlawn Dr *EGRIN* RH19 .... [ ]
   FIN/BW BN14 .... [ ]
Fairlawns *HORL* RH6 .... [ ]
   SHOR BN43 .... [ ]
Fairlea Cl *BURH* RH15 .... [ ]
Fairlead *LHPTN* BN17 .... [ ]
Fairlea Rd *EMRTH* P010 .... [ ]
Fairlie Gdns *BRI* BN1.................. [ ]
Fairlight Pl *ROTT* BN2 .... [ ]
Fairmead Rd *PUL/STOR* RH20...... [ ]
Fairmile Bottom *ARUN* BN18 ...... [ ]
Fair Vw *HORS* RH12 .... [ ]
Fairview Av *FERR* BN12 .... [ ]
Fairview Ri *BRI* BN1 .... [ ]
Fairview Rd *LAN/SOMP* BN15 ...... [ ]
Fairway *CRAWE* RH10................ [ ]
   CRAWW RH11 .... [ ]
   LHPTN BN17 .... [ ]
Fairway Cl *CRAWE* RH10 .... [ ]
Fairway Crs *PTSD* BN41 .... [ ]
The Fairway *BOGR* P021 .... [ ]
   HAV P09. .... [ ]
   LAN/SOMP BN15 .... [ ]
   MIDH GU29 .... [ ]
Faithfull Crs *PUL/STOR* RH20 ..... [ ]
Falcon Cl *CRAWW* RH11 .... [ ]
   SHOR BN43 .... [ ]
Falcon Gdns *LHPTN* BN17 .... [ ]

...nd Av *LHPTN* BN17 .... **250** B1
...nds Cl *MIDOS* PO22 .... **12** C3 🔢
...nds Dr *SWTR* RH13 .... **52** D7
...v Deer Cl *SWTR* RH13 .... **52** D8
...vfield Cl *HOVE* BN3 .... **235** K1 🔢
...vfield Crs *HOVE* BN3 .... **235** J1
...r Av *FERR* BN12 .... **253** F2
...er Cl *CRAWW* RH11 .... **2** C5 🔢
...R BN12 .... **253** G2
...ay Av *EGRIN* RH19 .... **36** D5
...ay Cl *SALV* BN13 .... **229** C5
...ay Rd *CRAWE* RH10 .... **31** K1
...mead *BOGR* PO21 .... **262** C1
...lls Crs *HORS* RH12 .... **114** D7
...gton Av *HWH* RH16 .... **112** B6
...gton Cl *HWH* RH16 .... **112** A6
...Acre *ANG/EP* BN16 .... **251** H1 🔢
...Av *HORS* RH12 .... **4** A4
...Cl *BIL* RH14 .... **46** C8
...WE RH10 .... **3** E2
...N RH19 .... **37** F3
... BN5 .... **161** G6
...S RH12 .... **51** F4
...T/KEY BN6 .... **164** E7
...OS PO22 .... **248** B6
...BN41 .... **234** E1
...Cnr *MIDOS* PO22 .... **248** A6
...eadow Wy *EMRTH* PO10 .... **214** B3
...La *RCCH* PO18 .... **215** K4
...eigh Cl *CRAWE* RH10 .... **32** C3 🔢
...Ms *HOVE* BN3 .... **236** D5 🔢
...Pl *BIL* RH14 .... **46** B8
...Rd *HOVE* BN3 .... **236** D5
... PO20 .... **258** A6
...vw *EMRTH* PO10 .... **190** D8
...Wy *ANG/EP* BN16 .... **250** D2
...H RH15 .... **165** J2
...H BN42 .... **234** E4
...way Cl *HOVE* BN3 .... **235** H1
...mbe La *RHWH* RH17 .... **141** F6
...mbe Rd *WTHG* BN11 .... **9** F5
...ell Cl *CCH* PO19 .... **7** E2 🔢
...Cl *SELS* PO20 .... **241** J7
...La *SELS* PO20 .... **241** J7
...old Rd *STEY/UB* BN44 .... **183** K7
...am Av *HPPT/KEY* BN6 .... **165** G6
...am Cl *CRAWW* RH11 .... **55** C3
...am La *HASM* GU27 .... **40** C2
...am Rd *PSF* GU32 .... **89** F3
...irst Rd *MIDOS* PO22 .... **223** F5
...st Rd *BURH* RH15 .... **139** K6
...roes *LHPTN* BN17 .... **226** C8
...RHWH RH17 .... **111** F5
...s Cl *BIL* RH14 .... **102** A4
...t Wy *LHPTN* BN17 .... **250** C2
...ers Wy *BURH* RH15 .... **139** G6
...Ri *HFD* BN5 .... **161** G5
...e La *HORS* RH12 .... **29** C4
... *HORS* RH12 .... **4** B3
...ge Av *CRAWE* RH10 .... **32** D4
...ge Cl *EGRIN* RH19 .... **22** A8
...ge Ct *EGRIN* RH19 .... **21** J8
...ge Rd *EGRIN* RH19 .... **21** J8
...Rd *CRAWE* RH10 .... **20** E8
...rt La *LING* RH7 .... **21** K2
...st Rd *EGRIN* RH19 .... **22** A4
...t Wy *HORS* RH12 .... **77** F2
...m Gdns *MIDOS* PO22 .... **247** F6
...m Rd *MIDOS* PO22 .... **13** E4
...m Wy *MIDOS* PO22 .... **13** F3
...OS PO22 .... **247** F6
... *HWH* RH16 .... **112** A6
...Cl *SWTR* RH13 .... **52** D7
...Crs *CRAWE* RH10 .... **2** A6
...y *LAN/SOMP* BN15 .... **232** A5 🔢
...ndy La *CRAWE* RH10 .... **34** C2
... *EPSF* GU31 .... **89** G8
...le Rd *BURH* RH15 .... **165** H2
...PO19 .... **219** C1
... BN3 .... **236** D4
...le Wk *ANG/EP* BN16 .... **227** J5 🔢
...n La *HASM* GU27 .... **40** D8
...wn *CRAWE* RH10 .... **32** D1
...wn Gdns *MIDOS* PO22 .... **13** F3 🔢
...l Cl *CRAWE* RH10 .... **34** D2 🔢
...l Rd *HORL* RH6 .... **18** D4
...rst Cl *BRI* BN1 .... **213** J5
...W RH11 .... **2** A1
...rst Crs *BIL* RH14 .... **213** H6
...rst Dr *FERR* BN12 .... **252** E1
...rst Gdns *BOGR* PO21 .... **262** A1
...rst Rd *LIPH* GU30 .... **64** B8
...d *PUL/STOR* RH20 .... **180** A2
...rst Rd *HORS* RH12 .... **4** C2
...ood Ri *BRI* BN1 .... **212** D6
...rs Cl *CRAWE* RH10 .... **3** F5 🔢
...Cl *FERR* BN12 .... **252** C3
...Gdns *MIDOS* PO22 .... **13** F3
... Grange Gdns
... . **252** C1 🔢
...ham La *FERR* BN12 .... **252** C2
...ham Wy *FERR* BN12 .... **252** C3
... La *FERR* BN12 .... **228** D8

Ferring Marine *FERR* BN12 .... **252** D3
Ferring St *FERR* BN12 .... **252** C1
Ferry Rd *LHPTN* BN17 .... **249** H5
   SHOR BN43 .... **233** H5
Fetherston Rd *LAN/SOMP* BN15 .... **231** K4
Feversham Cl *SHOR* BN43 .... **233** K5
Field Cl *ARUN* BN18 .... **223** H2
   BURH RH15 .... **138** E7
   LAN/SOMP BN15 .... **231** K5
Fieldend *HORS* RH12 .... **52** D6 🔢
Field End *PUL/STOR* RH20 .... **180** C1
Fieldgate Cl *SWTR* RH13 .... **78** E7
The Fieldings *SWTR* RH13 .... **105** F4
Field Pl *LHPTN* BN17 .... **249** K2
   LIPH GU30 .... **38** B8
Field Rd *SELS* PO20 .... **257** J4
Fields End *HWH* RH16 .... **112** B7
Fieldway *HASM* GU27 .... **40** E4
   HPPT/KEY BN6 .... **165** K8
   HWH RH16 .... **112** B3
Fifth Av *FIN/BW* BN14 .... **230** C3
   LAN/SOMP BN15 .... **232** A4
Filbert Crs *CRAWW* RH11 .... **30** E5
Filey Cl *CRAWW* RH11 .... **30** D7
Fincham Cl *ANG/EP* BN16 .... **251** H2
Finchdean Rd *HAV* PO9 .... **190** A1
Finches Cl *LAN/SOMP* BN15 .... **231** K6
   LHPTN BN17 .... **225** J7
   SWTR RH13 .... **134** C8 🔢
Finches Gdns *HWH* RH16 .... **112** C3
Finches La *HWH* RH16 .... **112** C3
   PUL/STOR RH20 .... **156** A3
Finches Park Rd *HWH* RH16 .... **112** C3
Finch Gdns *MIDOS* PO22 .... **12** A1
Findon By-pass *FIN/BW* BN14 .... **205** H5
Findon Cl *HOVE* BN3 .... **211** K8 🔢
Findon Dr *MIDOS* PO22 .... **247** H5
Findon Rd *CRAWW* RH11 .... **2** A1
   FIN/BW BN14 .... **205** K7
   FIN/BW BN14 .... **229** K1
Findon Wy *HORS* RH12 .... **50** D8
Finians Fld *SWTR* RH13 .... **103** K1
Finisterre Wy *LHPTN* BN17 .... **250** C3
Finsbury Cl *CRAWW* RH11 .... **55** G1 🔢
Finsbury Rd *ROTT* BN2 .... **11** D4
Fircroft Av *LAN/SOMP* BN15 .... **231** K3
Fircroft Cl *BRI* BN1 .... **212** E8
Fircroft Crs *ANG/EP* BN16 .... **251** F1
Firlands *HWH* RH16 .... **112** B7 🔢
Firle Cl *CRAWE* RH10 .... **3** D1
Firle Rd *LAN/SOMP* BN15 .... **231** K2
   ROTT BN2 .... **11** F4
Firs Av *MIDOS* PO22 .... **247** F6
Firs Av West *MIDOS* PO22 .... **247** F6
Firsdown Cl *SALV* BN13 .... **229** J1 🔢
Firsdown Rd *SALV* BN13 .... **229** J1
First Av *EMRTH* PO10 .... **215** H3
   FIN/BW BN14 .... **230** C3
   HOVE BN3 .... **236** A5
   LAN/SOMP BN15 .... **232** A5
   MIDOS PO22 .... **247** J5
   SELS PO20 .... **258** A6
   SELS PO20 .... **258** E1
The Firs *LIPH* GU30 .... **38** B8
Firtoft Cl *BURH* RH15 .... **139** H8
Fir Tree Av *HASM* GU27 .... **39** K5
Fir Tree Cl *CRAWW* RH11 .... **79** J8
   PUL/STOR RH20 .... **156** B5
   SWTR RH13 .... **79** J8
Fir Tree La *PUL/STOR* RH20 .... **156** B5
Fir Tree Wy *HPPT/KEY* BN6 .... **165** G7
   MIDOS PO22 .... **12** B5
Fishbourne Rd (East) *CCH* PO19 .... **218** C5
Fishbourne Rd (West) *CCH* PO19 .... **218** B5
Fisher Cl *CRAWE* RH10 .... **3** F5
Fishergate Cl *PTSD* BN41 .... **234** E4 🔢
Fisher La *MFD/CHID* GU8 .... **44** A4
   SELS PO20 .... **243** J4
The Fishermans *EMRTH* PO10 .... **214** E3 🔢
Fisherman Wk *BOGR* PO21 .... **262** A2 🔢
   SELS PO20 .... **265** F5
   SHOR BN43 .... **233** F6 🔢
Fishers Cl *ANG/EP* BN16 .... **250** D5
Fishers Ct *HORS* RH12 .... **4** B3
Fishersgate Ter *PTSD* BN41 .... **234** E4
Fish La *BOGR* PO21 .... **262** C1
   SELS PO20 .... **264** C3
Fitchet Cl *CRAWW* RH11 .... **2** A1
Fittleworth Cl *FERR* BN12 .... **229** F7 🔢
Fittleworth Dr *MIDOS* PO22 .... **247** G5
Fittleworth Rd *BIL* RH14 .... **100** B5
Fitzalan Rd *ARUN* BN18 .... **225** H1
   HORS RH12 .... **3** F2
   LHPTN BN17 .... **250** A2
Fitzherbert Dr *ROTT* BN2 .... **11** F2
Fitzwilliam Cl *BOGR* PO21 .... **245** H7 🔢
Five Acres *CRAWE* RH10 .... **3** D1
   RCCH PO18 .... **192** E6
Five Oaks Rd *SWTR* RH13 .... **75** J3
Flag Sq *SHOR* BN43 .... **233** H5
Flansham La *MIDOS* PO22 .... **247** G4
Flansham Pk *MIDOS* PO22 .... **247** G5
Flatt Rd *RCCH* PO18 .... **216** B3
Flaxman Av *CCH* PO19 .... **218** D5

Flax Mean *MIDOS* PO22 .... **247** F6
Fleet Cl *LHPTN* BN17 .... **250** C3
The Fleet *PUL/STOR* RH20 .... **127** H8
Fleming Wy *CRAWE* RH10 .... **31** J1
Fletcher Cl *BOGR* PO21 .... **261** J1
   CRAWE RH10 .... **3** D5 🔢
Fletcher Pl *SELS* PO20 .... **243** J2
Fletcher Rd *FIN/BW* BN14 .... **9** E1
Fletchers *SWTR* RH13 .... **77** F8 🔢
Fletchers Cl *SWTR* RH13 .... **5** D6
Fletchers Fld *LIPH* GU30 .... **38** B8
Fletcher's La *RCCH* PO18 .... **241** H2
   SELS PO20 .... **241** H2
Fletcher Wy *ANG/EP* BN16 .... **227** H5
   BOGR PO21 .... **12** B4
Flint Cl *ANG/EP* BN16 .... **251** H1 🔢
   CRAWE RH10 .... **32** B8
   PTSD BN41 .... **235** F1
Florence Av *HOVE* BN3 .... **235** H3
Florence Cl *SELS* PO20 .... **241** H7
Florence Pl *BRI* BN1 .... **11** D1
Florence Rd *BRI* BN1 .... **10** C2
   CCH PO19 .... **7** E3
The Florets *STEY/UB* BN44 .... **208** D2 🔢
Florida Cl *FERR* BN12 .... **252** D3
Florida Gdns *FERR* BN12 .... **252** D3 🔢
Florida Rd *FERR* BN12 .... **252** D5
Floridanlia Cl *LAN/SOMP* BN15 .... **231** H6
Flower Farm Cl *HFD* BN5 .... **161** H6
Foamcourt Waye *FERR* BN12 .... **252** C2
Folders Cl *BURH* RH15 .... **165** K2
Folders La *BURH* RH15 .... **165** J2
Follett Cl *BOGR* PO21 .... **262** B2
Follis Gdns *CCH* PO19 .... **218** B4
Folly La *EPSF* GU31 .... **88** D8
   PUL/STOR RH20 .... **151** J8
Fonthill Rd *HOVE* BN3 .... **236** B3
Fontwell Av *SELS* PO20 .... **222** D2
Fontwell Cl *ANG/EP* BN16 .... **250** D3
   ARUN BN18 .... **222** D1
   FIN/BW BN14 .... **230** A3
Fontwell Rd *CRAWE* RH10 .... **3** F6 🔢
   SELS PO20 .... **265** H3
Forbes Cl *CRAWE* RH10 .... **56** B1 🔢
Fordingbridge Cl *HORS* RH12 .... **4** B6
Ford La *ARUN* BN18 .... **224** D7
   SWTR RH13 .... **159** K4
Ford Manor Rd *LING* RH7 .... **23** F1
Ford Rd *ARUN* BN18 .... **224** B8
Fordwater Gdns *ARUN* BN18 .... **224** B8
Fordwater La *CCH* PO19 .... **219** G1
Fordwater Rd *CCH* PO19 .... **195** G3
   RCCH PO18 .... **195** G2
Foredown Cl *PTSD* BN41 .... **235** F1 🔢
Foredown Dr *PTSD* BN41 .... **235** F2
Foredown Rd *PTSD* BN41 .... **211** F8
Forest Cl *CRAWE* RH10 .... **34** D3
   SWTR RH13 .... **52** D7
   SWTR RH13 .... **78** E5
Forest Cnr *LISS* GU33 .... **62** A4
Forester Rd *CRAWE* RH10 .... **3** D7
Forestfield *CRAWE* RH10 .... **32** B7
    .... **5** F4
Forest Lane Cl *LIPH* GU30 .... **52** D7 🔢
Forest Oaks *SWTR* RH13 .... **52** D7
Forest Ri *LISS* GU33 .... **62** A5
Forest Rd *FIN/BW* BN14 .... **230** D5
   HORS RH12 .... **52** D7
   MIDH GU29 .... **121** K5
Forest Vw *CRAWE* RH10 .... **3** E6
Forest View Rd *EGRIN* RH19 .... **36** C5
Forest Wy *EGRIN* RH19 .... **37** F6
Forge *ANG/EP* BN16 .... **251** H1
   CCH PO19 .... **6** A6
   HORS RH12 .... **50** A4
   PTSD BN41 .... **235** F1
Forge La *CRAWE* RH10 .... **3** F2 🔢
    HORS RH12 .... **50** A4
Forge Rd *CRAWE* RH10 .... **3** F2
The Forge *HORS* RH12 .... **50** E4
   SWTR RH13 .... **105** F2
Forge Wy *BIL* RH14 .... **102** A3
   BURH RH15 .... **139** F7
Forge Wd *CRAWE* RH10 .... **18** D8
Forrester Rd *SWTR* RH13 .... **134** B8
Fort Hvn *SHOR* BN43 .... **234** A5
Fort Rd *LHPTN* BN17 .... **249** J1
Forty Acre La *EPSF* GU31 .... **117** F8
Foster La *PUL/STOR* RH20 .... **157** K6
Fosters Cl *ANG/EP* BN16 .... **251** G3
Foundry Cl *SWTR* RH13 .... **5** D3
Foundry La *HASM* GU27 .... **40** C5
   SWTR RH13 .... **5** D3
Foundry Rd *ARUN* BN18 .... **223** K4
Fountains Cl *BRI* BN1 .... **10** C4
Fountains Cl *BRI* BN1 .... **237** H1 🔢
   CRAWW RH11 .... **30** E7 🔢
Fourth Av *FIN/BW* BN14 .... **230** D4
   HOVE BN3 .... **236** B5
   LAN/SOMP BN15 .... **232** A5
   MIDOS PO22 .... **247** G7 🔢
Fowey Cl *SHOR* BN43 .... **233** K5
Fowler Cl *CRAWE* RH10 .... **32** C7
Foxbridge La *BIL* RH14 .... **71** J2
Foxbury *EMRTH* PO10 .... **191** C7

Fox Cl BURH RH15 .... 165 F2 ⓐ
CRAWW RH11 .... 2 A1
Fox Ct PUL/STOR RH20 .... 179 K2
Foxdale Dr ANG/EP BN16 ...... 227 H7
Fox Dell PUL/STOR RH20 .... 179 K2
Foxes Cl SWTR RH13 .... 105 F4
Foxes Cft MIDSS PO22 .... 223 G5
Foxfield Cottages
  SWTR RH13 .... 105 H4
Foxfields PUL/STOR RH20 ...... 156 A3
Foxglove Av HORS RH12 .... 5 D1
Foxglove Cl BURH RH15 .... 138 D7
Foxglove Wy ANG/EP BN16 ... 226 C8 ⓐ
Fox Hl HWH RH16 .... 140 A2
Fox Hill Cl HWH RH16 .... 140 A2
Fox Hill Village HWH RH16 .... 140 B3
Foxhole La RHWH RH17 .... 137 F1
Foxholes HORS RH12 .... 48 B5
Foxhunters Rd PTSD BN41 ... 210 D8 ⓐ
Fox Lea FIN/BW BN14 .... 205 J6
Foxleigh Cha HORS RH12 .... 5 E2 ⓐ
Foxley La SALV BN13 .... 229 K3
Fox Rd HASM GU27 .... 40 A5
  MIDH GU29 .... 122 C1
Foxwarren HWH RH16 .... 111 J6 ⓐ
Foxwarren Cl SELS PO20 .... 257 J4
Fox Wy PTSD BN41 .... 210 E8
Foxwells RHWH RH17 .... 83 G2
Framfield Cl CRAWW RH11 ..... 30 E3
The Framptons ANG/EP BN16 ... 226 B3 ⓐ
France La SALV BN13 .... 228 B5
Franciscan Wy LHPTN BN17 ... 249 K2
Francis Edwards Wy
  CRAWW RH11 .... 54 C1 ⓐ
Francis Rd HWH RH16 .... 112 D3
Francis St BRI BN1 .... 10 C5
Frandor Rd BOGR PO21 .... 245 H6
Frankland Md PUL/STOR RH20 ... 181 J5 ⓐ
Franklands Cl BURH RH15 ...... 165 G3
  FIN/BW BN14 .... 229 K2
Franklands Gdns BURH RH15 ... 165 G3
Franklands Wy BURH RH15 .... 165 G5
Frankland Ter EMRTH PO10 ... 214 E3 ⓐ
Franklin Pl CRAWE RH10 .... 32 C6
  PTSD BN41 .... 235 G4
  ROTT BN2 .... 11 E3
  SALV BN13 .... 229 J4
  SHOR BN43 .... 234 A3
Franklin St ROTT BN2 .... 11 E3
Franklynn Rd HWH RH16 ...... 112 B8
Frankton Av HWH RH16 .... 112 C8 ⓐ
Frant Rd HOVE BN3 .... 236 A1
Frarydene EMRTH PO10 .... 215 H3
Fraser Cl SELS PO20 .... 265 G4
Fraser Gdns EMRTH PO10 ...... 215 J1
Frederick Pl BRI BN1 .... 10 C4
Frederick Rd CRAWE RH10 ..... 218 C4 ⓐ
Free St BRI BN1 .... 10 B4
Freehold St SHOR BN43 .... 233 G4
Freehold Ter ROTT BN2 .... 11 D2
Freek's La BURH RH15 .... 139 G5
Freeland Cl CCH PO19 .... 218 C5
Freeman Cl SELS PO20 .... 223 F2
Freeman Rd HORS RH12 .... 50 E3
Freemans Cl BIL RH14 .... 102 A3 ⓐ
Freemans Rd PTSD BN41 ...... 234 D3
Freeways SELS PO20 .... 264 D3
Frenches PUL/STOR RH20 .. 180 B1 ⓐ
Frenches Md BIL RH14 .... 102 A3
French Gdns HWH RH16 .... 112 B5
Frenchmans Rd PSF GU32 ...... 88 C7
Freshbrook Cl LAN/SOMP BN15 ... 232 A6 ⓐ
Freshbrook Rd LAN/SOMP BN15 ... 232 B6
Freshfield Bank FROW RH18 .... 61 J1
Freshfield Cl CRAWE RH10 ...... 3 F4 ⓐ
Freshfield La RHWH RH17 ...... 114 A3
Freshfield Pl ROTT BN2 .... 11 E5
Freshfield Rd ROTT BN2 .... 11 E5
Freshfields Cl LAN/SOMP BN15 ... 231 K5
Freshfields Dr LAN/SOMP BN15 ... 231 K5
Freshfield St ROTT BN2 .... 11 E5
Freshwind Wy ROTT BN2 ...... 11 E5
Freya Cl HORS PO22 .... 247 K7
Friar Cl BRI BN1 .... 213 G7
Friar Crs BRI BN1 .... 213 F8
Friar Rd BRI BN1 .... 213 G7
Friars Cl HPPT/KEY BN6 .... 164 E7
Friars Oak Rd HPPT/KEY BN6 ... 164 E6
Friars Rookery CRAWE RH10 .... 3 D3
Friar Wk BRI BN1 .... 213 F7
  SALV BN13 .... 229 K8
Friary Cl MIDSS PO22 .... 247 J6
Friary La CCH PO19 .... 6 C3
Friary Wy CRAWE RH10 .... 3 D4 ⓐ
Friday St HORS RH12 .... 28 A6
  HORS RH12 .... 5 H3 ⓐ
Friends Cl CRAWW RH11 .... 31 H2 ⓐ
Friston Wk CRAWW RH11 ...... 30 E4
Frith Pk EGRIN RH19 .... 22 C8
Frith Rd BOGR PO21 .... 245 J6
  HOVE BN3 .... 236 A3
Frobisher Cl FERR BN12 .... 229 H7
Frobisher Gdns EMRTH PO10 ... 214 D3 ⓐ
Frobisher Rd BOGR PO21 ...... 261 J1
Frobisher Wy ANG/EP BN16 ... 251 G3

FERR BN12 .... 229 H7
Froggetts La CRAN GU6 .... 25 G2
Fry Cl CRAWW RH11 .... 55 F2
Fry Crs BURH RH15 .... 138 E6
Fryern Cl PUL/STOR RH20 ..... 180 A1
Fryern Rd PUL/STOR RH20 .... 156 B8
Fryland La HFD BN5 .... 135 K7
  SWTR RH13 .... 135 J7
Fulbeck Av SALV BN13 .... 229 F5
Fulham Cl CRAWW RH11 .... 55 F1
Fullers Wk LHPTN BN17 .... 249 G6
Fulmar Cl CRAWW RH11 .... 30 B6 ⓐ
  HOVE BN3 .... 236 D2
Fulmar Dr EGRIN RH19 .... 22 E8
Fulmar Rd SELS PO20 .... 221 G2
The Furlongs STEY/UB BN44 ... 207 K1
Furnace Dr CRAWE RH10 .... 3 E5
Furnace Farm Rd CRAWE RH10 ... 3 F5
Furnace Pde CRAWE RH10 ...... 3 F5
Furnace Pl CRAWE RH10 .... 3 F5
Furnace Rd CRAWE RH10 ...... 20 E8
Furners La HFD BN5 .... 161 J6
Furners Md HFD BN5 .... 161 H7
Furnston Gv EMRTH PO10 ..... 215 J2
Furse Feld BOGR PO21 .... 262 D1
Furze Cl SALV BN13 .... 229 H1
Furze Common Rd
  PUL/STOR RH20 .... 156 D5
Furzedown LHPTN BN17 .... 250 A3
Furzefield CRAWW RH11 .... 2 A2
  SELS PO20 .... 257 J2
Furzefield Cha EGRIN RH19 .... 22 C5
Furzefield Cl ANG/EP BN16 ... 227 H4
Furzefield Rd EGRIN RH19 ..... 22 C5
  HORS RH12 .... 52 D6
Furzeholme SALV BN13 .... 229 J1 ⓐ
Furze La EGRIN RH19 .... 21 K8
Furze Meadow HPPT/KEY BN6 ... 163 H3
Furzen La HORS RH12 .... 24 E8
Furze Rd HORS RH12 .... 48 B3
  SALV BN13 .... 229 H1
Furze Vw BIL RH14 .... 75 F5
Fushia Cl HAV PO9 .... 190 A7

G

Gableson Av BRI BN1 .... 212 B7
The Gables HORS RH12 .... 4 C5 ⓐ
  SWTR RH13 .... 105 F3
Gabriel Rd CRAWE RH10 .... 56 C1
Gage Cl CRAWE RH10 .... 34 E2
Gage Rdg FROW RH18 .... 61 J2
Gaggle Wd SWTR RH13 .... 78 E5
Gainsboro Rd BOGR PO21 ... 12 B5 ⓐ
Gainsborough Dr FIN/BW BN14 ... 230 E4
Gainsborough Dr SELS PO20 ... 265 F4
Gainsborough Rd CRAWE RH10 ... 55 K1
Gaisford Cl FIN/BW BN14 .... 8 C2 ⓐ
Gaisford Rd FIN/BW BN14 .... 8 B2
Galahad Rd CRAWW RH11 ... 30 C5 ⓐ
Gales Dr CRAWE RH10 .... 3 E3
Gales Pl CRAWE RH10 .... 3 E3
Galliers Cl BRI BN1 .... 213 H5
Galsworthy Cl FERR BN12 ..... 229 F8 ⓐ
Galsworthy Rd FERR BN12 ..... 229 F8
Gamecock Ter SELS PO20 ..... 221 F2
Gander Cl BURH RH15 .... 139 G6 ⓑ
Gander Gn HWH RH16 .... 112 B4
Gander Hl HWH RH16 .... 112 B4
Gandersgate La BIL RH14 .... 99 G4
Gannon Rd WTHG BN11 .... 9 F3
Garbitts La EGRIN GU31 .... 91 F8
Garden Av SELS PO20 .... 258 A5
Garden Cl ANG/EP BN16 .... 227 J4
  EGRIN RH19 .... 36 D4
  LAN/SOMP BN15 .... 231 J5
  PTSD BN41 .... 235 G3
  PUL/STOR RH20 .... 180 B1
  SHOR BN43 .... 233 K2
Garden Ct BOGR PO21 .... 262 B1
Garden Crs MIDSS PO22 .... 223 G6
Gardeners Cl HORS RH12 .... 50 E3
Gardeners Gn HORS RH12 ...... 28 E5
Gardener St PTSD BN41 .... 234 E3
Garden House La EGRIN RH19 ... 36 C4
The Gardens PTSD BN41 .... 235 G3
  PUL/STOR RH20 .... 127 G8
  RCCH PO18 .... 193 F8
  STHW BN42 .... 234 D4
Garden Wood Cl PUL/STOR RH20 ... 156 B5
Garden Wood Rd EGRIN RH19 ... 35 K1
Gardner La CRAWE RH10 .... 34 D3
Gardner Rd PTSD BN41 .... 234 E4
Gardner St BRI BN1 .... 10 C5 ⓑ
Garland Av EMRTH PO10 ...... 190 D8
Garland Cl CCH PO19 .... 7 D4
Garland Rd EGRIN RH19 .... 36 B2
Garland Sq SELS PO20 .... 221 F1
Garrett Cl CRAWE RH10 .... 32 C7 ⓐ
Garrick Rd FIN/BW BN14 .... 9 D2

The Garrones CRAWE RH10 3
Garsons Rd EMRTH PO10 2
Garton Cl CRAWW RH11 3
Gaskyns Cl HORS RH12 ....
Gasson Wood Rd CRAWW RH11
Gaston Wy RCCH PO18 ....
Gatcombe Cl SALV BN13 22
Gateford Dr HORS RH12 ....
Gatehouse La BURH RH15 1
  EPSF GU31 ....
  HPPT/KEY BN6 ....
Gates Cl CRAWE RH10 5
Gatesmead HWH RH16 1
The Cattons BURH RH15 1
Gatwick Rd CRAWE RH10 1
  HORL RH6 ....
Gatwick Wy HORL RH6 ....
Gay St PUL/STOR RH20 ....
Gay Street La PUL/STOR RH20 ...
Geary Cl HORL RH6 ....
Geddes Wy EPSF GU31 ....
Gemini Cl CRAWW RH11 ....
Genoa Cl ANG/EP BN16 ....
Gentles La LIPH GU30 ....
George Denyer Cl HASM GU27 ...
George Iv Wk MIDSS PO22 ....
Georges La PUL/STOR RH20 ....
George St HOVE BN3 ....
  PTSD BN41 23
  ROTT BN2 1
George V Av FERR BN12 ....
  LAN/SOMP BN15 ....
  WTHG BN11 ....
Georgia Av FIN/BW BN14 ....
Georgian Cl CRAWE RH10 ......
Georgian Gdns ANG/EP BN16 ... 25
Gerald Cl BURH RH15 ....
Gerald Rd WTHG BN11 ....
Gerard St BRI BN1 ....
Gibbons Cl CRAWE RH10 ....
Giblets La HORS RH12 ....
Giblets Wy HORS RH12 ....
Gibson Rd SELS PO20 ....
Gibson Wy BOGR PO21 ....
Giffards Cl EGRIN RH19 3
Gifford Rd RCCH PO18 ....
Gilbert Rd CCH PO19 ....
The Gilberts ANG/EP BN16 2
Giles Cl ARUN BN18 ....
Gilham La FROW RH18 ....
Gillett Ct SWTR RH13 ....
Gillham's La HASM GU27 ....
Gilligan Cl HORS RH12 ....
The Gilligans BURH RH15 ....
Gillway SELS PO20 ....
Gilmore Rd CCH PO19 ....
Gilpin Cl CCH PO19 ....
Gilwynes BOGR PO21 ....
Ginhams Rd CRAWW RH11 ....
The Glades EGRIN RH19 ....
The Glade BOGR PO21 ....
  CRAWE RH10 ....
  SWTR RH13 ....
Gladonian Rd LHPTN BN17 ....
Gladstone Pl ROTT BN2 ....
Gladstone Rd ARUN BN18 ......
  BURH RH15 ....
  HORS RH12 ....
  PTSD BN41 ....
Gladstone Ter LHPTN BN17 2
Gladys Rd HOVE BN3 ....
Glamis Ct BOGR PO21 ....
Glamis St BOGR PO21 ....
Glaseby La PUL/STOR RH20 ....
Glasshouse La BIL RH14 ....
Glastonbury Rd HOVE BN3 .....
Glatting La PUL/STOR RH20 ....
Glaziers La MIDH GU29 ....
Gleave Cl EGRIN RH19 ....
Glebe Cl CRAWE RH10 ....
  LAN/SOMP BN15 2
  SELS PO20 ....
  STHW BN42 ....
Glebe Field Rd SELS PO20 .....
Glebelands BIL RH14 ....
  CRAWE RH10 ....
  PUL/STOR RH20 ....
Glebelands Cl SHOR BN43 2
Glebe Rd EPSF GU31 ....
  HASM GU27 ....
  RHWH RH17 1
  SALV BN13 ....
Glebeside Av FIN/BW BN14 ....
Glebeside Cl FIN/BW BN14 .....
The Glebe CRAWE RH10 ....
  EGRIN RH19 ....
  HWH RH16 ....
  SELS PO20 ....
Glebe Vw RHWH RH17 ....
Glebe Vls HOVE BN3 ....
Glebe Wy BIL RH14 ....
  LAN/SOMP BN15 ....
Glenbarrie Wy FERR BN12 ......
Glencathara Rd BOGR PO21 ....

Crs SELS PO20 .... 265 F4
Dl HAV PO9 .... 190 B2
dale Cl HORS RH12 .... 5 F1
dale Rd BURH RH15 .... 165 H1
VE BN3 .... 236 D4
dor Rd HOVE BN3 .... 235 J5
dyne Cl EGRIN RH19 .... 36 E3
dyne Wy EGRIN RH19 .... 36 E3
eig Cl BOGR PO21 .... 245 H5
Falls Av BRI BN1 .... 213 G4
Gdns FERR BN12 .... 252 D1
ea GSHT GU26 .... 40 A2
ea Hollow GSHT GU26 .... 40 A3
Ri BRI BN1 .... 212 B6
Rise Cl BRI BN1 .... 212 B6
len SALV BN13 .... 230 A1
TR RH13 .... 105 G1 ⬚
iew Cl CRAWE RH10 .... 3 E1
ville Rd ANG/EP BN16 .... 250 E3
Vue EGRIN RH19 .... 36 C2
sway MIDOS PO22 .... 12 C4
wood Av MIDOS PO22 .... 12 C4
wood Rd EMRTH PO10 .... 215 H2
n Av HOVE BN3 .... 235 H1
le Pl LHPTN BN17 .... 225 K8
er Dr BOGR PO21 .... 261 J1
cester Cl PSF GU32 .... 88 B8
cester La LHPTN BN17 .... 249 K2
cester Pl BRI BN1 .... 10 C4
PTN BN17 .... 249 K2
TT BN2 .... 10 C4 ⬚
cester Rd BOGR PO21 .... 13 D5
BN1 .... 10 B4
RH RH15 .... 139 F8
AWE RH10 .... 55 J1
PTN BN17 .... 249 J2
cester St BRI BN1 .... 10 C4
cester Wy CCH PO19 .... 219 F2
er's Rd HORL RH6 .... 16 B4
le Av FERR BN12 .... 252 D1
le Cl FERR BN12 .... 252 D1
le Pl HORS RH12 .... 4 B5 ⬚
le Rd ROTT BN2 .... 11 F4
t Rd LHPTN BN17 .... 250 A2
ard Cl CRAWE RH10 .... 32 B8
nan Cl BOGR PO21 .... 245 F8 ⬚
talls La STEY/UB BN44 .... 183 J8
vin Cl EMRTH PO10 .... 190 C8
vin Rd HOVE BN3 .... 235 H3
vin Wy RCCH PO18 .... 218 A3
s Cl CRAWW RH11 .... 2 B4
La CRAWW RH11 .... 2 A3
Park Rd CRAWW RH11 .... 2 B4
rest Av LHPTN BN17 .... 225 J7
en Acre ANG/EP BN16 .... 251 K3
GR PO21 .... 261 H3
en Avenue ANG/EP BN16 .... 251 K2
en Avenue Cl ANG/EP BN16 .... 251 K3
en Flds LIPH GU30 .... 38 D8
en Hl LHPTN BN17 .... 139 K8
en La SWTR RH13 .... 159 K5
inch Cl CRAWW RH11 .... 2 C1
RS RH12 .... 51 J4
ng Cl CRAWE RH10 .... 32 C6 ⬚
ng La SWTR RH13 .... 79 F4
mid Rd HOVE BN3 .... 10 A3
mith Rd FIN/BW BN14 .... 9 E2
tone Cl HOVE BN3 .... 212 B8
tone Crs HOVE BN3 .... 236 A1
tone La HOVE BN3 .... 236 B3
tone Rd HOVE BN3 .... 236 B4
tone Vls HOVE BN3 .... 236 B4
tone Wy HOVE BN3 .... 236 A1
lub La PUL/STOR RH20 .... 155 H4
er BRI BN1 .... 213 H8
inks La SELS PO20 .... 265 F22
inks Rd MIDOS PO22 .... 13 F2
acres MIDOS PO22 .... 223 G6
new Cl ARUN BN18 .... 224 A8
win Cl CRAWW RH11 .... 30 C6
wins Cl EGRIN RH19 .... 22 B8
wood Av MIDOS PO22 .... 13 E3
wood Cl ANG/EP BN16 .... 251 C1
WE RH10 .... 3 F6 ⬚
H GU29 .... 122 A6
wood Ct EMRTH PO10 .... 215 J3
wood Gdns SELS PO20 .... 244 A5
wood Rd SALV BN13 .... 230 A2
e Green Cl HORS RH12 .... 4 C2
egreen La PUL/STOR RH20 .... 131 G8
en Av BOGR PO21 .... 12 C4 ⬚
PO19 .... 6 A6
OS PO22 .... 12 C3
R BN43 .... 233 J4
en Cl HWH RH16 .... 112 A5
en Rd BRI BN1 .... 237 F1
RH RH15 .... 139 J7
RTH PO10 .... 215 F4
RS RH12 .... 4 C3
H RH16 .... 112 A5
/SOMP BN15 .... 231 K5
D BN41 .... 234 E4
R BN43 .... 233 H4

WTHG BN11 .... 9 D3 ⬚
Goreside La RHWH RH17 .... 111 F3
Goring Cha FERR BN12 .... 228 E7
Goring Rd FERR BN12 .... 253 G1 ⬚
   FERR BN12 .... 253 G1
   STEY/UB BN44 .... 207 K1
   WTHG BN11 .... 253 K1
Goring's Md SWTR RH13 .... 4 C6
Goring St FERR BN12 .... 228 E8
   FERR BN12 .... 252 E1
Goring Wy FERR BN12 .... 229 F8
   SWTR RH13 .... 134 C7
Gorling Cl CRAWW RH11 .... 30 C6 ⬚
Gorringe Cl SHOR BN43 .... 234 B4
Gorringes Brook HORS RH12 ...... 4 C1
Gorse Av ANG/EP BN16 .... 252 C1
   FIN/BW BN14 .... 230 B5
   MIDOS PO22 .... 247 H5
Gorse Bank Cl PUL/STOR RH20 .. 157 G8
Gorse Cl CRAWE RH10 .... 33 H1
   CRAWW RH11 .... 55 F5
   PTSD BN41 .... 210 D7
Gorse End HORS RH12 .... 4 C2
Gorselands BIL RH14 .... 102 C3
Gorse La SALV BN13 .... 229 J1
Gorse Rd EPSF GU31 .... 89 G8
Gosden Cl CRAWE RH10 .... 3 F4 ⬚
Gosden Rd LHPTN BN17 .... 250 B1
Gospond Rd MIDOS PO22 .... 222 E6
Gossamer La BOGR PO21 ...... 245 F8
Gossops Dr CRAWW RH11 .... 30 E6
Gossops Green La CRAWW RH11 30 E6
Gostrode La MFD/CHID GU8 .... 42 E5
Goudhurst Cl CRAWE RH10 ..... 32 E5
Gower Rd HWH RH16 .... 112 A7
Gowers Cl RHWH RH17 .... 84 A3
Grace Rd CRAWW RH11 .... 54 E2
Graffham Cl CCH PO19 .... 195 G8
   CRAWW RH11 .... 2 A1
Grafton Av MIDOS PO22 .... 247 G5
Grafton Cl ANG/EP BN16 ...... 250 E1 ⬚
Grafton Dr LAN/SOMP BN15 .. 231 J5
Grafton Gdns LAN/SOMP BN15 . 231 J5
Grafton Pl WTHG BN11 .... 9 D4 ⬚
Grafton Rd SELS PO20 .... 265 F6
   WTHG BN11 .... 9 D4
Graham Av BRI BN1 .... 212 E7
   PTSD BN41 .... 210 D7
Graham Crs PTSD BN41 .... 210 D7
Graham Rd ARUN BN18 .... 247 K1
   WTHG BN11 .... 9 D4
Grailands Cl HASM GU27 .... 66 E5
Granary La SELS PO20 .... 264 E3
Granary Wy HORS RH12 .... 77 F2
   LHPTN BN17 .... 225 K7 ⬚
Grand Av HOVE BN3 .... 236 C5
   HPPT/KEY BN6 .... 166 F7
   LAN/SOMP BN15 .... 232 A4
   LHPTN BN17 .... 225 J8
   WTHG BN11 .... 8 A4
Grand Junction Rd BRI BN1 ...... 10 C6
Grand Pde ROTT BN2 .... 10 C5
Grand Parade Ms ROTT BN2 .. 10 C5 ⬚
Grange Cl BRI BN1 .... 10 A1
   BURH RH15 .... 139 J6
   CRAWE RH10 .... 3 F1
   FERR BN12 .... 252 D1
Grange Ct BOGR PO21 .... 262 B2
Grange Crs CRAWE RH10 .... 34 B4
Grange Field Wy BOGR PO21 .. 262 A1
Grange La SELS PO20 .... 265 H1
Grange Park Rd FERR BN12 ... 252 C2
Grange Rd CRAWE RH10 .... 34 C4
   HOVE BN3 .... 235 J4
   MIDH GU29 .... 122 B4
   PSF GU32 .... 116 C1
   STHW BN42 .... 234 C4
Grange Wy SWTR RH13 .... 105 F1
Grangeways BRI BN1 .... 212 E6 ⬚
Grangewood Dr BOGR PO21 ... 262 A1 ⬚
Granston Wy CRAWE RH10 ..... 34 E3
Grant Cl SELS PO20 .... 264 E4 ⬚
Grantham Rd BRI BN1 .... 10 C1
Grantmead LAN/SOMP BN15 .. 232 A4 ⬚
Grant St ROTT BN2 .... 11 D3
Granville Rd HOVE BN3 .... 10 A3
   LHPTN BN17 .... 250 A3
Grasmere Av LAN/SOMP BN15 . 231 H5
Grasmere Gdns HORS RH12 ... 52 D5 ⬚
Grassmere Cl LHPTN BN17 .... 226 C8 ⬚
   MIDOS PO22 .... 13 E4
Gratten La HFD BN5 .... 136 D8
Grattons Dr CRAWE RH10 .... 32 C2
The Grattons SWTR RH13 .... 49 J8
Gratwicke Cl BIL RH14 .... 102 B5
Gratwicke Rd WTHG BN11 .... 8 C4
Gravelly Crs LAN/SOMP BN15 . 232 B5
Gravelye Cl HWH RH16 .... 112 D6
Gravelye La HWH RH16 .... 112 D6
Graveney Rd CRAWE RH10 ...... 32 C6 ⬚
Gravett Ct BURH RH15 .... 165 F1
Gravetye Cl CRAWE RH10 .... 3 F5 ⬚
Gravits La BOGR PO21 .... 245 J7

Graydon Av CCH PO19 .... 6 A5
Grays Cl HASM GU27 .... 41 G3
Grayswood Av SELS PO20 ...... 258 A5
Grayswood Rd HASM GU27 ..... 41 F3
Great College St ROTT BN2 ..... 11 E6
Greatham Br PUL/STOR RH20 . 154 A6
Greatham Rd CRAWE RH10 ..... 32 C8
   FIN/BW BN14 .... 229 K2
Great Hanger EPSF GU31 .... 89 F8
Greatpin Cft PUL/STOR RH20 . 127 G8
Grebe Crs SWTR RH13 .... 5 F6
Greenacre PUL/STOR RH20 ... 179 K2 ⬚
Greenacres CRAWE RH10 .... 32 B6
   HORS RH12 .... 4 B3
   PUL/STOR RH20 .... 158 A5
   SHOR BN43 .... 233 G3
   STEY/UB BN44 .... 207 K1
Greenacres Ring ANG/EP BN16 227 H5
Greenbank MIDOS PO22 .... 223 G6
Green Bushes Cl ANG/EP BN16 250 D3 ⬚
Green Cl STHW BN42 .... 234 C4 ⬚
   SWTR RH13 .... 105 F1
Greencourt Dr BOGR PO21 .... 245 J6
Greenfield PUL/STOR RH20 ... 175 K1
Greenfield Cl BRI BN1 .... 213 G6
   LIPH GU30 .... 38 C6 ⬚
Green Field Cl STHW BN42 .... 234 C3 ⬚
Greenfield Crs BRI BN1 .... 213 F6
Greenfield Rd CCH PO19 .... 7 D1
   SWTR RH13 .... 49 H8
Greenfields EPSF GU31 .... 118 E4 ⬚
   LHPTN BN17 .... 225 H8
   LISS GU33 .... 62 A7
Greenfields Cl EPSF GU31 ..... 118 E3
   HORS RH12 .... 5 F1
Greenfields Rd HORS RH12 ...... 5 F2
Greenfields Wy HORS RH12 ...... 5 F1
Greenfield Wy PUL/STOR RH20 180 C1
Greenfinch Wy HORS RH12 ...... 51 K4
Greengates PETW GU28 .... 96 B1
Green Hedges Av EGRIN RH19 .. 36 E3 ⬚
Green Hedges Cl EGRIN RH19 . 36 B1
Greenhill Pk HWH RH16 .... 140 C1
Greenhill Wy HWH RH16 .... 140 C1
Greenhurst La PUL/STOR RH20 156 C6
Greenland Cl SALV BN13 .... 229 J4
Greenland Rd SALV BN13 ...... 229 J5
Greenlands Cl BURH RH15 .... 165 H3
Greenlands Dr BURH RH15 .... 165 H3
Green La RDKG RH5 .... 15 F3
   CCH PO19 .... 7 D2
   CRAWE RH10 .... 3 D1
   CRAWE RH10 .... 20 B7
   CRAWE RH10 .... 32 D5
   HASM GU27 .... 40 D7
   HORL RH6 .... 19 E5
   HORS RH12 .... 28 A7
   RCCH PO18 .... 216 D3
   RCCH PO18 .... 217 G5
   SELS PO20 .... 220 B7
   SELS PO20 .... 242 E5
   SELS PO20 .... 244 B1
   SELS PO20 .... 259 H2
   SELS PO20 .... 264 E5
   SWTR RH13 .... 133 H2
Green Lane Cl ARUN BN18 .... 225 F1 ⬚
Greenlea Av BOGR PO21 .... 261 J1
Greenleas HOVE BN3 .... 235 H1
Green Mdw HWH RH16 .... 112 D3
Greenoaks LAN/SOMP BN15 .. 231 K3
Green Pk FERR BN12 .... 228 D6
Green Park Cnr RHWH RH17 .. 140 C7
Green Rdg BRI BN1 .... 212 B6
Green Rd RHWH RH17 .... 140 C6
Greensand Cl GSHT GU26 .... 40 C1
   HASM GU27 .... 40 E4
Greenstede Av EGRIN RH19 ..... 22 D7
The Green BOGR PO21 .... 261 H3
   CRAWE RH10 .... 19 H8
   HOVE BN3 .... 236 C1
   PUL/STOR RH20 .... 180 D1
Greentree La SWTR RH13 ..... 134 E6
Greentrees LAN/SOMP BN15 .. 231 J5 ⬚
Greentrees Crs LAN/SOMP BN15 231 J5
Green Wk CRAWE RH10 .... 3 E1
Greenway HORS RH12 .... 51 G8
Green Wy MIDOS PO22 .... 247 K6
Green Park Cnr RHWH RH17 .. 116 A5
Greenways BOGR PO21 .... 261 J2
   HWH RH16 .... 112 B5
   STHW BN42 .... 234 D2
Greenways Crs FERR BN12 .... 252 D2
   SHOR BN43 .... 233 J2
The Green Wy FERR BN12 ..... 229 F7
Greenwich Cl CRAWW RH11 ... 55 G1 ⬚
Greenwood Av MIDOS PO22 ... 12 A2
Greenwood Cl MIDOS PO22 ... 12 A2
Greenwood Dr ANG/EP BN16 . 227 H8
Greet Rd LAN/SOMP BN15 .... 231 K4
Gregory Cl CRAWE RH10 .... 56 C1
Gregsons HORS RH12 .... 50 E3
Grenehurst Wy EPSF GU31 ..... 88 D8
Grenville Cl FERR BN12 .... 229 H8 ⬚
Grenville Cl FERR BN12 .... 229 G8
   LIPH GU30 .... 38 C7

Grenville Gdns *CCH* PO10 .... 6 B5
Grenville St *BRI* BN1 .... 10 B5
Gresham Pl *HFD* BN5 .... 161 F5
Gresham Wk *CRAWE* RH10 .... 3 D6 **6**
Grevatt's La *LHPTN* BN17 .... 248 A4
Grevatt's La West *ARUN* BN18 .... 247 K3
Greville Gn *EMRTH* PO10 .... 190 C7
Grey Alders *HWH* RH16 .... 112 D5
Greyfriars *BOGR* PO21 .... 236 D3
Greyfriars Cl *BOGR* PO21 .... 245 H8
   SALV BN13 .... 230 A5
Greyfriars La *PUL/STOR* RH20 .... 180 A3
Greyhound Slip *CRAWE* RH10 ...... 32 D4 **6**
Greynville Cl *BOGR* PO21 .... 261 K1
Greystoke Ms *FERR* BN12 .... 252 C1 **6**
Greystoke Rd *FERR* BN12 .... 252 C1
Greystone Av *BOGR* PO21 .... 245 H4
   SALV BN13 .... 229 K6
Gribble La *SELS* PO20 .... 220 D4
Grier Cl *CRAWW* RH11 .... 30 C6 **6**
Griffin Crs *LHPTN* BN17 .... 225 K7
Griffith's Av *LAN/SOMP* BN15 .... 231 K3
Grinstead Av *LAN/SOMP* BN15 ...... 232 A5
Grinstead La *EGRIN* RH19 .... 60 A3
   LAN/SOMP BN15 .... 232 A5
Grisedale Cl *CRAWW* RH11 .... 2 B5 **6**
Groombridge Wy *HORS* RH12 .... 77 F2
Groomsland Dr *BURH* RH14 .... 102 A5
The Grooms *CRAWE* RH10 .... 32 D3
Grosvenor Gdns *BOGR* PO21 .... 244 E8 **6**
Grosvenor Rd *CCH* PO19 .... 8 B6
   EGRIN RH19 .... 36 B2
   WTHG BN11 .... 9 D4 **6**
Grosvenor St *ROTT* BN2 .... 11 D5 **6**
Grosvenor Wy *BOGR* PO21 .... 244 E8 **6**
Grouse Rd *SWTR* RH13 .... 54 A8
Grove Crs *LHPTN* BN17 .... 250 A1
Grove Hl *ROTT* BN2 .... 11 D4
Grovelands Cl *BURH* RH15 .... 165 F2 **6**
The Grovelands
   LAN/SOMP BN15 .... 232 A7 **6**
Grove La *PETW* GU28 .... 126 A5
   PUL/STOR RH20 .... 156 B5
Grove Pk *CCH* PO19 .... 218 D5
Grove Rd *BURH* RH15 .... 165 H1
   CCH PO19 .... 7 D4
   FIN/BW BN14 .... 230 C5
   SELS PO20 .... 264 E5
Grove St *PETW* GU28 .... 125 K4
   ROTT BN2 .... 11 D4
The Grove *CRAWW* RH11 .... 2 B3
   EMRTH PO10 .... 191 F8
   FERR BN12 .... 252 C1 **6**
   HORL RH6 .... 18 B1
   HWH RH16 .... 112 D8
   LIPH GU30 .... 38 B7
   MIDOS PO22 .... 13 F4
Guernsey Cl *CRAWW* RH11 .... 54 E1
Guernsey Farm La *MIDOS* PO22 .... 247 G6
Guernsey Rd *FERR* BN12 .... 252 D3 **6**
Guilden Rd *CCH* PO19 .... 7 D3
Guildford Cl *EMRTH* PO10 .... 215 H2
   FIN/BW BN14 .... 8 A2 **6**
Guildford Pl *CCH* PO19 .... 219 F2
Guildford Rd *ANG/EP* BN16 .... 251 K3
   FIN/BW BN14 .... 8 A3
   HORS RH12 .... 47 H3
   HORS RH12 .... 49 F4
   HORS RH12 .... 77 G1
Guildford St *BRI* BN1 .... 10 B4 **6**
Guildhall St *CCH* PO19 .... 6 C2 **6**
Guilford Rd *BRI* BN1 .... 10 B4
Guillards Oak *MIDH* GU29 .... 122 A4
Guinevere Rd *CRAWW* RH11 .... 30 C5 **6**
Gunning Cl *CRAWW* RH11 .... 30 E8
Gunns Farm *LIPH* GU30 .... 64 C1
Gunwin Ct *BOGR* PO21 .... 262 A1
Gutner La *HISD* PO11 .... 238 A2
Gwynne Gdns *EGRIN* RH19 .... 36 A1

H

Habin Hl *EPSF* GU31 .... 91 F7
Hackenden Cl *EGRIN* RH19 .... 22 C8
Hackenden La *EGRIN* RH19 .... 22 C8
Haddington Cl *HOVE* BN3 .... 236 B5
Haddington St *HOVE* BN3 .... 236 B4 **6**
Hadlands *BOGR* PO21 .... 261 H2 **6**
Hadley Av *FIN/BW* BN14 .... 230 D5
Hadley Cl *MIDOS* PO22 .... 247 J5
Hadlow Cl *ROTT* BN2 .... 11 D4
Hadlow Wy *LAN/SOMP* BN15 ...... 232 B5
Hadmans Cl *HORS* RH12 .... 4 B6
Hadrian Av *STHW* BN42 .... 234 D3
Haglands Copse
   PUL/STOR RH20 .... 156 B1 **6**
Haglands La *PUL/STOR* RH20 ...... 156 B6 **6**
Haig Av *BRI* BN1 .... 213 K5
Haigh Cl *LAN/SOMP* BN15 .... 232 D5
Hailsham Cl *ANG/EP* BN16 .... 227 K2 **6**
Hailsham Rd *WTHG* BN11 .... 253 K2

Hale Cl *SELS* PO20 .... 258 A5
Hales Fld *HASM* GU27 .... 40 E5
Halewick Cl *LAN/SOMP* BN15 ...... 231 J5 **6**
Halewick La *LAN/SOMP* BN15 ...... 231 J3
Haleybridge Wk *SELS* PO20 .... 221 F2
Half Moon Hl *HASM* GU27 .... 40 E5
Half Moon La *SALV* BN13 .... 229 K3
Halfrey Cl *RCCH* PO18 .... 218 A4
Halfrey Rd *RCCH* PO18 .... 218 A4
Halifax Cl *CRAWE* RH10 .... 32 C2
Halifax Dr *SALV* BN13 .... 229 H5
Halland Cl *CRAWE* RH10 .... 3 F2 **6**
Hall Av *FIN/BW* BN14 .... 230 A4
Hall Cl *FIN/BW* BN14 .... 230 A4
Hallett Rd *ROTT* BN2 .... 11 F3
Halley Cl *CRAWW* RH11 .... 55 F2
Halliford Dr *MIDOS* PO22 .... 223 G6
Halliwick Gdns *MIDOS* PO22 .... 247 F7
Hallsland *CRAWE* RH10 .... 34 E3
Halyburton Rd *HOVE* BN3 .... 235 H3
Halnaker Barn La *RCCH* PO18 ...... 197 J7
Halnaker Gdns *BOGR* PO21 .... 261 K1
Halsbury Cl *WTHG* BN11 .... 9 E3
Halsbury Rd *WTHG* BN11 .... 9 F3
Halsford La *EGRIN* RH19 .... 35 K1
Halsford Park Rd *EGRIN* RH19 ...... 36 A1
Halson Cl *BOGR* PO21 .... 12 A4
Hambledon Pl *BOGR* PO21 .... 12 A5
Hamble Gdns *SALV* BN13 .... 229 G4
Hamble Rd *LAN/SOMP* BN15 ...... 231 H5
Hambleton Hl *CRAWW* RH11 .... 2 B5
Hamble Wy *SALV* BN13 .... 229 G4
Hambrook *BURH* RH15 .... 165 J2 **6**
Hambrook Hl (North) *RCCH* PO18 .. 192 B8
Hambrook Hl (South) *RCCH* PO18 .. 216 B1
Ham Cl *WTHG* BN11 .... 231 G1 **6**
Hamilton Cl *ANG/EP* BN16 .... 226 D8 **6**
   FIN/BW BN14 .... 9 E1
   PTSD BN41 .... 210 E8
Hamilton Dr *ANG/EP* BN16 .... 226 D8
Hamilton Gdns *BOGR* PO21 .... 262 A1 **6**
   RCCH PO18 .... 217 G4
Hamilton Rd *BRI* BN1 .... 10 B2
   HORS RH12 .... 4 A4
   LAN/SOMP BN15 .... 231 K4
   LISS GU33 .... 62 D1
Ham La *EMRTH* PO10 .... 215 H4
   RHWH RH17 .... 113 G8
   SELS PO20 .... 221 F4
Ham Manor Cl *ANG/EP* BN16 ...... 227 F7
Ham Manor Wy *ANG/EP* BN16 .... 227 G7
Hammer Hl *HASM* GU27 .... 39 J7
   RHWH RH17 .... 82 A8
Hammer La *CSHT* GU26 .... 39 J3
   HASM GU27 .... 39 J6
   LIPH GU30 .... 59 G5
   MIDH GU29 .... 92 D7
Hammerpond Rd *SWTR* RH13 .... 78 C5
   SWTR RH13 .... 79 K5
Hammerwood Copse
   HASM GU27 .... 39 K6 **6**
Hammerwood Rd *EGRIN* RH19 ...... 37 J5
Hammingden La *EGRIN* RH19 .... 59 C8
   RHWH RH17 .... 85 G4
Hammond Dr *SALV* BN13 .... 229 H5
Hammonds Gdns *BURH* RH15 ...... 165 F2 **6**
Hammonds Rdg *BURH* RH15 .... 164 E2
Hammy Cl *SHOR* BN43 .... 233 K3
Hammy La *SHOR* BN43 .... 233 K3
Hammy Wy *SHOR* BN43 .... 233 K3
Hampden Cl *CRAWE* RH10 .... 32 E2 **6**
   MIDOS PO22 .... 247 K6 **6**
Hampden Rd *ROTT* BN2 .... 11 E3
Hampers La *PUL/STOR* RH20 .... 181 F3
Hampshire Av *BOGR* PO21 .... 12 A3
Hampstead Rd *BRI* BN1 .... 236 D2
Hampton Ct *BOGR* PO21 .... 245 H7
Hampton Flds *LHPTN* BN17 .... 249 K1
Hampton Pl *BRI* BN1 .... 10 A5
Hampton St *BRI* BN1 .... 10 A5 **6**
Hampton Wy *EGRIN* RH19 .... 36 D4
Ham Rd *SELS* PO20 .... 259 H5
   SHOR BN43 .... 233 H4
   WTHG BN11 .... 231 G1
Hamsey Rd *EGRIN* RH19 .... 59 J5
Hamshire Hl *RHWH* RH17 .... 80 D7
Hamsland *RHWH* RH17 .... 86 A7
Hamstead Meadow *RCCH* PO18 .. 216 C4
Ham Wy *WTHG* BN11 .... 231 G1 **6**
Hanbury La *HWH* RH16 .... 112 C6
Hanbury Rd *CRAWW* RH11 .... 30 C6
Handcross Rd *RHWH* RH17 .... 56 C8
   SWTR RH13 .... 79 K7
Handford Wy *RHWH* RH17 .... 80 B5
Hangers Wy *EPSF* GU31 .... 116 A7
Hanger Wy *EPSF* GU31 .... 89 F8
Hangleton Cl *HOVE* BN3 .... 235 H1
Hangleton Gdns *HOVE* BN3 .... 235 H2
Hangleton Gra *FERR* BN12 .... 228 C8 **6**
Hangleton La *FERR* BN12 .... 228 B7
   HOVE BN3 .... 235 G1
   PTSD BN41 .... 235 F1
Hangleton Manor Cl *HOVE* BN3 .... 235 G1

Hangleton Rd *HOVE* BN3 .... 23▮
Hangleton Valley Dr *HOVE* BN3 .... 21▮
Hangleton Wy *HOVE* BN3 .... 23▮
Hanlye La *RHWH* RH17 .... 11▮
Hannah Sq *CCH* PO19 .... 1▮
Hannington Pl *HPPT/KEY* BN6 ...... 16▮
Hanover Cl *CRAWE* RH10 ....
   PUL/STOR RH20 177
   SELS PO20 .... 26▮
Hanover Ct *MIDH* GU29 122
Hanover Crs *ROTT* BN2 .... 11▮
Hanover Gdns *SWTR* RH13 .... 13▮
Hanover Ms *ROTT* BN2 ....
Hanover St *ROTT* BN2 ....
Hanover Ter *ROTT* BN2 ....
Hanover Wk *PUL/STOR* RH20 .... 18▮
Harbolets Rd *BIL* RH14 .... 13▮
   PUL/STOR RH20 .... 13▮
Harborough Cl *PUL/STOR* RH20 .. 155▮
Harborough Dr *PUL/STOR* RH20 .... 15▮
Harborough Gorse
   PUL/STOR RH20 .... 1▮
Harborough Hl *PUL/STOR* RH20 ...... 1▮
Harborough Meadow
   PUL/STOR RH20 .... 1▮
Harbour Ct *RCCH* PO18 ....
Harbour Rd *BOGR* PO21 ....
   RCCH PO18 ....
Harbour View Rd *BOGR* PO21 .... 26▮
   RCCH PO18 ....
   RCCH PO18 ....
   SHOR BN43 ....
Harcourt Wy *SELS* PO20 .... 2▮
Hardbarrow Woods
   PUL/STOR RH20 .... 1▮
Hardham Cl *ANG/EP* BN16 .... 250▮
   CRAWW RH11 ....
Hardham Rd *CCH* PO19 ....
Hard's Hl *SWTR* RH13 ....
The Hard *MIDOS* PO22 ....
Hardwick Rd *HOVE* BN3 ....
Hardwick Wy *HOVE* BN3 ....
Hardy Cl *CRAWE* RH10 .... 32▮
   HORS RH12 ....
   MIDOS PO22 ....
   SHOR BN43 .... 233▮
Harebell Cl *ANG/EP* BN16 .... 226▮
Harebell Dr *PTSD* BN41 ....
Harefield Av *SALV* BN13 ....
Harefield Rd *MIDOS* PO22 ....
Hare La *CRAWW* RH11 ....
   SELS PO20 ....
Haresfield Ter *SELS* PO20 ....
Harefoot Cl *RCCH* PO18 .... 1▮
Hares La *RCCH* PO18 ....
Harewood Cl *CRAWE* RH10 ....
Harlands Cl *RHWH* RH17 ....
Harlands Rd *HWH* RH16 ....
Harlech Cl *SALV* BN13 ....
Harmans Md *EGRIN* RH19 ....
Harmony Cl *CRAWW* RH11 .... 3▮
Harmony Dr *SELS* PO20 ....
Harmsworth Crs *HOVE* BN3 .... 21▮
Harold Rd *CRAWE* RH10 ....
   EMRTH PO10 ....
Haroldslea *HORL* RH6 ....
Haroldslea Cl *HORL* RH6 ....
Haroldslea Dr *HORL* RH6 ....
Harper Dr *CRAWE* RH10 ....
Harrier Wy *EPSF* GU31 ....
Harrington Pl *BRI* BN1 ....
Harrington Rd *BRI* BN1 ....
Harrington Vls *BRI* BN1 ....
Harriots Cl *SWTR* RH13 ....
Harris Cl *CRAWW* RH11 ....
Harris La *HORN* PO8 ....
Harrison Ct *FIN/BW* BN14 ....
Harrison Rd *FIN/BW* BN14 ....
Harrow Dr *SELS* PO20 ....
Harrow La *PSF* GU32 ....
Harrow Rd *WTHG* BN11 ....
Harsfold Cl *ANG/EP* BN16 ....
Harsfold Rd *ANG/EP* BN16 ....
Hartfield Av *BRI* BN1 ....
Harting Cl *FERR* BN12 ....
Harting Ct *CRAWW* RH11 ....
Harting Down *EPSF* GU31 ....
Harting Rd *LHPTN* BN17 ....
The Hartings *MIDOS* PO22 ....
Hartington Pl *ROTT* BN2 ....
Hartington Rd *ROTT* BN2 ....
Hartington Ter *ROTT* BN2 ....
Hartington Vls *HOVE* BN3 ....
Hartland Ct *EMRTH* PO10 ....
Harvest Cl *HWH* RH16 ....
Harvester Cl *CCH* PO19 ....
Harvesters *HORS* RH12 ....
   HWH RH16 ....
Harvest Hl *EGRIN* RH19 ....
   RHWH RH17 ....
Harvest Rd *CRAWE* RH10 ....
Harvey Cl *CRAWW* RH11 ....
Harvey Rd *FERR* BN12 ....

varden Cl *CRAWE* RH10	34 E3	
wood Av *FERR* BN12	229 H7	
wood Rd *LHPTN* BN17	249 J1	
/TR RH13	5 D4	
Woods Cl *EGRIN* RH19	36 D4	
wood's La *EGRIN* RH19	36 D3	
RIN RH14	36 D5	
e Dr *HASM* GU27	40 D6	
emere Rd *EMRTH* PO10	215 H1	
SM GU27	66 D5	
H GU20	38 D7	
er's La *RCCH* PO18	170 E6	
ett Av East *CRAWE* RH10	3 E3	
ett Av West *CRAWE* RH10	2 C4	
AWW RH11	2 C3	
ngbourne La *PETW* GU28	125 J6	
ocks Ct *CRAWW* RH11	30 D8	
ocks Rd *HPPT/KEY* BN6	164 B6	
e Hl *HASM* GU27	41 F6	
ings Cl *BOGR* PO21	245 H7	
ings Rd *CRAWE* RH10	32 B2	
TT BN2	11 E2	
HG BN11	8 A5	
n End *FROW* RH18	61 K1	
hetts Dr *HASM* GU27	39 J5	
ngate *HORL* RH6	17 K1	
ngate Rd *RHWH* RH17	111 G5	
ngate La *RHWH* RH17	111 G5	
n Hl *HASM* GU27	66 D2	
hlands *HORS* RH12	52 C4	
WH RH17	111 F5	
n La *HASM* GU27	66 D1	
s GU33	62 C7	
erleigh Cl *BOGR* PO21	245 J6	
erleigh Gdns *BOGR* PO21	245 J6	
nt Rd *EMRTH* PO10	214 B3	
lock Cl *MIDOS* PO22	13 E5	
lock Rd *BOGR* PO21	12 B4	
BN1	10 B1	
n Gdns *CRAWE* RH10	34 C2	
ngate *HORS* RH12	5 E2	
n Rd *BIL* RH14	48 B8	
RH14	74 D4	
nside *SHOR* BN43	233 F6	
nstoke Ct *EGRIN* RH19	219 G2	
aven *ANG/EP* BN16	250 C2	
rsham Cl *CRAWE* RH10	3 E3	
ce Cl *ANG/EP* BN16	251 G2	
esbourne Rd *HORS* RH12	5 E2	
esmoor Rd *CRAWW* RH11	30 C7	
hurst Rd *BRI* BN1	213 K5	
hurst Wk *CRAWE* RH10	32 B7	
kins Cl *BOGR* PO21	261 J1	
OR BN43	234 B2	
kins Crs *SHOR* BN43	234 B1	
kins Cl *CRAWE* RH10	3 D5	
OR BN43	234 B2	
sfold La East *HASM* GU27	66 C5	
sfold La West *HASM* GU27	66 C5	
s Pl *MIDOS* PO22	12 A2	
ey Rd *ANG/EP* BN16	250 D1	
nead *CRAWE* RH10	34 E3	
rth Rd *CRAWE* RH10	32 B6	
h Av *CRAWE* RH10	3 F3	
WE RH10	3 F4	
h Cl *CRAWE* RH10	3 F5	
horn Cl *BURH* RH15	139 K6	
PO19	6 B2	
WW RH11	31 G3	
RS RH12	4 B3	
H GU29	121 K5	
horn Crs *FIN/BW* BN14	230 D5	
horn Gdns *FIN/BW* BN14	230 D5	
horn Rd *BOGR* PO21	12 B3	
BW BN14	230 C5	
TN BN17	225 K7	
awthorns *BURH* RH15	139 G6	
/STOR RH20	156 C4	
horn Wy *PTSD* BN41	210 E8	
/STOR RH20	180 E1	
arn Dr *HORS* RH12	52 A4	
on Cl *BOGR* PO21	261 K2	
s Cl *PTSD* BN41	235 G3	
H PO18	194 E4	
s La *SWTR* RH13	75 G2	
sy Rd *LAN/SOMP* BN15	74 D6	
y's Gdns *MIDOS* PO22	13 F4	
nd Rd *HWH* RH16	112 D6	
ng Gdns *SALV* BN13	229 J2	
ng Ri *SALV* BN13	229 J2	
es Rd *FIN/BW* BN14	8 A2	
es Wy *FIN/BW* BN14	8 B2	
'd *CCH* PO19	7 D5	
ards *CRAWE* RH10	32 D2	
ards Cl *MIDOS* PO22	13 F3	
ards Heath Rd *RHWH* RH17	83 H3	
ards Rd *BRI* BN1	213 G5	
H RH16	112 A8	
bank Cl *EPSF* GU31	89 F7	
T GU30	38 C3	
Cl *CRAWE* RH10	34 E3	
WW RH11	31 G2	
D BN41	211 F8	
SWTR RH13	105 G2	
Hazeldene Meads *BRI* BN1	212 D8	
BURH RH15	165 H2	
GSHT GU26	40 A2	
Hazelgrove Rd *HWH* RH16	112 A7	
HORS RH12	77 F2	
Hazelhurst Dr *CRAWE* RH10	32 E5	
Hazelmead Dr *ANG/EP* BN16	251 J2	
Hazel Rd *MIDOS* PO22	12 A2	
Hazel Wy *CRAWE* RH10	34 D3	
Hazelwick Av *CRAWE* RH10	3 F1	
Hazelwick Mill La *CRAWE* RH10	3 F1	
CRAWE RH10	32 B3	
Hazelwick Rd *CRAWE* RH10	3 F2	
Hazelwood Cl *CRAWW* RH11	30 C5	
Hazelwood Cl *CRAWE* RH10	34 B3	
FIN/BW BN14	9 F1	
MIDH GU29	94 B8	
PUL/STOR RH20	181 F1	
Hazelwood Rd *SWTR* RH13	134 C8	
Head Down *EPSF* GU31	89 F8	
Headley Cl *CRAWE* RH10	32 D2	
Headley Rd *LIPH* GU30	38 A5	
Hearn Cl *SELS* PO20	220 E2	
Hearnfield Rd *LHPTN* BN17	225 K7	
Heath Cl *HORS* RH12	50 E8	
HPPT/KEY BN6	163 H7	
SELS PO20	243 G3	
SWTR RH13	79 F5	
Heathcote Dr *EGRIN* RH19	35 K1	
Heather Bank *HWH* RH16	111 J6	
Heather Cl *CRAWE* RH10	4 C2	
HORS RH12	4 C2	
RCCH PO18	193 F8	
Heatherfield *EPSF* GU31	116 B6	
Heatherlands *PUL/STOR* RH20	180 D1	
Heather La *PUL/STOR* RH20	155 K6	
SALV BN13	229 J1	
Heather Wy *PUL/STOR* RH20	180 D2	
Heatherstone Rd *WTHG* BN11	231 G8	
Heatherton Ms *EMRTH* PO10	190 D8	
Heatherway *LING* RH7	21 H4	
Heather Wy *PUL/STOR* RH20	180 D2	
Heatherwood *MIDH* GU29	121 K3	
Heathfield *CRAWE* RH10	32 D2	
Heathfield Av *ANG/EP* BN16	227 H8	
Heathfield Cl *MIDH* GU29	122 A4	
SALV BN13	229 K6	
Heathfield Copse *PUL/STOR* RH20	155 K6	
Heathfield Crs *PTSD* BN41	210 D7	
Heathfield Dr *PTSD* BN41	210 D8	
Heathfield Gdns *MIDH* GU29	122 A4	
Heathfield Gn *MIDH* GU29	122 A4	
Heathfield Pk *MIDH* GU29	121 K4	
Heathfield Pl *MIDOS* PO22	12 C1	
Heath Rd *EPSF* GU31	88 E8	
HWH RH16	112 A6	
Heath Rd East *EPSF* GU31	117 F1	
Heath Rd West *EPSF* GU31	116 E1	
Heath Wy *HORS* RH12	4 C2	
Hebe Rd *SHOR* BN43	233 G4	
Hechle Wd *BOGR* PO21	262 C1	
Hedge End Rd *MIDOS* PO22	223 G5	
Hedgehog La *HASM* GU27	40 D6	
Hedgerow Gdns *EMRTH* PO10	190 D8	
Hedgers Hl *ARUN* BN18	223 K2	
Hedgeside *CRAWW* RH11	55 G2	
Hedgeway *MIDOS* PO22	247 H6	
Heene Pl *WTHG* BN11	8 B5	
Heene Rd *WTHG* BN11	8 B5	
Heene Ter *WTHG* BN11	8 B5	
Heene Wy *WTHG* BN11	8 B4	
Heghbrook Wy *BOGR* PO21	262 D1	
The Heights *BRI* BN1	212 B6	
FIN/BW BN14	230 A1	
Helena Cl *PTSD* BN41	235 G2	
Helston Dr *EMRTH* PO10	190 C8	
Helyer's Gn *LHPTN* BN17	249 J1	
Henderson Rd *CRAWW* RH11	55 F1	
Henderson Wk *STEY/UB* BN44	184 A7	
Hendon Av *ANG/EP* BN16	250 C4	
Hendon St *ROTT* BN2	11 E5	
Henfield Cl *FERR* BN12	228 C7	
Henfield Rd *HFD* BN5	185 G7	
STEY/UB BN44	208 D2	
Henfield Wy *HOVE* BN3	211 K8	
MIDOS PO22	247 H5	
Henge Wy *PTSD* BN41	235 F2	
Hengist Cl *HORS* RH12	77 G2	
Henley Cl *CRAWE* RH10	32 D8	
Henry Av *ANG/EP* BN16	250 C2	
Henry Burt Wy *BURH* RH15	164 E2	
Henry St *BOGR* PO21	12 C1	
Henshaw Cl *CRAWW* RH11	30 D7	
Henson Rd *CRAWE* RH10	32 B4	
Henty Cl *ARUN* BN18	223 K3	
CRAWW RH11	30 C8	
Henty Gdns *CCH* PO19	6 A2	
Henty Rd *FERR* BN12	252 D3	
FIN/BW BN14	8 B3	
Henwood Down *EPSF* GU31	88 E8	
Hepplewhite Cl *CRAWW* RH11	55 F2	
Herald Dr *CCH* PO19	6 C4	
Herbert Rd *BRI* BN1	237 F1	
LAN/SOMP BN15	231 H2	
Hercules Pl *MIDOS* PO22	247 H6	
Hereford Cl *CCH* PO19	219 F2	
CRAWE RH10	55 J1	
Hereford St *ROTT* BN2	11 D5	
Herington Rd *ARUN* BN18	225 F1	
Herm Cl *CRAWW* RH11	54 E1	
Hermione Cl *FERR* BN12	228 B8	
Hermitage Cl *SELS* PO20	243 K2	
Hermitage La *EGRIN* RH19	36 D3	
Hermitage Rd *EGRIN* RH19	22 B8	
Hermits Rd *CRAWE* RH10	3 E1	
Hermonger La *HORS* RH12	48 D1	
Herm Rd *FERR* BN12	252 D3	
Herne Gdns *ANG/EP* BN16	251 F1	
Herne La *ANG/EP* BN16	251 F1	
Herne Rd *EPSF* GU31	88 E8	
Heron Cl *CRAWW* RH11	2 B1	
MIDOS PO22	12 A1	
RCCH PO18	194 E4	
SELS PO20	264 C3	
Herondale *HASM* GU27	40 A5	
Heron Md *BOGR* PO21	261 G4	
Heron Pl *EGRIN* RH19	36 D3	
Heron Quay *EMRTH* PO10	214 E4	
Herons Cl *BIL* RH14	99 H1	
CRAWE RH10	20 C6	
Herons Lea *CRAWE* RH10	20 C6	
Herontye Dr *EGRIN* RH19	36 D3	
Heron Wy *SWTR* RH13	5 F5	
Herrick Cl *CRAWE* RH10	32 C5	
Hersee Wy *SELS* PO20	264 D4	
Hertford Cl *BOGR* PO21	245 H7	
Hertford Rd *BRI* BN1	237 H1	
WTHG BN11	9 D3	
Heston Av *BRI* BN1	213 F4	
Heston Gv *BOGR* PO21	261 K2	
Hewart's La *BOGR* PO21	245 F8	
Hewitts *HFD* BN5	161 G7	
Hewitts End *HFD* BN5	161 G7	
Hewshott Gv *LIPH* GU30	38 E6	
Hewshott La *LIPH* GU30	38 D6	
Hexham Cl *CRAWE* RH10	32 E5	
Heyshott Cl *LAN/SOMP* BN15	232 A3	
Hickman's Cl *HWH* RH16	112 D3	
Hickman's La *HWH* RH16	112 C3	
Hickstead Cl *RHWH* RH17	137 G6	
Hide Gdns *ANG/EP* BN16	250 D1	
Highams Hl *CRAWW* RH11	30 D6	
Highbank *BRI* BN1	212 C6	
High Bar La *PUL/STOR* RH20	156 D5	
Highbarn *FIN/BW* BN14	205 J4	
High Beeches La *RHWH* RH17	81 H1	
High Beech La *HWH* RH16	112 B3	
Highbrook Cl *ROTT* BN2	237 K1	
Highbury Gv *HASM* GU27	40 E3	
Highclere Wy *SALV* BN13	229 F6	
High Cl *PTSD* BN41	234 E2	
Highcroft Av *MIDOS* PO22	12 C3	
Highcroft Cl *MIDOS* PO22	13 D5	
Highcroft Crs *MIDOS* PO22	13 D5	
Highcroft Dr *HORS* RH12	48 C2	
Highcroft Rd *EGRIN* RH19	59 J5	
Highcroft Vls *BRI* BN1	10 A1	
Highdown *STHW* BN42	234 D2	
Highdown Av *SALV* BN13	8 A1	
Highdown Cl *FERR* BN12	228 C8	
STHW BN42	234 D2	
Highdown Ct *CRAWE* RH10	32 B8	
Highdown Dr *LHPTN* BN17	226 A8	
Highdown Rd *HOVE* BN3	10 A3	
Highdown Wy *FERR* BN12	228 C8	
HORS RH12	52 B4	
Highercombe Rd *HASM* GU27	41 G3	
Highfield *LHPTN* BN17	225 H8	
Highfield Cl *ANG/EP* BN16	227 D2	
MIDH GU29	122 C1	
Highfield Crs *BRI* BN1	213 G6	
Highfield Dr *HPPT/KEY* BN6	164 B6	
Highfield Gdns *ANG/EP* BN16	250 D2	
LISS GU33	62 B7	
MIDOS PO22	12 C3	
Highfield La *LIPH* GU30	64 D1	
SELS PO20	220 E4	
Highfield Rd *EGRIN* RH19	22 B8	
MIDOS PO22	12 C3	
PSF GU32	88 D7	
SALV BN13	230 A5	
Highfields *FROW* RH18	61 K1	
Highgate Dr *BOGR* PO21	245 H4	
Highgate Rd *FROW* RH18	61 K2	
Highground La *MIDOS* PO22	223 F7	
Highgrove Gdns *WTHG* BN11	8 B4	
Highland Av *HASM* GU27	12 A4	
Highland Cl *EMRTH* PO10	214 C3	
Highland Ct *HWH* RH16	112 A7	
Highland Rd *CCH* PO19	219 G2	
EMRTH PO10	214 C2	
HWH RH16	112 B8	
Highlands Av *SWTR* RH13	5 D5	
Highlands Cl *HPPT/KEY* BN6	165 G8	

SALV BN13 .... 229 J2
Highlands Crs SWTR RH13 .... 5 D5 🄳
Highlands Dr BURH RH15 .... 139 G7
Highlands Rd PTSD BN41 .... 235 F2
SWTR RH13 .... 5 E5
The Highlands RHWH RH17 .... 111 F3
High La HASM GU27 .... 40 E3
Highleigh Rd SELS PO20 .... 259 H1
High Meadow MIDH GU29 .... 147 K3
High Oaks CRAWW RH11 .... 2 A5
High Park Av HOVE BN3 .... 211 J8
High Pitfold GSHT GU26 .... 39 G7
High Point HWH RH16 .... 112 C8
High Ridge Cl ARUN BN18 .... 225 F2
High Seat Gdns BIL RH14 .... 102 B2
High Spinney PUL/STOR RH20 ... 156 C6 🄳
Highstanding La MIDH GU29 ...... 122 C5
Highstead La PETW GU28 .... 95 K1
High St ANG/EP BN16 .... 227 H6
ARUN BN18 .... 178 A4
ARUN BN18 .... 201 H8
BIL RH14 .... 102 B3
BOGR PO21 .... 12 C5
CRAWW RH11 .... 2 C3 🄳
EGRIN RH19 .... 36 D3
EMRTH PO10 .... 214 D3
EPSF GU31 .... 88 D8
EPSF GU31 .... 116 B6
FIN/BW BN14 .... 205 J6
HASM GU27 .... 41 F5
HFD BN5 .... 161 H7
HORS RH12 .... 28 E5
HPPT/KEY BN6 .... 163 K5
HPPT/KEY BN6 .... 164 A6
HPPT/KEY BN6 .... 165 K8
HWH RH16 .... 112 D3
LHPTN BN17 .... 249 K2 🄳
PETW GU28 .... 126 A3
PTSD BN41 .... 234 E2
PUL/STOR RH20 .... 180 B2
RCCH PO18 .... 216 C5
RHWH RH17 .... 56 B7
RHWH RH17 .... 56 E5
RHWH RH17 .... 81 G3
RHWH RH17 .... 84 D5
RHWH RH17 .... 110 E5
ROTT BN2 .... 11 D5
SALV BN13 .... 8 A1
SELS PO20 .... 220 E5
SELS PO20 .... 264 E4
SHOR BN43 .... 233 G4
STEY/UB BN44 .... 183 K8
STEY/UB BN44 .... 208 C1
SWTR RH13 .... 134 C8
WTHG BN11 .... 9 E4
High Street Gn MFD/CHID GU8 .... 43 J2
The High St CRAWW RH11 .... 2 C3
High Titten ARUN BN18 .... 177 K6
High Trees BOGR PO21 .... 262 C1
HWH RH16 .... 112 B6
SELS PO20 .... 243 G2
Highview LAN/SOMP BN15 .... 231 K2
High Vw SALV BN13 .... 229 K2
Highview Av North BRI BN1 ...... 212 E5
Highview Av South BRI BN1 .... 212 E6
Highview Rd BRI BN1 .... 212 E5 🄳
SELS PO20 .... 222 D4
Highview Wy BRI BN1 .... 212 E6
Highway Cl ROTT BN2 .... 237 K1
Highways PTSD BN41 .... 235 F1 🄳
The Highway ROTT BN2 .... 237 K1
High Weald Landscape Trail
EGRIN RH19 .... 36 B4
EGRIN RH19 .... 59 F6
RHWH RH17 .... 111 H2
Hilary Rd CCH PO19 .... 6 A2
Hildon Cl SALV BN13 .... 229 H6
Hillary Cl EGRIN RH19 .... 36 E1
Hillbank Cl PTSD BN41 .... 210 D8
Hillbarn Av LAN/SOMP BN15 ... 231 J3
Hill Barn La FIN/BW BN14 .... 230 C4
Hillbarn La RCCH PO18 .... 147 J5
Hill Brow HOVE BN3 .... 212 C6
Hillbrow Rd BRI BN1 .... 212 C7
Hillcrest BRI BN1 .... 212 C6
Hill Crest EGRIN RH19 .... 22 C5
Hillcrest Cl CRAWE RH10 .... 32 D5
PUL/STOR RH20 .... 158 A6
RHWH RH17 .... 141 H1
Hillcrest Dr PUL/STOR RH20 .... 158 A7
Hillcrest La RHWH RH17 .... 113 H8
Hillcrest Pk PUL/STOR RH20 .... 155 F1
Hillcroft PTSD BN41 .... 234 D1
Hill Dr HOVE BN3 .... 212 B8
Hill Farm Cl HASM GU27 .... 40 B6 🄳
Hill Farm La PUL/STOR RH20 ... 128 C2
Hill Farm Wy SWTR BN42 .... 234 B1
Hillfield Rd SELS PO20 .... 264 E5
Hill House Cl CRAWE RH10 .... 34 C7
Hillhouse La HORS RH12 .... 47 G2
Hillingdale CRAWW RH11 .... 55 G2
Hill La EPSF GU31 .... 144 C1
MIDOS PO22 .... 223 F2
Hillmead CRAWW RH11 .... 30 D5
Hill Md HORS RH12 .... 51 G8

Hill Pl CRAWW RH11 .... 2 B4 🄳
Hillrise Av LAN/SOMP BN15 ..... 231 J3
Hill Rd HASM GU27 .... 40 E5
LHPTN BN17 .... 250 A1
Hillsboro Rd BOGR PO21 .... 12 B4
Hills Farm La HORS RH12 .... 77 F2
Hillside CRAWE RH10 .... 34 D5
HORS RH12 .... 77 G1
PTSD BN41 .... 235 G2
ROTT BN2 .... 237 K1
STHW BN42 .... 234 D2
Hillside Av FIN/BW BN14 .... 230 B4
Hillside Cl CRAWW RH11 .... 2 A5
EGRIN RH19 .... 22 C8
Hillside Crs ANG/EP BN16 .... 227 J6
LAN/SOMP BN15 .... 231 J3
PUL/STOR RH20 .... 180 D1
Hillside Wk PUL/STOR RH20 .... 180 E1 🄳
RHWH RH17 .... 111 J5
Hillside Wy BRI BN1 .... 212 C7
Hills Pl HORS RH12 .... 77 C1
Hills Rd STEY/UB BN44 .... 207 J1
Hill Ter ARUN BN18 .... 201 F8
Hill Top BRI BN1 .... 212 B6
Hill Top Cl PTSD BN41 .... 234 D1
Hilltop Rd EGRIN RH19 .... 59 G5
Hillview Crs ANG/EP BN16 .... 251 J1
Hillview Gdns CRAWW RH11 ..... 55 G3 🄳
Hillview Ri FIN/BW BN14 .... 229 K2
Hillview Rd FIN/BW BN14 .... 229 K1
Hillybarn Rd CRAWW RH11 .... 50 A2
Hilton Pk SELS PO20 .... 257 K3
Hinde Rd MIDOS PO22 .... 247 G6
Hindhead Cl CRAWW RH11 .... 2 B5 🄳
Hindhead Rd HASM GU27 .... 40 B5
Hindle Cl PUL/STOR RH20 .... 156 B4
Hinton Cl BRI BN1 .... 237 J1
Hislop Wk BOGR PO21 .... 12 C5 🄳
Hither Gn EMRTH PO10 .... 215 J1
Hoadlands EPSF GU31 .... 88 E7
Hoad La HWH RH16 .... 84 F7
Hobart Cl SALV BN13 .... 229 G4
Hobbs Rd CRAWW RH11 .... 54 E2
Hobbs Wy ANG/EP BN16 .... 250 E2
Hobdens La RHWH RH17 .... 84 C4
Hoblands HWH RH16 .... 112 D4
Hobs Acre STEY/UB BN44 .... 208 D2
Hocken Md CRAWE RH10 .... 32 D3
Hodgkin Cl CRAWE RH10 .... 32 B6
Hoe Ct LAN/SOMP BN15 .... 232 C2
Hoefield La RCCH PO18 .... 147 J6
Hoe La ARUN BN18 .... 224 C4
MIDOS PO22 .... 246 E3
RCCH PO18 .... 241 G2
Hoewood HFD BN5 .... 185 G4
Hogarth Rd CRAWE RH10 .... 3 E6
HOVE BN3 .... 235 K4
Hoggarth Cl EPSF GU31 .... 88 E7
Hog La ARUN BN18 .... 178 A4
Hogspudding La RDKG RH5 .... 14 E1
Hogwood Rd BIL RH14 .... 45 J8
Holbein Rd CRAWE RH10 .... 3 E6
Holbrook School La HORS RH12 .. 51 K4
The Holdens RCCH PO18 .... 216 D5
Holder Rd CRAWE RH10 .... 32 B8 🄳
Holders HPPT/KEY BN6 .... 163 G5
Holdfast La HASM GU27 .... 41 H3
Hole St PUL/STOR RH20 .... 182 B1
Holford Gn SELS PO20 .... 265 G4 🄳
Holland Cl BOGR PO21 .... 245 H6
Holland Ms HOVE BN3 .... 236 D6
Holland Rd HOVE BN3 .... 236 D5
STEY/UB BN44 .... 183 K8
Hollands Fld HORS RH12 .... 50 E7
Hollands La HFD BN5 .... 160 B8
Hollands Rd HFD BN5 .... 161 F6
Holland St ROTT BN2 .... 11 D4
Hollands Wy EGRIN RH19 .... 22 E7
HORS RH12 .... 51 F3
Hollin Ct CRAWE RH11 .... 31 J2
Hollingbourne Crs CRAWW RH11 . 55 G3 🄳
Hollingbury Copse BRI BN1 ...... 213 G7
Hollingbury Crs BRI BN1 .... 11 D1
Hollingbury Gdns FIN/BW BN14 . 206 A8
Hollingbury Park Av BRI BN1 ... 237 G1
Hollingbury Pl BRI BN1 .... 11 D1
Hollingbury Ri BRI BN1 .... 213 H8
Hollingbury Ri West BRI BN1 .... 237 G1
Hollingbury Rd BRI BN1 .... 11 D1
Hollingbury Ter BRI BN1 .... 237 G1 🄳
Hollingdean La BRI BN1 .... 11 D2
Hollingdean Rd ROTT BN2 .... 11 D2
Hollingdean St BRI BN1 .... 11 D1
Hollingdean Ter BRI BN1 .... 11 D1
Hollist La EPSF GU31 .... 118 E7 🄳
MIDH GU29 .... 93 K8
The Hollow CRAWW RH11 .... 30 D6
EGRIN RH19 .... 59 H5
HWH RH16 .... 112 D6
PUL/STOR RH20 .... 156 B2
PUL/STOR RH20 .... 177 G3
PUL/STOR RH20 .... 181 J3

Hollybank La EMRTH PO10 19
Hollybush Rd CRAWE RH10 2
CRAWE RH10 2
HORS RH12 2
PUL/STOR RH20 1
PUL/STOR RH20 180
SALV BN13 22
Hollycombe Cl LIPH GU30 6
Holly Ct PUL/STOR RH20 180
Holly Dr LHPTN BN17 22
Hollyhock Wy ANG/EP BN16 226
Hollyridge HASM GU27 40
Holly Rd HWH RH16 1
Holman Cl CRAWW RH11 55
Holmans RHWH RH17 8
Holmbury Cl CRAWW RH11 1
SHOR BN43 2
Holmbush La HFD BN5 1
Holmbush Wy MIDH GU29 1
STHW BN42 2
Holmcroft CRAWE RH10 2
Holmcroft Gdns FIN/BW BN14 ... 2
Holmes Av HOVE BN3 2
Holmesdale Rd BURH RH15 1
Holmes La ANG/EP BN16 2
Holmfield Cl ANG/EP BN16 250
Holming End HORS RH12 52
Holm Oaks SWTR RH13 1
Holmsted Hl RHWH RH17 1
Holt Down EPSF GU31 1
The Holt BURH RH15 1
PUL/STOR RH20 1
Holtye Av EGRIN RH19 2
Holtye Rd EGRIN RH19 2
EGRIN RH19 2
Holyrood Pl CRAWW RH11 2
Home Cl CRAWE RH10 2
Home Farm Rd BRI BN1 2
Homefield Av MIDOS PO22 2
Homefield Crs ARUN BN18 2
Homefield Rd EMRTH PO10 1
WTHG BN11 2
Homelands Av ANG/EP BN16 2
Homelands Copse HASM GU27 2
Home Platt EGRIN RH19 2
Home Rd BRI BN1 2
Homestall Rd EGRIN RH19 2
Homestead La BURH RH15 1
Home Wy EPSF GU31 2
Homewood FIN/BW BN14 2
Homing Gdns MIDOS PO22 2
Honer La SELS PO20 2
Honeybridge La PUL/STOR RH20 . 1
SWTR RH13 1
Honey Cft HOVE BN3 2
Honey La ANG/EP BN16 2
Honeysuckle Cl ANG/EP BN16 ... 226
LAN/SOMP BN15 2
Honeysuckle La CRAWW RH11 2
SALV BN13 2
Honeysuckle Wk HORS RH12 2
Honeywood La RDKG RH5 2
Honeywood Rd SWTR RH13 2
The Hooe LHPTN BN17 2
Hooklands La SWTR RH13 2
Hook La SELS PO20 2
BOGR PO21 2
EGRIN RH19 2
MIDOS PO22 2
RCCH PO18 2
RHWH RH17 2
SELS PO20 2
Hook Lane Cl BOGR PO21 2
The Hooks HFD BN5 2
Hop Garden La SELS PO20 2
The Hop Gdn EPSF GU31 2
The Hopgarton BOGR PO21 24
Hornbeam Wy MIDH GU29 2
Horndean Cl CRAWE RH10 3
Horndean Rd EMRTH PO10 2
Hornet Rd EMRTH PO10 2
The Hornet CCH PO19 2
Horn La HFD BN5 2
Hornshill La HORS RH12 2
Horns La BOGR PO21 2
Horsebridge Hl BIL RH14 2
Horsefield Rd SELS PO20 2
Horsemere Green La LHPTN BN17 . 2
Horseshoe Cl CRAWE RH10 3
The Horse Shoe SELS PO20 2
Horsgate La RHWH RH17 2
Horsham Rd RDKG RH5 2
RDKG RH5 2
BIL RH14 ....

l RH14 .... 74 E5
AN GU6 .... 25 F2
AWW RH11 .... 2 B4
AWW RH11 .... 54 C1
I/BW BN14 .... 205 J4
RS RH12 .... 28 C7
RS RH12 .... 54 B1
PTN BN17 .... 250 B1
TW GU28 .... 126 A2
WH RH17 .... 80 E4
EY/UB BN44 .... 183 J6
ham Rd West LHPTN BN17 .... 250 B1
ted La EGRIN RH19 .... 59 K7
WH RH17 .... 86 D7
ton Rd BRI BN1 .... 11 D1
kins Pl EGRIN RH19 .... 22 D7
pital Vls HWH RH16 .... 140 B1
ham Gdns MIDOS PO22 .... 13 D4 1
ham Wy BOGR PO21 .... 12 C4
ghton Br ARUN BN18 .... 177 K7
ghton La PUL/STOR RH20 .... 177 G4
ghton Rd CRAWE RH10 .... 32 C8 6
Vls HOVE BN3 .... 236 B5
Park Gdns HOVE BN3 .... 236 B3
Park Rd HOVE BN3 .... 236 C2
Park Vls HOVE BN3 .... 236 B3
Park Wy HOVE BN3 .... 236 C2
Pl HOVE BN3 .... 236 B6
St HOVE BN3 .... 236 A5
ard Av BURH RH15 .... 138 E7
LS PO20 .... 257 G4
ard Pl BRI BN1 .... 10 B3
PTN BN17 .... 249 K2 2
ard Rd ARUN BN18 .... 225 G1
AWW RH11 .... 54 B1
N/SOMP BN15 .... 231 J2
PTN BN17 .... 249 J2
TT BN2 .... 11 E3
TR RH13 .... 5 F3
ard St WTHG BN11 .... 8 C3
ards Wy ANG/EP BN16 .... 250 D4 3
ard Ter BRI BN1 .... 10 B3
ake Cl CRAWW RH11 .... 30 B6
e La MIDH GU29 .... 149 F2
son Cl SALV BN13 .... 229 H5
son Dr ANG/EP BN16 .... 251 F3
son Rd CRAWE RH10 .... 3 D5
es Cl BOGR PO21 .... 245 H7
es Rd ROTT BN2 .... 11 D2
ber Av SALV BN13 .... 229 G4
ber Cl LHPTN BN17 .... 250 B3
V BN13 .... 229 G4
phrey's Gap SHOR BN43 .... 233 J5
phrys Rd WTHG BN11 .... 9 D4 4
redsteddle La SELS PO20 .... 258 C1
tanton Cl CRAWW RH11 .... 30 B6 3
er Rd CRAWW RH11 .... 2 C6
RTH PO10 .... 214 E7
ers Cha LIPH GU30 .... 38 B6
ers Cl BOGR PO21 .... 261 K2 1
ers Md SWTR RH13 .... 134 C8
ers Race CCH PO19 .... 194 D8
ers Rd LISS GU33 .... 62 D1
ers Wy CCH PO19 .... 195 F8
ingdon Wy BURH RH15 .... 139 K6
sbottom La LISS GU33 .... 62 B8
nds La MFD/CHID GU8 .... 45 F2
y Rd SALV BN13 .... 229 J5
Av HORS RH12 .... 4 C4
HG BN11 .... 253 K1
Cl ARUN BN18 .... 178 A4
WW RH11 .... 30 D7
H GU30 .... 38 A6
Cottages ARUN BN18 .... 178 A4
Ct HORS RH12 .... 4 C4
Crs PTSD BN41 .... 235 F3
Farm Rd EGRIN RH19 .... 36 B3
field LAN/SOMP BN15 .... 231 K6 1
I/SOMP BN15 .... 231 K6 1
field Cl HWH RH16 .... 140 C1 1
Gdns HPPT/KEY BN6 .... 163 K5
Hl BRI BN1 .... 213 J6
lands BIL RH14 .... 102 A4
ton Cl FIN/BW BN14 .... 230 A3
ton Gv PUL/STOR RH20 .... 179 K1
ton La PUL/STOR RH20 .... 155 J7
Rd ANG/EP BN16 .... 251 G1
RS RH12 .... 4 C4
PT/KEY BN6 .... 164 D7
twood Av EMRTH PO10 .... 215 J2
twood La HWH RH16 .... 140 B3 1
WH RH17 .... 86 B2
on Rd BRI BN1 .... 213 H8
Dr CRAWW RH11 .... 30 C6
La STEY/UB BN44 .... 208 D2
Sq STEY/UB BN44 .... 208 D1 1
St STEY/UB BN44 .... 208 D1
ds Cl CRAWE RH10 .... 3 F4
rs's La RCCH PO18 .... 170 C2
n Rd PSF GU32 .... 88 D8
rion Ct CRAWW RH11 .... 30 C7 3
e Cl WTHG BN11 .... 8 A5
e Rd BRI BN1 .... 237 G1
HG BN11 .... 8 A5

I

Icarus Wy MIDOS PO22 .... 247 G6
Iden Hurst HPPT/KEY BN6 .... 164 A4
Ifield Av CRAWW RH11 .... 2 B2
CRAWW RH11 .... 30 E2
Ifield Dr CRAWW RH11 .... 30 E4
Ifield Gn CRAWW RH11 .... 30 E2
Ifield Rd CRAWW RH11 .... 2 B3
HORL RH6 .... 16 C6
Ifield St CRAWW RH11 .... 30 D3
Ifield Wd CRAWW RH11 .... 30 B2
Ifold Bridge La BIL RH14 .... 45 J7
Ifoldhurst BIL RH14 .... 71 J1
Ilex Cl ANG/EP BN16 .... 250 D3
Ilex Wk HISD PO11 .... 238 A8
Ilex Wy FERR BN12 .... 253 F1
MIDOS PO22 .... 247 J5
Imberhorne La EGRIN RH19 .... 21 K8
Imberhorne Wy EGRIN RH19 .... 21 K8
Infirmary Dr SWTR RH13 .... 76 E5
Infirmary Ter CCH PO19 .... 6 B1
Ingham Dr BRI BN1 .... 213 K5
Ingle Green Cl FERR BN12 .... 252 C3 3
Ingleside Crs LAN/SOMP BN15 .... 232 A6
Ingleside Rd LAN/SOMP BN15 .... 232 A6 2
Inglewood Dr BOGR PO21 .... 261 J2
Ingram Cl ANG/EP BN16 .... 250 D2
HORS RH12 .... 77 G1
Ingram Crs HOVE BN3 .... 235 J4 1
Ingram Crs East HOVE BN3 .... 235 J4
Ingram Crs West HOVE BN3 .... 235 J4
Ingram Rd STEY/UB BN44 .... 207 J1
Ingram's Green La MIDH GU29 .... 120 C5
MIDH GU29 .... 146 B1
Inholmes Cl BURH RH15 .... 165 H1
Inholmes Park Rd BURH RH15 .... 139 H8
Inkpen La FROW RH18 .... 61 K2
Inlands Rd RCCH PO18 .... 215 K2
Inmans La PSF GU32 .... 89 F6
Innerwyke Cl MIDOS PO22 .... 247 F6 1
Innes Rd HORS RH12 .... 5 E3
Innovation Dr HPPT/KEY BN6 .... 164 D1
Inval Hl HASM GU27 .... 40 E3
Inverness Rd ROTT BN2 .... 11 E2 3
Inwood Crs BRI BN1 .... 236 D2
Inwood Rd LISS GU33 .... 62 A8
Iona Cl CRAWW RH11 .... 2 A6
Iona Wy HWH RH16 .... 112 A7 3
Iping La MIDH GU29 .... 92 E7
Iping Rd LIPH GU30 .... 92 B1
Irene Av LAN/SOMP BN15 .... 231 K4
Irvine Rd LHPTN BN17 .... 249 K3
Irving Wk CRAWE RH10 .... 3 D6
Irwin Dr HORS RH12 .... 51 G8
Isaac's La BURH RH15 .... 139 F5
Isabel Crs HOVE BN3 .... 235 J3
Isfield Rd BRI BN1 .... 237 J1
Island La SELS PO20 .... 264 C3
Island Loop SELS PO20 .... 264 C3
Islingword Pl ROTT BN2 .... 11 E4
Islingword Rd ROTT BN2 .... 11 D3
Islingword St ROTT BN2 .... 11 D4
Itchen Cl PSF GU32 .... 116 C1
Itchenor Rd SELS PO20 .... 240 D4
Itchingfield Rd SWTR RH13 .... 76 A3 1
Ivanhoe Cl CRAWW RH11 .... 31 H2
Ivanhoe Pl MIDOS PO22 .... 247 G6
Iveagh Cl CRAWW RH11 .... 55 G2
Ivory Pl ROTT BN2 .... 11 D4
Ivory Wk CRAWW RH11 .... 30 C8 2
Ivy Arch Cl FIN/BW BN14 .... 205 K5
Ivy Arch Rd FIN/BW BN14 .... 9 D3
Ivy Cl PUL/STOR RH20 .... 158 A6
SELS PO20 .... 222 B4
SWTR RH13 .... 104 E2
Ivy Crs MIDOS PO22 .... 12 C3
Ivydale Rd BOGR PO21 .... 245 J7
Ivydene Crs RCCH PO18 .... 216 B4
Ivy Dene La EGRIN RH19 .... 37 H5
Ivydore Av SALV BN13 .... 229 H3
Ivydore Cl SALV BN13 .... 229 H4
Ivy La MIDOS PO22 .... 12 C3
PUL/STOR RH20 .... 158 A5
SELS PO20 .... 222 B4
Ivy Pl HOVE BN3 .... 236 D6 5
WTHG BN11 .... 8 B5

J

Jackdaw Cl CRAWW RH11 .... 2 B1
Jackdaw La HORS RH12 .... 5 D2
Jacken Cl MIDOS PO22 .... 247 G7
Jackrells La SWTR RH13 .... 77 H8
Jackson Rd CRAWW RH11 .... 55 F3
Jackson St ROTT BN2 .... 11 D3
Jacobean Cl CRAWE RH10 .... 32 C6
James Cl SALV BN13 .... 229 K5
James St SELS PO20 .... 265 F5
James Watt Wy CRAWE RH10 .... 18 A7
Jane Murray Wy BURH RH15 .... 164 E2
HPPT/KEY BN6 .... 138 C7
Janes Cl BURH RH15 .... 139 J6
Janes La BURH RH15 .... 139 J6
PETW GU28 .... 96 C8
Jan Smuts Cl LISS GU33 .... 62 D2
Japonica Cl SHOR BN43 .... 233 K2
Japonica Wy HAV PO9 .... 190 A7
Jarvis La STEY/UB BN44 .... 183 K8
Jarvis Rd ARUN BN18 .... 201 F8
Jasmine Cl ANG/EP BN16 .... 226 C8 8
Javelin Rd EMRTH PO10 .... 214 E8
Jay Cl SWTR RH13 .... 105 G1
Jays Cl LHPTN BN17 .... 249 K1
Jay's La HASM GU27 .... 41 K8
The Jays BURH RH15 .... 138 E7
Jefferies RHWH RH17 .... 86 A7
Jefferies La FERR BN12 .... 253 G2
Jeffreys Av CCH PO19 .... 219 G2
Jengers Md BIL RH14 .... 102 B2
Jenner Rd CRAWE RH10 .... 17 K8
Jeremy's La RHWH RH17 .... 109 F5
Jerrard Rd SELS PO20 .... 220 E1
Jersey Rd CRAWW RH11 .... 54 E1
FERR BN12 .... 252 D2
Jersey St ROTT BN2 .... 11 D4
Jervis Av ANG/EP BN16 .... 251 F2
Jesmond Rd HOVE BN3 .... 235 J4
Jesters BURH RH15 .... 139 J4
The Jetty MIDOS PO22 .... 248 A7
Jevington Cl SALV BN13 .... 229 F6
Jevington Dr ROTT BN2 .... 11 F1
Jew St BRI BN1 .... 10 C5 8
Jib Cl ANG/EP BN16 .... 226 C8 9
Jobes RHWH RH17 .... 83 F2
Job's La HPPT/KEY BN6 .... 138 A5
Jobson's La HASM GU27 .... 68 A3
John Arundel Rd CCH PO19 .... 6 A2
Johnson Dr BURH RH15 .... 139 K8
Johnson Wk CRAWE RH10 .... 2 C6
Johnson Wy ARUN BN18 .... 248 B1
John St BOGR PO21 .... 12 C5 2
ROTT BN2 .... 11 D5
SHOR BN43 .... 233 G4
Jolesfield CRAWW RH11 .... 30 D8
SWTR RH13 .... 134 B7
Jolliffe Rd SELS PO20 .... 257 G4
Jones Sq SELS PO20 .... 265 F5
Jordans Cl CRAWW RH11 .... 2 C1
Jordans Crs CRAWW RH11 .... 31 H2
The Jordans EGRIN RH19 .... 36 C3
Joyce Cl LHPTN BN17 .... 225 J8
Joys Cft CCH PO19 .... 7 D2
Jubilee Av ANG/EP BN16 .... 250 E1
Jubilee Cl HWH RH16 .... 112 C7
Jubilee Rd BURH RH15 .... 164 E1
CCH PO19 .... 6 C2
HORS RH12 .... 48 B3
PTSD BN41 .... 234 E3
Jubilee Wk CRAWE RH10 .... 3 F3 2
Jubilee Wy PUL/STOR RH20 .... 156 D8
Judge's Ter EGRIN RH19 .... 36 C3 3
Juggs La PUL/STOR RH20 .... 156 C2
The Juggs PUL/STOR RH20 .... 156 C2
Julian Rd HOVE BN3 .... 10 A3
Junction Cl ARUN BN18 .... 248 B1
BURH RH15 .... 139 J7
Junction Rd BURH RH15 .... 165 H1
June Cl BOGR PO21 .... 261 G3
June La MIDH GU29 .... 121 K3
June Mdw MIDH GU29 .... 121 K3
Juniper Cl MIDOS PO22 .... 247 J5 2
PTSD BN41 .... 211 F8 1
SALV BN13 .... 229 G6
Juniper Rd CRAWW RH11 .... 31 G2
Jupp's La FERR BN12 .... 229 F8
Jura Cl CRAWW RH11 .... 2 A6
Jury La SELS PO20 .... 242 D6
Juxon Cl CCH PO19 .... 6 C4
CRAWW RH11 .... 30 D7

K

Kearsley Dr FIN/BW BN14 .... 230 A2
Keats Cl HORS RH12 .... 52 A4
Keats Pl EGRIN RH19 .... 36 B2 3
Keats Wk BOGR PO21 .... 12 A5
Keble Cl BOGR PO21 .... 245 H8
CRAWE RH10 .... 32 D2
Keelson Wy ANG/EP BN16 .... 250 C1
Keepers Wd CCH PO19 .... 195 F8
Kelly Rd HOVE BN3 .... 236 D2
Kelsey Av EMRTH PO10 .... 215 J2
Kelsey Cl LISS GU33 .... 62 A6
Kelso Cl CRAWE RH10 .... 32 E4
SALV BN13 .... 229 J7
Kelvin La CRAWE RH10 .... 31 K1
Kelvin Wy CRAWE RH10 .... 31 K1
Kemnal Pk HASM GU27 .... 41 F3
Kemps HPPT/KEY BN6 .... 163 K5
Kempshott Rd HORS RH12 .... 4 A3
Kemp St BRI BN1 .... 10 C4
Kemp Town Pl ROTT BN2 .... 11 F6 8
Kendal Cl LHPTN BN17 .... 226 C8 10

Kendale Cl *CRAWE* RH10 .... 56 C1
Kendal Rd *CRAWE* BN3 .... 235 K3
  LAN/SOMP BN15 .... 231 J5
Kenilworth Cl *CRAWW* RH11 .... 55 F1
Kenilworth Rd *BOGR* PO21 .... 245 J7
Kenlegh *BOGR* PO21 .... 262 C1
Kenmara Cl *CRAWE* RH10 .... 32 B2
Kenmara Ct *CRAWE* RH10 .... 32 B1
Kenmure Av *EGRIN* RH19 .... 22 B8
Kennedy Av *EGRIN* RH19 .... 22 B8
Kennedy Rd *SWTR* RH13 .... 4 C6
Kennel Hl *RCCH* PO18 .... 196 A4
Kennel La *HORL* RH6 .... 17 H1
  SWTR RH13 .... 134 A1
Kennet Cl *CRAWW* RH11 .... 320 D6
  SALV BN13 .... 229 H4
Kennet Rd *PSF* GU32 .... 116 C1
Kensington Gdns *BRI* BN1 .... 10 C4
Kensington Pl *BRI* BN1 .... 10 C4
Kensington Rd *CCH* PO19 .... 7 E3
  CRAWW RH11 .... 55 F1
Kensington St *BRI* BN1 .... 10 C4
Kent Cl *SHOR* BN43 .... 234 A4
Kenton Rd *HOVE* BN3 .... 235 H4
Kent Rd *CCH* PO19 .... 7 D2
  LHPTN BN17 .... 249 K1
Kents Rd *HWH* RH16 .... 112 B8
Kent St *SWTR* RH13 .... 136 A5
Kentstreet La *SWTR* RH13 .... 136 A2
Kenwards *BRI* BN1 .... 213 K4
Kerves La *SWTR* RH13 .... 78 A5
Kestrel Cl *CRAWW* RH11 .... 2 B1
  HORS RH12 .... 5 D2
  HOVE BN3 .... 236 D3
  SELS PO20 .... 257 K5
Kestrel Ct *BOGR* PO21 .... 261 G4
Kestrel Wy *LHPTN* BN17 .... 225 J7
Keswick Cl *CRAWW* RH11 .... 30 D7
  FERR BN12 .... 229 H6
Ketche's La *RHWH* RH17 .... 114 C4
  UCK TN22 .... 114 C5
Ketch Rd *LHPTN* BN17 .... 250 C3
Kewell's Cnr *SELS* PO20 .... 241 J6
Kew Gdns *BOGR* PO21 .... 245 H7
Kew St *BRI* BN1 .... 10 B4
Keymer Ct *BURH* RH15 .... 165 H1
Keymer Crs *FERR* BN12 .... 253 G2
Keymer Gdns *BURH* RH15 .... 165 H2
Keymer Pde *BURH* RH15 .... 165 H1
Keymer Pk *HPPT/KEY* BN6 .... 165 H8
Keymer Rd *BRI* BN1 .... 213 H5
  BURH RH15 .... 165 H5
  CRAWW RH11 .... 30 C8
  HPPT/KEY BN6 .... 165 F8
Keymer Wy *FERR* BN12 .... 253 G2
Keynor La *SELS* PO20 .... 259 K3
Keysford La *HWH* RH16 .... 85 G8
Kidborough Rd *CRAWW* RH11 .... 30 D7
Kidbrook *HWH* RH16 .... 112 E5
Kidders La *HFD* BN5 .... 161 F3
Kidd Rd *CCH* PO19 .... 219 H2
Kidmans Cl *HORS* RH12 .... 5 E1
Killinghurst La *HASM* GU27 .... 42 A5
Kilmore Cl *FIN/BW* BN14 .... 205 J5
Kilnbarn Wy *HWH* RH16 .... 139 K1
Kilnfield Rd *HORS* RH12 .... 48 B3
Kiln Flds *HASM* GU27 .... 40 E3
Kiln La *EPSF* GU31 .... 116 A7
  HWH RH16 .... 112 D6
The Kiln *BURH* RH15 .... 139 J8
Kilnwood Cl *SELS* PO20 .... 265 G4
Kilnwood La *HORS* RH12 .... 29 J8
Kilwich Cl *MIDOS* PO22 .... 247 H5
Kimber Cl *LAN/SOMP* BN15 .... 231 K6
Kimberley La *CRAWE* RH10 .... 32 B4
  LISS GU33 .... 62 C1
  ROTT BN2 .... 11 F2
Kimbers *F* GU32 .... 88 C7
Kimbridge Rd *SELS* PO20 .... 257 K5
Kindersley Cl *EGRIN* RH19 .... 23 F8
Kinfauns Dr *SALV* BN13 .... 229 H1
King Alfred Cl *STEY/UB* BN44 .... 183 K8
King Edward Av *FIN/BW* BN14 .... 9 D2
King Edward Cl *FIN/BW* BN14 .... 9 E2
  SWTR RH13 .... 76 D5
King Edward Rd *SWTR* RH13 .... 76 D5
Kingfisher Cl *CRAWE* RH10 .... 32 A2
  SALV BN13 .... 229 G6
Kingfisher Ri *EGRIN* RH19 .... 36 D3
Kingfisher Wy *HORS* RH12 .... 4 B2
King George Av *EGRIN* RH19 .... 22 A8
  EPSF GU31 .... 88 D7
King George Gdns *CCH* PO19 .... 6 B1
King George Rd *SHOR* BN43 .... 234 A3
King George Vi Av *HOVE* BN3 .... 211 K8
King George Vi Dr *HOVE* BN3 .... 212 A8
King Pl *BRI* BN1 .... 10 C5
King's Arms Hl *ARUN* BN18 .... 201 H8
King's Av *CCH* PO19 .... 6 B5
King's Barn La *STEY/UB* BN44 .... 184 A6
King's Barn Vls *STEY/UB* BN44 .... 184 A8
Kingsbridge Ms *SALV* BN13 .... 229 H4

Kingsbury Rd *BRI* BN1 .... 10 C3
Kingsbury St *BRI* BN1 .... 10 C3
Kings Cl *ARUN* BN18 .... 223 K8
  LAN/SOMP BN15 .... 232 B6
Kings Copse *EGRIN* RH19 .... 36 D3
Kingscote Hl *CRAWW* RH11 .... 2 B1
Kings Ct *SELS* PO20 .... 265 F3
Kings Crs *SHOR* BN43 .... 233 F6
Kings Dr *BOGR* PO21 .... 261 J3
  HPPT/KEY BN6 .... 165 F2
  MIDH GU29 .... 93 K4
  SHOR BN43 .... 233 F5
King's Esp *HOVE* BN3 .... 236 A6
Kingsey Av *EMRTH* PO10 .... 214 C5
Kingsfernsden La *PSF* GU32 .... 88 E6
Kingsfield *PUL/STOR* RH20 .... 180 C1
Kingsfold Cl *BIL* RH14 .... 102 B5
Kings Gap *SHOR* BN43 .... 233 F6
King's Gdns *HOVE* BN3 .... 236 B6
Kingsham Av *CCH* PO19 .... 7 D4
Kingsham Rd *CCH* PO19 .... 6 C4
Kingsland *RDKG* RH5 .... 14 C2
Kingsland Cl *PUL/STOR* RH20 .... 180 C1
  SHOR BN43 .... 234 A4
Kingsland Rd *FIN/BW* BN14 .... 230 E5
Kings La *PUL/STOR* RH20 .... 153 J4
  PUL/STOR RH20 .... 155 H1
  SWTR RH13 .... 77 G7
  SWTR RH13 .... 135 K3
Kingslea *SWTR* RH13 .... 5 D4
Kingsley Cl *FIN/BW* BN14 .... 9 F2
Kingsley Rd *BRI* BN1 .... 236 D2
  CRAWW RH11 .... 30 E8
Kingsmead *LHPTN* BN17 .... 225 J6
  MIDOS PO22 .... 13 E4
Kingsmead *STEY/UB* BN44 .... 207 K2
Kingsmead Pl *HORS* RH12 .... 50 D8
Kingsmead Rd *HORS* RH12 .... 248 A5
  MIDOS PO22 .... 248 A5
Kings Ms *HOVE* BN3 .... 236 B5
Kingsmill Rd *MIDOS* PO22 .... 223 G5
King's Pde *BOGR* PO21 .... 262 D1
Kingspit La *PETW* GU28 .... 126 C4
Kings Platt *SWTR* RH13 .... 132 C3
Kings Ride *BURH* RH15 .... 165 K2
King's Rd *BRI* BN1 .... 10 C6
  EMRTH PO10 .... 214 C5
  HASM GU27 .... 40 C5
  HWH RH16 .... 140 B1
  LAN/SOMP BN15 .... 232 A6
  PSF GU32 .... 88 B7
  STHW BN42 .... 234 B2
  SWTR RH13 .... 5 D4
King's Stone Av *STEY/UB* BN44 .... 208 B1
King's Ter *EMRTH* PO10 .... 214 D3
Kingsthorpe Rd *HOVE* BN3 .... 235 J3
Kingston Bay Rd *SHOR* BN43 .... 234 A5
Kingston Broadway *SHOR* BN43 .... 234 A2
Kingston Cl *HOVE* BN3 .... 235 J1
  SHOR BN43 .... 234 A2
Kingston La *ANG/EP* BN16 .... 251 K2
  SHOR BN43 .... 234 B4
Kingston Wy *SHOR* BN43 .... 234 A4
King St *ARUN* BN18 .... 201 G8
  BRI BN1 .... 10 C5
  EMRTH PO10 .... 191 F9
  EMRTH PO10 .... 214 E3
  FIN/BW BN14 .... 9 D2
Kings Wk *SHOR* BN43 .... 233 F6
Kings Wy *BURH* RH15 .... 165 J2
Kingsway *BOGR* PO21 .... 262 D2
  HOVE BN3 .... 235 K5
  SELS PO20 .... 265 G5
Kingswood *PUL/STOR* RH20 .... 156 A4
Kingswood Cl *CRAWW* RH11 .... 55 G3
Kingswood Firs *GSHT* GU26 .... 39 J1
Kingswood La *GSHT* GU26 .... 39 J1
Kingswood Rd *ROTT* BN2 .... 10 C5
Kinnell Ct *EMRTH* PO10 .... 214 D3
Kinniburgh Dr *LING* RH7 .... 22 E2
Kipling Av *FERR* BN12 .... 229 F8
Kipling Cl *CRAWE* RH10 .... 32 C3
Kipling Ct *SWTR* RH13 .... 5 F3
Kipling Wy *EGRIN* RH19 .... 36 A2
Kirdford Cl *ANG/EP* BN16 .... 250 D3
  BURH RH15 .... 165 J2
  CRAWW RH11 .... 30 E3
Kirdford Rd *ARUN* BN18 .... 225 G1
Kirkby Cl *RCCH* PO18 .... 197 F8
Kirkland Cl *ANG/EP* BN16 .... 250 D2
Kitchener Cl *LISS* GU33 .... 62 C1
Kites Cl *CRAWW* RH11 .... 2 C5
Kithurst Cl *ANG/EP* BN16 .... 250 D2
  CRAWW RH11 .... 2 C5
  FERR BN12 .... 229 F7
Kithurst Crs *FERR* BN12 .... 229 F7
Kithurst Farm Rd *PUL/STOR* RH20 .... 179 K3
Kithurst La *PUL/STOR* RH20 .... 180 A2
Kithurst Pk *PUL/STOR* RH20 .... 179 K2
Kitsmead *CRAWE* RH10 .... 33 G1
Kittiwake *CRAWW* RH11 .... 30 D3
Knepp Cl *CRAWE* RH10 .... 32 C5
Knighton Cl *CRAWE* RH10 .... 32 D1
Knightscroft Av *ANG/EP* BN16 .... 250 E3
Knightscroft Cl *ANG/EP* BN16 .... 250 D3

Knight's Hl *RCCH* PO18 17
Knob Hl *HORS* RH12 5
Knockhundred La *GSHT* GU26 3
Knockhundred Rw *MIDH* GU29 12
Knole Cl *CRAWE* RH10 32
Knole Gv *EGRIN* RH19 2
Knoll Cl *HOVE* BN3 23
Knowle Cl *CRAWE* RH10 1
Knowle Dr *CRAWE* RH10 1
Knowles Meadow *LISS* GU33 9
The Knowle *RHWH* RH17 1
Knoyle Rd *BRI* BN1 21
Kymer Gdns *HPPT/KEY* BN6 16
Kynon Gdns *MIDOS* PO22 24
Kyoto Ct *BOGR* PO21 26

L

Laburnum Av *HOVE* BN3 23
Laburnum Cl *FERR* BN12 252
  LAN/SOMP BN15 231
Laburnum Gv *CCH* PO19 7
  MIDOS PO22 2
Laburnum Wy *HWH* RH16 1
Lackenhurst La *SWTR* RH13 10
Lacock Cl *SELS* PO20 2
Ladbroke Hurst *LING* RH7 ....
Ladies Mile Cl *BRI* BN1 2
Ladies' Mile Rd *BRI* BN1 21
Ladydell Rd *WTHG* BN11 ....
Lady Margaret Rd *CRAWW* RH11 ....
Ladymead *BURH* RH15 139
Ladymead Cl *CRAWE* RH10 32
Ladysmith Rd *ROTT* BN2 1
Lagness Rd *SELS* PO20 2
Lagoon Rd *BOGR* PO21 2
Lagwood Cl *HPPT/KEY* BN6 1
Laine Cl *BRI* BN1 2
Laines Rd *STEY/UB* BN44 2
Lake La *ARUN* BN18 2
  MIDOS PO22 2
Lake Rd *CCH* PO19 ....
Lakers Meadow *BIL* RH14 10
Lakeside *HORS* RH12 ....
  MIDH GU29 1
Lakeside Dr *SWTR* RH13 1
Lake Vw *BOGR* PO21 2
Lake View Rd *CRAWE* RH10 2
  EGRIN RH19 ....
Lambert's La *MIDH* GU29 1
Lambeth Cl *CRAWW* RH11 ....
Lambleys La *FIN/BW* BN14 23
Lambourn Cl *EGRIN* RH19 22
Lambourne Cl *BRI* BN1 2
  CRAWE RH10 ....
Lambourne La *LIPH* GU30 ....
Lambourne Rd *BRI* BN1 2
Lambs Crs *HORS* RH12 ....
Lambs Farm Cl *HORS* RH12 ....
Lambs Farm Rd *HORS* RH12 ....
Lambs Green Rd *HORS* RH12 ....
Lammas Cl *LHPTN* BN17 2
Lamorna Gdns *FERR* BN12 252
  SELS PO20 222
Lamorna Gv *FIN/BW* BN14 2
Lanark Cl *SWTR* RH13 ....
Lancaster Cl *CRAWE* RH10 32
Lancaster Dr *EGRIN* RH19 ....
Lancaster Pl *MIDOS* PO22 ....
Lancaster Rd *BRI* BN1 2
  FERR BN12 2
Lancastrian Gra *CCH* PO19 ....
Lancelot Cl *CRAWW* RH11 3
Lancing Cl *CRAWW* RH11 ....
  LAN/SOMP BN15 ....
Lancing Pk *LAN/SOMP* BN15 2
Landseer Dr *SELS* PO20 2
Landseer Rd *HOVE* BN3 2
Lane End Dr *EMRTH* PO10 2
Lane End Rd *MIDOS* PO22 2
Lanercost Rd *CRAWW* RH11 2
The Lane *BIL* RH14 2
  CCH PO19 2
Lanfranc Rd *FIN/BW* BN14 2
Langbury Cl *FERR* BN12 2
Langbury La *FERR* BN12 2
Langdale Av *CCH* PO19 ....
Langdale Cl *LAN/SOMP* BN15 23
Langdale Gdns *HOVE* BN3 2
Langdale Rd *CRAWW* RH11 3
  HOVE BN3 2
Langham Gdns *WTHG* BN11 ....
Langhurst Cl *HORS* RH12 ....
Langhurst La *HORS* RH12 ....
Langhurstwood Rd *HORS* RH12 ....
Langley Dr *CRAWW* RH11 ....
Langley Gv *BOGR* PO21 2
Langley La *CRAWW* RH11 ....
Langley Pde *CRAWW* RH11 ....
Langley Pl *CRAWW* RH11 3
Langley Wk *CRAWW* RH11 ....
Langmead Cl *LHPTN* BN17 24
Langridge Dr *EGRIN* RH19 3

... BN41 ..... 235 F1
...dge La HWH RH16 ..... 112 C6
...dge La BURH RH15 ..... 138 E6
...tone Cl CRAWE RH10 ..... 32 C8
...en Cl SELS PO20 ..... 264 E5
...en La HPPT/KEY BN6 ..... 163 J3
...on Rd CCH PO19 ..... 6 A2
... SW BN14 ..... 9 D2
...ry Rd CRAWW RH11 ..... 55 F2
...own Cl HORS RH12 ..... 52 D5
...owne Cl ANG/EP BN16 ..... 227 H5
...G BN11 ..... 8 A4
...owne Ct WTHG BN11 ..... 8 A4
...wne Ms HOVE BN3 ..... 236 D5
...wne Pl HOVE BN3 ..... 236 D6
...wne Rd ANG/EP BN16 ..... 227 H6
... BN3 ..... 236 D5
...N BN17 ..... 9 D2
...G BN11 ..... 8 A4
...wne Sq HOVE BN3 ..... 236 D6
...wne St HOVE BN3 ..... 236 D5
...wne Wy ANG/EP BN16 ..... 227 H5
...ds ANG/EP BN16 ..... 228 C8
... Cl HORS RH12 ..... 5 F1
...g Cl SWTR RH13 ..... 5 E4
...l ANG/EP BN16 ..... 251 F2
...O19 ..... 219 F1
...U30 ..... 38 B8
...s PO22 ..... 12 B1
...End HORS RH12 ..... 4 A4
...STOR RH20 ..... 156 B4
...rches HORS RH12 ..... 52 E5
...eld Cl BOGR PO21 ..... 262 A2
...Vy HWH RH16 ..... 112 D7
...ibe Rd PSF GU32 ..... 116 B2
...cres SELS PO20 ..... 264 E4
...l SHOR BN43 ..... 234 A4
...d Cl LAN/SOMP BN15 ..... 232 B6
...d Wy BRI BN1 ..... 213 G7
... HOVE BN3 ..... 211 J8
... Rd HORL RH6 ..... 17 H4
... CRAWW RH11 ..... 2 B1
...U30 ..... 38 A4
...r Wy SWTR RH13 ..... 77 G8
...er Rd ANG/EP BN16 ..... 251 J2
...ere CRAWE RH10 ..... 19 K8
... Rd SELS PO20 ..... 264 E5
... Cl CRAWW RH11 ..... 31 H2
... Rd WTHG BN11 ..... 253 K2
...r CRAWE RH10 ..... 32 D6
...Cl EMRTH PO10 ..... 215 H1
...on Rd HORS RH12 ..... 5 E2
...y La RHWH RH17 ..... 87 H3
...Cl BURH RH15 ..... 139 K3
...E RH10 ..... 3 F6
...BN13 ..... 229 G6
...Dene EGRIN RH19 ..... 36 D2
...w MIDOS PO22 ..... 12 B2
...nt PUL/STOR RH20 ..... 154 E1
...rels HFD BN5 ..... 161 C6
...RH13 ..... 105 F1
...Vk SWTR RH13 ..... 5 E6
...on Rd BRI BN1 ..... 236 E1
...Cl CRAWW RH11 ..... 30 D6
...BN12 ..... 228 E7
...Down Rd RCCH PO18 ..... 194 E4
...e RH10 ..... 195 F8
...st PSF GU32 ..... 88 C7
...er Hl SHOR BN43 ..... 233 K2
...er St ROTT BN2 ..... 11 D6
...on Cl CRAWW RH11 ..... 30 D4
...on Rd FIN/BW BN14 ..... 230 B5
...t FERR BN12 ..... 229 G8
...Wy ANG/EP BN16 ..... 251 J2
...ns ANG/EP BN16 ..... 251 J4
...OMP BN15 ..... 231 J4
...n BOGR PO21 ..... 262 B2
...ce Av ANG/EP BN16 ..... 251 F1
...ce Cl SELS PO20 ..... 265 F5
...ce Rd HOVE BN3 ..... 235 K4
...a HWH RH16 ..... 112 C6
...CRAWW RH11 ..... 30 C6
...s La HFD BN5 ..... 160 E6
...s Rd PTSD BN41 ..... 234 E4
...ne MIDOS PO22 ..... 248 A6
...e EMRTH PO10 ..... 215 H3
...RAWW RH11 ..... 30 D6
...n La PUL/STOR RH20 ..... 153 H1
...t Court Rd BRI BN1 ..... 212 E8
... Cl MIDOS PO22 ..... 247 K6
... Rd RCCH PO18 ..... 217 G6
... MIDOS PO22 ..... 12 B3
...s ANG/EP BN16 ..... 227 G8
...ttle La CCH PO19 ..... 7 E3
...d HORL RH6 ..... 17 K2
...eld Rd LAN/SOMP BN15 ..... 231 J6
...ol La SWTR RH13 ..... 5 F3
...: BOGR PO21 ..... 262 B1
... SALV BN13 ..... 229 F6
...RH13 ..... 105 G1

Leeward Cl SALV BN13 ..... 229 K6
Leeward Rd LHPTN BN17 ..... 250 B2
SALV BN13 ..... 229 K6
Legion Wy SELS PO20 ..... 257 K5
Legsheath La EGRIN RH19 ..... 60 D4
Leicester St ROTT BN2 ..... 11 D5
Leicester Vls HORS RH12 ..... 235 H4
Leighlands CRAWE RH10 ..... 32 C3
Leigh Rd FIN/BW BN14 ..... 230 D5
Leighton Av FIN/BW BN14 ..... 230 E3
Leighton Rd HOVE BN3 ..... 236 A3
RHWH RH17 ..... 86 A2
Leinster Gdns MIDOS PO22 ..... 247 H6
Leith View Rd RHWH RH12 ..... 5 F2
Lemmington Wy HORS RH12 ..... 52 B4
Lenhurst Wy SALV BN13 ..... 229 K6
Lennox Rd CCH PO19 ..... 7 D2
HOVE BN3 ..... 235 K3
SHOR BN43 ..... 233 K3
WTHG BN11 ..... 9 D3
Lennox St BOGR PO21 ..... 12 C6
ROTT BN2 ..... 11 D5
Leonardslee Cl CRAWE RH10 ..... 32 B8
Leonard Wy SWTR RH13 ..... 5 E5
Leonora Dr BOGR PO21 ..... 261 J1
Leopold Cl MIDOS PO22 ..... 13 F2
Leopold Rd BRI BN1 ..... 13 F2
CRAWW RH11 ..... 2 B3
Lesser Foxholes SHOR BN43 ..... 233 F7
Letchworth Cl FERR BN12 ..... 252 C2
Level Mare La SELS PO20 ..... 198 B8
Leveret La CRAWW RH11 ..... 2 A1
Leverton Av MIDOS PO22 ..... 247 H7
Lewes Cl BOGR PO21 ..... 245 F7
CRAWE RH10 ..... 32 C5
Lewes Rd EGRIN RH19 ..... 36 D3
FROW RH18 ..... 37 J8
HWH RH16 ..... 112 D4
RHWH RH17 ..... 86 A7
RHWH RH17 ..... 87 H2
ROTT BN2 ..... 11 D5
Lewes St ROTT BN2 ..... 11 D4
Lewin Cl CRAWW RH11 ..... 55 G2
Leyfield CRAWE RH10 ..... 32 B8
Lewis Cl SALV BN13 ..... 229 F6
Lewis La ARUN BN18 ..... 224 B8
Lewis Rd CCH PO19 ..... 7 D2
EMRTH PO10 ..... 190 E8
LAN/SOMP BN15 ..... 231 K3
SELS PO20 ..... 264 E4
Leybourne Cl CRAWW RH11 ..... 55 G2
Leyfield CRAWW RH11 ..... 55 G2
Leylands Pk BURH RH15 ..... 139 H6
Leylands Rd BURH RH15 ..... 139 G7
Ley Rd MIDOS PO22 ..... 13 F3
The Leys HASM GU27 ..... 66 C6
RCCH PO18 ..... 172 A4
Leyton Lea RHWH RH17 ..... 110 E5
Library Pl WTHG BN11 ..... 9 F4
Lichfield Gdns BOGR PO21 ..... 245 G8
Lidsey Cl CRAWE RH10 ..... 32 C7
Lidsey Rd MIDOS PO22 ..... 222 B3
Lifeboat Wy SELS PO20 ..... 265 F6
Lilac La CCH PO19 ..... 7 D2
MIDOS PO22 ..... 247 J5
SALV BN13 ..... 229 F6
Lillywhite Cl BURH RH15 ..... 139 F6
Limbourne La PUL/STOR RH20 ..... 127 H8
Limbrick Cl FERR BN12 ..... 229 G8
Limbrick La FERR BN12 ..... 229 G8
Limbrick Wy FERR BN12 ..... 229 F7
Lime Av HORS RH12 ..... 5 F3
Lime Cha PUL/STOR RH20 ..... 180 B1
Lime Cl CCH PO19 ..... 7 D2
CRAWE RH10 ..... 19 H8
CRAWW RH11 ..... 31 G2
Lime Kiln Rd SWTR RH13 ..... 78 E3
Lime Rd FIN/BW BN14 ..... 205 J4
Limes Av HORL RH6 ..... 18 B2
Limes Cl LIPH GU30 ..... 38 C4
The Limes ARUN BN18 ..... 223 K8
EGRIN RH19 ..... 21 J6
Lime Tree Av FIN/BW BN14 ..... 230 A1
Lime Tree Cl ANG/EP BN16 ..... 251 H3
Limmard Wy MIDOS PO22 ..... 247 G7
Limmer La MIDOS PO22 ..... 13 F4
Linacre Dr CRAN GU6 ..... 24 A5
HORS RH12 ..... 24 A8
Lincett Av SALV BN13 ..... 229 K7
Lincett Dr SALV BN13 ..... 229 K8
Linchmere Pl CRAWW RH11 ..... 30 E4
Linchmere Rd HASM GU27 ..... 39 J8
Linch Rd HASM GU27 ..... 65 G8
MIDH GU29 ..... 93 H6
Lincoln Av PO21 ..... 244 E7
Lincoln Cl CRAWE RH10 ..... 3 D6
Lincoln Cottages ROTT BN2 ..... 11 D4
Lincoln Gn CCH PO19 ..... 219 F2
Lincoln Rd PTSD BN41 ..... 235 F4
SALV BN13 ..... 229 K7
Lincoln St ROTT BN2 ..... 11 D4
Lincoln Wd RHWH RH17 ..... 111 J6
Linden Av EGRIN RH19 ..... 36 A1
Linden Cl CRAWE RH10 ..... 3 D6
HORS RH12 ..... 5 D3

Linden Gv HWH RH16 ..... 112 C5
Linden Pk LHPTN BN17 ..... 249 J2
Linden Rd BOGR PO21 ..... 12 A4
LHPTN BN17 ..... 249 J2
Lindens Cl EMRTH PO10 ..... 190 D8
Lindfield Rd RHWH RH17 ..... 84 E5
Lindsey Rd MIDOS PO22 ..... 13 F2
Lindum Rd SALV BN13 ..... 229 K6
Lindum Wy SALV BN13 ..... 229 K6
Lineside Wy LHPTN BN17 ..... 249 H1
Linfield Copse PUL/STOR RH20 ..... 156 D5
Lingfield Cl SALV BN13 ..... 229 K5
Lingfield Dr CRAWE RH10 ..... 32 E4
Lingfield Rd EGRIN RH19 ..... 22 B8
Lingfield Wy SELS PO20 ..... 265 G4
Link Hl PUL/STOR RH20 ..... 179 K2
Link La PUL/STOR RH20 ..... 154 E1
Links Av MIDOS PO22 ..... 13 E4
Links Cl PTSD BN41 ..... 235 G3
Links Rd FIN/BW BN14 ..... 230 A3
LAN/SOMP BN15 ..... 232 B5
PTSD BN41 ..... 235 G3
The Link CRAWW RH11 ..... 2 C3
Link Wy BOGR PO21 ..... 261 H2
The Linkway BRI BN1 ..... 13 D1
Linnet Cl EPSF GU31 ..... 117 G1
Linton Rd HOVE BN3 ..... 235 K5
Lintott Gdns SWTR RH13 ..... 5 D4
Lionel Av MIDOS PO22 ..... 247 G5
Lion La CRAWE RH10 ..... 34 C7
GSHT GU26 ..... 40 B2
Lion Md HASM GU27 ..... 40 B5
Lion Rd BOGR PO21 ..... 261 H1
Lion St CCH PO19 ..... 6 C3
Liphook Cl BRI BN1 ..... 11 E1
Liphook Rd HASM GU27 ..... 39 G7
Lisher Rd LAN/SOMP BN15 ..... 232 B4
Lisle Wy EMRTH PO10 ..... 190 C8
Lismore Crs CRAWW RH11 ..... 2 A6
Lister Av EGRIN RH19 ..... 36 C5
Listers RHWH RH17 ..... 108 D2
Litten Ter CCH PO19 ..... 6 C2
Little Ashfield MIDH GU29 ..... 122 A3
Little Babbsham BOGR PO21 ..... 262 B1
Little Barn Pl LISS GU33 ..... 62 B7
Little Bentswood HWH RH16 ..... 112 B6
Little Black Hl HWH RH16 ..... 112 D4
Little Boultons SELS PO20 ..... 243 F5
Little Breach CCH PO19 ..... 6 B1
Little Bridges Cl SWTR RH13 ..... 105 F2
Little Cl SWTR RH13 ..... 105 F4
Little Comptons SWTR RH13 ..... 5 E5
Little Copse Rd HPPT/KEY BN6 ..... 164 E6
Littlecote PETW GU28 ..... 125 K4
Little Crabtree CRAWW RH11 ..... 2 B2
Little Dipper's PUL/STOR RH20 ..... 154 E1
Little Dr FERR BN12 ..... 252 C2
Little Dro STEY/UB BN44 ..... 207 K2
Little East St BIL RH14 ..... 102 B2
Littlefield Cl SELS PO20 ..... 265 F4
Littlefield Rd CCH PO19 ..... 7 D4
Little Finches SWTR RH13 ..... 134 C8
Little Gables SALV BN13 ..... 229 K5
Little Grebe HORS RH12 ..... 4 B2
Littlehampton Rd ANG/EP BN16 ..... 228 A8
FERR BN12 ..... 229 F7
SALV BN13 ..... 229 J6
Little Hatch HORS RH12 ..... 5 E2
Little Haven La HORS RH12 ..... 5 E2
Littlehaven La HORS RH12 ..... 5 E3
Littleheath Rd ARUN BN18 ..... 198 C8
Little High St BOGR PO21 ..... 12 B6
SHOR BN43 ..... 233 G4
WTHG BN11 ..... 9 D3
Little Hl PUL/STOR RH20 ..... 156 A3
Little King St EGRIN RH19 ..... 36 C2
Little London CCH PO19 ..... 6 C3
Little Pembrokes WTHG BN11 ..... 8 A3
Little Preston St BRI BN1 ..... 10 A5
Littlestone Rd SALV BN13 ..... 229 J5
Little Western St BRI BN1 ..... 10 A5
Littleworth La SWTR RH13 ..... 134 C7
Liverpool Gdns WTHG BN11 ..... 9 D4
Liverpool Rd WTHG BN11 ..... 9 D4
Liverpool Ter WTHG BN11 ..... 9 D4
Livesay Crs FIN/BW BN14 ..... 9 D4
Livingstone Rd BURH RH15 ..... 139 F8
CRAWE RH10 ..... 3 D5
HOVE BN3 ..... 236 B4
SWTR RH13 ..... 4 C6
Livingstone St ROTT BN2 ..... 11 F5
Lizard Head LHPTN BN17 ..... 250 C1
Lloyd Cl HOVE BN3 ..... 236 C3
Lloyd Goring Cl ANG/EP BN16 ..... 227 H5
Lloyd Rd HOVE BN3 ..... 236 C3
Loats La BOGR PO21 ..... 245 H4
Lobster La SELS PO20 ..... 264 C3
Lobs Wood La PUL/STOR RH20 ..... 180 B1
Locke Rd LIPH GU30 ..... 38 D7
Lockgate Rd SELS PO20 ..... 242 C8
Lock La SELS PO20 ..... 241 K5
Locksash Cl SELS PO20 ..... 256 E1
Locksash La RCCH PO18 ..... 167 J3
Locks Crs PTSD BN41 ..... 235 F3

Locks HI *PTSD* BN41 .... 235 F2
Locks Meadow *LING* BN7 .... 22 E2 ◪
Lockwood CI *HORS* RH12 .... 5 F2 ◪
Loddon CI *SALV* BN13 .... 229 G3
Loder Gdns *FIN/BW* BN14 .... 8 C1
Loder PI *BRI* BN1 .... 237 F1
Loder Rd *BRI* BN1 .... 237 F1
Lodgebury CI *EMRTH* PO10 .... 215 J3
Lodge CI *CRAWW* RH11 .... 2 B3 ◪
　EGRIN RH19 .... 36 A2
　MIDOS PO22 .... 248 A6
　PTSD BN41 .... 234 D1 ◪
Lodge Ct *BOGR* PO21 .... 262 E1
　SHOR BN43 .... 233 G2
Lodge Hill La *HPPT/KEY* BN6 .... 165 J7
Lodgelands CI *RHWH* RH17 .... 167 H5
Lodge La *HAV* PO9 .... 165 G8
　HPPT/KEY BN6 .... 165 G8
Lodsworth Rd *BOGR* PO21 .... 244 D5
Lombard St *PETW* GU28 .... 125 K3 ◪
Lomond Av *BRI* BN1 .... 213 G4
London La *RHWH* RH17 .... 111 F5
London Rd *ARUN* BN18 .... 198 D3
　ARUN BN18 .... 200 E5
　BOGR PO21 .... 12 C5
　BRI BN1 .... 10 C3
　BRI BN1 .... 212 D3
　BURH RH15 .... 139 F8 ◪
　CRAWE RH10 .... 57 G2
　CRAWW RH11 .... 2 C2
　CRAWW RH11 .... 17 J8
　EGRIN RH19 .... 36 C2
　EPSF GU31 .... 89 J5
　FROW RH18 .... 37 J7
　HFD BN5 .... 161 G4
　HORL RH6 .... 18 A3
　HORS RH12 .... 4 B5
　HPPT/KEY BN6 .... 164 E6
　HPPT/KEY BN6 .... 187 H1
　PUL/STOR RH20 .... 38 C7
　PUL/STOR RH20 .... 153 H6
　PUL/STOR RH20 .... 158 A7
　PUL/STOR RH20 .... 181 J4
　RHWH RH17 .... 57 F8
　RHWH RH17 .... 83 F3
　RHWH RH17 .... 86 E7
　RHWH RH17 .... 110 E3
London St *WTHG* BN11 .... 8 C3
London Ter *BRI* BN1 .... 10 C3
Lone Oak *HORL* RH6 .... 19 H2
Long Acre *CRAWE* RH10 .... 264 E5
Longacre *SELS* PO20 .... 62 A7
Longacre CI *LISS* GU33 .... 62 A7
Longacre Crs *RHWH* RH17 .... 111 F3
Longacre La *SELS* PO20 .... 264 E5
Longbridge Rd *HORL* RH6 .... 17 K2
Longbrook Wk *HORL* RH6 .... 17 K2 ◪
Longbrook *BOGR* PO21 .... 13 G5
Long Copse La *EMRTH* PO10 .... 190 D7
Longdene Rd *HASM* GU27 .... 40 D5
Long Down *EPSF* GU31 .... 89 F7
Longfellow Rd *WTHG* BN11 .... 8 B3
Longfield Rd *EMRTH* PO10 .... 190 C8
Longford Rd *BOGR* PO21 .... 205 F7
Long Furlong *SALV* BN13 .... 228 C2
　SALV BN13 .... 204 C7
Longfurlong La *SALV* BN13 .... 204 C7
Long La *SWTH* RH13 .... 107 H3
Longhurst *BURH* RH15 .... 165 K1
Longhurst Rd *CRAWW* RH11 .... 54 E2
Longland Av *PUL/STOR* RH20 ..... 180 A1
Longlands *FIN/BW* BN14 .... 230 D3
Longlands Gld *FIN/BW* BN14 ...... 230 D3
Longlands Rd *EMRTH* PO10 .... 215 H3
　SELS PO20 .... 257 J5
Longlands Spinney *FIN/BW* BN14 . 230 D3
Long La *ARUN* BN18 .... 200 C3
　RCCH PO18 .... 144 D8
Long Md *ARUN* BN18 .... 223 H2
Long Meadow *FIN/BW* BN14 .... 205 K7
Longmere Rd *CRAWW* RH11 .... 2 C1
Longmoor Rd *LISS* GU33 .... 62 A1
Long Park Cnr *HPPT/KEY* BN6 .... 189 K1
Longport Rd *MIDOS* PO22 .... 247 F7
Long Rd *PSF* GU32 .... 88 E6
Longships *ANG/EP* BN16 .... 250 C1
The Loop *MIDOS* PO22 .... 247 G7
Loose La *FIN/BW* BN14 .... 231 C6
　LAN/SOMP BN15 .... 231 H5
Loppetts Rd *CRAWE* RH10 .... 3 E5
Lordings La *PUL/STOR* RH20 ...... 156 D4
Lordings Rd *BIL* RH14 .... 101 H6
Loriners *CRAWE* RH10 .... 2 C6 ◪
Lorna Rd *HOVE* BN3 .... 236 D4
Lorne Rd *BRI* BN1 .... 10 C2
Lotts La *LAN/SOMP* BN15 .... 231 J5
Loudoun Rd *LHPTN* BN17 .... 249 J2 ◪
Love La *EPSF* GU31 .... 88 C7
Loveletts *CRAWW* RH11 .... 30 E6
Lovells CI *BOGR* PO21 .... 261 J1
Lover's Wk *BRI* BN1 .... 10 B2
Loveys Rd *ARUN* BN18 .... 247 K1 ◪
Lowdells CI *EGRIN* RH19 .... 22 B7

Lowdells Dr *EGRIN* RH19 .... 22 B7
Lowdells La *EGRIN* RH19 .... 22 A8
Lowe CI *CRAWW* RH11 .... 55 F3
Lower Barn *HORS* RH12 .... 5 E2
Lower Beach Rd *SHOR* BN43 ...... 233 H5
Lower Bognor Rd *BOGR* PO21 .... 245 G7
　SELS PO20 .... 244 D5
Lower Church Rd *BURH* RH15 .... 139 F8
Lower Dene *EGRIN* RH19 .... 36 C2
Lower Dr *STHW* BN42 .... 234 C2
Lower Faircox *HFD* BN5 .... 161 F6
Lower Hanger *HASM* GU27 .... 39 J5
Lower Heyshott *EPSF* GU31 .... 88 E7
Lower Home La *RCCH* PO18 .... 240 E2
Lower Market St *HOVE* BN3 .... 236 D6 ◪
Lower Md *EPSF* GU31 .... 89 F8
Lower Mere *EGRIN* RH19 .... 36 D3
Lower Rd *HASM* GU27 .... 41 H1
　RCCH PO18 .... 195 G6
Lower Rock Gdns *ROTT* BN2 .... 11 D6 ◪
Lower Station Rd *BIL* RH14 .... 102 B5
　HFD BN5 .... 161 F7
Lower St *HASM* GU27 .... 40 D5
　PUL/STOR RH20 .... 153 F2
　PUL/STOR RH20 .... 154 D1
Lower Tanbridge Wy *HORS* RH12 . 4 A5 ◪
Lower Wardown *EPSF* GU31 .... 89 F7
Lowfield CI *HWH* RH16 .... 49 H5
　SWTH RH13 .... 49 H8
Lowfield Wy *HORL* RH6 .... 17 J6 ◪
Lowlands Rd *BURH* RH15 .... 139 H6
Lowther Rd *BRI* BN1 .... 237 G1
　SALV BN13 .... 229 K4
Loxwood Wk *CRAWW* RH11 .... 30 D4 ◪
Loxwood *ANG/EP* BN16 .... 227 K8 ◪
Loxwood Av *FIN/BW* BN14 .... 8 B1
Loxwood Rd *BIL* RH14 .... 47 F7
　BIL RH14 .... 71 G1
　CRAN GU6 .... 46 B3
Lucas CI *EGRIN* RH19 .... 36 D2 ◪
Lucas Fld *HASM* GU27 .... 40 A5 ◪
Lucas Gra *HWH* RH16 .... 111 K6
Lucas La *HORS* RH12 .... 50 E3
Lucastes Av *HWH* RH16 .... 111 J5
Lucastes La *RHWH* RH17 .... 111 J5
Lucas Wy *HWH* RH16 .... 111 J6
Lucerne CI *PTSD* BN41 .... 235 F2
Lucerne Ct *BOGR* PO21 .... 262 B1
Lucerne Dr *CRAWE* RH10 .... 32 D7
Lucerne Rd *BRI* BN1 .... 10 B1
Lucking La *MIDOS* PO22 .... 247 K6
Ludlow CI *BOGR* PO21 .... 262 B1 ◪
Luffs Meadow *PETW* GU28 .... 68 E4
Lullington Av *HOVE* BN3 .... 235 K3
Lulworth CI *CRAWW* RH11 .... 30 E8 ◪
Lumley Rd *EMRTH* PO10 .... 214 E2
Lunce's HI *RHWH* RH17 .... 140 B3
Lundy CI *ANG/EP* BN16 .... 250 C3
　CRAWW RH11 .... 2 B6
Lupin CI *ANG/EP* BN16 .... 226 C8
Lurgashall *BURH* RH15 .... 165 J2 ◪
Lutener Rd *MIDH* GU29 .... 122 B3
Luther St *ROTT* BN2 .... 11 E3
The Luth *BIL* RH14 .... 100 E3
Lutman St *EMRTH* PO10 .... 190 C7
Lutyens CI *CRAWW* RH11 .... 30 C7 ◪
Luxford CI *HORS* RH12 .... 5 E2 ◪
Luxford Rd *HWH* RH16 .... 112 D4
Luxfords La *EGRIN* RH19 .... 37 F5
　EGRIN RH19 .... 22 D8
Luxford Wy *BIL* RH14 .... 102 A4
The Lychgates *ARUN* BN18 .... 223 K7
Lye La *RCCH* PO18 .... 193 K7
Lyminster Av *BRI* BN1 .... 213 G6
Lyminster Rd *ARUN* BN18 .... 225 K2
　LHPTN BN17 .... 225 K6
Lynch Down *RCCH* PO18 .... 192 D5
Lynchet CI *BRI* BN1 .... 237 J1
Lynchet Down *BRI* BN1 .... 237 J1
Lynchets Crs *HOVE* BN3 .... 211 H8
The Lynchette *SHOR* BN43 .... 233 H2
Lynchet Wk *BRI* BN1 .... 237 J1
Lynchmere Av *LAN/SOMP* BN15 . 231 K3
Lyndhurst CI *CRAWW* RH11 .... 2 C4
Lyndhurst Farm CI *EGRIN* RH19 . 21 F7
Lyndhurst Rd *CCH* PO19 .... 7 D3
　HOVE BN3 .... 236 D4
　WTHG BN11 .... 9 E3
Lyndum CI *EPSF* GU31 .... 88 D8
Lyn Rd *SALV* BN13 .... 229 G5
Lynton CI *HPPT/KEY* BN6 .... 164 B6
Lynton Park Av *EGRIN* RH19 .... 36 E1
Lynton Rd *PSF* GU32 .... 88 C7
Lyntons *PUL/STOR* RH20 .... 154 C1
Lynton St *ROTT* BN2 .... 11 E3
Lynwick St *HORS* RH12 .... 48 B3
Lynwood Crt *HORS* RH12 .... 56 C1
Lyon CI *CRAWE* RH10 .... 3 F6
　HOVE BN3 .... 236 D4
Lyons CI *SWTR* RH13 .... 49 H8
Lyons Rd *SWTR* RH13 .... 49 J8
Lyon St *BOGR* PO21 .... 12 C5

Lyons Wy *FIN/BW* BN14 ....
Lyoth La *HWH* RH16 ....
Lyric CI *CRAWE* RH10 ....
Lysander Wy *SELS* PO20 ....
Lytton Dr *CRAWE* RH10 ....

M

Mackerel La *SELS* PO20 ....
Mackie Av *BRI* BN1 ....
　HPPT/KEY BN6 ....
Macklin Rd *MIDOS* PO22 ....
Macleod Rd *SWTR* RH13 ....
Madehurst CI *ANG/EP* BN16 ......
　ROTT BN2 ....
Madehurst Ct *CRAWW* RH11 .....
Madehurst Wy *LHPTN* BN17 ......
Madeira Av *HORS* RH12 ....
　MIDOS PO22 ....
　WTHG BN11 ....
Madeira Dr *ROTT* BN2 ....
Madeira PI *ROTT* BN2 ....
Madeline Rd *EPSF* GU31 ....
Madgwick La *RCCH* PO18 ....
Mafeking Rd *ROTT* BN2 ....
Magdalene CI *CRAWE* RH10 ......
Magnolia CI *SALV* BN13 ....
　SWTR RH13 ....
Magpie La *SELS* PO20 ....
　SWTR RH13 ....
Magpie Rd *HORN* PO8 ....
Maidenbower Dr *CRAWE* RH10...
Maidenbower La *CRAWE* RH10 ...
Maidenbower PI *CRAWE* RH10 ...
Maiden La *CRAWW* RH11 ....
Maidment CI *HFD* BN5 ....
Main Dr *MIDOS* PO22 ....
Main Rd *ARUN* BN18 ....
　EMRTH PO10 ....
　RCCH PO18 ....
　RCCH PO18 ....
　SELS PO20 ....
Mainstone Rd *HOVE* BN3 ....
Maisemore Gdns *EMRTH* PO10 ..
Major CI *BRI* BN1 ....
Major's HI *CRAWE* RH10 ....
Malcolm CI *FERR* BN12 ....
Malcolm Gdns *HORL* RH6 ....
Malcolm Rd *SELS* PO20 ....
Maldon Rd *BRI* BN1 ....
Malham CI *CRAWE* RH10 ....
Malin Rd *ANG/EP* BN16 ....
Mallard CI *HASM* GU27 ....
　HORS RH12 ....
Mallard Crs *BOGR* PO21 ....
Mallard PI *EGRIN* RH19 ....
Mallard Wy *HFD* BN5 ....
Mallion's La *RHWH* RH17 ....
Mallon Dene *ANG/EP* BN16 ....
Mallory Rd *HOVE* BN3 ....
Mallow CI *HORS* RH12 ....
Malthouse CI *ARUN* BN18 ....
　LAN/SOMP BN15 ....
Malthouse La *HPPT/KEY* BN6 ....
　RCCH PO18 ....
　ROTT BN2 ....
Malthouse Mdw *LIPH* GU30 ....
Malthouse Pas *LHPTN* BN17 ......
Malthouse Rd *CRAWE* RH10 ......
　SELS PO20 ....
The Maltings *BURH* RH15 ....
　EPSF GU31 ....
　LIPH GU30 ....
Maltravers Dr *LHPTN* BN17 ......
Maltravers Rd *LHPTN* BN17 ......
Maltravers St *ARUN* BN18 ....
Malvern CI *WTHG* BN11 ....
Malvern Ms *EMRTH* PO10 ....
Malvern Rd *CRAWW* RH11 ....
　LISS GU33 ....
Malvern St *HOVE* BN3 ....
Malvern Wy *BOGR* PO21 ....
Manaton CI *HWH* RH16 ....
Manchester St *ROTT* BN2 ....
Manet Sq *MIDOS* PO22 ....
Manhood La *SELS* PO20 ....
Manitoba Wy *SALV* BN13 ....
Manley's HI *PUL/STOR* RH20 ....
Manning CI *EGRIN* RH19 ....
Manning Rd *CCH* PO19 ....
　LHPTN BN17 ....
Mannings CI *CRAWE* RH10 ....
Manor Av *HPPT/KEY* BN6 ....
Manor CI *ANG/EP* BN16 ....
　BURH RH15 ....
　CCH PO19 ....
　HASM GU27 ....
　HFD BN5 ....
　LAN/SOMP BN15 ....
　MIDOS PO22 ....
　PUL/STOR RH20 ....
　STHW BN42 ....
　WTHG BN11 ....
Manor Dr *RHWH* RH17 ....

Farm Cl *SELS* PO20 .... 265 F3
Farm Ct *SELS* PO20 .... 265 F3
fields *CRAWW* RH11 .... 54 B1
Flds *LIPH* GU30 .... 38 D7
RH13 .... 5 F3
Gdns *EMRTH* PO10 .... 215 H2
/KEY BN6 .... 163 K5
Hall Rd *STHW* BN42 .... 234 C3
La *SELS* PO20 .... 265 G3
RH13 .... 78 D3
Pk *BOGR* PO21 .... 261 H2
Pl *BOGR* PO21 .... 12 B6
Rd *ANG/EP* BN16 .... 250 D1
EP BN16 .... 251 J3
RH15 .... 139 J7
TH PO10 .... 215 H2
RH12 .... 5 E2
/KEY BN6 .... 163 K5
SOMP BN15 .... 231 K3
BN41 .... 235 F2
PO20 .... 265 F4
UB BN44 .... 208 E1
BN11 .... 8 B4
Royal *CRAWE* RH10 .... 31 J2
Vls *RCCH* PO18 .... 217 G6
Wy *BOGR* PO21 .... 261 J2
TH PO10 .... 215 H2
BN5 .... 161 H6
SOMP BN15 .... 161 H6
S PO22 .... 232 B4
S PO22 .... 248 B6
ergh Rd *CCH* PO19 .... 219 H2
Rd *SHOR* BN43 .... 233 K3
Rd *ARUN* BN18 .... 225 K2
eld Cl *WTHG* BN11 .... 231 G7
eld Rd *BOGR* PO21 .... 12 A3
BN3 .... 235 J4
BN11 .... 231 G8
n Cl *BURH* RH15 .... 139 K8
PUL/STOR RH20 .... 180 B2
g Rd *LHPTN* BN17 .... 249 K1
Cl *SELS* PO20 .... 258 B6
PETW GU28 .... 125 K4
BIL RH14 .... 102 A2
RH15 .... 139 H6
W RH11 .... 31 G2
H PO10 .... 214 D1
RH12 .... 5 F2
RH16 .... 112 D8
S PO22 .... 247 J5
BN13 .... 229 J2
own Cl *SWTR* RH13 .... 105 F1
Dr *BURH* RH15 .... 139 G6
RH19 .... 36 E2
Gdns *HOVE* BN3 .... 235 J2
S PO22 .... 12 B1
urst Rd *CCH* PO19 .... 195 G8
BN41 .... 234 E2
RH13 .... 106 B7
eaf *PUL/STOR* RH20 .... 153 J5
d *ARUN* BN18 .... 223 J3
14 .... 102 B4
ples *FERR* BN12 .... 252 D3
Vk *LAN/SOMP* BN15 .... 231 H4
s La *SELS* PO20 .... 242 A8
Gdns *ANG/EP* BN16 .... 250 D4
nts Cl *HPPT/KEY* BN6 .... 164 A5
nts Rd *HPPT/KEY* BN6 .... 164 A5
nts *W* BURH* RH15 .... 139 F6
s Rd *HORS* RH12 .... 26 D7
rches *HASM* GU27 .... 66 D6
RH12 .... 27 H6
wood *CCH* PO19 .... 195 G8
e Flds *RCCH* PO18 .... 216 E5
e Rd *SALV* BN13 .... 229 K5
Av *SELS* PO20 .... 6 A6
dens *CRAWW* RH11 .... 2 A2
Wy *EPSF* GU31 .... 88 E8
e *SHOR* BN43 .... 233 F5
ll Rd *PUL/STOR* RH20 .... 155 G1
et Cl *BOGR* PO21 .... 245 G1
et St *ROTT* BN2 .... 11 D6
r Rd *HOVE* BN3 .... 235 H3
Cl *EMRTH* PO10 .... 214 D3
v *HOVE* BN3 .... 235 H5
Cl *SELS* PO20 .... 257 H5
BN11 .... 8 A5
Crs *FERR* BN12 .... 253 H2
Dr *FERR* BN12 .... 252 E3
O20 .... 257 H4
O20 .... 265 G4
Dr West *BOGR* PO21 .... 262 D1
O20 .... 257 J2
Gdns *ROTT* BN2 .... 11 D6
O20 .... 264 D6
de *ROTT* BN2 .... 11 E6
BN11 .... 8 A5
Pl *WTHG* BN11 .... 9 E5
e *SHOR* BN43 .... 233 F6
errace Ms *ROTT* BN2 .... 11 E6
w *ROTT* BN2 .... 11 D5

Marine Wk *HISD* PO11 .... 238 B8
Marion Rd *CRAWE* RH10 .... 32 B8
Marisfield Pl *SELS* PO20 .... 265 G3
Marjoram Cl *SHOR* BN43 .... 233 K2
Market Av *CCH* PO19 .... 6 C3
Market Cl *MIDOS* PO22 .... 223 F5
Market Fld *STEY/UB* BN44 .... 183 K8
Market Pl *HWH* RH16 .... 111 K6
Market Sq *HORS* RH12 .... 4 B6
MIDH GU29 .... 122 B4
Market St *BOGR* PO21 .... 12 B6
BRI BN1 .... 10 C5
WTHG BN11 .... 9 D4
Markfield *MIDOS* PO22 .... 12 A2
Markway Cl *EMRTH* PO10 .... 214 B2
Markwick Ms *WTHG* BN11 .... 9 E3
Marlborough Ct *CCH* PO19 .... 7 F3
CRAWW RH11 .... 55 G1
HORS RH12 .... 4 C2
Marlborough Ct *BOGR* PO21 .... 245 H7
Marlborough Dr *BURH* RH15 .... 139 J8
Marlborough Ms *BRI* BN1 .... 10 B5
Marlborough Pk *HAV* PO9 .... 190 H8
Marlborough Pl *BRI* BN1 .... 10 C5
LAN/SOMP BN15 .... 231 H7
Marlborough Rd *FERR* BN12 .... 253 H1
Marlborough St *BRI* BN1 .... 10 B5
Marlborough Wy *FERR* BN12 .... 253 H1
Marle Av *BURH* RH15 .... 139 H7
Marles La *BIL* RH14 .... 74 A2
Marley Combe Rd *HASM* GU27 .... 40 A6
Marley Hanger *HASM* GU27 .... 40 C8
Marley La *HASM* GU27 .... 40 A6
The Marlinspike *SHOR* BN43 .... 233 J5
Marlow Dr *CRAWW* RH11 .... 2 C2
Marlow Dr *HWH* RH16 .... 112 D7
Marlowe Cl *MIDOS* PO22 .... 247 H5
Marlowe Rd *FIN/BW* BN14 .... 9 E1
Marlpit Cl *EGRIN* RH19 .... 22 C4
Marlpit La *EMRTH* PO10 .... 192 A7
SELS PO20 .... 220 D5
Marlpit Rd *EGRIN* RH19 .... 59 J5
Marlpost Rd *SWTR* RH13 .... 104 C2
Marmion Rd *HOVE* BN3 .... 235 K4
Marquis Wy *BOGR* PO21 .... 262 B2
Marringdean Rd *BIL* RH14 .... 180 B1
FIN/BW BN14 .... 205 K8
Marshall Av *BOGR* PO21 .... 12 A5
Marshall Cl *MIDOS* PO22 .... 223 F6
Marshall Rd *CRAWE* RH10 .... 32 C7
Marshalls Rw *BRI* BN1 .... 10 C5
Marshall Wy *HOVE* BN3 .... 235 K2
Marsh La *RCCH* PO18 .... 195 F4
RCCH PO18 .... 216 A7
SELS PO20 .... 220 C8
SELS PO20 .... 221 J1
SELS PO20 .... 244 B2
Marston Rd *FIN/BW* BN14 .... 9 E2
Martha Gunn Rd *ROTT* BN2 .... 11 F1
Martin Cl *CRAWW* RH11 .... 2 C1
Martin Rd *HOVE* BN3 .... 235 H2
Martins La *SELS* PO20 .... 241 K6
The Martins *CRAWE* RH10 .... 34 E3
Martlet Cl *CCH* PO19 .... 6 C4
Martlet Cl *PETW* GU28 .... 125 J4
Martlets *PUL/STOR* RH20 .... 156 A3
Martlets Cl *HORS* RH12 .... 4 B2
The Martlets *ANG/EP* BN16 .... 250 C4
CRAWE RH10 .... 3 D5
LAN/SOMP BN15 .... 231 J5
SHOR BN43 .... 233 H3
The Martlet *HOVE* BN3 .... 236 D3
Martlet Wy *BOGR* PO21 .... 261 G4
The Marts *HORS* RH12 .... 48 B4
Martyn Cl *HFD* BN5 .... 161 G6
Martyns Pl *EGRIN* RH19 .... 36 E3
Martyrs Av *CRAWW* RH11 .... 31 G2
Marvell Cl *CRAWE* RH10 .... 32 C3
Marylands *HWH* RH16 .... 112 B2
Marylands Crs *MIDOS* PO22 .... 13 G3
Masefield Rd *CRAWW* RH11 .... 30 C8
Mash Barn La *LAN/SOMP* BN15 .... 232 C4
Mason Cl *EGRIN* RH19 .... 36 C1
Mason Rd *CRAWE* RH10 .... 3 D5
Masons Fld *SWTR* RH13 .... 78 E5
Masons Wy *PUL/STOR* RH20 .... 128 E6
Massetts Rd *HORL* RH6 .... 17 K1
Matlock Rd *BRI* BN1 .... 236 D2
Matthews Dr *CRAWE* RH10 .... 56 C1
Matthey Pl *CRAWE* RH10 .... 32 D2
Maudlin La *STEY/UB* BN44 .... 207 K2
Maudlyn Cl *STEY/UB* BN44 .... 208 A2
Maudlyn Pk *STEY/UB* BN44 .... 207 K2
Maudlyn Pkwy *STEY/UB* BN44 .... 207 K2
Mauldmare Cl *BOGR* PO21 .... 262 C1
Maunsell Pk *CRAWE* RH10 .... 32 B5
Maxwell Rd *ARUN* BN18 .... 225 F2
LHPTN BN17 .... 249 J2
Maxwell Wy *CRAWE* RH10 .... 32 A2
Maybridge Crs *FERR* BN12 .... 229 G8
Maybridge Sq *FERR* BN12 .... 229 G7
Maybush Dr *RCCH* PO18 .... 216 A4
May Cl *FERR* BN12 .... 229 G7

MIDOS PO22 .... 12 C3
SELS PO20 .... 260 A3
Maydwell Av *SWTR* RH13 .... 75 F1
Mayes Cl *CRAWE* RH10 .... 32 C6
Mayes La *HORS* RH12 .... 27 F8
Mayfield *ANG/EP* BN16 .... 227 J8
CRAWE RH10 .... 32 D5
LING RH7 .... 22 E2
Mayfield Cl *BOGR* PO21 .... 261 J1
BRI BN1 .... 213 F6
FIN/BW BN14 .... 230 A3
Mayfield Crs *BRI* BN1 .... 213 F6
Mayfield Rd *BOGR* PO21 .... 245 J7
Mayfields *RHWH* RH17 .... 109 G7
Mayflower Cl *CRAWE* RH10 .... 32 D6
Mayflower Cl *CRAWE* RH16 .... 112 B7
Mayflower Rd *HWH* RH16 .... 112 B7
Mayflower Wy *ANG/EP* BN16 .... 227 J8
Mayhouse Rd *BURH* RH15 .... 165 F2
Mayo Rd *ROTT* BN2 .... 11 D2
Maypole La *ARUN* BN18 .... 223 K6
Maypole Rd *EGRIN* RH19 .... 36 B1
EGRIN RH19 .... 37 G5
Mayridge *SELS* PO20 .... 264 C3
May Rd *ROTT* BN2 .... 11 F3
May Tree Av *FIN/BW* BN14 .... 205 K8
Maytree Cl *ANG/EP* BN16 .... 227 H7
LAN/SOMP BN15 .... 231 H5
Maytree Wk *HOVE* BN3 .... 235 J2
Mcindoe Rd *EGRIN* RH19 .... 22 B8
Mciver Cl *EGRIN* RH19 .... 21 H7
Mckerchar Cl *LAN/SOMP* BN15 .... 232 B4
Mcnair Cl *SELS* PO20 .... 264 E3
Meades Cl *LING* RH7 .... 22 E2
The Meades *LING* RH7 .... 23 F2
Mead La *MIDOS* PO22 .... 13 D4
PUL/STOR RH20 .... 180 C1
Meadow Ap *CRAWE* RH10 .... 19 G3
Meadowbank Rd *BIL* RH14 .... 100 D3
Meadow Cl *CRAWE* RH10 .... 19 G8
HORS RH12 .... 5 F2
HOVE BN3 .... 212 B8
LIPH GU30 .... 38 C7
PTSD BN41 .... 235 F1
SELS PO20 .... 243 G3
WTHG BN11 .... 231 H8
Meadow Crs *WTHG* BN11 .... 231 G8
Meadowcroft *CRAWW* RH11 .... 30 C6
EGRIN RH19 .... 36 A1
Meadow Croft Cl *HORL* RH6 .... 18 C5
Meadow Dr *HWH* RH16 .... 112 A8
Meadow Farm La *HORS* RH12 .... 52 B4
Meadowfield Dr *CCH* PO19 .... 7 D2
Meadowland *SELS* PO20 .... 264 E5
Meadowlands *CRAWW* RH11 .... 2 B3
HAV PO9 .... 166 A8
Meadow La *BURH* RH15 .... 165 F2
HWH RH16 .... 112 A8
LAN/SOMP BN15 .... 232 A6
SELS PO20 .... 257 G1
Meadow Pk *ANG/EP* BN16 .... 251 K2
Meadow Rd *WTHG* BN11 .... 231 G8
Meadows *HPPT/KEY* BN6 .... 164 E6
Meadowside *ANG/EP* BN16 .... 227 J5
PUL/STOR RH20 .... 180 B2
Meadows Rd *SELS* PO20 .... 257 K4
The Meadows *ARUN* BN18 .... 223 H2
HOVE BN3 .... 211 G8
Meadow Sweet Cl *SALV* BN13 .... 228 E6
The Meadow *CRAWE* RH10 .... 19 G8
Meadow V *HASM* GU27 .... 40 C5
Meadowview Rd
LAN/SOMP BN15 .... 231 K5
Meadow Wk *MIDOS* PO22 .... 248 A6
Meadow Wy *BOGR* PO21 .... 261 J2
FERR BN12 .... 252 C1
LHPTN BN17 .... 250 B2
LIPH GU30 .... 38 C6
MIDOS PO22 .... 245 J3
PETW GU28 .... 125 J4
SELS PO20 .... 220 E2
SELS PO20 .... 222 B5
Mead Rd *CRAWE* RH10 .... 3 E2
Meads Av *HOVE* BN3 .... 211 G8
The Meads *BRI* BN1 .... 213 K6
EGRIN RH19 .... 36 C4
HASM GU27 .... 40 B5
Mead Sway *ARUN* BN18 .... 199 H7
The Mead *LIPH* GU30 .... 38 B6
PSF GU32 .... 116 B1
Meadvale *HORS* RH12 .... 77 F1
Meadway *ANG/EP* BN16 .... 251 F2
HASM GU27 .... 40 B5
Mead Wy *MIDH* GU29 .... 121 K5
Meadway *STHW* BN42 .... 234 B3
Meadway Crs *HOVE* BN3 .... 235 K1
The Meadway *SHOR* BN43 .... 233 H5
Measham Ct *FERR* BN12 .... 252 D2
Medina Pl *HOVE* BN3 .... 236 B6
Medina Ter *HOVE* BN3 .... 236 B6
Medina Vls *HOVE* BN3 .... 236 B6
Medlar Cl *CRAWW* RH11 .... 31 G2
Medmerry *SELS* PO20 .... 264 B3
Medway *CRAWE* RH10 .... 54 C6

Medway Cl *SALV* BN13 .... 229 H4 [5]
Medway Dr *EGRIN* RH19 .... 36 B5
Medway Rd *CRAWW* RH11 .... 30 D6
Medwin Wy *HORS* RH12 .... 4 B5
Meeds Rd *BURH* RH15 .... 165 G1
Meeting House La *BRI* BN1 .... 10 C5 [14]
Meiros Wy *PUL/STOR* RH20 .... 157 K6
Melbourne Av *FERR* BN12 .... 253 C1
Melbourne Rd *CCH* PO19 .... 7 D2
    FERR BN12 .... 253 C1
Melbourne St *ROTT* BN2 .... 11 E2
Melksham Cl *SWTR* RH13 .... 5 D5
Melrose Av *PTSD* BN41 .... 234 E2
    SALV BN13 .... 229 J7
Melrose Cl *BRI* BN1 .... 237 J1
    SALV BN13 .... 229 J7
Melrose Pl *PUL/STOR* RH20 .... 157 G8
Melton Cl *PUL/STOR* RH20 .... 156 C8
Melton Ct *PUL/STOR* RH20 .... 156 C8
Melton Dr *PUL/STOR* RH20 .... 156 B8
Melville Rd *HOVE* BN3 .... 10 A3
Melville Wy *FERR* BN12 .... 229 G7
Mendip Cl *ANG/EP* BN16 .... 251 J1 [3]
Mendip Crs *SALV* BN13 .... 229 J4
Mendip Rd *SALV* BN13 .... 229 J4
Meon Cl *PSF* GU32 .... 88 C7
Mercer Cl *CRAWE* RH10 .... 32 C5
Mercer Rd *HORS* RH12 .... 51 J3
Mercers Md *SWTR* RH13 .... 135 G2 [1]
Merchant St *BOGR* PO21 .... 12 B5 [1]
Mercury Cl *CRAWW* RH11 .... 30 C8
Meredith Rd *FIN/BW* BN14 .... 9 F7
Merevale *BRI* BN1 .... 237 H1
Mereworth Dr *CRAWE* RH10 .... 32 D3
Meridian Wy *EGRIN* RH19 .... 22 D5
Merle Wy *HASM* GU27 .... 66 C5
Merlin Cl *CRAWW* RH11 .... 30 C5 [4]
    HOVE BN3 .... 236 A3
Merlin Wy *EGRIN* RH19 .... 22 E8
    MIDOS PO22 .... 247 H5
Merrion Av *BOGR* PO21 .... 12 A3
Merry End *MIDOS* PO22 .... 247 J6
Merryfield Crs *ANG/EP* BN16 .... 227 J5
Merryfield Dr *HORS* RH12 .... 51 C8
    SELS PO20 .... 265 G4
Merryfield Rd *EPSF* GU31 .... 89 F7
    PUL/STOR RH20 .... 180 B1
Merryfield Wy *PUL/STOR* RH20 .... 180 B1
Merryhills La *BIL* RH14 .... 46 C6
Merryweather Rd *RCCH* PO18 .... 217 F6
Merrywood La *PUL/STOR* RH20 .... 156 E7
Mersey Cl *SALV* BN13 .... 229 G4
Mersey Rd *SALV* BN13 .... 229 G4
Mersham Gdns *FERR* BN12 .... 253 C1 [3]
Merton Av *ANG/EP* BN16 .... 250 B1
Merton Cl *BOGR* PO21 .... 245 G7 [1]
Merton Dr *LHPTN* BN17 .... 249 K1 [1]
Merton Rd *WTHG* BN11 .... 31 H1
Metcalf Wy *CRAWW* RH11 .... 31 H1
Meteor Rd *EMRTH* PO10 .... 214 E8
Mews Ct *EGRIN* RH19 .... 36 D5
Meyers Cl *HOVE* BN3 .... 211 G8 [3]
Meyners Cl *HOVE* BN3 .... 211 G8 [3]
Michael Crs *HORL* RH6 .... 18 A2
Michael Flds *FROW* RH18 .... 61 J1
Michelbourne Cl *BURH* RH15 .... 164 E2 [1]
Michel Gv *ANG/EP* BN16 .... 251 G2 [4]
Michell Cl *HORS* RH12 .... 77 G1 [1]
Micklam Cl *BOGR* PO21 .... 261 K1
Middlefield *SELS* PO20 .... 257 F2
Middlefield La *RCCH* PO18 .... 195 H3
Middle Meadow *LISS* GU33 .... 62 A7
Middle Onslow Cl *FERR* BN12 .... 228 C8 [3]
Middle Rd *BRI* BN1 .... 10 A1
    LAN/SOMP BN15 .... 231 K6
    SHOR BN43 .... 233 K4
    SWTR RH13 .... 134 C8
Middle St *BRI* BN1 .... 10 B5 [5]
    HORS RH12 .... 4 B5 [5]
    PETW GU28 .... 125 K3 [5]
    PTSD BN41 .... 235 H5
    SHOR BN43 .... 233 H4
Middleton Av *HOVE* BN3 .... 235 H5
Middleton Cl *SELS* PO20 .... 258 A5
Middleton Gdns *SELS* PO20 .... 221 F1
Middleton Rd *HORS* RH12 .... 77 G1
    MIDOS PO22 .... 247 G6
Middleton Wy *CRAWW* RH11 .... 30 C6
Middle Tyne *SALV* BN13 .... 229 H6
Middle Wy *ANG/EP* BN16 .... 252 B3
    BURH RH15 .... 139 H8
Midfields *BURH* RH15 .... 139 H7 [1]
Midfields Dr *BURH* RH15 .... 139 H8
Midfields Wk *BURH* RH15 .... 139 H7 [3]
Midgley Rd *CRAWE* RH10 .... 3 E1 [1]
Midhurst Cl *CRAWW* RH11 .... 30 E4 [1]
    FERR BN12 .... 252 D1
Midhurst Dr *FERR* BN12 .... 252 D1
Midhurst Rd *BRI* BN1 .... 252 D1
    HASM GU27 .... 40 D6
    HASM GU27 .... 66 D7
    LIPH GU30 .... 38 C8
    PETW GU28 .... 125 H4
Midhurst Wk *HOVE* BN3 .... 211 K8 [2]

The Midway *MIDOS* PO22 .... 13 F4
Mighell St *ROTT* BN2 .... 11 D5 [7]
Milborne Rd *CRAWE* RH10 .... 56 C1
Milbury Cl *FERR* BN12 .... 252 D3 [3]
Milcote Av *HOVE* BN3 .... 235 K5
Mile End La *SELS* PO20 .... 242 C1
Mile Oak Crs *STHW* BN42 .... 234 D2
Mile Oak Gdns *PTSD* BN41 .... 234 E2
Mile Oak Rd *PTSD* BN41 .... 210 D8
Miles Cl *ARUN* BN18 .... 248 B1
Millais *SWTR* RH13 .... 5 F4
Millais Cl *CRAWW* RH11 .... 54 D1 [1]
Millais Ct *SWTR* RH13 .... 5 F3 [1]
Milland La *LIPH* GU30 .... 64 A5
Milland Rd *LIPH* GU30 .... 92 B1
Mill Av *SHOR* BN43 .... 233 H2 [4]
Millbank *BURH* RH15 .... 139 H7
The Millbank *CRAWW* RH11 .... 30 D5
Mill Bay La *HORS* RH12 .... 4 A6
Millbrook Cl *LISS* GU33 .... 22 A7
Mill Cl *ANG/EP* BN16 .... 218 B5
    CCH PO19 .... 7 E1
    EGRIN RH19 .... 36 C4
    HASM GU27 .... 40 A5 [3]
    POY/PYE BN45 .... 187 G6
    PTSD BN41 .... 235 G2
    SWTR RH13 .... 107 J4
Mill Copse Rd *HASM* GU27 .... 40 D7
Millcroft *BRI* BN1 .... 212 D6
Millcroft Av *STHW* BN42 .... 234 C2
Millcroft Gdns *STHW* BN42 .... 234 C2
Millcross Rd *PTSD* BN41 .... 235 F2
Mill Dr *HFD* BN5 .... 161 H7
    HOVE BN3 .... 212 A8
Mill End *EMRTH* PO10 .... 215 F3
    HFD BN5 .... 161 G7
    PUL/STOR RH20 .... 156 A4
Millennium Cl *LAN/SOMP* BN15 .... 232 D5
Miller Rd *BRI* BN1 .... 10 A1
Millers Cl *ANG/EP* BN16 .... 251 F1
Millers Ga *HORS* RH12 .... 4 C1
The Millers *ARUN* BN18 .... 247 K1
Millers Wy *BURH* RH15 .... 139 C7
Mill Farm Rd *SWTR* RH13 .... 5 F3
Millfield *LAN/SOMP* BN15 .... 231 J4
    SWTR RH13 .... 105 G3
Millfield Cl *ANG/EP* BN16 .... 250 D4
    CCH PO19 .... 7 E1
Millfield Cottages *ROTT* BN2 .... 11 F6 [9]
Mill Gdns *SELS* PO20 .... 257 J4
Mill Green Rd *HWH* RH16 .... 112 A5
Mill Hl *SHOR* BN43 .... 209 G6
Mill Hill Cl *HWH* RH16 .... 112 A4
    SHOR BN43 .... 233 G2
Mill Hill Dr *SHOR* BN43 .... 233 G2
Mill Hill Gdns *SHOR* BN43 .... 233 G2
Mill House Gdns *WTHG* BN11 .... 8 A4
Mill La *ANG/EP* BN16 .... 251 F1
    ARUN BN18 .... 178 A5
    ARUN BN18 .... 199 C5
    ARUN BN18 .... 201 H8
    ARUN BN18 .... 223 H2
    CCH PO19 .... 218 B5
    CRAWE RH10 .... 20 A8
    CRAWW RH11 .... 30 A5
    EGRIN RH19 .... 21 F6
    EMRTH PO10 .... 215 F1
    EPSF GU31 .... 118 B8
    EPSF GU31 .... 119 K3
    EPSF GU31 .... 120 A3
    HASM GU27 .... 40 E7
    HPPT/KEY BN6 .... 138 A4
    HPPT/KEY BN6 .... 163 J1
    HPPT/KEY BN6 .... 188 E4
    LHPTN BN17 .... 225 K6
    LING RH7 .... 22 D1
    MIDH GU29 .... 121 C1
    MIDH GU29 .... 147 K3
    MIDH GU29 .... 148 B1
    POY/PYE BN45 .... 187 G6
    PSF GU32 .... 88 C3
    PSF GU32 .... 89 F5
    PTSD BN41 .... 235 F1
    PUL/STOR RH20 .... 156 A3
    PUL/STOR RH20 .... 157 K8
    PUL/STOR RH20 .... 180 B1
    RHWH RH17 .... 83 J2
    SALV BN13 .... 229 K1
    SELS PO20 .... 244 A4
    SELS PO20 .... 260 A4
    SELS PO20 .... 264 C4
    SHOR BN43 .... 233 G3
    SWTR RH13 .... 103 H8
    SWTR RH13 .... 107 J4
    SWTR RH13 .... 134 B6
Mill Md *PUL/STOR* RH20 .... 158 A7
Mill Park Rd *BOGR* PO21 .... 261 H1
Mill Pond Wy *ANG/EP* BN16 .... 251 H1
Mill Quay *EMRTH* PO10 .... 214 E4
Mill Race *HPPT/KEY* BN6 .... 164 E3
Mill Ri *BRI* BN1 .... 212 C6
Mill Rd *ANG/EP* BN16 .... 227 H6
    ARUN BN18 .... 199 H8
    ARUN BN18 .... 201 H8

BRI BN1
    BURH RH15
    CRAWE RH10
    EMRTH PO10
    LAN/SOMP BN15
    LISS GU33
    PTSD BN41
    PUL/STOR RH20
    STEY/UB BN44
    WTHG BN11
Mill Road Av *ANG/EP* BN16
Mill Straight *SWTR* RH13
Mill Stream Meadow
    HWH RH16 1
The Millstream *HASM* GU27
Millthorpe Rd *HORS* RH12
Mill Vale Mdw *LIPH* GU30
Millview Cl *BOGR* PO21
Mill View Rd *ARUN* BN18
Mill Wy *BIL* RH14
    EGRIN RH19
Mill Wd *BURH* RH15.
Millwood *EGRIN* RH19
Milne Cl *CRAWW* RH11
Milner Rd *ROTT* BN2
Milnthorpe Rd *HOVE* BN3
Milnwood Rd *HORS* RH12
Milton Av *ANG/EP* BN16.
Milton Cl *ANG/EP* BN16 2
    LAN/SOMP BN15
Milton Crs *EGRIN* RH19
Milton Dr *STHW* BN42
Milton Mount Av *CRAWE* RH10
    CRAWE RH10
Milton Rd *CRAWE* RH10
    HORS RH12
    HWH RH16
    ROTT BN2
    WTHG BN11
Milton St *WTHG* BN11
Mimmack Cl *STEY/UB* BN44
Mindlehem Av *EGRIN* RH19
The Minnels *HPPT/KEY* BN6
Minsted Rd *MIDH* GU29
Minton Rd *MIDOS* PO22
Mint Rd *LISS* GU33
Misbrooks Green Rd *RDKG* RH5
Mitchell Gdns *SWTR* RH13
Mitchells Rd *CRAWE* RH10
Mixon Cl *SELS* PO20
Moatfield La *SWTR* RH13
Moat La *PUL/STOR* RH20
Moat Rd *EGRIN* RH19
The Moat *PUL/STOR* RH20
Moat Wk *CRAWE* RH10
Moat Wy *FERR* BN12
Mocatta Rd *BURH* RH15
Modena Rd *HOVE* BN3
Moggs Md *EPSF* GU31
Mole Cl *CRAWW* RH11
Molecomb Broadwalk
    RCCH PO18
Molesworth St *HOVE* BN3
The Mole *LHPTN* BN17
Monarch Cl *CRAWW* RH11
Monarch's Wy *ARUN* BN18
    BRI BN1
    HAV PO9
    HOVE BN3
    PTSD BN41
    PUL/STOR RH20
    RCCH PO18
    RCCH PO18
    RCCH PO18
    SALV BN13
    SALV BN13
    SHOR BN43
    STEY/UB BN44
    STEY/UB BN44
    STHW BN42
Monastery La *PUL/STOR* RH20
Monkmead Copse
    PUL/STOR RH20
Monkmead La *PUL/STOR* RH20.
Monks Av *LAN/SOMP* BN15
Monks Cl *LAN/SOMP* BN15.
Monksfield *CRAWE* RH10
Monk's Hl *EMRTH* PO10
Monks La *RDKG* RH5
Monks Orch *PSF* GU32
Monks Wk *STEY/UB* BN44
Monks Wd *PSF* GU32
Monmouth St *HOVE* BN3
Mons Av *BOGR* PO21.
Montague Cl *SHOR* BN43
Montague Gdns *EPSF* GU31
Montague Pl *ROTT* BN2
    WTHG BN11
Montague Rd *MIDH* GU29
Montague St *ROTT* BN2
    WTHG BN11
Montagu Rd *CCH* PO19
Montalan Crs *SELS* PO20
Montefiore Rd *HOVE* BN3
Monterey Pines *MIDOS* PO22

s Hl *HWH* RH16	113	H3
...swood La *RHWH* RH17	113	K3
...ord Cl *SHOR* BN43	234	B3
...omeri Dr *ANG/EP* BN16	226	D8
...omery Dr *MIDOS* PO22	247	H5
...omery St *HOVE* BN3	235	K4
...elier Gdns *PUL/STOR* RH20	181	J3
...elier Pl *BRI* BN1	10	A4
...elier Rd *ANG/EP* BN16	251	J2
...N1	10	A5
...elier St *BRI* BN1	10	A4
...elier Ter *BRI* BN1	10	A4
...elier Vis *BRI* BN1	10	A4
...al Rd *ROTT* BN2	11	D4
...al Wy *SALV* BN13	229	G5
...se Cl *FERR* BN12	229	G8
...ent La *RCCH* PO18	191	K4
...ent Vw *ROTT* BN2	11	F4
...La *EGRIN* RH19	23	H4
RH13	5	D6 🔢
...oft Cl *CRAWW* RH11	2	A2
...Cl *SALV* BN13	229	F5
...ot Rd *SALV* BN13	229	F5
...ad Rd *HORS* RH12	52	D6
...n Wy *MIDOS* PO22	12	A2 🔢
...use La *MIDH* GU29	92	C5
...orings *EGRIN* RH19	21	J8
...OMP BN15	232	B3
...BN43	234	A3
...nd Rd *CRAWE* RH10	32	C8
...ark Crs *CRAWW* RH11	30	B6 🔢
...EGRIN* RH19	36	B1
...d *HASM* GU27	39	J6
...U33	62	B2
...t Dr *MIDOS* PO22	247	H5
...mbe Cl *CRAWW* RH11	30	D7 🔢
...mbe Rd *BRI* BN1	213	G5
...n Rd *RCCH* PO18	216	E6
...d Av *FIN/BW* BN14	230	E4
...*PUL/STOR* RH20	158	A7
...St *ROTT* BN2	10	C4
...gton Crs *HOVE* BN3	235	H4 🔢
...S PO22	13	F3
...Av *HORS* RH12	5	E2
...Wy *PUL/STOR* BN15	156	A4
...er Rd *HOVE* BN3	235	K3
...Cl *CRAWW* RH11	55	F3 🔢
...Rd *EGRIN* RH19	36	C4
...Rd *EMRTH* PO10	215	H3
...LISS GU33	62	A7
...dns *RCCH* PO18	218	B4
...atten Cl *CRAWW* RH11	55	G1 🔢
...I *CRAWE* RH10	32	C4
...elds *BRI* BN1	237	J1
...La *CCH* PO19	6	B3
...E RH10	34	C7
...loddy *RHWH* RH17	110	C8
...leasant *ARUN* BN18	201	G8
...BN2	11	D5 🔢
...nt *HASM* GU27	41	H1
...RH12	29	K2
...iew Rd *LAN/SOMP* BN15	231	J5
...ray *LAN/SOMP* BN15	232	A2
...ood Rd *EMRTH* PO10	215	H2
...020	265	C3
...tion Pl *BRI* BN1	10	B4 🔢
...a *STEY/UB* BN44	182	E4
...UB BN44	183	H7
...y's La *RCCH* PO18	217	J1
...y Dr *CRAWW* RH11	30	D7
...Cl *HOVE* BN3	235	J2
...Rd *CRAWW* RH11	55	C1
...ry La *RCCH* PO18	216	E3
...dge's La *RDKG* RH5	28	A3
...d Cl *CRAWW* RH11	30	B6
...N13	229	J5 🔢
...y Cl *BRI* BN1	213	F8 🔢
...BN12	229	G8
...N12	252	C1
...RH12	4	B2 🔢
...OMP BN15	232	A5 🔢
...BN43	234	B2
...y Gdns *FERR* BN12	253	C1 🔢
...y La *FERR* BN12	229	G8
...N12	253	C2
...KEY BN6	165	K8
...y Rd *CRAWW* RH11	31	F2 🔢
...d Pl *CCH* PO19	6	B3
...e Wy *ANG/EP* BN16	251	C1 🔢
...I Rd *RHWH* RH17	84	D4
...er *BURH* RH15	139	H7
...n Dr *SWTR* RH13	75	J8
...Av *BOGR* PO21	12	B3
...Ct *SWTR* RH13	52	D7
...Rd *SELS* PO20	264	D5
...Hl *HASM* GU27	41	F5
...e Av *EGRIN* RH19	36	C4
...Cl *ARUN* BN18	224	B8
...n *RHWH* RH16	111	K7
...n South *HWH* RH16	111	K7
...Hl *LING* RH7	22	E4
...s La *PUL/STOR* RH20	157	H8

Myrtle Crs *LAN/SOMP* BN15	231	J6
Myrtle Gv *ANG/EP* BN16	251	C2
Myrtle La *BIL* RH14	102	D4
Myrtle Rd *LAN/SOMP* BN15	231	K6
Mytten Bank *RHWH* RH17	111	F5 🔢
Mytten Cl *RHWH* RH17	111	F5

N

Nab Tower La *SELS* PO20	264	B3
Nab Wk *SELS* PO20	257	J5
Nagels Cl *SELS* PO20	257	K5
Naiad Gdns *MIDOS* PO22	247	H7 🔢
Naldrett Cl *HORS* RH12	5	E3
Naldretts La *HORS* RH12	48	A6
Namrik Ms *HOVE* BN3	236	A5
Nanson Rd *BRI* BN1	213	K5
Napier Wy *CRAWE* RH10	31	K2
Nappers Wd *HASM* GU27	66	C5
Nash La *RHWH* RH17	113	K7
Nash Rd *CRAWE* RH10	3	D6
Nash Wy *ARUN* BN18	223	H2
Natal Rd *ROTT* BN2	11	F1
Natts La *BIL* RH14	102	A4
Navarino Rd *WTHG* BN11	231	G8
Neale Cl *EGRIN* RH19	21	K8
Needles Cl *HORS* RH12	4	A6 🔢
Need's Hl *SWTR* RH13	134	A5
Nell Ball *BIL* RH14	70	E1
Nelson Cl *CRAWE* RH10	32	C6
LAN/SOMP BN15	231	K3
SELS PO20	221	F2
Nelson Rd *BOGR* PO21	245	J3
FERR BN12	229	H7
HORS RH12	4	A4
Nelson Rw *ARUN* BN18	224	B5
ROTT BN2	11	D5 🔢
Nepcote La *FIN/BW* BN14	205	J5
Nepfield Cl *FIN/BW* BN14	205	J6
Nep Town Rd *HFD* BN5	161	G7
Neptune Cl *CRAWW* RH11	30	C7 🔢
Neptune Ct *MIDOS* PO22	247	H7 🔢
Neptune Wy *ANG/EP* BN16	250	C3
Nesbitt Rd *ROTT* BN2	11	F1
Netherfion Cl *SELS* PO20	265	F4
SWTR RH13	77	F7
Netherwood *CRAWW* RH11	30	E8
Netherwoods Rd *SWTR* RH13	104	B5
Netley Cl *CRAWW* RH11	55	F3 🔢
Nettleton Av *SELS* PO20	220	E1
Nevile Cl *CRAWW* RH11	30	E8
Nevill Av *HOVE* BN3	235	K2
Nevill Cl *HOVE* BN3	236	A1
Nevill Gdns *HOVE* BN3	236	A1
Nevill Pl *HOVE* BN3	236	A1
Nevill Rd *HOVE* BN3	236	A1
Nevill Wy *HOVE* BN3	236	A1
Newark Pl *ROTT* BN2	11	D4
Newark Rd *CRAWE* RH10	3	E1
New Barn Cl *PTSD* BN41	235	F1
SHOR BN43	233	K2 🔢
New Barn Hl *RCCH* PO18	196	C6
New Barn La *PUL/STOR* RH20	155	K3
Newbarn La *BOGR* PO21	245	H4
HFD BN5	185	H1
MIDOS PO22	247	F5
RCCH PO18	191	J5
New Barn Rd *ARUN* BN18	177	K6
SHOR BN43	233	K2
Newbarn Rd *EPSF* GU31	116	A8
New Br *BIL* RH14	102	C6
Newbridge Cl *HORS* RH12	50	C8 🔢
Newbridge Rd *BIL* RH14	101	J3
New Brighton Rd *EMRTH* PO10	214	D1
Newbury La *RHWH* RH17	110	E6
Newbury Rd *CRAWE* RH10	32	D5
Newchapel Rd *LING* RH7	21	J1
New Church Rd *HOVE* BN3	235	H4
New Courtwick La *LHPTN* BN17	225	J7 🔢
New Cut *ARUN* BN18	201	H8 🔢
Newdigate Rd *HORS* RH12	29	F3
New Dorset St *BRI* BN1	10	B4
Newells La *RCCH* PO18	216	D1
SWTR RH13	107	F1
New England Ri *PTSD* BN41	210	E7
New England Rd *BRI* BN1	10	B3
HWH RH16	112	A7
New England St *BRI* BN1	10	C5 🔢
New Farthingdale *LING* RH7	22	S3
Newfield Rd *LISS* GU33	62	A5
SELS PO20	265	H3
Newhache *LING* RH7	22	E2
Newhall Cl *BOGR* PO21	245	H8
New Hall La *HFD* BN5	185	H4
Newham Cl *STEY/UB* BN44	183	J8
Newham La *STEY/UB* BN44	207	H1
Newhaven St *ROTT* BN2	11	D4
Newhouse La *PUL/STOR* RH20	157	G8
RCCH PO18	173	F4
Newland Rd *STEY/UB* BN44	208	D1

WTHG BN11	9	D3
Newlands *RHWH* RH17	83	F2
Newlands Cl *HPPT/KEY* BN6	165	G8
Newlands Crs *EGRIN* RH19	36	B1
Newlands La *CCH* PO19	218	D3
Newlands Pk *CRAWE* RH10	20	A8
Newlands Rd *CRAWW* RH11	2	B4
HORS RH12	4	B3
Newland St *WTHG* BN11	9	D3 🔢
New La *EPSF* GU31	144	B1
Newling Wy *SALV* BN13	229	J2
Newman Cl *CRAWE* RH10	32	C7 🔢
Newman's Gdns *LAN/SOMP* BN15	231	H4 🔢
Newmarket Rd *CRAWE* RH10	3	F6
ROTT BN2	11	E2 🔢
New Moorhead Dr *HORS* RH12	52	E5
New Pde *WTHG* BN11	9	F4
New Park Rd *CCH* PO19	6	C2
New Place Rd *PUL/STOR* RH20	128	E8
Newport Dr *CCH* PO19	218	E4
Newport Ms *WTHG* BN11	231	H8
Newport Rd *BURH* RH15	139	F8
Newport St *ROTT* BN2	11	D3 🔢
Newpound La *BIL* RH14	75	G8
Newpound La *BIL* RH14	100	E2
New Rd *ANG/EP* BN16	227	F8
BIL RH14	102	C1
BIL RH14	103	F1
BRI BN1	10	C5 🔢
EMRTH PO10	191	F8
HASM GU27	40	B6
HPPT/KEY BN6	189	F2
LHPTN BN17	249	K3
MIDH GU29	122	A5
MIDH GU29	123	G6
PETW GU28	124	E2
RCCH PO18	173	H2
RCCH PO18	196	C7
SALV BN13	229	C4
SHOR BN43	233	H4
STEY/UB BN44	208	D2
SWTR RH13	77	F7
Newstead Hall *HORL* RH6	18	D1
New Steine *ROTT* BN2	11	D6 🔢
ROTT BN2	11	D6 🔢
New St *CRAWE* RH10	3	F2
SWTR RH13	4	C5
WTHG BN11	9	D5 🔢
Newtimber Av *FERR* BN12	229	F8
Newtimber Dr *PTSD* BN41	234	E2
Newtimber Gdns *SHOR* BN43	233	H2 🔢
Newton Av *EGRIN* RH19	36	D5
Newton Cl *HWH* RH16	112	D4
Newton Rd *CRAWE* RH10	31	K1
HWH RH16	112	D4
New Town *CCH* PO19	6	C3 🔢
CRAWE RH10	19	H8
Newtown Av *BOGR* PO21	245	J5
Newtown Rd *HOVE* BN3	236	B3
LIPH GU30	38	B8
New Town Rd *PUL/STOR* RH20	179	K2
New Way La *HPPT/KEY* BN6	188	B1
Nicholsfield *BIL* RH14	46	B7
Nicolson Dr *SHOR* BN43	233	H3
Nightingale Cl *CRAWW* RH11	2	B1
EGRIN RH19	36	B4 🔢
PUL/STOR RH20	180	C2
Nightingale La *BURH* RH15	155	F5
PUL/STOR RH20	180	C2
RCCH PO18	192	A8
Nightingale Pk *PUL/STOR* RH20	180	C2
Nightingale Rd *HORS* RH12	4	C4
PSF GU32	116	B1 🔢
Nightingales *FIN/BW* BN14	205	J4
PUL/STOR RH20	156	B4
Nightingale Wk *BIL* RH14	102	B3
Nile St *BRI* BN1	10	C5 🔢
EMRTH PO10	214	D3
Nimbus Cl *LHPTN* BN17	250	C1
Niven Cl *CRAWE* RH10	32	D6 🔢
Nizells Av *HOVE* BN3	236	D4
Noahs Ark La *HWH* RH16	112	E4
Noel Gn *BURH* RH15	139	H7
Noel Ri *BURH* RH15	139	H7
Nonnington La *PETW* GU28	149	K2
The Nookery *ANG/EP* BN16	251	J2
Nor'bren Av *BOGR* PO21	245	J6
Norbury Cl *LAN/SOMP* BN15	232	B3
Norbury Dr *LAN/SOMP* BN15	232	A3
Nore Crs *EMRTH* PO10	214	B2
Nore Down Wy *RCCH* PO18	167	J3
Nore Farm Av *EMRTH* PO10	214	B2
Noreuil Rd *PSF* GU32	88	B8
Norfolk Buildings *BRI* BN1	10	A5 🔢
Norfolk Cl *BOGR* PO21	12	B6 🔢
CRAWW RH11	54	C1 🔢
HORL RH6	18	A1
Norfolk Gdns *LHPTN* BN17	250	B3
Norfolk Ms *BRI* BN1	10	A5 🔢
Norfolk Pl *LHPTN* BN17	250	B3 🔢
Norfolk Rd *BRI* BN1	10	A5
HORS RH12	4	C5
LHPTN BN17	250	B3
Norfolk Sq *BOGR* PO21	12	A6

BRI BN1 .... **10** A5
Norfolk St *BOGR* PO21 .... **12** C6 🅱
　BRI BN1 .... **236** D6
　WTHG BN11 .... **8** C3
Norfolk Ter *BRI* BN1 .... **10** A4
Norfolk Wy *MIDOS* PO22 .... **248** A6
Norman Cl *BIL* RH14 .... **102** C2
　LHPTN BN17 .... **250** B2
Norman Crs *SWTR* BN43 .... **233** H2
Normandy *HORS* RH12 .... **4** B6 🅱
Normandy Cl *CRAWE* RH10 .... **32** B7 🅱
　EGRIN RH19 .... **36** D3 🅰
Normandy Dr *ANG/EP* BN16 .... **251** H3
Normandy Gdns *HORS* RH12 .... **4** B6
Normandy La *ANG/EP* BN16 .... **251** J3
Normandy Rd *FIN/BW* BN14 .... **8** C2
Normanhurst Cl *ANG/EP* BN16 ...... **250** E3 🅱
　CRAWE RH10 .... **3** E3
　HOVE BN3 .... **235** J5
Norman Rd *BURH* RH15 .... **139** F8
Norman's Dr *MIDOS* PO22 .... **247** F5
Normanton Av *BOGR* PO21 .... **12** A5 🅱
Normanton St *ROTT* BN2 .... **11** E3 🅰
Norman Wy *MIDOS* PO22 .... **247** K6
　STEY/UB BN44 .... **183** K7
North Av *FERR* BN12 .... **253** J2
　MIDOS PO22 .... **247** K6
North Av South *MIDOS* PO22 .... **247** K7
North Bank *HPPT/KEY* BN6 .... **164** K7
North Bay *EMRTH* PO10 .... **214** E8
North Bersted St *MIDOS* PO22 .... **245** J4
Northbourne Cl *SHOR* BN43 .... **233** H3 🅱
Northbrook Cl *FIN/BW* BN14 .... **230** E5 🅱
Northbrook Rd *FIN/BW* BN14 .... **230** E5
Northcliffe Rd *MIDOS* PO22 .... **13** D2 🅰
North Cl *CRAWE* RH10 .... **3** E2
　PTSD BN41 .... **234** E1
North Common Rd *RHWH* RH17 .... **141** F6
Northcote Rd *BOGR* PO21 .... **245** J7
North Ct *HPPT/KEY* BN6 .... **164** E7
Northcourt Cl *FIN/BW* BN14 .... **251** F1
Northcourt Rd *FIN/BW* BN14 .... **8** C2
Northcroft *HFD* BN5 .... **161** F6
Northdown Ct *HORS* RH12 .... **5** E3
North Dr *ANG/EP* BN16 .... **227** H1
　ROTT BN2 .... **11** E4
Northease Cl *HOVE* BN3 .... **235** H1 🅱
Northease Dr *HOVE* BN3 .... **235** H1
Northease Gdns *HOVE* BN3 .... **211** J8 🅱
North End *HPPT/KEY* BN6 .... **165** K7
North End *PETW* GU28 .... **125** K2
Northend La *HPPT/KEY* BN6 .... **137** K8
North End Rd *ARUN* BN18 .... **223** K7
Northern Crs *SELS* PO20 .... **257** H4
North Farm Rd
　LAN/SOMP BN15 .... **232** A5 🅰
Northfield Av *SELS* PO20 .... **265** G4
Northfield Ri *HOVE* BN3 .... **211** H7
Northfield Rd *SALV* BN13 .... **230** A5 🅰
Northfields La *SELS* PO20 .... **222** B3
Northfield Wy *BRI* BN1 .... **213** C2
North Gdns *BRI* BN1 .... **10** B4
Northgate Av *CRAWE* RH10 .... **3** E2
Northgate Cl *LAN/SOMP* BN15 ...... **231** J5 🅰
Northgate Pl *CRAWE* RH10 .... **3** D2 🅱
Northgate Rd *CRAWW* RH11 .... **2** C5
North Ham Rd *LHPTN* BN17 .... **249** K2
North Heath Cl *HORS* RH12 .... **4** C2
North Heath La *HORS* RH12 .... **4** C2
North Holmes Cl *HORS* RH12 .... **52** D6
Northlands Av *HWH* RH16 .... **112** C8
Northlands *PUL/STOR* RH20 .... **156** C7
Northlands Rd *HORS* RH12 .... **50** D2
　HORS RH12 .... **52** A4
North La *ANG/EP* BN16 .... **250** D1
　ANG/EP BN16 .... **251** J2
　EGRIN RH19 .... **59** G6
　EPSF GU31 .... **116** C6
　EPSF GU31 .... **118** B7
　PTSD BN41 .... **234** E1
　RCCH PO18 .... **172** C2
　STEY/UB BN44 .... **182** C1
North Md *CRAWE* RH10 .... **3** E2
Northney La *HISD* PO11 .... **214** A7
North Pde *HORS* RH12 .... **4** B3
North Pl *BRI* BN1 .... **10** C5 🔢
　LHPTN BN17 .... **250** B3
North Pound *ARUN* BN18 .... **223** H2
North Rd *BRI* BN1 .... **10** B4 🅰
　CRAWE RH10 .... **3** F2
　HWH RH16 .... **112** C2
　LAN/SOMP BN15 .... **232** A6
　PSF GU32 .... **88** D7
　PTSD BN41 .... **234** E1
　RCCH PO18 .... **217** G4
　SELS PO20 .... **265** F4
Northside *RCCH* PO18 .... **194** E4
North St *BRI* BN1 .... **10** C5 🔢
　CCH PO19 .... **6** C3 🅱
　CRAWE RH10 .... **34** C7
　EMRTH PO10 .... **191** F7
　EMRTH PO10 .... **214** D2
　HORS RH12 .... **4** C5
　LHPTN BN17 .... **225** K8
　MIDH GU29 .... **122** B3

PETW GU28 .... **125** K2
PTSD BN41 .... **235** F4
PUL/STOR RH20 .... **180** B2
SHOR BN43 .... **233** G4
WTHG BN11 .... **9** D3
North Walls *CCH* PO19 .... **6** B3
Northway *BURH* RH15 .... **139** J7
North Wy *PETW* GU28 .... **125** J4
Northway Rd *LHPTN* BN17 .... **225** K7
Northwyke Cl *MIDOS* PO22 .... **247** G6
Northwyke Rd *MIDOS* PO22 .... **247** G6
Norton Cl *HOVE* BN3 .... **236** B5 🅱
Norton La *SELS* PO20 .... **221** K2
Norton Rd *HOVE* BN3 .... **236** B5
　LAN/SOMP BN15 .... **231** K6
Norway La *LHPTN* BN17 .... **226** B8
Norway St *PTSD* BN41 .... **235** G4
Norwich Rd *CCH* PO19 .... **6** B1
　CRAWE RH10 .... **3** F5
Norwoodhill Rd *HORL* RH6 .... **16** D2
Norwood La *PETW* GU28 .... **150** C3
Norwood La South *PETW* GU28 .... **150** C6
Nowhurst La *HORS* RH12 .... **50** A6
Nuffield Cl *BOGR* PO21 .... **245** G8 🅱
The Nurseries *BOGR* PO21 .... **244** E8 🅱
Nursery *ANG/EP* BN16 .... **251** J3
　EMRTH PO10 .... **190** D8
　HPPT/KEY BN6 .... **163** K4
　HWH RH16 .... **111** K6
　LAN/SOMP BN15 .... **231** K3
　MIDOS PO22 .... **225** F5
　PTSD BN41 .... **210** C7 🅱
　SHOR BN43 .... **233** K3
Nursery Gdns *LHPTN* BN17 .... **225** K8 🅱
Nurserylands *CRAWW* RH11 .... **30** C5
Nursery La *HORL* RH6 .... **17** H1
　RCCH PO18 .... **218** B4
　WTHG BN11 .... **8** C5
The Nursery *BURH* RH15 .... **139** J7
Nutbourne La *PUL/STOR* RH20 ...... **129** J7
Nutbourne Rd *FIN/BW* BN14 .... **8** B2
　PUL/STOR RH20 .... **155** J2
Nutcombe La *GSHT* GU26 .... **40** A2
Nutcroft *PUL/STOR* RH20 .... **128** E8 🅱
Nutham La *SWTR* RH13 .... **105** G2
Nuthurst Cl *CRAWW* RH11 .... **30** E4
Nuthurst Rd *SWTR* RH13 .... **78** E8
　SWTR RH13 .... **106** B6
Nuthurst St *SWTR* RH13 .... **106** C3
Nutley Av *FERR* BN12 .... **253** C2
Nutley Cl *FERR* BN12 .... **253** C2
　HOVE BN3 .... **211** K8 🅱
Nutley Crs *FERR* BN12 .... **253** C2
Nutley Dr *FERR* BN12 .... **253** C2
Nye La *HPPT/KEY* BN6 .... **189** K3
Nye Rd *BURH* RH15 .... **139** H8
Nyes Cl *HFD* BN5 .... **161** H6
Nyes La *SWTR* RH13 .... **77** F8
Nyetimber Cl *PUL/STOR* RH20 .... **156** A5
Nyetimber Copse *PUL/STOR* RH20.. **156** A4
Nyetimber Crs *BOGR* PO21 .... **261** J1
Nyetimber La *BOGR* PO21 .... **261** J1
　PUL/STOR RH20 .... **155** K4
Nyetimber Ml *BOGR* PO21 .... **261** J1
The Nyetimbers *BOGR* PO21 .... **261** H1
Nyewood La *BOGR* PO21 .... **12** A4
Nymans Cl *HORS* RH12 .... **52** C4
Nymans Ct *CRAWE* RH10 .... **32** B8 🅱
Nyton Rd *SELS* PO20 .... **221** J1
　SELS PO20 .... **222** C3

O

Oakapple Cl *CRAWW* RH11 .... **55** F2 🔢
　SWTR RH13 .... **135** G2
Oakapple Rd *STHW* BN42 .... **234** B3
Oak Av *CCH* PO19 .... **6** A2
　PUL/STOR RH20 .... **157** F8
Oak Bank *HWH* RH16 .... **112** B8
Oak Cl *BRI* BN1 .... **212** E8
　CCH PO19 .... **6** A2
　CRAWE RH10 .... **19** F8
　MIDOS PO22 .... **12** B3
　PUL/STOR RH20 .... **180** D1
　SALV BN13 .... **229** J2
　SWTR RH13 .... **105** F4
Oak Crt *EGRIN* RH19 .... **36** E3
Oakcroft Gdns *LHPTN* BN17 .... **226** B8
Oakdale Rd *HWH* RH16 .... **112** B8 🔢
Oak Dell *CRAWE* RH10 .... **32** C4
Oakdene Av *PTSD* BN41 .... **210** C8
Oakdene Cl *PTSD* BN41 .... **210** C8
Oakdene Crs *PTSD* BN41 .... **210** C8
Oakdene Gdns *PTSD* BN41 .... **210** C8
Oakdene Ri *PTSD* BN41 .... **210** C7
Oakdene Wy *PTSD* BN41 .... **210** C8
Oak End *ARUN* BN18 .... **224** E1
　PUL/STOR RH20 .... **156** B4
Oakenfield *BURH* RH15 .... **139** F6
Oakfield *BIL* RH14 .... **70** E1
Oakfield Av *SELS* PO20 .... **257** J4
Oakfield Cl *HWH* RH16 .... **112** C4

Oakfield Rd *SELS* PO20
　SWTR RH13 ....
Oakfields *RDKG* RH5 ....
　CRAWE RH10 ....
Oakfield Wy *EGRIN* RH19 ....
Oak Gv *BIL* RH14 ....
　MIDOS PO22 ....
Oak Hall Pk *BURH* RH15 ....
Oakhaven *CRAWE* RH10 ....
Oakhill Rd *SWTR* RH13 ....
Oakhurst *HFD* BN5 ....
　MIDH GU29 ....
Oakhurst Gdns *ANG/EP* BN16 ....
　EGRIN RH19 ....
Oakhurst La *BIL* RH14 ....
　HWH RH16 ....
Oaklands *BIL* RH14 ....
　HASM GU27 ....
　RHWH RH17 ....
Oaklands La *MIDH* GU29 ....
Oaklands Rd *HWH* RH16 ....
　PSF GU32 ....
Oaklands Wy *CCH* PO19 ....
Oak La *HORS* RH12 ....
Oakleigh Cl *WTHG* BN11 ....
Oakleigh Rd *FIN/BW* BN14 ....
　HORS RH12 ....
Oakley Cl *EGRIN* RH19 ....
Oakley Gdns *ANG/EP* BN16 ....
Oak Little *SWTR* RH13 ....
Oak Meadow *SELS* PO20 ....
Oakmeadow Cl *EMRTH* PO10 ....
Oakmead Rd *BURH* RH15 ....
Oak Rd *CRAWW* RH11 ....
　SWTR RH13 ....
Oakroyd Cl *BURH* RH15 ....
Oaks Cl *HORS* RH12 ....
　SELS PO20 ....
The Oaks *ANG/EP* BN16 ....
　BURH RH15 ....
　EGRIN RH19 ....
　HWH RH16 ....
Oak Tree Dr *EMRTH* PO10 ....
　LISS GU33 ....
Oak Tree Farm *RCCH* PO18 ....
Oak Tree La *HASM* GU27 ....
　SELS PO20 ....
Oak Tree Wy *SWTR* RH13 ....
Oak Wk *HORS* RH12 ....
Oak Wy *CRAWE* RH10 ....
Oakway *SWTR* RH13 ....
Oakwood *SWTR* RH13 ....
Oakwood Cl *BURH* RH15 ....
　MIDH GU29 ....
　SELS PO20 ....
Oakwood Gdns *BOGR* PO21 ....
Oakwood Rd *BURH* RH15 ....
　HWH RH16 ....
Oathall Av *HWH* RH16 ....
Oathall Rd *HWH* RH16 ....
Oatlands *CRAWW* RH11 ....
Oberon Wy *CRAWW* RH11 ....
Ocean Cl *FERR* BN12 ....
Ocean Dr *FERR* BN12 ....
Ockenden La *RHWH* RH17 ....
Ockenden Wy *HPPT/KEY* BN6 ....
Ockley Hl *HPPT/KEY* BN6 ....
Ockley La *BURH* RH15 ....
　HPPT/KEY BN6 ....
Ockley Rd *BOGR* PO21 ....
Ockley Wy *HPPT/KEY* BN6 ....
Offington Av *FIN/BW* BN14 ....
Offington Ct *FIN/BW* BN14 ....
Offington Dr *FIN/BW* BN14 ....
Offington Gdns *FIN/BW* BN14 ....
Offington La *FIN/BW* BN14 ....
Okehurst La *BIL* RH14 ....
Okehurst Rd *BIL* RH14 ....
Old Arundel Rd *RCCH* PO18 ....
Old Barn Cl *BOGR* PO21 ....
Old Barn Wy *STHW* BN42 ....
Old Boat Wk *BRI* BN1 ....
Old Bridge Rd *RCCH* PO18 ....
Old Brighton Rd (North)
　CRAWW RH11 ....
Old Brighton Rd South
　CRAWE RH10 ....
Old Brighton Rd (South)
　CRAWE RH10 ....
Old Broyle Rd *CCH* PO19 ....
Old Buddington La *MIDH* GU29 ... .
Oldbury Ct *HORS* RH12 ....
Old Coastguards *MIDOS* PO22 ....
Old Cottage Cl *SELS* PO20 ....
Old Court Cl *BRI* BN1 ....
Old Crawley Rd *HORS* RH12 ....
Old Denne Gdns *HORS* RH12 ....
Older Wy *ANG/EP* BN16 ....
Old Farm Cl *BOGR* PO21 ....
Old Farm Dr *SELS* PO20 ....
Old Farm La *EMRTH* PO10 ....
Old Farm Rd *BRI* BN1 ....
　SELS PO20 ....
Oldfield Crs *STHW* BN42 ....
Oldfield Rd *HORL* RH6 ....

rt Rd *SHOR* BN43 ..... **233** J5
ebe *HASM* GU27 ..... **66** D5
ildford Rd *HORS* RH12 ..... **50** E8
slemere Rd *HASM* GU27 ..... **40** E6
lbrook *HORS* RH12 ..... **52** A3
llow *CRAWE* RH10 ..... **33** F3
rsham Rd *CRAWW* RH11 ..... **2** A5
use La *BIL* RH14 ..... **103** F8
   PO9 ..... **167** H5
/STOR RH20 ..... **130** E3
   PO20 ..... **259** G4
ds Av *HPPT/KEY* BN6 ..... **165** C3
/H RH17 ..... **83** F2
ndon Rd *BRI* BN1 ..... **212** E6
/STOR RH20 ..... **153** K5
/STOR RH20 ..... **181** J3
anor CI *CRAWW* RH11 ..... **30** E3
anor House Gdns
   OS **247** F6
anor Rd *ANG/EP* BN16 ..... **250** D1
rtyrs *CRAWW* RH11 ..... **31** H2 ⊡
ad Rd *LHPTN* BN17 ..... **225** J6
d CI *BRI* BN1 ..... **212** E6
l Dr *PUL/STOR* RH20 ..... **180** B2
l La *PSF* GU31 ..... **89** F6
lmeads *HORS* RH12 ..... **4** B2
l PI *HASM* GU27 ..... **40** B4
/STOR RH20 ..... **155** F2
chards *CRAWE* RH10 ..... **32** E5
rk La *RHWH* RH17 ..... **111** G5 ⊡
rk La *RCCH* PO18 ..... **217** J8
tcham Ms *BRI* BN1 ..... **212** E6
BOGR PO21 ..... **262** B1
nt *MIDOS* PO22 ..... **247** J7
d Quarry *HASM* GU27 ..... **40** B7
ctory CI *EMRTH* PO10 ..... **191** F8 ⊡
ctory Dr *SELS* PO20 ..... **222** C4
ctory Gdns *STHW* RH42 ..... **234** B4
d Rectory *MIDOS* PO22 ..... **15** F4 ⊡
EGRIN RH19 ..... **36** D5
ts Farm Rd
/SOMP BN15 ..... **232** C5
hool CI *SELS* PO20 ..... **241** H7 ⊡
hool La *RDKG* RH5 ..... **14** D2
hool PI *BURH* RH15 ..... **165** F1
preham Rd *BRI* BN1 ..... **10** A3
 BN3 ..... **236** A3
/SOMP BN15 ..... **232** C3 ⊡
/ RH42 ..... **234** D3
tion CI *CRAWE* RH10 ..... **34** D4
ine *ROTT* BN2 ..... **10** C5 ⊡
ckham La *HWH* RH16 ..... **111** K4
ckhurst La *HORS* RH12 ..... **76** D2
k Mdw *RCCH* PO18 ..... **195** F6
rthing Rd *ANG/EP* BN16 ..... **251** K1
 CI *ROTT* BN2 ..... **11** E5
d *HOVE* BN3 ..... **235** J3
Rd *HORS* RH12 ..... **77** G2
 Meadow *SELS* PO20 ..... **222** B4
Whitby Rd *CCH* PO19 ..... **218** D4
Rd *CRAWE* RH10 ..... **32** D6
 Dr *FERR* BN12 ..... **252** E2
 CI *HORL* RH6 ..... **19** C1
BN13 ..... **229** G5
 Gdns *SALV* BN13 ..... **229** G5
d *WTHG* BN11 ..... **231** G8
 Rw *BRI* BN1 ..... **10** C5 ⊡ ⊡
/H PO10 ..... **214** D3
d Av *CCH* PO19 ..... **6** B2
/ W BN14 ..... **8** A1
BN3 ..... **236** A2
/SOMP BN15 ..... **232** A4
PO20 ..... **265** F5
d CI *BOGR* PO21 ..... **12** A5 ⊡
GU31 ..... **118** C7
 BN12 ..... **228** C8
 W BN14 ..... **8** B1
 N5 ..... **181** H5
 RH16 ..... **111** K3
 GU28 ..... **125** K4
 RH17 ..... **113** H8 ⊡
 BN43 ..... **233** G3
 BN42 ..... **234** D3
d Side *SELS* PO20 ..... **243** J2
chards *CRAWW* RH11 ..... **30** B6 ⊡
 St *CCH* PO19 ..... **6** B3
/ W RH11 ..... **2** C3
chard *BOGR* PO21 ..... **261** K2 ⊡

HASM GU27 ..... **40** B6
Orchard Wy *ARUN* BN18 ..... **198** E8
BURH RH15 ..... **139** F8 ⊡
EGRIN RH19 ..... **36** C2
HPPT/KEY BN6 ..... **163** K5
HWH RH16 ..... **111** K3
LAN/SOMP BN15 ..... **232** A4
MIDH GU29 ..... **122** B3
MIDOS PO22 ..... **12** B2
MIDOS PO22 ..... **223** F5
PUL/STOR RH20 ..... **128** E8
RHWH RH17 ..... **109** H3
Orchid Pk *HWH* RH16 ..... **112** E7
Orchid Vw *BRI* BN1 ..... **213** J5
Orde CI *CRAWE* RH10 ..... **32** D2
Oriel CI *CRAWE* RH10 ..... **32** C2 ⊡
MIDOS PO22 ..... **223** F5
Oriental PI *BRI* BN1 ..... **10** A5
Orient Rd *LAN/SOMP* BN15 ..... **232** E6
Orkney Ct *SALV* BN13 ..... **229** F6 ⊡
Orltons *HORS* RH12 ..... **29** H1
Orme Rd *WTHG* BN11 ..... **8** C3
Ormesby Crs *MIDOS* PO22 ..... **13** F2
Ormonde Av *CCH* PO19 ..... **7** D3
Ormonde Wy *SHOR* BN43 ..... **233** F5
Orpen PI *SELS* PO20 ..... **265** G4
Orpen Rd *HOVE* BN3 ..... **236** C5
Orwell Rd *PSF* GU32 ..... **116** C1
Osborn Crs *CCH* PO19 ..... **219** G2
Osborne CI *LAN/SOMP* BN15 ..... **231** J5
Osborne Crs *CCH* PO19 ..... **7** F3
Osborne Dr *LAN/SOMP* BN15 ..... **231** J5
Osborne Rd *BRI* BN1 ..... **237** F1
PSF GU32 ..... **88** C3
Osborne Vls *HOVE* BN3 ..... **236** C6
Osmonde CI *FIN/BW* BN14 ..... **8** C2 ⊡
Osmond Rd *HOVE* BN3 ..... **10** A3
Osmunda Bank *EGRIN* RH19 ..... **22** C5
Osmund CI *CRAWE* RH10 ..... **32** E5
Osney CI *CRAWW* RH11 ..... **2** B4
Osprey Gdns *MIDOS* PO22 ..... **12** B1
Osprey Quay *EMRTH* PO10 ..... **215** F4
Ostlers Vw *BIL* RH14 ..... **102** A4
Otard CI *SELS* PO20 ..... **265** F4
Otford CI *CRAWW* RH11 ..... **55** G3
Otter CI *CCH* PO19 ..... **6** A1
Otway CI *CRAWW* RH11 ..... **30** D3
Otway Rd *CCH* PO19 ..... **219** F2
Outerwyke Av *MIDOS* PO22 ..... **13** F2
Outerwyke Gdns *MIDOS* PO22 ..... **247** F5 ⊡
Outerwyke Rd *MIDOS* PO22 ..... **13** F2
Outram Rd *MIDOS* PO22 ..... **13** E5
The Oval *FIN/BW* BN14 ..... **205** J4
SALV BN13 ..... **229** K8
Oval Waye *FERR* BN12 ..... **252** C5
Overdene Dr *CRAWW* RH11 ..... **30** D3
Overdown Ri *PTSD* BN41 ..... **210** D7
Overdown Rd *MIDOS* PO22 ..... **247** F6
Overhill *STHW* RH42 ..... **234** C2
Overhill Dr *BRI* BN1 ..... **212** E6
Overhill Gdns *BRI* BN1 ..... **212** E6
Overhill Wy *BRI* BN1 ..... **212** E5
Overmead *SHOR* BN43 ..... **233** G3
Overstrand Av *ANG/EP* BN16 ..... **250** D4
Over St *BRI* BN1 ..... **10** C4
Overton Shaw *EGRIN* RH19 ..... **22** C8
Oving Rd *CCH* PO19 ..... **7** D3
SELS PO20 ..... **220** D4
Owen CI *BURH* RH15 ..... **165** F2
Owers Wy *SELS* PO20 ..... **257** H4
Owlbeech Wy *SWTR* RH13 ..... **52** D7
Owletts *CRAWE* RH10 ..... **32** D4 ⊡
Owlscastle CI *HORS* RH12 ..... **4** C2
Oxen Av *SHOR* BN43 ..... **233** H3
Oxford CI *SELS* PO20 ..... **257** J4
Oxford Ct *BRI* BN1 ..... **10** C3 ⊡
Oxford Dr *BOGR* PO21 ..... **245** G8
Oxford Ms *HOVE* BN3 ..... **236** C4
Oxford PI *BRI* BN1 ..... **10** C3 ⊡
Oxford Rd *CRAWE* RH10 ..... **55** J1
SWTR RH13 ..... **4** C5
WTHG BN11 ..... **8** C3
Oxford St *BOGR* PO21 ..... **12** A6 ⊡
BRI BN1 ..... **10** C3

P

Pacific Wy *SELS* PO20 ..... **265** F6
Packham Wy *BURH* RH15 ..... **139** F7 ⊡
Paddock CI *HASM* GU27 ..... **66** C2
Paddock Gdns *EGRIN* RH19 ..... **36** C3
Paddock La *ANG/EP* BN16 ..... **251** G3
Paddockhall Rd *HWH* RH16 ..... **111** K6
Paddockhurst La *RHWH* RH17 ..... **57** K7
Paddockhurst Rd *CRAWE* RH10 ..... **57** J2
CRAWW RH11 ..... **30** E6
Paddock La *LAN/SOMP* BN15 ..... **232** B6
Paddocks *MIDOS* PO22 ..... **264** E4
The Paddocks *LAN/SOMP* BN15 ..... **232** B6
STEY/UB BN44 ..... **184** D8
The Paddock *CRAWE* RH10 ..... **32** C4 ⊡
HASM GU27 ..... **40** C3
HOVE BN3 ..... **236** C2

LHPTN BN17 ..... **225** J5
MIDOS PO22 ..... **12** B3
SHOR BN43 ..... **233** F2
Paddock Wy *FIN/BW* BN14 ..... **205** J5
HASM GU27 ..... **41** J1
LIPH GU30 ..... **38** B6
PSF GU32 ..... **116** B1
Padwick Rd *SWTR* RH13 ..... **5** E5
Pages La *WTHG* BN11 ..... **231** G8
Pagewood CI *CRAWE* RH10 ..... **32** D7
Pagham CI *EMRTH* PO10 ..... **214** E3
Pagham Rd *BOGR* PO21 ..... **261** G3
SELS PO20 ..... **244** C6
Pain's Flat *RHWH* RH17 ..... **138** D3
Palace PI *BRI* BN1 ..... **10** C5 ⊡ ⊡
Palatine Rd *FERR* BN12 ..... **229** G7
Palings Wy *HASM* GU27 ..... **66** C6
The Pallant *FERR* BN12 ..... **229** F7
Pallingham Dr *CRAWE* RH10 ..... **32** C8
Pallingham La *BIL* RH14 ..... **128** B1
Palm Ct *SALV* BN13 ..... **229** J4
Palmeira Av *HOVE* BN3 ..... **236** C5
Palmeira Sq *HOVE* BN3 ..... **236** C6
Palmer CI *PUL/STOR* RH20 ..... **180** D1
Palmer PI *SELS* PO20 ..... **243** K2
Palmer Rd *ANG/EP* BN16 ..... **227** G5
CRAWE RH10 ..... **32** C8
Palmers Field Av *CCH* PO19 ..... **7** D1
Palmers Rd *EMRTH* PO10 ..... **214** D2
Palmerston Av *FERR* BN12 ..... **253** G1
Palmers Wy *SALV* BN13 ..... **229** H2
Pangdean La *HPPT/KEY* BN6 ..... **138** C7
Pangdene CI *BURH* RH15 ..... **164** E2
Pankhurst Av *ROTT* BN2 ..... **11** E4
Pannell CI *EGRIN* RH19 ..... **36** B2
Pannett *BURH* RH15 ..... **138** E7 ⊡
Panton CI *EMRTH* PO10 ..... **190** C8 ⊡
The Parade *BIL* RH14 ..... **46** B2
BOGR PO21 ..... **261** H4
CRAWE RH10 ..... **3** D2 ⊡
Paradise La *EMRTH* PO10 ..... **191** F7
Parchment St *CCH* PO19 ..... **6** B2
Parham CI *ANG/EP* BN16 ..... **250** D5 ⊡
FIN/BW BN14 ..... **229** K2 ⊡
LHPTN BN17 ..... **249** K1
ROTT BN2 ..... **11** F5
Parham Rd *CRAWW* RH11 ..... **30** D3
FIN/BW BN14 ..... **229** K2
Parish La *CRAWE* RH10 ..... **55** K5
Park Av *HOVE* BN3 ..... **235** J4
HPPT/KEY BN6 ..... **189** G5
SELS PO20 ..... **265** G4
SHOR BN43 ..... **233** J3
WTHG BN11 ..... **9** E5
Park CI *BURH* RH15 ..... **139** F8
FIN/BW BN14 ..... **230** A4
HASM GU27 ..... **41** H2
HOVE BN3 ..... **211** J8
PTSD BN41 ..... **235** F2
Park Copse *SELS* PO20 ..... **265** J2
Park Crs *EMRTH* PO10 ..... **214** B2
MIDH GU29 ..... **122** A3
PTSD BN41 ..... **234** E3
SELS PO20 ..... **265** H3
WTHG BN11 ..... **8** C4 ⊡
Park Crescent PI *ROTT* BN2. ..... **11** D3
Park Crescent Rd *ROTT* BN2. ..... **11** D3
Park Crescent Ter *ROTT* BN2. ..... **11** D3
Park Dr *ANG/EP* BN16 ..... **251** F1
ARUN BN18 ..... **248** A1
FERR BN12 ..... **252** D1
MIDOS PO22 ..... **247** H6
Parker CI *CRAWE* RH10 ..... **32** D7
Park Farm CI *HORS* RH12 ..... **51** K4
Parkfield *HORS* RH12 ..... **4** B4
Parkfield Av *BOGR* PO21 ..... **245** F8
Parkfield CI *CRAWW* RH11 ..... **30** D5
Parkfield Ct *SALV* BN13 ..... **8** A2
Parkfield Rd *SALV* BN13 ..... **8** A2
Parkgate Rd *RDKG* RH5 ..... **14** D1
Park HI *ROTT* BN2 ..... **11** D5
Parklands *SHOR* BN43 ..... **234** A3
Parklands Av *BOGR* PO21 ..... **12** A4
FERR BN12 ..... **253** H2
Parklands Ct *CCH* PO19 ..... **6** A2
HPPT/KEY BN6 ..... **165** F1
Park La *ARUN* BN18 ..... **199** G2
EMRTH PO10 ..... **191** F3
HASM GU27 ..... **66** D5
HWH RH16 ..... **113** F1
PUL/STOR RH20 ..... **157** H6
RCCH PO18 ..... **197** F6
RCCH PO18 ..... **241** H1
SELS PO20 ..... **221** K5
SELS PO20 ..... **265** G2
STHW RH42 ..... **234** B4
SWTR RH13 ..... **106** C5
SWTR RH13 ..... **53** K5
Parkmore Ter *BRI* BN1 ..... **10** B2
Park PI *ARUN* BN18 ..... **201** G8
Park Ri *HORS* RH12 ..... **4** A3
HOVE BN3 ..... **211** J8
PETW GU28 ..... **125** J4
Park Rd *ARUN* BN18 ..... **224** A8
BURH RH15 ..... **139** F8

EGRIN RH19 .... **22** C5
EGRIN RH19 .... **36** B2
EMRTH PO10 .... **215** H2
HASM GU27 .... **40** E5
HFD BN5 .... **161** C7
HORL RH6 .... **19** J2
HORS RH12 .... **53** H2
HWH RH16 .... **111** K7
MIDOS PO22 .... **123** H5
PETW GU28 .... **125** K3
PSF GU32 .... **88** D8
RCCH PO18 .... **196** B5
RHWH RH17 .... **81** F4
SELS PO20 .... **265** H3
SHOR BN43 .... **233** J3
SWTR RH13 .... **49** H8
WTHG BN11 .... **9** E3
Park Road Ter ROTT BN2 .... **11** D5
Parkside CRAWE RH10 .... **3** D3 ⊡
EGRIN RH19 .... **36** A2
HPPT/KEY BN6 .... **38** A1
SHOR BN43 .... **233** J2
Parkside Av LHPTN BN17 .... **250** B2
Parkside Ms CRAWW RH12 .... **4** C4 ⊡
The Parks PTSD BN41 .... **211** F8 ⊡
Park St HORS RH12 .... **4** C5
ROTT BN2 .... **11** D5
SWTR RH13 .... **149** C8
Park Ter BOGR PO21 .... **12** A6 ⊡
Park Ter East SWTR RH13 .... **4** C6
Park Ter West SWTR RH13 .... **4** C6
Park Vw CRAWW RH11 .... **2** B4
HWH RH16 .... **112** A5
Park View Rd HOVE BN3 .... **236** B2
Parkway BOGR PO21 .... **245** J8
Park Wy CRAWE RH10 .... **32** C5
HORS RH12 .... **4** B6
MIDH GU29 .... **122** D1
STHW BN42 .... **234** D3
Park Way Cl STHW BN42 .... **234** D3
The Parkway ANG/EP BN16 .... **251** F1
Parry Cl SWTR RH13 .... **52** E7
Parry Dr ANG/EP BN16 .... **250** D2
Parsonage Cl EPSF GU31 .... **89** F6
Parsonage Est EPSF GU31 .... **90** E7
HORS RH12 .... **4** C3
Parsonage La HFD BN5 .... **161** G6
Parsonage Wy HORS RH12 .... **5** D3
Parsons Cl HASM GU27 .... **40** E3
Parsons Gn HASM GU27 .... **40** E3
Parson's Hl ARUN BN18 .... **201** H8
Parsons Wk ARUN BN18 .... **223** J3
Parthings La HORS RH12 .... **77** F3
Partridge La RDKG RH5 .... **15** J3
HORS RH12 .... **29** C1
Paston Pl ROTT BN2 .... **11** F6
Pasture Hill Rd HWH RH16 .... **111** K5
The Pasture CRAWE RH10 .... **32** C5
Patcham By-pass BRI BN1 .... **212** B6
Patcham Gra BRI BN1 .... **212** C6
Patchdean BRI BN1 .... **213** F6
Patching Cl CRAWW RH11 .... **30** D4 ⊡
FERR BN12 .... **229** F7
Patchings SWTR RH13 .... **5** E4
Paterson Rd LISS GU33 .... **62** C1
Paterson Wilson Rd
  LHPTN BN17 .... **250** A2 ⊡
Pathfield Cl HORS RH12 .... **48** B4 ⊡
Pathfield Rd HORS RH12 .... **48** B4 ⊡
Pathfields HASM GU27 .... **41** F4
Path Link CRAWE RH10 .... **3** D2
Patricia Av FERR BN12 .... **253** H2
Patricia Cl FERR BN12 .... **253** H2
Patrick's Cl LISS GU33 .... **62** A7
Patrington Cl CRAWW RH11 .... **30** E8
Patterdale Cl CRAWW RH11 .... **30** D4 ⊡
Pavilion Buildings BRI BN1 .... **10** C5 ⊡
Pavilion Cl HPPT/KEY BN6 .... **164** E6
Pavilion Pde ROTT BN2 .... **10** C5 ⊡
Pavilion Rd FIN/BW BN14 .... **8** B3
Pavilion St ROTT BN2 .... **10** C5 ⊡
Pavilion Wy EGRIN RH19 .... **36** D1
Pax Cl CRAWW RH11 .... **30** C7
Paxmead Crs FIN/BW BN14 .... **231** F5
Payne Av HOVE BN3 .... **235** K3
Payne Cl BOGR PO21 .... **261** H3
  CRAWE RH10 .... **32** D3
Paynesfield Rd RHWH RH17 .... **109** G8
Paythorne Cl STHW BN42 .... **234** B2 ⊡
Paythorne Dro HFD BN5 .... **186** B6
Payton Dr BURH RH15 .... **165** F1
Peace Cl BRI BN1 .... **11** C1
Peacemaker Cl CRAWW RH11 .... **30** C7 ⊡
Peace Rd MIDH GU29 .... **148** C1
The Peacheries CCH PO19 .... **7** F3
Peachey Rd SELS PO20 .... **264** E5
Peacock Cl CCH PO19 .... **219** H7
Peacock La BRI BN1 .... **212** C4
Peacock's Hl SWTR RH13 .... **106** C5
Peacocks La PUL/STOR RH20 .... **157** C5
Peak La ANG/EP BN16 .... **252** A3
The Peak HAV PO9 .... **190** A4
Pearson Rd ARUN BN18 .... **225** F1
  CRAWE RH10 .... **32** B5
Peartree Cl BURH RH15 .... **138** E8

Peary Cl HORS RH12 .... **4** C1
Pease Cft EPSF GU31 .... **118** B8
Pebble Wk HTLY GU31 .... **226** C8 ⊡
Peckhams Copse La SELS PO20 .... **243** K1
Peeks Brook La HORL RH6 .... **18** E4
Peel Cl LHPTN BN17 .... **249** J1
Peerley Cl SELS PO20 .... **257** K5
Peerley Rd SELS PO20 .... **257** K5
Pegasus Cl HASM GU27 .... **39** K6
Pegasus Wy EGRIN RH19 .... **22** E8
Pegler Wy CRAWW RH11 .... **2** C3
Pegwell Cl CRAWW RH11 .... **30** D7
Pelham Ct CRAWW RH11 .... **55** F1
Pelham Dr CRAWW RH11 .... **54** E1
Pelham Pl CRAWW RH11 .... **55** F1
Pelham Rd HWH RH16 .... **112** C5
  SALV BN13 .... **229** K6
Pelham Sq BRI BN1 .... **10** C4 ⊡
Pelham St BRI BN1 .... **10** C4
Pelham Ter EMRTH PO10 .... **214** E3 ⊡
Pemberton Cl LAN/SOMP BN15 .... **232** A4 ⊡
Pembley Gn CRAWE RH10 .... **20** A8
Pembroke Av HOVE BN3 .... **236** A5
  WTHG BN11 .... **255** K1
Pembroke Crs HOVE BN3 .... **236** A4
Pembroke Gdns HOVE BN3 .... **236** A5
Pembroke Rd CRAWE RH10 .... **32** C2
Pembroke Wy BOGR PO21 .... **245** G7
Pembury Cl FIN/BW BN14 .... **9** D2 ⊡
  HWH RH16 .... **112** D8
Pembury Rd FIN/BW BN14 .... **9** D2
Penarth Gdns LHPTN BN17 .... **225** J6
Pendean BURH RH15 .... **165** J2 ⊡
Pende Cl LAN/SOMP BN15 .... **231** K3 ⊡
Pendine Av WTHG BN11 .... **231** C8
Penfold La ANG/EP BN16 .... **226** E8
Penfold Rd CRAWE RH10 .... **56** B1
  FIN/BW BN14 .... **9** E1
Penfolds Pl ARUN BN18 .... **225** J1
Penfold Wy STEY/UB BN44 .... **207** K1
Penhill Rd LAN/SOMP BN15 .... **232** B6
Penland Cl HWH RH16 .... **111** K4
Penland Rd HWH RH16 .... **111** K5
Penland's Ct STEY/UB BN44 .... **207** K1
Penlands V STEY/UB BN44 .... **207** J1
Penlands Ri STEY/UB BN44 .... **207** J1
Penlands Wy STEY/UB BN44 .... **207** K1
Penleigh Cl LAN/SOMP BN15 .... **232** B6
Penn Cl CRAWW RH11 .... **31** H2 ⊡
  MIDOS PO22 .... **247** J6
Penn Crs HWH RH16 .... **112** C6
Pennels Cl LIPH GU30 .... **92** B1
Pennine Cl CRAWW RH11 .... **2** A3 ⊡
Penns Ct STEY/UB BN44 .... **183** J7
Penns Pl EPSF GU31 .... **89** H8
Penns Rd PSF GU32 .... **88** C7
Pennycord Cl SELS PO20 .... **265** F6
Pennycress Av FERR BN12 .... **228** E6
Pennyfields MIDOS PO22 .... **247** G6
Penny La EMRTH PO10 .... **215** F3
Pensfold La HORS RH12 .... **48** C6
Penshurst Cl CRAWE RH10 .... **32** D4 ⊡
Penstone Pk LAN/SOMP BN15 .... **231** K5
Pentland Rd SALV BN13 .... **229** J5 ⊡
Penwarden Wy RCCH PO18 .... **217** G4
Penwith Dr HASM GU27 .... **39** K7
Peperham Rd HASM GU27 .... **40** E3
Peppard Rd CRAWE RH10 .... **32** D7
Pepper Dr BURH RH15 .... **164** E1 ⊡
  BURH RH15 .... **165** F2 ⊡
Peppering La ARUN BN18 .... **202** C4
Pepperscoombe La
  STEY/UB BN44 .... **184** C8
Peppersgate SWTR RH13 .... **107** J4
Pepper's La STEY/UB BN44 .... **159** J6
Perche Ct MIDH GU29 .... **121** K5 ⊡
Perching Dro HFD BN5 .... **186** C6
Percival Ter ROTT BN2 .... **11** F6 ⊡
Percy Rd HORS RH12 .... **4** C4
Peregrine Rd LHPTN BN17 .... **250** B1
Perimeter Rd East HORL RH6 .... **18** B4
Perimeter Rd North HORL RH6 .... **17** K3
Perimeter Rd South HORL RH6 .... **17** K6
Perrots La STEY/UB BN44 .... **207** J1
Perry Av EGRIN RH19 .... **22** C8
Perryfield La CRAWE RH10 .... **32** D4
Perryfield Rd CRAWW RH11 .... **2** C4
Perryfields BURH RH15 .... **138** E7
Perrylands HORL RH6 .... **16** D4
Perrylands La HORL RH6 .... **19** F1
Perryman's La RHWH RH17 .... **87** H8
Perrymount Rd HWH RH16 .... **112** A6
Perth Cl CRAWW RH11 .... **31** H2
Perth Wy HORS RH12 .... **5** E3
Pescott's Cl SELS PO20 .... **241** J6
Peskett Cl SWTR RH13 .... **75** K8
Peterborough Rd CRAWE RH10 .... **55** J7
Peterhouse Cl BOGR PO21 .... **245** H7 ⊡
Peter Rd LAN/SOMP BN15 .... **231** J7
Petersfield Rd EPSF GU31 .... **116** B6
  MIDH GU29 .... **121** K3
Peter's Cl SELS PO20 .... **264** B3
Peter's Pl SELS PO20 .... **264** B3
Peter Weston Pl CCH PO19 .... **7** D3
Petlands Gdns HWH RH16 .... **112** B6

Petlands Rd HWH RH16 .... **112** B6
Petworth Av FERR BN12 .... **253** K3
Petworth Ct CRAWW RH11 .... **30** D4 ⊡
Petworth Dr BURH RH15 .... **164** D1 ⊡
  HORS RH12 .... **48** B5
Petworth Rd BIL RH14 .... **36** A3
  BRI BN1 .... **169** G4
  HASM GU27 .... **40** C2
Pevensey Cl CRAWE RH10 .... **32** A2 ⊡
Pevensey Gdn WTHG BN11 .... **254** D5
Pevensey Rd BOGR PO21 .... **245** G7
  ROTT BN2 .... **11** J3
  SWTR RH13 .... **4** C6
  WTHG BN11 .... **254** D5
Peverel Rd CRAWW RH11 .... **30** D4
  SALV BN13 .... **229** K6
Peveril Cl LAN/SOMP BN15 .... **231** K4
Peveril Dr LAN/SOMP BN15 .... **231** K4
Phillips Cl CRAWE RH10 .... **32** C3
Philliswood La RCCH PO18 .... **217** F5
Phoenix Cl CCH PO19 .... **7** E3
Phoenix Crs STHW BN42 .... **234** C3
Phoenix La EGRIN RH19 .... **36** B2
Phoenix Ri ROTT BN2 .... **11** J2
  ROTT BN2 .... **11** J2
Phoenix Ri ROTT BN2 .... **11** J2
Phoenix Wy STHW BN42 .... **234** C3
Phrosso Rd WTHG BN11 .... **254** C5
Pickers Gn HWH RH16 .... **111** K5
Pickhurst La PUL/STOR RH20 .... **157** F3
Pickwell La RHWH RH17 .... **109** G8
Picton St ROTT BN2 .... **11** K2
Picts La SWTR RH13 .... **75** K8
Pier Rd LHPTN BN17 .... **250** A3
Piers Secombe Cl
  PUL/STOR RH20 .... **157** G4
Pigbush La BIL RH14 .... **57** J6
Pigeonhouse La ANG/EP BN16 .... **226** B7 ⊡
Piggery Hall La SELS PO20 .... **257** K5
  SELS PO20 .... **264** B3
The Pike PUL/STOR RH20 .... **157** F3
Pilgrims Cl FIN/BW BN14 .... **231** F5
Pilgrims Wk SALV BN13 .... **229** J6
Pilgrims Wy BOGR PO21 .... **245** G6
Pine Cl BIL RH14 .... **57** J6
  CRAWW RH11 .... **2** B4
  MIDH GU29 .... **122** D2
  PUL/STOR RH20 .... **157** F3
Pine Gdns HORL RH6 .... **19** J2
Pine Gv CCH PO19 .... **7** E3
  EGRIN RH19 .... **22** E7
Pineham Copse HWH RH16 .... **111** K6
Pinehurst BURH RH15 .... **165** H2 ⊡
  HORS RH12 .... **48** B5
Pinehurst Pk BOGR PO21 .... **261** H2
Pines Av FIN/BW BN14 .... **231** G5
Pine Shaw CRAWE RH10 .... **32** D4
The Pines ANG/EP BN16 .... **251** J6
  ARUN BN18 .... **202** C4
  HORS RH12 .... **48** B5
  HWH RH16 .... **112** A5
Pine Tree Cl HPPT/KEY BN6 .... **164** E6
Pine Trees Cl ANG/EP BN16 .... **251** J6
Pinetrees Cl CRAWE RH10 .... **32** D4
Pine View Cl HASM GU27 .... **40** E3
Pine Wk BOGR PO21 .... **261** H2
  LISS GU33 .... **62** B1
Pine Way Cl EGRIN RH19 .... **36** C2
Pinewood Cl ANG/EP BN16 .... **251** J6
  HORS RH12 .... **48** B5
Pinewood Ct MIDH GU29 .... **122** D2
Pinewood Gdns BOGR PO21 .... **245** H7
Pinewood Wy HWH RH16 .... **111** K6
  MIDH GU29 .... **122** D2
Pinkhurst La SWTR RH13 .... **76** A2
Pinks La SELS PO20 .... **264** B3
Pinland Rd SWTR RH13 .... **52** E7
Pipers Cl HOVE BN3 .... **235** K3
Pipers End SWTR RH13 .... **52** E7
Pipers La PETW GU28 .... **125** K3
  PETW GU28 .... **125** K3
Pitcroft La EPSF GU31 .... **118** B8
The Pitcroft CCH PO19 .... **7** F3
Pitfold Av HASM GU27 .... **39** K7
Pitfold Cl HASM GU27 .... **40** A7
Pit Rd HPPT/KEY BN6 .... **164** E6
Pitsham La MIDH GU29 .... **121** K8
Pitsham Wd MIDH GU29 .... **121** K8
Plainfields Av BRI BN1 .... **169** G4
Plainwood Cl CCH PO19 .... **7** F3
Plaistow Rd BIL RH14 .... **57** J6
  BIL RH14 .... **57** J6
  MFD/CHID GU8 .... **57** J6
  MFD/CHID GU8 .... **57** J6
Plantain Crs CRAWW RH11 .... **30** C7 ⊡
Plantation Cl SALV BN13 .... **229** J5 ⊡
Plantation Ri SALV BN13 .... **229** J5
Plantation Rd LISS GU33 .... **62** B1
The Plantation ANG/EP BN16 .... **251** J6
  PUL/STOR RH20 .... **157** F3
  SALV BN13 .... **229** J5
Plantation Wy PUL/STOR RH20 .... **157** F3
  SALV BN13 .... **229** J5
The Plat HORS RH12 .... **48** B5
Platts Meadow BIL RH14 .... **57** J6

att HWH RH16 ..... 112 D6
RH7 ..... 22 E3
atch La EGRIN RH19 ..... 60 C6
nt La EMRTH PO10 ..... 239 H2
n Cl CRAWW RH11 ..... 30 D3
n La HORS RH12 ..... 5 D2
Rd LING RH7 ..... 22 E1
Cl CRAWW RH11 ..... 2 B1
OS PO22 ..... 12 A1
PO20 ..... 257 K5
s Rd SWTR RH13 ..... 5 E4
nerden La HWH RH16 ..... 113 C1
ton Rd ROTT BN2 ..... 11 F4
ree Cross La SWTR RH13 ..... 75 K7
t La SWTR RH13 ..... 105 J2
a CRAWW RH11 ..... 17 G7
ub La RHWH RH17 ..... 111 F4
Cl FERR BN12 ..... 229 F7
St ARUN BN18 ..... 226 C5
s CRAWW RH11 ..... 30 E6
s Dr SWTR RH13 ..... 5 E5
's Hi SWTR RH13 ..... 105 G6
ro Cl FERR BN12 ..... 252 B2
r La HPPT/KEY BN6 ..... 164 A1
l Bil RH14 ..... 46 B7
H14 ..... 102 A3
opse La BIL RH14 ..... 46 B6
roft Rd HWH RH16 ..... 112 D4
eld Rd HORS RH12 ..... 48 B3
a SALV BN13 ..... 229 H4
Ms SALV BN13 ..... 229 H5
ti PUL/STOR RH20 ..... 156 C2
d SELS PO20 ..... 258 A6
BN43 ..... 233 H4
il Cl HORS RH12 ..... 4 C2
l Copse HORS RH12 ..... 4 C1
l Dr HORS RH12 ..... 51 K4
l Rd HORS RH12 ..... 4 B2
ly EGRIN RH19 ..... 37 F2
ood Rd CRAWE RH10 ..... 3 F1
arm FIN/BW BN14 ..... 205 K3
ourne La RHWH RH17 ..... 137 J6
a RCCH PO18 ..... 195 C6
a BRI BN1 ..... 10 C6
Md HASM GU27 ..... 40 E4
Av HOVE BN3 ..... 211 J8
Cl BRI BN1 ..... 237 F1
RH11 ..... 31 G2
BN3 ..... 211 J8
Rd SALV BN13 ..... 229 C6
plars ARUN BN18 ..... 224 A7
/KEY BN6 ..... 165 G5
RH13 ..... 5 D4
Wy MIDH GU29 ..... 122 A6
Cl SWTR RH15 ..... 77 G8
ster Cl SWTR RH13 ..... 105 C2
d Av BRI BN1 ..... 213 C5
d Wy CCH PO19 ..... 7 F1
ll Av BRI BN1 ..... 10 A2
ll Ms BRI BN1 ..... 10 A2
ll Pl BRI BN1 ..... 10 A2
ll Rd HOVE BN3 ..... 10 A2
ll St BRI BN1 ..... 10 A2
d Av HOVE BN3 ..... 235 J4
d Cl ANG/EP BN16 ..... 250 C1
d Pl ROTT BN2 ..... 11 E6
d Rd BURH RH15 ..... 139 F8
RH19 ..... 36 C3
BN3 ..... 235 H4
BN11 ..... 9 D4
d's Cl PSF GU32 ..... 89 F6
d St BRI BN1 ..... 10 B5
d Vls HOVE BN3 ..... 235 H4
outh La HWH RH16 ..... 112 B4
outh Rd LIPH GU30 ..... 39 C4
GU30 ..... 64 A5
outh Wd HWH RH16 ..... 112 B3
outh Wood Cl HWH RH16 ..... 112 B3
y STEY/UB BN44 ..... 207 J1
ice La SELS PO20 ..... 243 K2
v PUL/STOR RH20 ..... 180 C3
s Cft SWTR RH13 ..... 5 D5
Fld LISS GU33 ..... 62 A7
Gn SWTR RH15 ..... 135 G1
La BURH RH15 ..... 165 F2
Md LHPTN BN17 ..... 225 J8
La RCCH PO18 ..... 216 A7
r Cl MIDOS PO22 ..... 13 F3
's La FIN/BW BN14 ..... 230 B5
Cl BIL RH14 ..... 46 B6
GU28 ..... 125 K4
Farm Rd CCH PO19 ..... 7 D3
ield La BIL RH14 ..... 45 H8
Hill Pl CRAWE RH10 ..... 32 C5
La STEY/UB BN44 ..... 208 D1
RH13 ..... 78 E5
RH13 ..... 132 D3
RH13 ..... 135 F3
Rd ARUN BN18 ..... 223 H2
PO20 ..... 256 E2
st PETW GU28 ..... 125 K3
nd BURH RH15 ..... 139 F7
ross Rd HORL RH6 ..... 17 J2
Cl BURH RH15 ..... 138 D8
v BRI BN1 ..... 10 B4

Powis Rd BRI BN1 ..... 10 A4
Powis Sq BRI BN1 ..... 10 A4
Powis Vls BRI BN1 ..... 10 B4
Poynings Cl HOVE BN3 ..... 211 K8
Poynings Rd CRAWW RH11 ..... 30 B6
Poynter Rd HOVE BN3 ..... 236 A3
Poyntz Cl CCH PO19 ..... 6 B6
Pratton Av LAN/SOMP BN15 ..... 231 K4
Prawn Cl SELS PO20 ..... 264 D3
Preston Av ANG/EP BN16 ..... 251 F2
Preston Dro BRI BN1 ..... 237 F1
Preston Paddock ANG/EP BN16 ..... 251 G2
Preston Park Av BRI BN1 ..... 10 B1
Preston Rd BRI BN1 ..... 10 A1
BRI BN1 ..... 236 E1
Preston St BRI BN1 ..... 10 A5
Prestonville Rd BRI BN1 ..... 10 A4
Prestwick Cl CRAWW RH11 ..... 30 B6
Prestwick La HASM GU27 ..... 41 J1
Prestwood Cl CRAWW RH11 ..... 31 F7
Prestwood La CRAWW RH11 ..... 30 A1
Pretoria Av MIDH GU29 ..... 122 A4
Pretoria Cl LISS GU33 ..... 62 C1
Pretoria Rd MIDH GU29 ..... 122 A4
Price Wy RHWH RH17 ..... 84 D4
Priest Croft Cl CRAWW RH11 ..... 30 E5
Priestley Wy CRAWE RH10 ..... 18 A8
MIDOS PO22 ..... 247 H6
Prime Cl ARUN BN18 ..... 223 J3
Primrose Av HORL RH6 ..... 18 B2
Primrose Cl BURH RH15 ..... 138 D7
CRAWW RH11 ..... 2 A6
Primrose Copse HORS RH12 ..... 51 K4
Primrose La LISS GU33 ..... 62 D7
Prince Albert St BRI BN1 ..... 10 C5
Prince Av LAN/SOMP BN15 ..... 232 D6
Prince Charles Cl STHW BN42 ..... 234 D2
Princes Av HOVE BN3 ..... 236 A5
Princes Crs HOVE BN3 ..... 236 A5
ROTT BN2 ..... 11 D2
Princes Cft BOGR PO21 ..... 261 H2
Prince's Dr RCCH PO18 ..... 196 A2
Prince's Pl BRI BN1 ..... 10 C5
Princes Rd PSF GU32 ..... 88 B7
ROTT BN2 ..... 11 D2
Princess Anne Rd HORS RH12 ..... 48 B4
Princess Av BOGR PO21 ..... 262 D1
SALV BN13 ..... 229 K8
Princess Margaret Rd
HORS RH12 ..... 48 B4
Princes Sq HOVE BN3 ..... 236 A5
Princess Rd CRAWW RH11 ..... 2 B3
Prince's St ROTT BN2 ..... 10 C5
Prince William Cl FIN/BW BN14 ..... 230 A3
Prings La SWTR RH13 ..... 107 F3
Prinsep Rd HOVE BN3 ..... 236 A3
Prinsted La SWTR RH13 ..... 107 F8
Priors Acre RCCH PO18 ..... 197 F8
Priors Cl EMRTH PO10 ..... 215 J2
Priors Leaze La RCCH PO18 ..... 215 K2
Priors Wk CRAWE RH10 ..... 3 E3
Priors Waye BOGR PO21 ..... 261 H1
Priors Wd HASM GU27 ..... 40 B5
Priory Cl BOGR PO21 ..... 261 J5
LAN/SOMP BN15 ..... 231 H4
RCCH PO18 ..... 197 F8
SALV BN13 ..... 8 A2
Priory Fld STEY/UB BN44 ..... 208 C1
Priory Rd ANG/EP BN16 ..... 250 D1
ARUN BN18 ..... 225 F2
BURH RH15 ..... 165 G2
CCH PO19 ..... 6 C3
FROW RH18 ..... 60 E5
HPPT/KEY BN6 ..... 164 E6
Priory Wy HWH RH16 ..... 112 B7
Proctor Cl CRAWE RH10 ..... 32 C7
The Promenade EMRTH PO10 ..... 214 D4
Prospect Pl CRAWW RH11 ..... 2 B3
WTHG BN11 ..... 9 D5
Providence Pl BRI BN1 ..... 10 C3
Providence Ter WTHG BN11 ..... 9 E3
The Providence CCH PO19 ..... 6 B2
Pruetts La LISS GU33 ..... 89 K2
Pryors La BOGR PO21 ..... 261 K1
Puckshott Wy HASM GU27 ..... 41 J3
Pudding La HORL RH6 ..... 16 C3
Puffin Rd CRAWW RH11 ..... 30 D8
Pulborough Rd PUL/STOR RH20 ..... 179 K1
Pulborough Wy MIDOS PO22 ..... 247 H3
Pulens Crs EPSF GU31 ..... 89 G7
Pulens La EPSF GU31 ..... 89 G7
Punch Copse Rd CRAWE RH10 ..... 3 E2
Punches La SELS PO20 ..... 243 K6
Purbeck Pl LHPTN BN17 ..... 249 J2
Purcell Rd CRAWW RH11 ..... 30 D8
Purley Cl CRAWE RH10 ..... 32 D8
The Purrocks PSF GU32 ..... 88 D6
Purton Rd HORS RH12 ..... 4 A3
Putmans La EPSF GU31 ..... 117 K5
Puttock Cl HASM GU27 ..... 39 K6
Pycroft Cl HISD PO11 ..... 214 A8
Pyecombe St CRAWW RH11 ..... 30 D8
Pyecombe St POY/PYE BN45 ..... 188 A5
Pyrford Cl BOGR PO21 ..... 261 J3

Q

The Quadrangle FIN/BW BN14 ..... 205 J6
Quadrant BRI BN1 ..... 10 B5
The Quadrant FERR BN12 ..... 229 G8
HPPT/KEY BN6 ..... 165 G7
Quail Cl HORS RH12 ..... 51 K4
Quakers La HWH RH16 ..... 112 C6
Quantock Cl CRAWW RH11 ..... 2 A3
SALV BN13 ..... 229 K3
Quantock Rd SALV BN13 ..... 229 K3
The Quarries SWTR RH13 ..... 79 F5
Quarry Bank Rd BRI BN1 ..... 237 H1
Quarry Cl BURH RH15 ..... 139 K8
HORS RH12 ..... 5 E1
Quarry Hl RHWH RH17 ..... 111 J5
Quarry La CCH PO19 ..... 7 E4
Quarry Ri EGRIN RH19 ..... 22 E8
Quarry Wy SWTR RH13 ..... 105 F2
Quarterbrass Farm Rd
HORS RH12 ..... 51 K4
The Quashetts FIN/BW BN14 ..... 9 D1
Quayside LHPTN BN17 ..... 249 H2
Quebec St ROTT BN2 ..... 11 D4
Queen Alexandra Av HOVE BN3 ..... 212 A8
Queen Caroline Cl HOVE BN3 ..... 212 A8
Queen Elizabeth Av BURH RH15 ..... 165 F1
Queen Elizabeth Rd HORS RH12 ..... 48 B4
Queen Mary Av HOVE BN3 ..... 212 A8
Queen's Av CCH PO19 ..... 6 B5
Queensbury Ms BRI BN1 ..... 10 A5
Queens Crs BURH RH15 ..... 165 G1
Queensdown School Rd BRI BN1 .. 213 J8
Queens Dr HPPT/KEY BN6 ..... 165 F7
Queens Flds East BOGR PO21 ..... 245 H7
Queens Flds West BOGR PO21 ..... 245 G7
Queen's Gdns BRI BN1 ..... 10 C4
HOVE BN3 ..... 236 C6
Queens Ga HORL RH6 ..... 18 A3
Queens La ARUN BN18 ..... 225 H1
Queensmead BOGR PO21 ..... 261 G3
Queen's Park Ri ROTT BN2 ..... 11 E4
Queen's Park Rd ROTT BN2 ..... 11 D5
Queen's Park Ter ROTT BN2 ..... 11 E4
Queen's Pl BRI BN1 ..... 10 C3
HOVE BN3 ..... 236 C5
SHOR BN43 ..... 233 H4
Queen Sq BRI BN1 ..... 10 B5
Queen's Rd BRI BN1 ..... 10 B4
EGRIN RH19 ..... 36 C3
HWH RH16 ..... 112 A5
LAN/SOMP BN15 ..... 232 B7
PSF GU32 ..... 88 B7
STHW BN42 ..... 234 C2
WTHG BN11 ..... 8 C5
Queens Sq CRAWE RH10 ..... 2 C3
Queens St MIDH GU29 ..... 121 G1
Queen St ARUN BN18 ..... 201 H8
EMRTH PO10 ..... 214 E3
FIN/BW BN14 ..... 8 C2
LHPTN BN17 ..... 249 K2
SWTR RH13 ..... 4 C6
Queensway BOGR PO21 ..... 12 B5
CRAWE RH10 ..... 3 D3
EGRIN RH19 ..... 36 C3
LAN/SOMP BN15 ..... 232 A5
ROTT BN2 ..... 11 F4
SWTR RH13 ..... 4 B6
Queen Victoria Av HOVE BN3 ..... 212 A8
Querneby Cl SHOR BN43 ..... 234 B2
Quest Cl CCH PO19 ..... 7 D3

R

Racecourse Wy HORL RH6 ..... 17 K4
Rackfield HASM GU27 ..... 39 K4
Rackham Cl CRAWW RH11 ..... 2 C5
SALV BN13 ..... 229 K6
Rackham Rd ANG/EP BN16 ..... 250 D4
ARUN BN18 ..... 178 D4
SALV BN13 ..... 229 K6
Rackham St ARUN BN18 ..... 178 B4
PUL/STOR RH20 ..... 178 E3
Racton Rd EMRTH PO10 ..... 190 D8
Radford Rd CRAWE RH10 ..... 18 C7
MIDOS PO22 ..... 12 B3
Radinden Dr HOVE BN3 ..... 236 D2
Radinden Manor Rd HOVE BN3 ..... 236 C3
Radnor Cl SALV BN13 ..... 229 K7
Radnor Rd SALV BN13 ..... 229 K7
Raglan Av SALV BN13 ..... 229 J6
Railey Rd CRAWE RH10 ..... 3 D3
Railway Ap EGRIN RH19 ..... 36 B2
WTHG BN11 ..... 9 F3
Railway St BRI BN1 ..... 10 B4
Rainbow Wy PUL/STOR RH20 ..... 156 D8
Rake Rd LIPH GU30 ..... 91 K1
LISS GU33 ..... 62 B7
Rakers Rdg HORS RH12 ..... 4 C2
Raleigh Cl SHOR BN43 ..... 233 G5
Raleigh Crs FERR BN12 ..... 229 H8

Raleigh Rd *BOGR* PO21 .... 244 E8
Raleigh Wk *CRAWE* RH10 .... 3 D5 🗉
Raleigh Wy *FERR* BN12 .... 229 G7
Rambledown La *PUL/STOR* RH20... 156 A5
Ramblers Wy *CRAWW* RH11 .... 55 F2
Ramillies Gdns *MIDOS* PO22 .... 247 G6
Ramsey Cl *HORS* RH12 .... 4 C2
Ramshill *EPSF* GU31 .... 88 E7
Rams La *MFD/CHID* GU8 .... 45 G1
Ranelagh Vls *HOVE* BN3 .... 236 B3
Ranmore Cl *CRAWW* RH11 .... 55 G1
Ransome Cl *CRAWW* RH11 .... 30 B8
Ranville Cl *PETW* GU28 .... 125 J4 🗉
Ranworth Rd *MIDOS* PO22 .... 13 E3
Raphael Rd *HOVE* BN3 .... 235 K4
Rapley Av *PUL/STOR* RH20 .... 179 K1
Rascals Cl *SWTR* RH13 .... 105 F4
Rastrick Cl *BURH* RH15 .... 165 F2
Ratham La *RCCH* PO18 .... 217 G3
Rathlin Rd *CRAWW* RH11 .... 2 A6
Raughmere Dr *CCH* PO19 .... 195 F7
Raven La *CRAWW* RH11 .... 2 B1
Ravensbourne Av *SHOR* BN43 ...... 233 H2
Ravensbourne Cl *SHOR* BN43 .... 233 H2 🗉
Ravenscroft *PUL/STOR* RH20 .... 180 B3
Raven's Rd *SHOR* BN43 .... 233 H4
Ravens Wy *MIDOS* PO22 .... 12 A2
Ravenswood Rd *BURH* RH15 .... 139 H8
Raworth Cl *CRAWE* RH10 .... 32 C7 🗉
Raycroft Cl *BOGR* PO21 .... 262 C1 🗉
Rayden Cl *LHPTN* BN17 .... 250 M2
Rdffye Ct *HORS* RH12 .... 5 F3
Readon Cl *EPSF* GU31 .... 88 E7
Reapers Cl *HORS* RH12 .... 4 C2
Record Rd *EMRTH* PO10 .... 214 C2
Rectory Cl *PUL/STOR* RH20 .... 154 E1
  PUL/STOR RH20 .... 158 A6
  PUL/STOR RH20 .... 180 B2
  SHOR BN43 .... 234 B4
Rectory Farm Rd
  LAN/SOMP BN15 .... 231 H4
Rectory Gdns *FIN/BW* BN14 .... 8 C1
Rectory La *ANG/EP* BN16 .... 227 H6
  HORL RH6 .... 16 B4
  LIPH GU30 .... 38 D4
  PUL/STOR RH20 .... 154 D1
  PUL/STOR RH20 .... 157 H5
  SELS PO20 .... 2 🗉
Rectory Rd *FIN/BW* BN14 .... 8 A2
  PUL/STOR RH20 .... 180 B2 🗉
  SHOR BN43 .... 234 A4
Rectory Wk *LAN/SOMP* BN15 .... 231 H4
  PUL/STOR RH20 .... 180 B2 🗉
Red Admiral St *HORS* RH12 .... 5 D2
Redbridge La *RHWH* RH17 .... 56 B8
Redcross St *BRI* BN1 .... 10 C4
Red Deer Cl *SWTR* RH13 .... 52 D8
Redditch Cl *CRAWW* RH11 .... 54 C1
Redehall Rd *HORL* RH6 .... 19 H2
Redford Av *HORS* RH12 .... 4 A3
Redgarth Ct *EGRIN* RH19 .... 21 K8
Redgrave Dr *CRAWE* RH10 .... 32 D6
Redhill Cl *BRI* BN1 .... 212 C6
Redhill Dr *BRI* BN1 .... 212 C7
Red House Ct *EPSF* GU31 .... 91 F7
Redkiln Cl *SWTR* RH13 .... 5 E4
Redkiln Wy *SWTR* RH13 .... 5 E4
Redlands La *EMRTH* PO10 .... 190 D7
  SELS PO20 .... 240 D8
Red La *SWTR* RH13 .... 132 D2
Red Lion St *MIDH* GU29 .... 122 B4
Redvers Rd *ROTT* BN2 .... 11 F1
Redwing Cl *LHPTN* BN17 .... 225 J7 🗉
  SWTR RH13 .... 77 H8
Redwood Cl *CRAWE* RH10 .... 3 D1
  SALV BN13 .... 229 C6 🗉
Redwood Dr *HWH* RH16 .... 139 K1
Redwood Pl *BOGR* PO21 .... 262 B1 🗉
Reed Cl *PUL/STOR* RH20 .... 180 A2
Reedings *CRAWW* RH11 .... 30 B2
Reed Pond Wk *HWH* RH16 .... 112 C7
Reed's La *HPPT/KEY* BN6 .... 163 F3
  LISS GU33 .... 62 D5
  SWTR RH13 .... 77 H8
Reef Cl *LHPTN* BN17 .... 250 B3
Reeves Hl *BRI* BN1 .... 213 K6
Regal Dr *EGRIN* RH19 .... 36 D3
Regency Ms *BRI* BN1 .... 10 A5
Regency Rd *BRI* BN1 .... 10 B5
Regency Sq *BRI* BN1 .... 10 A5
Regent Cl *LAN/SOMP* BN15 .... 232 C5
Regent Hl *BRI* BN1 .... 10 B5
Regent Rw *BRI* BN1 .... 10 B5 🗉
Regents Cl *CRAWW* RH11 .... 55 G1
Regent St *BRI* BN1 .... 10 C5 🗉🗉
Regents Wy *BOGR* PO21 .... 245 H7
Regis Av *BOGR* PO21 .... 261 J2
Regis Ct *BOGR* PO21 .... 12 C5
Reigate Cl *CRAWE* RH10 .... 32 D2
Reigate Rd *BRI* BN1 .... 236 D2
  HORL RH6 .... 17 H1
  WTHG BN11 .... 253 K1
Renn Gdns *PUL/STOR* RH20 .... 157 J6
Renoir Ct *MIDOS* PO22 .... 245 J5

Renoir Ms *MIDOS* PO22 .... 245 J5
Renton Cl *BIL* RH14 .... 102 B3
Reservoir La *PSF* GU32 .... 88 D6
Rew La *CCH* PO19 .... 195 F8
Reynard Cl *HORS* RH12 .... 52 D6
Reynolds La *ARUN* BN18 .... 199 H7
Reynolds Pl *CRAWW* RH11 .... 2 B2 🗉
Reynolds Rd *CRAWW* RH11 .... 2 B2
  HOVE BN3 .... 235 K4
Rhodes Wy *CRAWE* RH10 .... 3 E5
Rice Br *RHWH* RH17 .... 137 C4
Rices Hl *EGRIN* RH19 .... 36 C2
Richardson Rd *HOVE* BN3 .... 235 K4
Richmond Av *BOGR* PO21 .... 245 J8
  CCH PO19 .... 219 G2
Richmond Cl *ANG/EP* BN16 .... 251 G1 🗉
Richmond Ct *CRAWE* RH10 .... 3 D4 🗉
  WTHG BN11 .... 8 C4 🗉
Richmond Pde *ROTT* BN2 .... 11 D4 🗉
Richmond Pl *ROTT* BN2 .... 10 C4
Richmond Rd *BOGR* PO21 .... 12 B5 🗉
  HORS RH12 .... a B3
  RCH PO18 .... 196 A8
  ROTT BN2 .... 11 D2
  WTHG BN11 .... 8 C4
Richmond Rd North *BOGR* PO21 .. 12 C4 🗉
Richmond St *ROTT* BN2 .... 11 D4
Richmond Wy *EGRIN* RH19 .... 36 D3
Rickfield *CRAWW* RH11 .... 30 E6 🗉
Rickman's La *BIL* RH14 .... 71 H3
The Ride *BIL* RH14 .... 71 J1
  BRI RH14 .... 10 B1
Ridge Cl *PTSD* RH41 .... 210 E7 🗉
Ridge Common La *PSF* GU32 .... 88 A5
Ridgehurst Dr *HORS* RH12 .... 77 F2
Ridgeside *CRAWE* RH10 .... 3 E3 🗉
Ridgeside Av *BRI* BN1 .... 212 E6
The Ridge *HORS* RH12 .... 48 C3
Ridgeway *EGRIN* RH19 .... 36 C4
Ridge Wy *HWH* RH16 .... 140 D1
Ridgeway Cl *STHW* BN42 .... 234 D2 🗉
The Ridgeway *BURH* RH15 .... 139 H7 🗉
  HASM GU27 .... 66 D5
  HORL RH6 .... 18 A2
  HORS RH12 .... 4 A3
The Ridgwy *MIDOS* PO22 .... 247 F7 🗉
The Ridings *ANG/EP* BN16 .... 251 H3
  ARUN BN18 .... 222 E1
  BOGR PO21 .... 261 K2
  BURH RH15 .... 165 J2
  CRAWE RH10 .... 32 D4
  LISS GU33 .... 62 B7
  STEY/UB BN44 .... 207 K2
Ridleys *EGRIN* RH19 .... 59 G5
Rife La *SELS* PO20 .... 264 C3
Rifeside Gdns *FERR* BN12 .... 228 C8 🗉
Rife Wy *FERR* BN12 .... 252 C1
  MIDOS PO22 .... 13 E4
Rigden Rd *HOVE* BN3 .... 236 C3
Riley Rd *ROTT* BN2 .... 11 F1
Rillside *CRAWE* RH10 .... 3 F6
Rill Wk *EGRIN* RH19 .... 37 F2
Rimmer Cl *CRAWW* RH11 .... 55 F3 🗉
Ringley Av *HORL* RH6 .... 18 A1
Ringley Rd *HORS* RH12 .... 5 D3
Ringmer Rd *SALV* BN13 .... 229 J6
Ring Rd *LAN/SOMP* BN15 .... 232 A2
Ringwood Cl *CRAWE* RH10 .... 3 D5
Ripley Rd *WTHG* BN11 .... 229 K8
Ripon Gdns *BOGR* PO21 .... 245 G8 🗉
The Rise *CRAWE* RH10 .... 32 C5
  EGRIN RH19 .... 36 D3
  HWH RH16 .... 112 D6
  PTSD BN41 .... 234 D1
  SWTR RH13 .... 134 C8
Ritchie Cl *CRAWE* RH10 .... 56 C1 🗉
Rival Moor Rd *EPSF* GU31 .... 117 F1
River Cl *SHOR* BN43 .... 233 H3
Riverhill La *PUL/STOR* RH20 ...... 126 D5
River La *PETW* GU28 .... 96 A7
  PUL/STOR RH20 .... 153 C7
River Md *CRAWW* RH11 .... 30 E2
  HORS RH12 .... 4 A6
Rivermead *PUL/STOR* RH20 ...... 155 F2
Riverside Rd *ARUN* BN18 .... 225 H1
  LHPTN BN17 .... 249 J2
Riverside *CCH* PO19 .... 7 D3
  FROW RH18 .... 37 J8
  HORL RH6 .... 18 A2
  HORS RH12 .... 77 G1
  PTSD BN41 .... 234 D1
  PUL/STOR RH20 .... 180 B1 🗉
  SHOR BN43 .... 233 H5
  STEY/UB BN44 .... 208 C1
Riverside Rd *SHOR* BN43 .... 233 H5
River's Rd *HWH* RH16 .... 83 K8
River St *EMRTH* PO10 .... 191 F7
Rixons Cl *RHWH* RH17 .... 86 A6
Rixons Orch *RHWH* RH17 .... 86 A6
Robell Wy *PUL/STOR* RH20 .... 156 C8
Roberts Cl *SWTR* RH13 .... 5 E4
Robertson Rd *BRI* BN1 .... 236 D1
Roberts Rd *LAN/SOMP* BN15 ..... 232 A7
  LISS GU33 .... 62 C1

Robert St *BRI* BN1 1
Robert Wy *HORS* RH12 ....
Robin Cl *CRAWW* RH11 ....
  EGRIN RH19 ....
  LHPTN BN17 ....
  SWTR RH13 ....
Robin Hood La *HORS* RH12 ....
Robin Rd *HPPT/KEY* BN6 ....
Robin's Cl *SELS* PO20 ....
Robins Dr *BOGR* PO21 ....
Robins La *MIDH* GU29 ....
Robinson Cl *LAN/SOMP* BN15 .. 2🗉
Robinson Rd *CRAWW* RH11 ....
Robson Rd *WTHG* BN11 ....
Rochester Cl *CCH* PO19 ....
  SALV BN13 .... 22🗉
Rochester Gdns *HOVE* BN3 ....
Rochester St *ROTT* BN2 ....
Rochester Wy *BOGR* PO21 ....
Rockall Cl *ANG/EP* BN16 .... 22🗉
Rock Gdns *BOGR* PO21 ....
Rock Gv *ROTT* BN2 ....
Rockingham Cl *SALV* BN13 ....
Rock La *PUL/STOR* RH20 ....
Rock Pl *ROTT* BN2 ....
Rock Rd *PUL/STOR* RH20 ....
Rocks La *RHWH* RH17 ....
The Rocks *EGRIN* RH19 ....
Rocky La *HWH* RH16 ....
Rodmell Rd *SALV* BN13 ....
Rodney Cl *BOGR* PO21 2
Rodney Crs *ARUN* BN18 ....
Roebuck Cl *SWTR* RH13 ....
Roedale Rd *BRI* BN1 ....
Roedean Rd *SALV* BN13 ....
Roedeer Copse *HASM* GU27 .....
Roffey's Cl *CRAWE* RH10 ....
Rogate Cl *LAN/SOMP* BN15 ......
  SALV BN13 ....
Rogate Rd *SALV* BN13 ....
Roger's La *FIN/BW* BN14 ....
Rolfe Dr *BURH* RH15 ....
Rollaston Pk *ARUN* BN18 ....
Romaine Cl *BURH* RH15 ....
Roman Acre *LHPTN* BN17 ....
Roman Crs *STHW* BN42 ....
Roman Landing *SELS* PO20 ......
Roman Rd *HOVE* BN3 ....
  STEY/UB BN44 ....
  STHW BN42 ....
Roman Wk *LAN/SOMP* BN15 .....
Roman Wy *BIL* RH14 ....
  CCH PO19 ....
  STHW BN42 ....
Romany Cl *PTSD* BN41 ....
Romany Rd *SALV* BN13 ....
Romney Broadwalk *MIDOS* PO22
Romney Garth *SELS* PO20 2
Romney Rd *WTHG* BN11 ....
Romsey Cl *BRI* BN1 ....
Rona Cl *CRAWW* RH11 ....
Rookcross La *SWTR* RH13 ....
Rookery Cl *BRI* BN1 ....
Rookery La *SELS* PO20 ....
The Rookery *EMRTH* PO10 ....
Rookery La *HWH* RH16 ....
Rook Wy *HORS* RH12 ....
Rookwood La *SELS* PO20 ....
Rookwood Pk *HORS* RH12 ....
Rookwood Rd *SELS* PO20 ....
Ropeland Wy *HORS* RH12 ....
Ropes La *HASM* GU27 ....
Ropetackle *SHOR* BN43 ....
Rope Wk *LHPTN* BN17 ....
  SHOR BN43 ....
Rosamund Rd *CRAWE* RH10 .....
Rose Av *MIDOS* PO22 ....
Rosebarn Cl *BURH* RH15 ....
Rosebery Av *FERR* BN12 ....
Rose Cottage La *RHWH* RH17 ....
Rosecroft Cl *LAN/SOMP* BN15 ..
Rosedale Cl *CRAWW* RH11 ....
Rose Green Rd *BOGR* PO21 ....
Rosehill *BIL* RH14 ....
Rose Hl *ROTT* BN2 ....
Rose Hill Cl *BRI* BN1 ....
Rose Hill Ter *BRI* BN1 ....
Roseleigh Gdns *RHWH* RH17 ....
Rosemary Av *STEY/UB* BN44 .....
Rosemary Cl *BOGR* PO21 ....
  PUL/STOR RH20 ....
  RHWH RH17 ....
  STEY/UB BN44 ....
Rosemary Dr *SHOR* BN43 ....
Rosemary La *CRAN* GU6 ....
  HORL RH6 ....
  HORL RH6 ....
  PETW GU28 ....
Rosemead *LHPTN* BN17 ....
Rose Wk *FERR* BN12 ....
Rosier Wy *BIL* RH14 ....
Rossalyn Cl *BOGR* PO21 ....
Ross Cl *BOGR* PO21 ....
  CRAWE RH10 ....
Rossiter Rd *LAN/SOMP* BN15 ....

St Mary's Wy *LHPTN* BN17 .... 250 B2 🔲
St Matthew's Rd *WTHG* BN11 .... 8 C3
St Maur's Rd *FERR* BN12 .... 252 C1
St Michaels Cl *PETW* GU28 .... 68 E4
St Michael's Pl *BRI* BN1 .... 10 A4
St Michaels Rd *EGRIN* RH19 .... 36 C1
  PTSD BN41 .... 235 F4
  WTHG BN11 .... 8 B4
St Michaels Wy *SWTR* RH13 .... 134 B8
St Nicholas' La *MIDOS* PO22 .... 247 K6
St Nicholas Rd *BRI* BN1 .... 10 B3
  PTSD BN41 .... 235 F4
  RCCH PO18 .... 194 E4
St Nicolas La *SHOR* BN43 .... 233 F3
St Osmund Rd *FERR* BN12 .... 252 B1
St Pancras *CCH* PO19 .... 6 C3
St Patrick's La *LISS* GU33 .... 62 C6
St Patrick's Rd *HOVE* BN3 .... 236 A4
St Paul's Av *WTHG* BN11 .... 231 H7
St Paul's Ct *HWH* RH16 .... 112 B6
St Paul's Rd *CCH* PO19 .... 6 B1
St Paul's St *ROTT* BN2 .... 11 D2
St Peter's Av *HISD* PO11 .... 238 A1
St Peters Cl *BOGR* PO21 .... 245 G7
  HOVE BN3 .... 235 K1
  SWTR RH13 .... 135 G2
St Peter's Crs *SELS* PO20 .... 265 F3
St Peters Rd *BURH* RH15 .... 139 G7
  CRAWW RH11 .... 2 B5 🔲
  HISD PO11 .... 238 A1
  PSF GU32 .... 88 D8
  PTSD BN41 .... 235 F4
St Peter's Sq *EMRTH* PO10 .... 214 D3
St Philips Ms *HOVE* BN3 .... 235 K4
St Raphael's Rd *WTHG* BN11 .... 253 K1 🔲
St Richard's Ct *BOGR* PO21 .... 245 F8
St Richard's Rd *PTSD* BN41 .... 235 F4
  SELS PO20 .... 222 C4
St Richard's Wy *BOGR* PO21 .... 245 F8
St Roche's Cl *RCCH* PO18 .... 195 F4
St Sampson Rd *CRAWW* RH11 .... 54 D1
St Stephens Cl *HASM* GU27 .... 40 E4
St Swithun's Cl *EGRIN* RH19 .... 36 D2 🔲
St Thomas Dr *BOGR* PO21 .... 261 G3
St Thomas's Rd *FIN/BW* BN14 .... 8 B2
St Valerie Rd *WTHG* BN11 .... 8 A5
St Vincent Cl *CRAWE* RH10 .... 32 D6 🔲
St Wilfreds Cl *SELS* PO20 .... 265 H3 🔲
St Wilfreds Rd *BURH* RH15 .... 139 H7
  FIN/BW BN14 .... 9 D2
St Wilfrid Rd *CCH* PO19 .... 218 D4
St Wilfrid's Wy *HWH* RH16 .... 112 A7
St Winefride's Rd *LHPTN* BN17 .... 250 A5
St Winifred's Cl *BOGR* PO21 .... 12 A6 🔲
Sake Ride La *HFD* BN5 .... 161 G2
Salehurst Rd *CRAWE* RH10 .... 32 E5
Salisbury Rd *CRAWE* RH10 .... 55 J1
  HOVE BN3 .... 236 C5
  WTHG BN11 .... 9 D4
Salisbury Wy *CCH* PO19 .... 219 F2 🔲
Salt Box Cl *SWTR* RH13 .... 103 K1
Saltdean Cl *CRAWW* RH11 .... 2 C6
Salterns Cl *HISD* PO11 .... 238 A8
Salterns Rd *CRAWE* RH10 .... 32 C8
Saltham La *SELS* PO20 .... 244 A2
Salthill La *CCH* PO19 .... 218 C3
Salthill Rd *CCH* PO19 .... 218 B4
The Saltings *ANG/EP* BN16 .... 250 C1
  LAN/SOMP BN15 .... 232 B6 🔲
  SELS PO20 .... 241 J7
  SHOR BN43 .... 233 F5
Saltings Wy *STEY/UB* BN44 .... 208 C3
Salvington Cl *SALV* BN13 .... 229 H4 🔲
Salvington Gdns *SALV* BN13 .... 229 K5
Salvington Hl *SALV* BN13 .... 229 J2
Salvington Rd *CRAWW* RH11 .... 30 D8
  SALV BN13 .... 229 J4
Samaritan Cl *CRAWW* RH11 .... 30 C7 🔲
Samphire Cl *CRAWW* RH11 .... 30 E8 🔲
Samphire Dr *SALV* BN13 .... 228 E6
Sampsons Dr *SELS* PO20 .... 220 E4 🔲
Sanctuary La *PUL/STOR* RH20 .... 181 G2
Sandfield Av *LHPTN* BN17 .... 225 K7
Sandgate La *PUL/STOR* RH20 .... 180 E1
Sandgate Rd *BRI* BN1 .... 237 G1
Sandhawes Hl *EGRIN* RH19 .... 22 E7 🔲
Sandhill La *CRAWE* RH10 .... 34 D4
  PUL/STOR RH20 .... 181 J3
Sandhills Rd *SWTR* RH13 .... 75 K8
Sandown Av *FERR* BN12 .... 253 G2
Sandown Cl *FERR* BN12 .... 253 G2
Sandown Rd *ROTT* BN2 .... 11 F3
  STHW BN42 .... 234 B5
Sandpiper Cl *CRAWW* RH11 .... 30 B7 🔲
Sandridge La *HWH* RH16 .... 112 B2
Sandringham Cl *HOVE* BN3 .... 212 A8 🔲
  SELS PO20 .... 258 A6
Sandringham Dr *HOVE* BN3 .... 212 A8
Sandringham Ms *SALV* BN13 .... 229 H4 🔲
Sandringham Rd *CCH* PO19 .... 7 F3 🔲
  CRAWW RH11 .... 55 F1
  PSF GU32 .... 88 D7

Sandringham Wy *BOGR* PO21 .... 12 A4
Sandrock *HASM* GU27 .... 40 E5
  MIDH GU29 .... 121 K3
Sandrocks Wy *HWH* RH16 .... 140 A1
Sands La *HFD* BN5 .... 185 C5
The Sands *PUL/STOR* RH20 .... 157 K6
Sandwich Rd *WTHG* BN11 .... 253 K2
Sandy Cl *EPSF* GU31 .... 89 C8
Sandygate La *SWTR* RH13 .... 79 H8
Sandy La *CRAWE* RH10 .... 34 C3
  EGRIN RH19 .... 36 C2
  EGRIN RH19 .... 59 C5
  GSHT GU26 .... 40 B3
  HASM GU27 .... 39 J4
  HASM GU27 .... 41 G2
  HFD BN5 .... 161 F7
  LISS GU33 .... 62 E8
  MIDH GU29 .... 121 J3
  PUL/STOR RH20 .... 157 K6
  PUL/STOR RH20 .... 181 F2
  RCCH PO18 .... 193 H7
  RHWH RH17 .... 87 C3
Sandymount Av *MIDOS* PO22 .... 12 A3
Sandymount Cl *MIDOS* PO22 .... 12 B2
Sandy Rd *BOGR* PO21 .... 261 H4
Sandy V *HWH* RH16 .... 139 K7
San Feliu Ct *EGRIN* RH19 .... 37 F1
Sangers Dr *HORL* RH6 .... 17 K1
Sanyhils Av *BRI* BN1 .... 213 F4
Sargent Cl *CRAWE* RH10 .... 55 K1 🔲
Sarisbury Cl *MIDOS* PO22 .... 13 F3 🔲
Sark Cl *CRAWW* RH11 .... 54 E1 🔲
Sark Gdns *FERR* BN12 .... 252 D2
Satinwood Cl *MIDOS* PO22 .... 247 J5
Saturn Cl *CRAWW* RH11 .... 30 C7 🔲
Saucelands La *SWTR* RH13 .... 131 J4
Saunders Cl *CRAWE* RH10 .... 32 B5
Saunders Hl *BRI* BN1 .... 213 K4
Saunders Park Vw *ROTT* BN2 .... 11 E4
Savernake Wk *CRAWE* RH10 .... 3 E6
Saville Gdns *BIL* RH14 .... 102 B6
Savill Rd *HWH* RH16 .... 112 C3
Sawyers Cl *BURH* RH15 .... 165 K2
Saxby Rd *BURH* RH15 .... 138 D7
Saxifrage Wy *SALV* BN13 .... 228 E6
Saxon Cl *ANG/EP* BN16 .... 227 K8
  BIL RH14 .... 102 B2
  BOGR PO21 .... 261 G3
Saxon Crs *HORS* RH12 .... 4 A3
Saxon Rd *CRAWE* RH10 .... 32 E6
  HOVE BN3 .... 235 H5
  STEY/UB BN44 .... 184 B8
Saxons *SHOR* BN43 .... 233 H2
Saxony Rd *FIN/BW* BN14 .... 8 C2
Sayers Cl *SWTR* RH13 .... 5 D5
The Sayers *EGRIN* RH19 .... 36 A2
Scallops Cl *CRAWE* RH10 .... 3 F2
Scallows Cl *CRAWE* RH10 .... 3 F2
Scamps Hl *HWH* RH16 .... 112 E5
Scant Rd *RCCH* PO18 .... 192 D8
Scant Rd (East) *RCCH* PO18 .... 216 C1
Scant Rd (West) *RCCH* PO18 .... 216 C1
Scarborough Rd *BRI* BN1 .... 236 D2 🔲
School Cl *BURH* RH15 .... 165 F1
  HORS RH12 .... 5 F1 🔲
  PUL/STOR RH20 .... 127 C8
  STHW BN42 .... 234 C4 🔲
School Dell *RCCH* PO18 .... 192 E8
School Hl *ARUN* BN18 .... 185 C6
  FIN/BW BN14 .... 205 J5
  HORS RH12 .... 51 F5
  PUL/STOR RH20 .... 180 B2
School La *ARUN* BN18 .... 225 H1 🔲
  EGRIN RH19 .... 37 H5
  EMRTH PO10 .... 191 F6
  EMRTH PO10 .... 214 D7
  FROW RH18 .... 61 K1
  MIDH GU29 .... 121 F2
  PETW GU28 .... 95 K8
  POY/PYE BN45 .... 188 C5
  PSF GU32 .... 88 E5
  PUL/STOR RH20 .... 151 K7
  PUL/STOR RH20 .... 153 C1
  PUL/STOR RH20 .... 180 A2
  PUL/STOR RH20 .... 181 J5
  RCCH PO18 .... 167 K1
  RCCH PO18 .... 215 K4
  RCCH PO18 .... 217 C6
  RHWH RH17 .... 86 C7
  SELS PO20 .... 222 D4
  SELS PO20 .... 243 K1
  SELS PO20 .... 264 E3
  STEY/UB BN44 .... 159 K6
  STEY/UB BN44 .... 183 K8
  SWTR RH13 .... 132 C2
School Rd *ARUN* BN18 .... 178 A4
  BIL RH14 .... 100 E2
  HASM GU27 .... 40 B6
  HOVE BN3 .... 235 K4
  STEY/UB BN44 .... 208 C3
Scory Cl *CRAWW* RH11 .... 30 E8 🔲
Scotland La *HASM* GU27 .... 40 D6
Scotlands Cl *HASM* GU27 .... 40 D6
Scotlands Dr *HASM* GU27 .... 40 D6 🔲

Scotland St *ROTT* BN2 ....
Scotney Cl *LAN/SOMP* BN13 229
Scott Cl *BOGR* PO21 ....
Scott Rd *CRAWE* RH10 ....
  HOVE BN3 23
Scott St *BOGR* PO21 ....
Scratchings La *PETW* GU28 ....
Sea Av *ANG/EP* BN16 ....
Seabrook Cl *BOGR* PO21 ....
Sea Cl *FERR* BN12 ....
  MIDOS PO22 ....
Seacourt Cl *BOGR* PO21 26
Sea Dr *FERR* BN12 ....
  MIDOS PO22 ....
Seafield Av *FERR* BN12 ....
Seafield Cl *SELS* PO20 ....
Seafield Rd *ANG/EP* BN16 ....
  HOVE BN3 ....
Seafields *EMRTH* PO10 ....
  SELS PO20 ....
Seafield Wy *SELS* PO20 ....
Seaford Rd *CRAWW* RH11 ....
  HOVE BN3 ....
Sea Gv *SELS* PO20 ....
Seagull Cl *SELS* PO20 ....
Seagull La *EMRTH* PO10 ....
Seahaven Gdns *SHOR* BN43 23
Sea La *BOGR* PO21 ....
  FERR BN12 ....
  FERR BN12 ....
  FERR BN12 ....
  MIDOS PO22 ....
Sea Lane Cl *ANG/EP* BN16 ....
  FERR BN12 ....
Sea Lane Gdns *FERR* BN12 ....
Seal Rd *SELS* PO20 ....
Seal Sq *SELS* PO20 ....
Seamill Park Av *WTHG* BN11 ....
Seamill Park Crs *WTHG* BN11 ....
Seamill Wy *WTHG* BN11 ....
Sea Pl *FERR* BN12 ....
Searle's Vw *HORS* RH12 ....
Sea Rd *ANG/EP* BN16 ....
  LHPTN BN17 ....
  MIDOS PO22 ....
Seaside Av *LAN/SOMP* BN15 ....
Seaside Cl *LAN/SOMP* BN15 ....
Seaside Rd *LAN/SOMP* BN15 ....
Seaton Cl *LHPTN* BN17 ....
Seaton La *LHPTN* BN17 ....
Seaton Pk *LHPTN* BN17 ....
Seaton Rd *LHPTN* BN17 ....
Seaview Av *ANG/EP* BN16 ....
Seaview Ct *LAN/SOMP* BN15 ....
Seaview Rd *ANG/EP* BN16 ....
  HISD PO11 ....
Sea View Rd *WTHG* BN11 ....
Seaward Dr *SELS* PO20 ....
Seawaves Cl *ANG/EP* BN16 ....
Sea Wy *BOGR* PO21 ....
  MIDOS PO22 ....
  MIDOS PO22 ....
Second Av *EMRTH* PO10 ....
  FIN/BW BN14 ....
  HOVE BN3 ....
  LAN/SOMP BN15 ....
  MIDOS PO22 ....
  SELS PO20 ....
  SELS PO20 ....
Sedbury Rd *LAN/SOMP* BN15 ....
Sedgefield Cl *CRAWE* RH10 ....
Sedgewick Cl *CRAWE* RH10 ....
Sedgewick Rd *BRI* BN1 ....
Sedgwick La *SWTR* RH13 ....
Sefter Rd *BOGR* PO21 ....
Sefton Av *BOGR* PO21 ....
Sefton Cl *SALV* BN13 ....
Sefton Rd *PTSD* BN41 ....
Selangor Av *EMRTH* PO10 ....
Selborne Cl *PSF* GU32 ....
Selborne Pl *HOVE* BN3 2
Selborne Rd *HOVE* BN3 ....
  LHPTN BN17 ....
  WTHG BN11 ....
Selborne Wy *ANG/EP* BN16 ....
Selbourne Cl *CRAWE* RH10 ....
Selby Ct *HWH* RH16 ....
Selden La *SALV* BN13 ....
  WTHG BN11 ....
Selden Rd *WTHG* BN11 ....
Selden's Ms *SALV* BN13 2
Selden's Wy *SALV* BN13 ....
Selham Cl *CCH* PO19 ....
  CRAWW RH11 ....
Selham Dr *BRI* BN1 ....
Selham Rd *MIDH* GU29 ....
Selhurst Cl *ANG/EP* BN16 ....
Selhurstpark Rd *RCCH* PO18 ....
Selkirk Cl *SALV* BN13 ....
Selsey Av *BOGR* PO21 ....
Selsey Cl *SALV* BN13 ....
Selsey Rd *CCH* PO19 ....
  CRAWW RH11 ....
  SELS PO20 ....
  SELS PO20 ....

...eld Dr ROTT BN2 ... 213 K8
...eld Rd CRAWE RH10 ... 34 C8
...IN RH19 ... 58 E4
...VH RH17 ... 84 D2
...y La LHPTN BN17 ... 250 B1
...n Av LHPTN BN17 ... 225 K8
...n Cl BOGR PO21 ... 245 H7
...WE RH10 ... 32 C2
...ey Rd BRI BN1 ... 10 C1
...T/KEY BN6 ... 164 E7
...on Cl HWH RH16 ... 111 J6
...on Rd HWH RH16 ... 111 K6
...Wy HORS RH12 ... 5 D2
...e Rd HORL RH6 ... 17 K3
...e Cl BOGR PO21 ... 262 C1
...th Av LAN/SOMP BN15 ... 232 A3
...ls Rd MIDH GU29 ... 121 H3
...n Rd CRAWE RH10 ... 32 C6
...St ROTT BN2 ... 11 E3
...Cl HORL RH6 ... 16 D4
...ur Rd CRAWW RH11 ... 54 E1
...ur Sq ROTT BN2 ... 11 F6
...ur St ROTT BN2 ... 11 F6
...eton Rd CRAWE RH10 ... 3 D6
...ells Cl LAN/SOMP BN15 ... 232 B4
...ells Rd LAN/SOMP BN15 ... 232 B8
...sbury Av FERR BN12 ... 229 J8
...sbury Pl BRI BN1 ... 10 C2
...sbury Rd ANG/EP BN16 ... 250 E3
...BN1 ... 10 C2
...WE RH10 ... 32 D7
...speare Rd WTHG BN11 ... 8 B3
...speare St HOVE BN3 ... 236 A3
...ourne Crs SELS BN20 ... 258 B6
...brook La FROW RH18 ... 61 K2
...ock Cl CHI PO19 ... 7 D1
...P PO18 ... 217 G6
...on Gdns FIN/BW BN14 ... 230 D5
...on Rd FIN/BW BN14 ... 230 D5
...on Wy FIN/BW BN14 ... 230 D5
...ys Cl HORS RH12 ... 77 G3
...in Rd ROTT BN2 ... 11 E2
...on Cl ANG/EP BN16 ... 250 C3
...eloes Rd ANG/EP BN16 ... 227 H5
...n Cl CRAWE RH10 ... 3 F6
...thorne Cl CRAWW RH11 ... 30 D5
...thorne Crs PTSD BN41 ... 235 F4
...s Wood La HPPT/KEY BN6 ... 186 E1
...Cl LHPTN BN17 ... 248 A6
...La SWTR RH13 ... 104 D3
...Rd CRAWE RH10 ... 3 C2
...HI EPSF GU31 ... 89 F6
...water Dr MIDS PO22 ... 12 B2
...ngdean La BURH RH15 ... 139 G7
...ell Cl PTSD BN41 ... 211 F8
...down Cl PETW GU28 ... 126 A4
...down Dr PETW GU28 ... 125 K4
...Fold Av ANG/EP BN16 ... 251 G1
...La MIDS GU29 ... 122 B3
...Pen La STEY/UB BN44 ... 183 K8
...St PSF GU31 ... 88 D8
...wash La RCCH PO18 ... 195 F6
...PO20 ... 240 B8
...el Br UCK TN22 ... 115 F7
...eld Cl CRAWE RH10 ... 32 E7
...eld Mill La UCK TN22 ... 115 C3
...Rd SALV BN13 ... 229 G5
...n Cl CRAWE RH10 ... 32 D6
...idge Rd ARUN BN18 ... 199 J7
...le Av PTSD BN41 ... 235 F4
...le Crs PTSD BN41 ... 235 F4
...le Rd PTSD BN41 ... 234 E3
...Cl CRAWE RH10 ... 32 C3
...Dr HORS RH12 ... 50 C8
...Rd BOGR PO21 ... 245 J8
...RH19 ... 36 B2
...RH12 ... 4 A4
...BN3 ... 235 K4
...GBN11 ... 8 C4
...RHWH RH17 ... 83 J3
...Ct SWTR RH13 ... 5 F4
...eld Wy BRI BN1 ... 237 H1
...one HWH RH16 ... 112 D3
...erd Cl CRAWE RH10 ... 2 C6
...erds Cft BRI BN1 ... 212 C8
...erdsgrove La EGRIN RH19 ... 23 K6
...erd's Hl HWH RH16 ... 40 E5
...erds La PETW GU27 ... 95 K5
...erds Rd BURH RH15 ... 139 F7
...IN BN14 ... 206 A8
...erds Wk HPPT/KEY BN6 ... 164 E6
...erds Wy HORS RH12 ... 5 F2
...GU30 ... 38 D8
...rd Wy PTSD BN41 ... 210 E8
...ey Cl CRAWW RH11 ... 2 A6
...eys HWH RH16 ... 139 K1
...rne La CCH PO19 ... 6 B2
...urne Cl HOVE BN3 ... 211 H8
...urne La SELS PO20 ... 264 C3
...urne Rd HOVE BN3 ... 211 H8
...urne Wy HOVE BN3 ... 211 H8
...ooke Cl SALV BN13 ... 229 H5
...an Cl EGRIN RH19 ... 36 A2
...an Rd FIN/BW BN14 ... 9 D1
...an Ter HOVE BN3 ... 236 A3

Sherlock Av CCH PO19 ... 6 A2
Shermanbury Dr
PUL/STOR PO20 ... 180 A1
Shermanbury Rd FIN/BW BN14 ... 8 B2
Sherwood Cl LISS GU33 ... 62 A4
MIDOS PO22 ... 12 A2
Sherwood Dr HWH RH16 ... 111 J6
Sherwood Rd MIDOS PO22 ... 12 A3
Sherwood Wk CRAWE RH10 ... 3 E6
Shetland Cl CRAWE RH10 ... 32 E4
Shetland Cl SALV BN13 ... 229 F6
Shillinglee Rd BIL RH14 ... 44 D8
MFD/CHID GU8 ... 43 F6
Shingle Rd SHOR BN43 ... 233 J5
Shingle Wk SELS PO20 ... 257 J5
Shipfield BOGR PO21 ... 262 C1
Shipleybridge La HORL RH6 ... 19 F6
Shipley Ct LIPH GU30 ... 38 B8
Shipley Paygate SWTR RH13 ... 132 D2
Shipley Rd CRAWW RH11 ... 30 E5
SWTR RH13 ... 104 B3
Ship St BRI BN1 ... 10 B5 11
EGRIN RH19 ... 36 C3
SHOR BN43 ... 233 G4
Shipton Green La SELS PO20 ... 240 E7
Shire Pde CRAWE RH10 ... 32 D4
Shirley Av HOVE BN3 ... 236 B1
Shirley Cl ANG/EP BN16 ... 251 F3
BOGR PO21 ... 261 H3
FIN/BW BN14 ... 230 B4
SHOR BN43 ... 234 A3
Shirley Dr FIN/BW BN14 ... 230 B4
HOVE BN3 ... 236 C2
MIDOS PO22 ... 13 F2
Shirley Rd HOVE BN3 ... 236 C3
Shirleys Gdn MIDOS PO22 ... 13 F3
Shirley St HOVE BN3 ... 236 B2
Shooting Fld STEY/UB BN44 ... 183 K6
Shopfield Cl ANG/EP BN16 ... 250 E1
Shop La RCCH PO18 ... 195 G6
Shopsdam Rd LAN/SOMP BN15 ... 232 B7
Shopwhyke Rd SELS PO20 ... 220 A4
Shorecroft BOGR PO21 ... 262 C2
Shoreham By-pass
LAN/SOMP BN15 ... 232 A3
Shoreham Rd CRAWE RH10 ... 32 C8
HFD BN5 ... 185 G4
STEY/UB BN44 ... 208 D3
Shore Rd RCCH PO18 ... 216 E8
SELS PO20 ... 257 H5
Shoreside Wk SELS PO20 ... 257 H5
Short Cl CRAWW RH11 ... 2 C1
Short Furlong LHPTN BN17 ... 250 B2
Short Gallop CRAWE RH10 ... 32 D4
Shortsfield Cl HORS RH12 ... 4 B2
Shottermill HORS RH12 ... 52 C4
Shovelstrode La EGRIN RH19 ... 37 J1
Shripney La MIDOS PO22 ... 245 K3
Shripney Rd MIDOS PO22 ... 12 C3
MIDOS PO22 ... 246 B2
Shrubbs Dr MIDOS PO22 ... 247 K6
Sickle Rd HASM GU27 ... 40 B6
Sidehill Dr PTSD BN41 ... 234 D1
Sideways La HORL RH6 ... 17 C2
Sidlesham La SELS PO20 ... 241 K6
Silchester Cl CRAWW RH11 ... 30 E8
Sillwood Pl BRI BN1 ... 10 A5
Sillwood Rd BRI BN1 ... 10 A5
Sillwood St BRI BN1 ... 10 A5
Silver Birch Cl LISS GU33 ... 62 A7
Silver Birch Dr MIDOS PO22 ... 247 J5
SALV BN13 ... 229 F6
Silver Birches HFD BN5 ... 185 H4
HWH RH16 ... 112 C7
Silverdale Av HOVE BN3 ... 236 D4
Silverdale Cl BOGR PO21 ... 261 H5
Silverdale Dr LAN/SOMP BN15 ... 231 J6
Silverdale Rd BURH RH15 ... 165 H1
HOVE BN3 ... 236 D4
Silver Gld PUL/STOR PO20 ... 156 C5
Silver La BIL RH14 ... 102 B4
Silverlea Gdns HORL RH6 ... 18 C1
Silverston Av BOGR PO21 ... 262 D1
Silvertrees EMRTH PO10 ... 214 D1
Silver Wy SELS PO20 ... 258 B6
Silver Wd PUL/STOR PO20 ... 155 K4
Silver Wood Copse
PUL/STOR PO20 ... 155 K4
Simmons Cl HISD PO11 ... 238 A3
Sinclair Cl CRAWE RH10 ... 32 C7
Sincox La SWTR RH13 ... 131 J5
Singleton Cl BOGR PO21 ... 261 K2
FERR BN12 ... 228 D7
Singleton Crs FERR BN12 ... 228 D8
Singleton Rd BRI BN1 ... 213 G5
HORS RH12 ... 50 D8
Singleton Wy BURH RH15 ... 165 J2
Sinnocks PUL/STOR PO20 ... 156 C2
Sir George's Pl STEY/UB BN44 ... 183 J6
Siskin Cl HORS RH12 ... 5 D2
Sissinghurst Cl CRAWE RH10 ... 32 D4
Six Acres Cl SWTR RH13 ... 103 K1
Skeyne Dr PUL/STOR PO20 ... 154 E1

Skiff La BIL RH14 ... 72 B5
Skye Cluan Cl MIDOS PO22 ... 223 F5
Skylark Vw CRAWW RH12 ... 51 K4
Slade La EPSF GU31 ... 90 C7
Slattsfield Cl SELS PO20 ... 265 G4
Slaugham Ct CRAWW RH11 ... 30 D8
Slaugham La RHWH RH17 ... 80 E7
Sleets Rd HORS RH12 ... 50 E8
Slider's La UCK TN22 ... 114 E4
Slimbridge Rd BURH RH15 ... 139 F8
Slindon Bottom Rd ARUN BN18 ... 198 E2
Slindon Rd FIN/BW BN14 ... 230 D5
Slinfold Wk CRAWW RH11 ... 30 A2
Slinford Cl ROTT BN2 ... 11 F5
Slipper Rd EMRTH PO10 ... 214 E4
Slonk Hill Rd SHOR BN43 ... 233 J1
Sloughbrook Cl HORS RH12 ... 5 E1
Sloughgreen La RHWH RH17 ... 109 K2
Slugwash La RHWH RH17 ... 140 D6
Smallcroft Cl LHPTN BN17 ... 249 J2
Smallcutts Av EMRTH PO10 ... 215 H2
Smalls Md CRAWW RH11 ... 2 B3
Smithbarn SWTR RH13 ... 5 F4
Smith Cl CRAWE RH10 ... 2 C6
Smithers Hill La SWTR RH13 ... 132 B3
Smith La EMRTH PO10 ... 239 G2
Smock Aly PUL/STOR PO20 ... 156 C5
Smokyhouse La PETW GU28 ... 123 K6
Smolletts EGRIN RH19 ... 36 A3
Smugglers End RHWH RH17 ... 81 G3
Smugglers' La RDKG RH5 ... 26 E4
RCCH PO18 ... 240 E2
SWTR RH13 ... 75 H8
Smugglers Wk FERR BN12 ... 253 J2
Smugglers Wy SWTR RH13 ... 103 K1
Snapes Rd PUL/STOR PO20 ... 156 D8
Snell Hatch CRAWW RH11 ... 2 A3
Snipe La HASM GU27 ... 66 C2
Snowdrop Cl ANG/EP BN16 ... 226 D8
CRAWW RH11 ... 54 E1
Snowdrop La HWH RH16 ... 112 E7
Snowflakes La HWH RH16 ... 113 F5
Snow Hl CRAWE RH10 ... 20 B7
Snowhill La CRAWE RH10 ... 20 B8
Soane Cl ANG/EP BN16 ... 30 C7
Solent Cl ANG/EP BN16 ... 226 C8 13
Solent Rd SELS PO20 ... 257 J5
Solent Wy EMRTH PO10 ... 214 A4
SELS PO20 ... 264 E6
Solway Av BRI BN1 ... 213 F4
Solway Cl LHPTN BN17 ... 250 C1
Somergate HORS RH12 ... 77 F1
Somerhill Av HOVE BN3 ... 236 D4
Somerhill Rd HOVE BN3 ... 236 D5
Somerley La SELS PO20 ... 258 C2
Somersbury La CRAN GU6 ... 24 D1
Somerset Cl SALV BN13 ... 8 A1
Somerset Gdns MIDOS PO22 ... 12 B3
Somerset Rd ANG/EP BN16 ... 251 K1
FERR BN12 ... 252 D3
Somerset St ROTT BN2 ... 11 E5
Somerstown CCH PO19 ... 6 B2
Somerton Gn MIDOS PO22 ... 13 E3
Somerville Dr CRAWE RH10 ... 32 C2
Sompting Av HOVE BN14 ... 9 D1
Sompting By-pass FIN/BW BN14 ... 230 E4
Sompting Rd FIN/BW BN14 ... 9 E1
LAN/SOMP BN15 ... 231 K5
Sopers La STEY/UB BN44 ... 207 H4
Sorrel Cl CRAWW RH11 ... 54 E1
Sorrel Rd HORS RH12 ... 5 D2
South Acre EPSF GU31 ... 118 B8
Southall Av ROTT BN2 ... 11 F1
ROTT BN2 ... 237 K1
Southampton St ROTT BN2 ... 11 D4
South Ash STEY/UB BN44 ... 183 K7
South Av BOGR PO21 ... 245 G8
FERR BN12 ... 253 J2
HPPT/KEY BN6 ... 164 A6
ROTT BN2 ... 11 E5
South Bank CCH PO19 ... 6 B5
HPPT/KEY BN6 ... 164 E8
South Bay EMRTH PO10 ... 214 E8
Southbourne Av EMRTH PO10 ... 215 F3
Southbrook CRAWW RH11 ... 55 G2
Southbrook Rd RCCH PO18 ... 192 E8
South Cl BURH RH15 ... 138 E8
CRAWE RH10 ... 3 E2
Southcote Av SELS PO20 ... 257 H4
Southcourt Cl ANG/EP BN16 ... 251 G1
Southcourt Rd FIN/BW BN14 ... 8 C3
Southdean Cl MIDOS PO22 ... 247 K6
Southdean Dr MIDOS PO22 ... 247 K6
Southdown Av BRI BN1 ... 10 C1
PTSD BN41 ... 235 C3
Southdown Cl HORS RH12 ... 52 C1
HWH RH16 ... 139 K1
MIDH GU29 ... 121 K5
Southdown Pl BRI BN1 ... 10 C1
Southdown Rd BOGR PO21 ... 12 B5
BRI BN1 ... 10 C1
PTSD BN41 ... 234 E1
SHOR BN43 ... 233 H4
STHW BN42 ... 234 C4
South Downs Wy ARUN BN18 ... 178 A6

EPSF GU31 ..... 144 E2
HFD BN5 ..... 210 D1
HPPT/KEY BN6 ..... 189 J4
PETW GU28 ..... 150 C7
POY/PYE BN45 ..... 188 E5
PUL/STOR RH20 ..... 175 K4
SHOR BN43 ..... 181 K7
SHOR BN43 ..... 209 K1
STEY/UB BN44 ..... 207 G4
Southdown Ter STEY/UB BN44 ..... 184 A8 🔟
Southdown View Cl FIN/BW BN14 ..... 9 F1 🔟
Southdown View Rd FIN/BW BN14 ..... 9 E1
Southdown View Wy
FIN/BW BN14 ..... 230 E5 🔃
Southdown Wy PUL/STOR RH20 ..... 156 D8
South Dr ANG/EP BN16 ..... 227 F8
BURH BN15 ..... 138 E8
FERR BN12 ..... 252 C5
PO22 ..... 247 G6
Southern Rd SELS PO20 ..... 265 F5
Southey Rd WTHG BN11 ..... 8 C5
South Farm Rd FIN/BW BN14 ..... 230 C5
Southfield Rd FIN/BW BN14 ..... 9 D1
Southfields Cl CCH PO19 ..... 6 B6
Southfields Rd LHPTN BN17 ..... 250 B2
Southgate Av CRAWE RH10 ..... 2 C6
Southgate Dr CRAWE RH10 ..... 2 C5
Southgate Rd CRAWW RH11 ..... 2 C5
South Gv PETW GU28 ..... 125 K4 🔃
SWTR RH13 ..... 4 C6
South Holmes Rd SWTR RH13 ..... 52 D7
Southlands EGRIN RH19 ..... 36 C4
Southlands La PUL/STOR RH20 ..... 156 C4
Southlands Pk MIDH GU29 ..... 122 A6
South La ARUN BN18 ..... 177 H8
EMRTH PO10 ..... 116 B7
EPSF GU31 ..... 116 B7
PETW GU28 ..... 124 D4
Southleigh Rd EMRTH PO10 ..... 190 D8
Southleys HASM GU27 ..... 190 D8
South Lodge Cl BURH RH15 ..... 139 F7 🔃
Southmount ROTT BN2 ..... 11 D1
Southon Cl PTSD BN41 ..... 210 D8
Southover Pl ROTT BN2 ..... 11 D3
Southover Rd BOGR PO21 ..... 12 B5 🔃
Southover St ROTT BN2 ..... 11 D4
Southover Wy SELS PO20 ..... 243 G3
South Pallant CCH PO19 ..... 6 C5
South Pas LHPTN BN17 ..... 250 B3
South Pier Rd HORL RH6 ..... 18 A4
South Rd BRI BN1 ..... 10 A1
HWH RH16 ..... 112 A7
LIPH GU30 ..... 64 C2
MIDOS PO22 ..... 13 E3
RHWH RH17 ..... 140 E7
Southsea Av FERR BN12 ..... 253 J1
Southside PUL/STOR RH20 ..... 155 F1
South Strd ANG/EP BN16 ..... 251 J3
South St BRI BN1 ..... 10 B5
CCH PO19 ..... 6 C5
EMRTH PO10 ..... 214 D4
HORS RH12 ..... 4 B5
HPPT/KEY BN6 ..... 165 K8
LAN/SOMP BN15 ..... 232 A6
MIDH GU29 ..... 122 B4
PTSD BN41 ..... 234 E2
RHWH RH17 ..... 110 E6
SALV BN13 ..... 8 A2
SWTR RH13 ..... 134 C8
WTHG BN11 ..... 9 D4
South Ter LHPTN BN17 ..... 249 K3
South Vw ANG/EP BN16 ..... 251 K3
HPPT/KEY BN6 ..... 165 K6
South View Cl CRAWE RH10 ..... 20 A8
Southview Cl SHOR BN43 ..... 234 A4
STHW BN42 ..... 234 C2 🔟
Southview Dr WTHG BN11 ..... 8 A4
Southview Gdns WTHG BN11 ..... 253 K1
Southview Rd MIDOS PO22 ..... 247 F7
STHW BN42 ..... 234 C3
South View Ter HFD BN5 ..... 161 G7
South Vw MIDOS PO22 ..... 247 H6
Southwark Cl CRAWW RH11 ..... 55 F1 🔃
Southwark Wk BOGR PO21 ..... 245 G7 🔃
Southwater Cl FERR BN12 ..... 229 F8 🔃
ROTT BN2 ..... 11 F4
Southways Av FIN/BW BN14 ..... 230 E5
Southwick Cl EGRIN RH19 ..... 36 B1
Southwick Sq STHW BN42 ..... 234 C4
Southwick St STHW BN42 ..... 234 C4
Southwold Cl SALV BN13 ..... 229 J2
South Woodlands BRI BN1 ..... 212 E7
The Spain PSF GU32 ..... 88 C8
Sparks Ct LHPTN BN17 ..... 249 K2
Spark's La RHWH RH17 ..... 110 E1
Sparrow Wy HPPT/KEY BN6 ..... 138 D8
Sparshott Rd SELS PO20 ..... 265 F6
Spartan Cl EMRTH PO10 ..... 214 E8
Spear Hl PUL/STOR RH20 ..... 158 A4
Speedwell Cl SALV BN13 ..... 228 E6 🔃
Speedwell Wy HORS RH12 ..... 5 D2

Spencer Av HOVE BN3 ..... 211 H8
Spencer Rd EMRTH PO10 ..... 190 C7
LAN/SOMP BN15 ..... 231 K6
Spencers La HORL RH6 ..... 16 D2
Spencers Pl HORS RH12 ..... 4 A3
Spencers Rd CRAWW RH11 ..... 2 B4
HORS RH12 ..... 4 A4
Spencer St BOGR PO21 ..... 12 C4
Spey Cl SALV BN13 ..... 229 G3
Spicers Cl BURH RH15 ..... 139 F6 🔃
Spierbridge Rd PUL/STOR RH20 ..... 180 A1
Spiers Wy HORL RH6 ..... 18 B2 🔟
Spindle Cl HAV PO9 ..... 190 A8
Spindle Warren HAV PO9 ..... 190 A8 🔟
Spindle Wy CRAWE RH10 ..... 3 E4
Spinnaker Cl LHPTN BN17 ..... 250 C2
Spinnaker Gra HISD PO11 ..... 214 A7
Spinnals Gv STHW BN42 ..... 234 B4
Spinney Cl CRAWE RH10 ..... 34 E3
HORS RH12 ..... 52 D5 🔃
HPPT/KEY BN6 ..... 164 C6
SELS PO20 ..... 264 E3
Spinney La PUL/STOR RH20 ..... 156 A6
SELS PO20 ..... 240 E5
Spinney North PUL/STOR RH20 ..... 155 F1
The Spinney ANG/EP BN16 ..... 251 J3 🔃
BOGR PO21 ..... 245 G8 🔃
CRAWW RH11 ..... 2 A5
HASM GU27 ..... 40 E3
HOVE BN3 ..... 212 C8
HPPT/KEY BN6 ..... 165 F6
PUL/STOR RH20 ..... 154 C7
RHWH RH17 ..... 111 K4
SELS PO20 ..... 240 D6
Spinney Wk MIDOS PO22 ..... 223 F4
Spitalfield La CCH PO19 ..... 7 D2
Spitalmead La STEY/UB BN44 ..... 182 D2
Spooners Rd HORS RH12 ..... 5 F3
Springate Rd STHW BN42 ..... 234 D3
Springbank CCH PO19 ..... 219 F2
Spring Copse CRAWE RH10 ..... 19 J8
Springfarm Rd HASM GU27 ..... 40 A6
Springfield BOGR PO21 ..... 261 H1
EGRIN RH19 ..... 22 B7
Springfield Cl ANG/EP BN16 ..... 251 J3
RCCH PO18 ..... 195 F4
RHWH RH17 ..... 109 F5
SELS PO20 ..... 241 K6
Springfield Crs HORS RH12 ..... 4 A5
Springfield La SWTR RH13 ..... 53 K7
Springfield Park Rd HORS RH12 ..... 4 A5
Springfield Rd BRI BN1 ..... 10 C2
CRAWW RH11 ..... 2 B4
HORS RH12 ..... 4 B5
Spring Gdns BRI BN1 ..... 10 C5
CRAWE RH10 ..... 19 J8
EMRTH PO10 ..... 214 D3
PUL/STOR RH20 ..... 181 J1
Spring La HPPT/KEY BN6 ..... 188 E3
HWH RH16 ..... 112 D2
SWTR RH13 ..... 49 G8
Spring Meadow FROW RH18 ..... 61 K2
Spring Plat CRAWE RH10 ..... 32 C5
Spring St BRI BN1 ..... 10 A5 🔟
Spring Wy EGRIN RH19 ..... 22 E7
Spronketts La RHWH RH17 ..... 108 C7
Sproule Cl ARUN BN18 ..... 248 B1
Sproutes La SWTR RH13 ..... 131 G3
Spurgeon Cl CRAWW RH11 ..... 2 B2 🔃
Spy La BIL RH14 ..... 46 C7
Squadron Dr SALV BN13 ..... 229 F5
The Square CRAWW RH11 ..... 2 C3 🔃
EMRTH PO10 ..... 191 F8 🔃
EPSF GU31 ..... 118 B7
MIDOS PO22 ..... 223 F5
PSF GU32 ..... 88 D8
Squires Cl CRAWE RH10 ..... 34 C3
Squirrel Cl CRAWW RH11 ..... 31 F2 🔃
Squirrels Copse PUL/STOR RH20 ..... 157 G8
Stable Cl CRAWE RH10 ..... 32 D8
Stable Fld MIDOS PO22 ..... 248 B6
Stable La FIN/BW BN14 ..... 205 J5
Stackfield Rd CRAWW RH11 ..... 30 C6
Stafford Rd BRI BN1 ..... 10 A2
CRAWW RH11 ..... 30 E2
PSF GU32 ..... 88 D6
Staffords Cl ANG/EP BN16 ..... 250 D1 🔟
Staffords Pl HORL RH6 ..... 18 B1
Stafford Wy HPPT/KEY BN6 ..... 165 G8
Stag Cl HFD BN5 ..... 161 G5
Stagelands CRAWW RH11 ..... 2 A1
Stairbridge La RHWH RH17 ..... 137 J3
Stakers La SWTR RH13 ..... 105 H3
Stalham Wy MIDOS PO22 ..... 13 F2
Stallard Cl EMRTH PO10 ..... 214 C2
Stall House La PUL/STOR RH20 ..... 129 J4
Stammers Hl HFD BN5 ..... 186 D7
Stanbridge Cl CRAWW RH11 ..... 30 C5 🔃
Stanbridge Rd RHWH RH17 ..... 84 C4
Stanbrok Cl BOGR PO21 ..... 245 G8 🔃
Stanbury Ct RCCH PO18 ..... 217 F4
Standean Cl BRI BN1 ..... 213 K5
Standen Cl EGRIN RH19 ..... 21 J8
Standen Pl HORS RH12 ..... 52 C4

Standgrove Pl RHWH RH17 .....
Standinghall La CRAWE RH10 .....
Standon La RDKG RH5 .....
Stane St RDKG RH5 .....
BIL RH14 .....
BIL RH14 .....
PUL/STOR RH20 .....
RCCH PO18 .....
SWTR RH13 .....
Stane Street Cl PUL/STOR RH20 .....
Stanford Av BRI BN1 .....
HPPT/KEY BN6 .....
Stanford Cl HOVE BN3 .....
HPPT/KEY BN6 1
MIDOS PO22 .....
Stanford Orch HORS RH12 5
Stanford Rd BRI BN1 .....
Stanford Wy HORS RH12 .....
Stan Hl HORL RH6 .....
Stanhope Rd LHPTN BN17 .....
WTHG BN11 .....
Stanier Cl CRAWE RH10 .....
Stanley Av BOGR PO21 .....
CRAWE RH10 .....
Stanley Rd BRI BN1 .....
EMRTH PO10 .....
LHPTN BN17 .....
PTSD BN41 .....
WTHG BN11 .....
Stanley St ROTT BN2 .....
Stanmer Park Rd BRI BN1 .....
Stanmer St BRI BN1 2
Stanmer Vis BRI BN1 .....
Stanmore Gdns BOGR PO21 2
Stanmore La MIDOS PO22 .....
MIDOS PO22 .....
Stanstead Cl HAV PO9 .....
Stanton Dr CCH PO19 .....
Stanton Rd PSF GU32 .....
Stanwater La MIDH GU29 .....
Staplecross Ct CRAWW RH11 .....
Staplefield Rd RHWH RH17 .....
RHWH RH17 .....
Staple La RCCH PO18 .....
Staples Barn HFD BN5 .....
Staples Barn La HFD BN5 .....
Staples Hl SWTR RH13 .....
Stapleton Ct BOGR PO21 .....
Stapley Rd HOVE BN3 .....
Starling Cl HPPT/KEY BN6 .....
Star Rd SWTR RH13 .....
Station Ap HPPT/KEY BN6 1
RHWH RH17 .....
Station Approach Rd
HORL RH6 .....
Station Cl SWTR RH13 .....
Station Hl CRAWE RH10 .....
Station Rd ANG/EP BN16 .....
ANG/EP BN16 .....
ARUN BN18 .....
BIL RH14 .....
BIL RH14 .....
BOGR PO21 .....
BRI BN1 .....
BURH RH15 .....
CRAWE RH10 .....
CRAWE RH10 .....
EGRIN RH19 .....
EGRIN RH19 .....
EPSF GU31 .....
FROW RH18 .....
HFD BN5 .....
HORS RH12 .....
HORS RH12 .....
HORS RH12 .....
HORS RH12 .....
LIPH GU30 .....
MIDH GU29 .....
PETW GU28 .....
PSF GU32 .....
PUL/STOR RH20 .....
RCCH PO18 .....
RHWH RH17 .....
STEY/UB BN44 .....
STHW BN42 .....
SWTR RH13 .....
SWTR RH13 .....
SWTR RH13 .....
SWTR RH13 .....
SWTR RH13 .....
WTHG BN11 .....
Station St BRI BN1 1
Station Wy CRAWE RH10 1
Stavely Gdns CCH PO19 1
Stean Furlong LHPTN BN17 .....
Stedham La MIDH GU29 .....
Steele Cl PUL/STOR RH20 .....
Steels La RCCH PO18 .....
Steep Cl FIN/BW BN14 .....
Steepdown Rd LAN/SOMP BN15 .....
Steep La FIN/BW BN14 .....
Steeple Vw SALV BN13 .....
Steeres Hl HORS RH12 .....
Steers La CRAWE RH10 .....

e Gdns *ROTT* BN2 .... 10 C5 🔟
e La *BRI* BN1 .... 10 C5 🔟
e St *ROTT* BN2 .... 10 C6
Rd *EMRTH* PO10 .... 215 H1
o Dr *BIL* RH14 .... 102 A3
oswood Wy *MIDOS* PO22 .... 225 G5 🔟
tennings *EGRIN* RH19 .... 22 A8
en Cl *CRAWW* RH11 .... 31 H2 🔟
enson Dr *EGRIN* RH19 .... 36 D5
enson Pl *CRAWE* RH10 .... 32 B5
enson Wy *CRAWE* RH10 .... 32 B5
ens Rd *BRI* BN1 .... 237 H5
ey Cl *CRAWE* RH10 .... 32 C7 🔟
way *LHPTN* BN17 .... 250 C2
nage Rd *CRAWW* RH11 .... 54 C1
nson Rd *ROTT* BN2 .... 11 E5
ards Ri *ARUN* BN18 .... 225 F2
Gdns *WTHG* BN11 .... 9 E4
e St *BOGR* PO21 .... 12 B5
teyne *BOGR* PO21 .... 12 B6
HG BN11 .... 9 E4
ing Av *HOVE* BN3 .... 211 K8
ing By-pass *STEY/UB* BN44.... 208 B2
ing Cl *CRAWE* RH10 .... 3 D1
R BN12 .... 229 F8 🔟
/SOMP BN15 .... 231 K3
ing Crs *PUL/STOR* RH20 .... 180 A1
ing Rd *SHOR* BN43 .... 208 D5
R RH13 .... 133 J4
dns *HASM* GU27 .... 40 B5
g Cl *BURH* RH15 .... 139 J7
WE RH10 .... 32 B6
g Court Rd *BURH* RH15 .... 139 J7
g Pl *HOVE* BN3 .... 236 A5
g Rd *CCH* PO19 .... 6 C3
g Wy *BOGR* PO21 .... 262 B5
IN RH19 .... 23 F8
R RH13 .... 5 D5
p Wy *CRAWE* RH10 .... 32 D4
ey Hollow *HASM* GU27 .... 40 C3
ey Ri *HASM* GU27 .... 40 C5
oridge Gdns *CCH* PO19 .... 6 A6
oridge Rd *CCH* PO19 .... 6 B5
croft Rd *RHWH* RH17 .... 83 G2
er Rd *BOGR* PO21 .... 12 A6
ands Cl *RHWH* RH17 .... 111 F3
s Cl *HORL* RH6 .... 18 B1
s La *RCCH* PO18 .... 195 H7
S PO20 .... 257 J4
s Rd *PUL/STOR* RH20 .... 181 J5
well Rd *EGRIN* RH19 .... 36 C5
am La *EPSF* GU31 .... 89 J3
GU33 .... 89 J1
Abbott Rd *WTHG* BN11 .... 9 D4 🔟
Rd *ARUN* BN18 .... 201 J1
s Cl *CRAWE* RH10 .... 32 C7 🔟
age Cl *MIDOS* PO22 .... 12 B2
chat Cl *EPSF* GU31 .... 117 G1
Cl *SALV* BN13 .... 229 K5
croft Cl *HOVE* BN3 .... 211 K7
crop Cl *CRAWW* RH11 .... 2 A6 🔟
cross La *HWH* RH16 .... 85 F8
field Cl *CRAWE* RH10 .... 2 C4
fields *ANG/EP* BN16 .... 250 E2
field Wy *BURH* RH15 .... 139 F6
hall La *RHWH* RH17 .... 83 H4
ham Cl *PSF* GU32 .... 88 B7
ham Pk *PSF* GU32 .... 88 B7
nam Rd *HOVE* BN3 .... 235 K4
hill Crs *BOGR* PO21 .... 244 D8
house La *SWTR* RH13 .... 134 D3
house Rd *LIPH* GU30 .... 38 D7
hurst Ct *ROTT* BN2 .... 11 E4 🔟
hurst Rd *SALV* BN13 .... 229 K6
La *SALV* BN13 .... 229 K5
eigh Av *BRI* BN1 .... 213 F5
eigh Cl *BRI* BN1 .... 213 F5
N RH19 .... 36 D1 🔟
oit La *HFD* BN5 .... 160 D6
ound Rd *HPPT/KEY* BN6 ..... 164 E7
Quarry Rd *RHWH* RH17 .... 87 H4
rs Cl *HORL* RH6 .... 17 H3
cy Rd *PTSD* BN41 .... 234 E1
ry Rd *PTSD* BN41 .... 234 E1
St *BRI* BN1 .... 10 A5
ybrook *HORS* RH12 .... 77 F2
y La *RHWH* RH17 .... 57 G6
PO20 .... 258 C7
R BN43 .... 233 A3
y Stile Cl *BOGR* PO21 .... 261 K1 🔟
y Stile La *BOGR* PO21 .... 261 K2
am Cl *FIN/BW* BN14 .... 8 B1 🔟
am Rd *CRAWE* RH10 .... 32 C8
/STOR RH20 .... 154 A2
eadow *PUL/STOR* RH20 .... 180 B1
gton Cl *HOVE* BN3 .... 235 J1 🔟
PO18 .... 218 B4
gton Ri *FIN/BW* BN14 .... 205 K7
gton Rd *PUL/STOR* RH20 .. 156 E8
/STOR RH20 .... 181 F3
Rd *CCH* PO19 .... 7 E2
Cl *PSF* GU32 .... 116 C1
BN13 .... 229 G3
Rd *SALV* BN13 .... 229 G3
l Cl *CRAWE* RH10 .... 32 D7 🔟

The Strand *FERR* BN12 .... 229 H8
    FERR BN12 .... 252 C5
Strand Wy *MIDOS* PO22 .... 247 F7
Strange Gdn *BOGR* PO21 .... 262 B2 🔟
Strathfield Cl *HWH* RH16 .... 112 B7 🔟
Strathmoor Gdns *MIDH* GU29 123 B2 🔟
Strathmore Cl *SALV* BN13 ...... 229 J7
Strathmore Rd *CRAWW* RH11 .. 30 E2
    SALV BN13 .... 229 J7
Stratton Ct *MIDOS* PO22 .... 13 D3
Strawberry La *PUL/STOR* RH20 157 F7
Stream Cl *RCCH* PO18 .... 217 F6 🔟
Stream La *PUL/STOR* RH20 .... 155 K2
Stream Pk *EGRIN* RH19 .... 21 J8
Street End La *SELS* PO20 .... 242 E8
Street End Rd *SELS* PO20 ...... 242 E8
Streetfield Rd *SWTR* RH13 ...... 49 H8
Street Hl *CRAWE* RH10 .... 32 E6
Street La *RHWH* RH17 .... 84 C3
The Street *ANG/EP* BN16 .... 250 D2
    ANG/EP BN16 .... 251 H1
    ARUN BN18 .... 223 J3
    ARUN BN18 .... 223 H2
    BIL RH14 .... 70 E1
    HORL RH6 .... 16 C4
    HPPT/KEY BN6 .... 163 G5
    LAN/SOMP BN15 .... 232 A3
    MIDH GU29 .... 121 G2
    PUL/STOR RH20 .... 155 J1
    PUL/STOR RH20 .... 157 F4
    PUL/STOR RH20 .... 177 G4
    PUL/STOR RH20 .... 181 H5
    RCCH PO18 .... 197 F7
    RHWH RH17 .... 108 D3
    SALV BN13 .... 228 B1
    SALV BN13 .... 228 C2
    SELS PO20 .... 240 D4
    SHOR BN43 .... 233 F2
    STEY/UB BN44 .... 208 B1
    SWTR RH13 .... 49 H7
    SWTR RH13 .... 135 G1
Stretch Hl *PUL/STOR* RH20 ... 127 G6
Strettington La *RCCH* PO18 ... 196 C8
Strettons Copse *LIPH* GU30 ..... 64 B8
Strickland Cl *CRAWW* RH11 .... 30 C6 🔟
Stride Cl *CCH* PO19 .... 7 E2
Stringer Wy *BRI* BN1 .... 213 F8
Strood Cl *RHWH* RH17 .... 140 E8
Strood La *HORS* RH12 .... 50 C4
Stroud Green Dr *BOGR* PO21 .. 245 H6
Stroudley Cl *CRAWE* RH10 ..... 32 B6 🔟
Strudgate Cl *CRAWE* RH10 .... 32 B7 🔟
Stuart Cl *CRAWE* RH10 .... 32 C6 🔟
    WTHG BN11 .... 9 F2
Stuart Wy *EGRIN* RH19 .... 36 D3
Stubcroft La *SELS* PO20 .... 258 A4
Stubfield *HORS* RH12 .... 51 G8
Stubpond La *LING* RH7 .... 21 F4
Stumblemead *RHWH* RH17 ..... 83 G5
Stumblets *CRAWE* RH10 .... 32 C4 🔟
Stumps La *RCCH* PO18 .... 217 G7
Sturges Rd *BOGR* PO21 .... 12 B5
Sturt Av *HASM* GU27 .... 40 B6
Sturt Rd *HASM* GU27 .... 40 C7
Sudbury Cl *BOGR* PO21 .... 261 K2 🔟
Sudeley Pl *ROTT* BN2 .... 11 F6
Sudeley St *ROTT* BN2 .... 11 F6
Sudeley Ter *ROTT* BN2 .... 11 F6 🔟
Sudley Gdns *BOGR* PO21 .... 12 C5
Sudley Rd *BOGR* PO21 .... 12 C5
Suffolk Cl *HORL* RH6 .... 18 A1 🔟
Suffolk St *HOVE* BN3 .... 235 K5
Sugar La *RHWH* RH17 .... 85 K6
Sugden Rd *WTHG* BN11 .... 9 F3
Sugworth Cl *HWH* RH16 .... 111 K4 🔟
Sullington Copse *PUL/STOR* .. 180 C1
Sullington Gdns *FIN/BW* BN14 . 205 K7
Sullington Hl *CRAWW* RH11 .... 2 C5 🔟
Sullington La *PUL/STOR* RH20 . 180 D3
Sullington Md *HORS* RH12 ...... 50 E8
Sullington Wy *SHOR* BN43 .... 233 J3
Sullivan Dr *CRAWW* RH11 .... 30 C8
    CRAWW RH11 .... 54 C1
Sultan Rd *EMRTH* PO10 .... 214 D2
Summer Cl *PTSD* BN41 .... 234 D1
Summerdale Rd *HOVE* BN3 .... 235 H1
Summerdown Cl *SALV* BN13 . 229 F6 🔟
Summerfield Rd *SELS* PO20 ... 256 E1
Summerfields *FIN/BW* BN14 .. 205 J5
Summerhill Cl *HWH* RH16 ...... 112 A4
    MIDOS PO22 .... 247 G5
Summerhill Dr *HWH* RH16 .... 112 B4
    MIDOS PO22 .... 247 G5
Summerhill Gra *HWH* RH16 .. 112 B4
Summerhill La *HWH* RH16 .... 112 B4
Summer La *BOGR* PO21 .... 261 G2
Summerley La *MIDOS* PO22 .. 247 F6
Summersdale Rd *CCH* PO19 .. 219 G2
Summersdeane *STHW* BN42 .. 234 D2
Summersvere Cl *CRAWE* RH10 . 32 K2
Sumner Rd *EPSF* GU31 .... 116 B6
Sumners *RHWH* RH17 .... 84 C1
Sun Brow *HASM* GU27 .... 40 B6
Sundale La *MIDOS* PO22 .... 247 J6

Sunderland Cl *SELS* PO20 ..... 221 F1 🔟
Sundew Cl *CRAWW* RH11 .... 54 E1 🔟
Sunneymead *SELS* PO20 .... 265 F5 🔟
Sunningdale Cl *CRAWW* RH11 .. 2 C5 🔟
Sunningdale Gdns *MIDOS* PO22 12 A1
Sunningdale Rd *SALV* BN13 ... 229 H5
Sunninghill Av *HOVE* BN3 ...... 235 J1
Sunninghill Cl *HOVE* BN3 ...... 235 J1 🔟
Sunny Av *CRAWH* RH10 .... 34 C3
Sunnybox La *ARUN* BN18 .... 199 H7
Sunny Cl *FERR* BN12 .... 253 J2
Sunnycroft Cl *RHWH* RH17 ... 141 G1
Sunnydale Av *BRI* BN1 .... 213 G5
Sunnydale Cl *BRI* BN1 .... 213 G5
Sunnyhill Cl *CRAWE* RH10 ...... 34 C3 🔟
Sunnymead *CRAWW* RH11 .... 2 C3
Sunnymead Cl *MIDOS* PO22 .. 248 A6
Sunnymead Dr *SELS* PO20 .... 265 F5
Sunny Wy *RCCH* PO18 .... 217 F6
Sunnywood Dr *HWH* RH16 .... 111 K8
Sun Park Cl *BOGR* PO21 .... 245 J5
Sunset La *PUL/STOR* RH20 .... 156 A6
Sunte Av *HWH* RH16 .... 112 B4
Sunte Cl *HWH* RH16 .... 112 A4
Sunvale Av *HASM* GU27 .... 39 K5
Sunvale Cl *HASM* GU27 .... 39 K5 🔟
Surrenden Cl *BRI* BN1 .... 213 F7
Surrenden Crs *BRI* BN1 .... 212 E8
Surrenden Holt *BRI* BN1 .... 213 F8
Surrenden Pk *BRI* BN1 .... 213 G7
Surrenden Ri *CRAWW* RH11 ... 55 C5 🔟
Surrenden Rd *BRI* BN1 .... 213 F8
Surrey St *ARUN* BN18 .... 225 G1
    BRI BN1 .... 10 B4 🔟
    LHPTN BN17 .... 249 K3
    WTHG BN11 .... 8 C5
Surrey Whf *ARUN* BN18 .... 225 H1
Surry St *SHOR* BN43 .... 233 H4
Sussex Border Pth *RDKG* RH5... 25 J6
    RDKG RH5 .... 27 H3
    BRI BN1 .... 211 K1
    BRI BN1 .... 212 E3
    CRAWE RH10 .... 33 K1
    EGRIN RH19 .... 35 F4
    EMRTH PO10 .... 190 D8
    EMRTH PO10 .... 214 D8
    EPSF GU31 .... 117 K6
    HASM GU27 .... 67 H2
    HAV PO9 .... 166 B7
    HORL RH6 .... 17 G3
    HORL RH6 .... 18 E3
    HORN PO8 .... 142 A7
    HORS RH12 .... 28 E4
    LIPH GU33 .... 63 F5
    LISS GU35 .... 63 F3
    MFD/CHID GU8 .... 42 D6
    MFD/CHID GU8 .... 44 E5
    PTSD BN41 .... 210 C5
    PTSD BN41 .... 210 E2
    RHWH RH17 .... 86 B3
Sussex Dr *BOGR* PO21 .... 261 H2
Sussex Gdns *ANG/EP* BN16 .. 250 E1 🔟
    EPSF GU31 .... 116 D1
    HWH RH16 .... 112 D8
Sussex Gv *SELS* PO20 .... 258 B6
Sussex Pl *ROTT* BN2 .... 11 D4 🔟
Sussex Rd *EPSF* GU31 .... 116 E1
    HOVE BN3 .... 236 B7 🔟
    HWH RH16 .... 112 A8
    LAN/SOMP BN15 .... 232 E5
    WTHG BN11 .... 9 D3
Sussex St *BOGR* PO21 .... 12 C5 🔟
    LHPTN BN17 .... 249 K1
    ROTT BN2 .... 11 D5
Sussex Wy *BURH* RH15 .... 138 C6
Sutherland Cl *ANG/EP* BN16 .. 250 D2 🔟
    BOGR PO21 .... 12 B5 🔟
Sutherland Rd *ROTT* BN2 .... 11 E5
Sutton Av *ANG/EP* BN16 .... 250 E3
Sutton Cl *MIDOS* PO22 .... 13 E2
Swainsthorpe Cl *HWH* RH16 . 112 B8 🔟
Swaledale Cl *CRAWW* RH11 ..... 2 B6 🔟
Swallowfield *LING* RH7 .... 22 E1 🔟
Swallowfield Cl *SWTR* RH13 ... 78 E6
Swallow Rd *CRAWW* RH11 .... 2 B1
Swallows Cl *LAN/SOMP* BN15 232 E6
Swallows Green Dr *SALV* BN13 229 G6
Swallows La *SWTR* RH13 .... 133 F7
Swallowtail Rd *HORS* RH12 ...... 5 D1
Swan Barn Rd *HASM* GU27 ..... 41 F5
Swanbourne Cl *LAN/SOMP* BN15 232 B3
Swanbourne Rd *LHPTN* BN17 . 225 K8
Swan Cl *EMRTH* PO10 .... 214 E3
    PUL/STOR RH20 .... 180 A1
    SWTR RH13 .... 105 G1
Swan Dene *BOGR* PO21 .... 261 G4
Swanfield Dr *CCH* PO19 .... 7 D2
Swan La *HORL* RH6 .... 16 D4
Swann Cl *BURH* RH15 .... 139 K8
Swann Wy *HORS* RH12 .... 50 E8
Swansea Gdns *BOGR* PO21 ... 12 A6 🔟
Swans Ghyll *FROW* RH18 .... 37 J8
Swan St *PSF* GU32 .... 88 C8
Swan Vw *PUL/STOR* RH20 .... 154 E2 🔟
Sweetlands *HPPT/KEY* BN6 ... 165 H6 🔟

Swift Cl HPPT/KEY BN6 .... 138 D8
Swift La CRAWW RH11 .... 2 C1
Swift Rd EMRTH PO10 .... 214 E8
Swift Wy LHPTN BN17 .... 225 J7
Swillage La ANG/EP BN16 .... 227 J2
Swindon Rd HORS RH12 .... 4 A3
Swiss Gdns SHOR BN43 .... 283 C4
Swissland Hl EGRIN RH19 .... 22 C5
Sycamore Av HORS RH12 .... 52 E6
Sycamore Cl ANG/EP BN16 .... 227 H7
   CRAWW RH11 .... 31 G2
   PTSD BN41 .... 211 G8
Sycamore Dr EGRIN RH19 .... 36 E2
Sycamore Rd MIDOS PO22 .... 12 B3
Sydney Rd HWH RH16 .... 112 A5
Sydney St BRI BN1 .... 10 C4
Sylvan Cl HWH RH16 .... 112 D7
Sylvan Rd CRAWE RH10 .... 3 F5
   LAN/SOMP BN15 .... 231 H5
Sylvan Wy BOGR PO21 .... 12 A5
Sylvester Wy HOVE BN3 .... 211 G8
Sylvia Cl BOGR PO21 .... 261 H2
Symbister Rd PTSD BN41 .... 235 G4
Syresham Gdns HWH RH16 .... 112 A7

T

Tabard Ga BOGR PO21 .... 261 J4
Tack Lee Rd ARUN BN18 .... 223 K8
Talbot Cl BRI BN1 .... 213 K5
Talbot La HORS RH12 .... 4 B6
Talbot Rd LHPTN BN17 .... 249 J2
Tallis Cl CRAWW RH11 .... 30 D8
Talman Cl CRAWW RH11 .... 30 C6
Tamar Av SALV BN13 .... 229 G3
Tamar Cl CRAWE RH10 .... 32 C6
   SALV BN13 .... 229 G4
Tamarisk Cl MIDOS PO22 .... 12 B3
Tamarisk Wk SELS PO20 .... 257 J5
Tamarisk Wy ANG/EP BN16 .... 251 G5
   FERR BN12 .... 252 D3
Tamar Wy SELS PO20 .... 221 F1
Tamplin Ter ROTT BN2 .... 11 D4
Tamworth Rd HOVE BN3 .... 235 G5
Tanbridge Pk HORS RH12 .... 77 G2
Tanbridge Pl HORS RH12 .... 4 A6
Tandridge Rd HOVE BN3 .... 235 J5
Tangle Oak EGRIN RH19 .... 21 G7
Tangmere Gdns BOGR PO21 .... 262 A1
Tangmere Rd BRI BN1 .... 213 G5
   CRAWW RH11 .... 30 D5
   SELS PO20 .... 220 B4
Tankerdale La PSF GU32 .... 89 G3
Tanners Fld RHWH RH17 .... 140 C6
Tanners La HASM GU27 .... 40 E4
Tanners Md RHWH RH17 .... 81 J6
Tannery Cl SWTR RH13 .... 49 G8
Tansy Md PUL/STOR PO20 .... 179 K1
Tanyard Av EGRIN RH19 .... 36 E3
Tanyard Cl CRAWE RH10 .... 32 C8
   SWTR RH13 .... 5 D6
Tanyard La RHWH RH17 .... 87 G7
   STEY/UB BN44 .... 183 J8
Tarmount La SHOR BN43 .... 233 H4
Tarner Rd ROTT BN2 .... 11 D4
Tarragon Wy SHOR BN43 .... 234 A2
Tarrant St ARUN BN18 .... 225 H1
Tarrant Whf ARUN BN18 .... 225 H1
Tarring Rd WTHG BN11 .... 8 B3
Tasman Cl ANG/EP BN16 .... 251 F3
Tasman Wy SALV BN13 .... 229 G4
Tate Crs BURH RH15 .... 139 F6
Tates Wy HORS RH12 .... 48 B4
Tavern Ct HASM GU27 .... 66 D5
Taverner Rd CCH PO19 .... 7 D5
Tavistock Down BRI BN1 .... 237 J1
Tavy Cl SALV BN13 .... 229 G5
Tavy Rd SALV BN13 .... 229 G5
Taw Cl SALV BN13 .... 229 H4
Taylors Fld MIDH GU29 .... 122 A5
Taylor's La RCCH PO18 .... 217 G7
Taylors Rd MIDH GU29 .... 122 A5
Teal Cl HORS RH12 .... 4 B2
Teal La SELS PO20 .... 264 C3
Teasel Cl CRAWW RH11 .... 2 A6
Teazle Cl EPSF GU31 .... 117 G1
Teesdale CRAWW RH11 .... 2 B6
Teg Cl PTSD BN41 .... 235 G1
Telegraph La EPSF GU31 .... 144 E1
Telegraph St ROTT BN2 .... 11 E6
Telford Pl CRAWE RH10 .... 3 D4
Telgarth Rd FERR BN12 .... 252 C3
Telham Ct CRAWW RH11 .... 30 D8
Templars Cl MIDOS PO22 .... 247 H5
The Templars FIN/BW BN14 .... 230 E4
Temple Cl CRAWE RH10 .... 32 D6
Temple Gdns HOVE BN3 .... 10 A4
Temple Gv BURH RH15 .... 138 D7
Temple La RDKG RH5 .... 14 A5
Temple Rd LISS GU33 .... 62 A5
Templesheen Rd MIDOS PO22 .... 248 B6
Temple St BRI BN1 .... 10 A5

Tenacre Cl CCH PO19 .... 7 D1
Ten Acres WTHG BN11 .... 231 G8
Tenantry Rd ROTT BN2 .... 11 F2
Tennis Rd HOVE BN3 .... 235 J5
Tennyson Av ANG/EP BN16 .... 250 C2
Tennyson Cl CRAWE RH10 .... 32 B3
   HORS RH12 .... 5 D1
Tennyson Ri EGRIN RH19 .... 36 A2
Tennyson Rd BOGR PO21 .... 245 J8
   WTHG BN11 .... 8 C4
Tennyson's La HASM GU27 .... 41 G7
Terminus Pl BRI BN1 .... 10 B3
   LHPTN BN17 .... 249 K2
Terminus Rd BRI BN1 .... 10 B3
   CCH PO19 .... 6 A4
   LHPTN BN17 .... 249 J2
Terminus St BRI BN1 .... 10 B4
Tern Rd CRAWW RH11 .... 30 B6
The Terrace LAN/SOMP BN15 .... 232 A7
Terringes Av SALV BN13 .... 229 J6
Terry Rd CRAWW RH11 .... 55 F2
Terwick La EPSF GU31 .... 120 A3
Test Cl PSF GU32 .... 116 C2
Testers Cl SWTR RH13 .... 105 C4
Test Rd LAN/SOMP BN15 .... 231 H5
Teville Pl WTHG BN11 .... 8 C3
Teville Rd WTHG BN11 .... 8 C3
Thackeray Rd FIN/BW BN14 .... 9 F2
Thakeham Cl ANG/EP BN16 .... 227 K8
   FERR BN12 .... 252 E1
Thakeham Copse PUL/STOR RH20... .... 181 F1
Thakeham Dr FERR BN12 .... 252 E1
Thakeham Rd PUL/STOR RH20 .... 180 D1
Thalassa Rd WTHG BN11 .... 231 H8
Thames Cl LHPTN BN17 .... 250 C3
   ROTT BN2 .... 11 D5
Thames Wy SALV BN13 .... 229 H4
Thatcher Cl CRAWE RH10 .... 2 C6
Thatchers Cl BURH RH15 .... 165 K2
   HORS RH12 .... 5 K3
Thatchway Cl LHPTN BN17 .... 249 K1
The Thatchway ANG/EP BN16 .... 227 C6
Theatre La CCH PO19 .... 6 C3
The Denture ARUN BN18 .... 176 B7
Thelton Av HORS RH12 .... 50 D8
Theobalds Rd BURH RH15 .... 139 J5
Thesiger Cl WTHG BN11 .... 231 G7
Thesiger Rd WTHG BN11 .... 231 G7
Theydon Cl CRAWE RH10 .... 3 F5
Thicket La RCCH PO18 .... 197 K6
Third Av FIN/BW BN14 .... 230 D4
   HOVE BN3 .... 236 B6
   LAN/SOMP BN15 .... 232 A4
   MIDOS PO22 .... 247 F7
   SELS PO20 .... 258 A6
   SELS PO20 .... 258 D3
Thirlmere Crs FIN/BW BN14 .... 231 H6
Thirlmere Rd CRAWW RH11 .... 30 B7
Thirlmere Wy MIDOS PO22 .... 247 F6
Thistledowne Gdns EMRTH PO10 ... . 215 F3
Thistle Wy SWTR RH13 .... 77 J2
Thistledown V BIL RH14 .... 45 K7
Thompson Rd BRI BN1 .... 11 E1
   MIDOS PO22 .... 247 F7
Thomson Cl SALV BN13 .... 229 F5
Thorgate Rd LHPTN BN17 .... 225 H8
Thornbank Crs PTSD BN41 .... 211 F8
Thorn Cl EPSF GU31 .... 117 C1
Thorncroft Rd LHPTN BN17 .... 250 A1
Thorndean Dr RHWH RH17 .... 109 H4
Thorndean Rd ROTT BN2 .... 213 K8
Thornden SWTR RH13 .... 135 C3
Thorndene Av BOGR PO21 .... 12 A4
Thorndyke Cl CRAWE RH10 .... 32 D6
Thorney Dr SELS PO20 .... 264 D5
Thorney Old Pk EMRTH PO10 .... 239 H2
Thorney Rd EMRTH PO10 .... 215 F6
Thornham La EMRTH PO10 .... 215 H5
Thornhill Av BRI BN1 .... 213 G4
Thornhill Cl HOVE BN3 .... 235 J1
Thornhill Ri PTSD BN41 .... 210 E7
Thornhill Wy PTSD BN41 .... 210 E7
Thorn Rd WTHG BN11 .... 8 C5
Thornscroft STEY/UB BN44 .... 183 K7
Threals Copse PUL/STOR RH20 .... 156 C6
Threal's La PUL/STOR RH20 .... 156 C5
Three Acres HORS RH12 .... 77 C3
Three Bridges Rd CRAWE RH10 .... 3 E3
   CRAWE RH10 .... 32 B5
Three Gates La HASM GU27 .... 41 F4
Threestile Rd HORS RH12 .... 51 F2
Thrusloes BOGR PO21 .... 262 C1
Thurbarns Hl RDKG RH5 .... 14 A2
Thurlow Rd WTHG BN11 .... 9 E3
Thurne Wy HORS RH12 .... 48 B4
Thyme Cl SHOR BN43 .... 234 A2
Ticehurst Cl CRAWE RH10 .... 32 E5
Tichborne St BRI BN1 .... 10 C5
Tideway Rd ANG/EP BN16 .... 250 C3
Tidy St BRI BN1 .... 10 C4
Tilbury Pl ROTT BN2 .... 11 D5
Tilbury Wy ROTT BN2 .... 11 D4
Tile Barn La SELS PO20 .... 258 B2
Tilers Cl BURH RH15 .... 139 K8

Tilgate Cl ROTT BN2 ....
Tilgate Dr CRAWE RH10 ....
Tilgate Pde CRAWE RH10 ....
Tilgate Pl CRAWE RH10 ....
Tilgate Wy CRAWE RH10 ....
Tilletts La HORS RH12 ....
Tillinghurst La RHWH RH17 ....
Tillotson Cl CRAWE RH10 ....
Tillstone Cl ROTT BN2 23
Tillstone St ROTT BN2 ....
Tilmore Gdns PSF GU32 ....
Tilmore Rd PSF GU32 ....
Tiltwood Dr CRAWE RH10 ....
Timber Cl SALV BN13 22
Timberham Farm Rd HORL RH6...
Timberlands CRAWW RH11 5
   PUL/STOR RH20 ....
Timberlea Cl PUL/STOR RH20 ....
Timberleys LHPTN BN17 ....
Timber MI SWTR RH13 ....
Timbermill Ct HASM GU27 4
The Timbers SWTR RH13 ....
Tindal Cl BURH RH15 1
Tinghall BOGR PO21 ....
Tinsley Gn CRAWE RH10 ....
Tinsley La CRAWE RH10 ....
Tinsley La North CRAWE RH10 ....
Tinsley La South CRAWE RH10 ....
Tintern Cl BRI BN1 ....
Tintern Rd CRAWW RH11 ....
Tinwood La RCCH PO18 ....
Tipper La EPSF GU31 ....
Tisbury Rd HOVE BN3 ....
Titchfield Cl BURH RH15 ....
Titch Hl LAN/SOMP BN15 ....
Tithe Barn La BOGR PO21 ....
Tithe Barn Wy BOGR PO21 ....
Tithe Gn ANG/EP BN16 ....
Tithe Orch EGRIN RH19 ....
Titian Rd HOVE BN3 ....
Titmus Dr CRAWE RH10 ....
Titnore La FERR BN12 ....
   SALV BN13 ....
Titnore Wy FERR BN12 ....
Tivoli Crs BRI BN1 ....
Tivoli Crs North BRI BN1 ....
Tivoli Pl BRI BN1 ....
Tivoli Rd BRI BN1 ....
Toat La PUL/STOR RH20 ....
Toddington La LHPTN BN17 ....
Toddington Pk LHPTN BN17 ....
Toftwood Cl CRAWE RH10 ....
Tollgate Hl CRAWW RH11 ....
Tollgate La RHWH RH17 11
Tollhouse Cl CCH PO19 ....
Tompset's Bank FROW RH18...
Tomtits La FROW RH18...
Tongdean Av HOVE BN3 ....
Tongdean La BRI BN1 ....
Tongdean Ri BRI BN1 ....
Tongdean Rd HOVE BN3 ....
Toomey Rd STEY/UB BN44 ....
Top Rd ARUN BN18 ....
   EGRIN RH19...
Top St RHWH RH17 ....
Torberry Dr EPSF GU31 ....
Toronto Cl SALV BN13 22
Toronto Dr HORL RH6...
Toronto Ter ROTT BN2 ....
Torrance Cl HOVE BN3 2
Torridge Cl SALV BN13 ....
Torton Hill Rd ARUN BN18 ....
Tor Wy EPSF GU31 ....
Tote La MIDH GU29 ....
Totland Rd ROTT BN2 ....
Tottington Dr HFD BN5 ....
Tottington Wy SHOR BN43 2
Tower Cl CCH PO19 ....
   EGRIN RH19...
Towergate BRI BN1 ....
Tower House Cl RHWH RH17 ....
Tower Rd HORS RH12 ....
   LAN/SOMP BN15 ....
   LIPH GU30 ....
   ROTT BN2 ....
   WTHG BN11 ....
Towers Rd STEY/UB BN44 ....
Tower St CCH PO19 ....
   EMRTH PO10 ....
Town Barn Rd CRAWW RH11 ....
Town Cross Av BOGR PO21 ....
Town La EPSF GU31 ....
   RCCH PO18 ....
Town Md CRAWW RH11 ....
Townsend Crs LHPTN BN17 ....
Tozer Wy CCH PO19 ....
Trafalgar Ct BRI BN1 1
Trafalgar La BRI BN1 ....
Trafalgar Pl BRI BN1 1
Trafalgar Rd HORS RH12 ....
Trafalgar Rd PTSD BN41 ....
Trafalgar St BRI BN1 ....
Tramway Cl SELS PO20...
Trap La RDKG RH5 ....
Treadcroft Dr HORS RH12 ....
Tredcroft Rd HOVE BN3...

Av HASM GU27 .... 40 B3
mans Rd RWHW RH17 .... 113 K1
ops SWTR RH13 .... 105 F4
iew CRAWW RH11 .... 55 G2
il Cl HORS RH12 .... 5 D2
il Crs CRAWW RH11 .... 54 E1
erth Rd CCH PO19 .... 219 G1
dle Gn BOGR PO21 .... 245 H8
ear Cl SWTR RH13 .... 5 D5
: Cl CRAWW RH11 .... 30 D7
/SOMP BN15 .... 231 J5
Rd WTHG BN11 .... 253 J1
wn Gdns SELS PO20 .... 265 G5
nne Plat CRAWE RH10 .... 32 D4 🔟
or Cl WTHG BN11 .... 8 C4
ord Cl CRAWW RH11 .... 30 D5
gle Rd HASM RH16 .... 112 A8
t RDKG RH5 .... 14 A3
y Cl CRAWE RH10 .... 32 C3
y Rd HPPT/KEY BN6 .... 164 A5
y St ROTT BN2 .... 11 D3
y Wy BOGR PO21 .... 245 H7
RN BN17 .... 250 B3
HI LAN/SOMP BN15 .... 231 K3
am Cl LAN/SOMP BN15 ...... 231 G4
Pl MIDOS PO22 .... 247 G6
Cl CRAWW RH11 .... 30 B7
n Cl CRAWE RH10 .... 32 C8
n Rd EPSF GU31 .... 119 K3
La SWTR RH13 .... 104 A3
Rd HASM GU27 .... 40 A3
nede RHWH RH17 .... 83 C2
Blue Prec LHPTN BH17 ...... 225 K8
ers RHWH RH17 .... 81 F3
gh Dr PTSD BN41 .... 210 E7
gh Rd STEY/UB BN44 .... 208 D1
gh Wy SHOR BN43 .... 233 J2
le Cl RCCH PO18 .... 194 E5
le Md HORS RH12 .... 4 B2
le View Cl MIDOS PO22 ..... 223 F5
Cl CCH PO19 .... 219 F2
Crs BOGR PO21 .... 245 G8
r's HI HPPT/KEY BN6 .... 162 D4
el Wy MIDOS PO22 .... 247 F7
Av EMRTH PO10 .... 190 C7
Cl CCH PO19 .... 219 F1
WE RH10 .... 32 D6
IN RH19 .... 36 D4 🔟
BW BN14 .... 205 J5
T GU26 .... 39 K1
E BN3 .... 235 K1
OS PO22 .... 247 H6
/STOR RH20 .... 155 H2
Dr SELS PO20 .... 222 B3
/UB BN44 .... 184 C8
Gdns BURH RH15 .... 139 F7 🔟
Village PUL/STOR RH20 ... 157 G8
Fld MIDH GU29 .... 121 K5 🔟
Meadow MIDH GU29 .... 122 A4
es Plat HORS RH12 .... 50 E4
idge Crs LIPH GU30 .... 38 B6
idge La LIPH GU30 .... 38 B5
neade CRAWW RH11 ..... 30 C6 🔟
ate STEY/UB BN44 .... 183 K8 🔟
nny La EMRTH PO10 .... 215 J1
y La BURH RH15 .... 139 H8 🔟
ull Rd CCH PO19 .... 7 D2
Ct EGRIN RH19 .... 22 E8
Rd FIN/BW BN14 .... 230 E5
s Hill Rd CRAWE RH10 ..... 20 B8
WE RH10 .... 32 E5
WE RH10 .... 34 B1
N RH19 .... 35 J6
s Md PUL/STOR RH20 .... 179 K1
s Mill Cl HWH RH16 .... 111 K4
s Mill Rd HWH RH16 .... 111 K5
s Wy BURH RH15 .... 139 F7 🔟
Wy SELS PO20 .... 265 G5 🔟
ke Cl CCH PO19 .... 6 B6
ke Pl CRAWW RH11 .... 2 C1
ke Rd ARUN BN18 .... 178 B5
Cl ROTT BN2 .... 11 F5
Md MIDOS PO22 .... 247 K6
y Gdns CRAWE RH10 .... 31 J3
ore Av CRAWW RH11 .... 31 J2
ore Crs CRAWW RH11 ...... 31 J2 🔟
ore La CRAWE RH10 .... 1 J1
ck Cl CRAWW RH11 .... 30 E7
d Cl CRAWE RH10 .... 32 C7
La CRAWW RH11 .... 30 D2
nam La HPPT/KEY BN6 ..... 162 E2
n Cl STHW BN42 .... 234 C4
n La EGRIN RH19 .... 21 C7
itten BURH RH15 .... 139 H7 🔟
/KEY BN6 .... 163 G5
V BN42 .... 234 C4
Wy SALV BN13 .... 8 A2
arns La RCCH PO18 .... 194 D5
ile Ash Rd SWTR RH13 ..... 75 K8
ays BIL RH14 .... 46 C1 🔟
d Cl CRAWW RH11 .... 30 D5
d Gdns SALV BN13 .... 229 J5
d Rd BRI BN1 .... 213 K5

SALV BN13 .... 229 J5
Twyhurst Ct EGRIN RH19 .... 22 B8 🔟
Twyne Cl CRAWW RH11 ..... 30 D7
Tye La ARUN BN18 .... 223 J2
Tylden Wy HORS RH12 .... 5 E1
Tyler's Gn RHWH RH17 ...... 111 H7
Tyler Rd CRAWE RH10 .... 2 C6
Tylston Meadow LIPH GU30 .. 38 B6 🔟
Tyne Cl CRAWE RH10 .... 32 C6
SALV BN13 .... 229 G4
Tyne Wy BOGR PO21 .... 245 F7
The Tynings LAN/SOMP BN15 .. 232 A6 🔟
Tythe Barn RHWH RH17 .... 109 G8
Tythe Barn Rd SELS PO20 .. 265 F5

U

Ullswater Dr ANG/EP BN16 .. 226 C8
Ullswater Gv MIDOS PO22 .. 247 J5
Ullswater Rd LAN/SOMP BN15 .. 231 H6
Underdown Rd STHW BN42 .. 234 C4
Underhill La HPPT/KEY BN6 .. 188 E3
Underhill Rd RDKG RH5 .... 14 D3
Undermill Rd STEY/UB BN44 .. 208 D1
Underwood Cl CRAWE RH10 .. 34 D3 🔟
Underwood Rd HASM GU27 .. 40 B4
Union Pl WTHG BN11 .... 9 D4
Union Rd LISS GU33 .... 62 D1
Union Rd ROTT BN2 .... 10 C5
Union St BRI BN1 .... 10 C5 🔟
Upfield HORL RH6 .... 18 A4
Upfield Cl HORL RH6 .... 18 A1
Uphill Wy SELS PO20 .... 243 F3
Uplands Av SALV BN13 .... 229 F3
Uplands Cl HASM GU27 .... 41 F3
Uplands Cl BRI BN1 .... 237 J1
HAV PO9 .... 190 A1
Uppark Gdns HORS RH12 ...... 5 E1
Uppark Wy MIDOS PO22 .... 247 H5
Upper Abbey Rd ROTT BN2 .. 11 F6
Upper Bedford St BRI BN1 ... 11 E6
Upper Bognor Rd BOGR PO21 .. 12 C4 🔟
MIDOS PO22 .... 13 E5

Upper Boundstone La

LAN/SOMP BN15 .... 231 K3
Upper Brighton Rd FIN/BW BN14 .. 230 E4
LAN/SOMP BN15 .... 231 G4
Upper Dr ANG/EP BN16 ...... 251 K3
Upper Dr FROW RH18 .... 61 K1
The Upper Dr HOVE BN3 ..... 236 C3
Upperfield MIDH GU29 ...... 122 B1 🔟
Upper Gardner St BRI BN1 .. 10 C4 🔟
Upper Gloucester Rd BRI BN1 .. 10 C4 🔟
Upper Hamilton Rd BRI BN1 .. 10 A2
Upper Heyshott EPSF GU31 .. 88 E8
Upper High St WTHG BN11 ... 9 E3
Upper Hollingdean Rd BRI BN1 .. 11 D1
Upper Kingston La STHW BN42 .. 234 B1
Upper Lewes Rd ROTT BN2 .. 11 D3
Upper Market St HOVE BN3 .. 236 D6 🔟
Upper Mt HASM GU27 .... 41 H2
Upper North St BRI BN1 ... 10 B5 🔟
Upper Park Pl ROTT BN2 ... 11 D5 🔟
Upper Rock Gdns ROTT BN2 .. 11 D6
Upper St James's St ROTT BN2 .. 11 D6
Upper St Johns Rd BURH RH15 .. 139 G8
Upper Shoreham Rd SHOR BN43 .. 233 G3
STHW BN42 .... 234 B2
Upper Station Rd HFD BN5 ... 181 F6
Upper St PUL/STOR RH20 ... 157 F6
Upper Sudeley St ROTT BN2 .. 11 F6 🔟
Upperton Rd PETW GU28 ... 125 F1
Upper Wardown EPSF GU31 .. 89 F7
Upper Wellington St ROTT BN2 .. 11 E3
Upper West Dr FERR BN12 .. 252 C1
Upper West La LAN/SOMP BN15 .. 232 A4
Upper Winfield Av BRI BN1 .. 213 F5
Upton Av STHW BN42 .... 234 C2
Upton Gdns SALV BN13 ...... 229 K7
Upton Rd CCH PO19 .... 6 B5
SALV BN13 .... 229 K7
Upways Cl SELS PO20 .... 265 F2
Ursula Av SELS PO20 .... 264 E5
Ursula Av North SELS PO20 .. 264 E5 🔟
Ursula Sq SELS PO20 .... 264 E6

V

Vale Av BRI BN1 .... 212 E4
FIN/BW BN14 .... 229 K1
Valebridge Dr BURH RH15 .. 139 J5 🔟
Valebridge Dr BURH RH15 .. 139 J6 🔟
Valebridge Rd BURH RH15 .. 139 J6
Vale Dr FIN/BW BN14 .... 229 K1
HORS RH12 .... 4 A5
Vale Gdns PTSD BN41 .... 235 F4
Valencia Rd WTHG BN11 .... 8 A3
Valentine Cl FIN/BW BN14 .. 230 B4 🔟
Valentine Dr BURH RH15 ... 138 E7
Valentines Gdns BOGR PO21 .. 261 K1 🔟

Valentines Lea PETW GU28 .. 68 E3
Valerie Cl PTSD BN41 .... 235 F1
Vale Rd HWH RH16 .... 139 K1
PTSD BN41 .... 235 G4
Valetta Pk EMRTH PO10 .... 214 C3
Valetta Rd EMRTH PO10 .... 239 H2
Vale Wk FIN/BW BN14 .... 229 K1
Valewood Cl BIL RH14 ...... 103 H2
Valewood La BIL RH14 .... 103 J2
Valewood Rd HASM GU27 ... 40 E3
Valiant Rd EMRTH PO10 .... 239 H2
Vallance Cl BURH RH15 ..... 138 E7
Vallance Gdns HOVE BN3 ... 236 A5
Vallance Rd HOVE BN3 .... 236 A5
Valley Cl BRI BN1 .... 212 C7
Valley Dr BRI BN1 .... 212 C7
Valley Rd LAN/SOMP BN15 .. 231 J3
PTSD BN41 .... 234 E1
Valley Side LIPH GU30 .... 38 B6
Vanbrugh Cl CRAWW RH11 .. 30 C8 🔟
Vancouver Cl SALV BN13 ... 229 H5 🔟
Vancouver Dr CRAWW RH11 . 31 H2
Vancouver Rd SALV BN13 .. 229 G5
Van Dyck Pl MIDOS PO22 .. 245 J5
Vanguard Wy EGRIN RH19 .. 23 K6
Vann Bridge Cl HASM GU27 .. 66 C5
Vanners CRAWE RH10 .... 3 D2 🔟
Vann Rd HASM GU27 .... 66 C5
Vanzell Rd MIDH GU29 ..... 122 C2
Varey Rd SALV BN13 .... 229 F5
Varndean Cl BRI BN1 .... 212 E8
Varndean Dr BRI BN1 .... 212 E8
Varndean Gdns BRI BN1 .... 212 E8
Varndean Holt BRI BN1 ..... 212 F8
Varndean Rd BRI BN1 .... 212 E8
Varsity Rd EMRTH PO10 .... 239 H2
Vauxhall Wy PSF GU32 .... 88 C8
Velyn Av CCH PO19 .... 7 D3
Ventnor Vls HOVE BN3 ...... 236 B5
Venus La BOGR PO21 .... 261 F4
Veras Wk PUL/STOR RH20 .. 181 C2
Verbania Wy EGRIN RH19 .... 37 F2
Verdley Pl HASM GU27 .... 66 E8
Vere Rd BRI BN1 .... 10 C2
Vermont Dr ANG/EP BN16 .. 251 J2
Vermont Wy ANG/EP BN16 .. 251 J2
Vernon Cl ANG/EP BN16 .... 250 E2
HORS RH12 .... 5 F3
Vernon Ter BRI BN1 .... 10 A5
Veronica Cl ANG/EP BN16 .. 251 J5 🔟
Veronica Wy ROTT BN2 ...... 11 D6
Viaduct Rd BRI BN1 .... 10 C3
ROTT BN2 .... 11 D3
Vicarage Flds SALV BN13 .. 229 H4
Vicarage La ANG/EP BN16 .. 251 H2
HASM GU27 .... 13 E4
MIDOS PO22 .... 13 B5
PETW GU28 .... 125 F1
RHWH RH17 .... 117 H1
RHWH RH17 .... 113 H8
STEY/UB BN44 .... 183 K8
Vicarage Rd CRAWE RH10 .. 34 C4
Victoria Av BURH RH15 .... 138 E3 🔟
MIDH GU29 .... 122 C2
Victoria Cl BURH RH15 .... 138 E3 🔟
MIDH GU29 .... 122 A4 🔟
Victoria Dr BOGR PO21 ...... 12 A4
SELS PO20 .... 222 B4
Victoria Gv HOVE BN3 ...... 236 C5 🔟
Victoria Park Gdns WTHG BN11 .. 8 C3 🔟
Victoria Pl BRI BN1 .... 10 A4 🔟
Victoria Rd BOGR PO21 .... 12 A6
BRI BN1 .... 10 A4
BURH RH15 .... 164 E1
CCH PO19 .... 7 E3
CRAWW RH11 .... 2 B3
EMRTH PO10 .... 214 C2
HWH RH16 .... 113 B8
PTSD BN41 .... 235 F3
RHWH RH17 .... 83 G2
SHOR BN43 .... 233 G4
STHW BN42 .... 234 B4
WTHG BN11 .... 8 C3
Victoria Rd South BOGR PO21 .. 12 A6 🔟
Victoria St BRI BN1 .... 10 A4
SWTR RH13 .... 4 C5
Victoria Wy BURH RH15 ... 165 F1
EGRIN RH19 .... 36 D4
Victor Rd EMRTH PO10 ..... 239 H2
Victory Rd HORS RH12 .... 4 A4
View Ter LING RH7 .... 22 E5
The View BOGR PO21 .... 261 H3
The Village Barn BRI BN1 .. 212 E4
Village St RDKG RH5 .... 14 D2
PSF GU32 .... 89 F5
Vinall Gdns HORS RH12 ...... 50 D7
Vincent Cl LAN/SOMP BN15 .. 231 K5 🔟
SWTR RH13 .... 5 D5
Vincent Rd SELS PO20 ...... 264 D5
Vineries Cl SALV BN13 ...... 230 A5 🔟
The Vineries BURH RH15 .. 139 K8
Vine St BRI BN1 .... 10 C4 🔟
Vinnetrow Rd SELS PO20 .. 220 A8
Vinson Rd LISS GU33 .... 62 A7

Viscount Dr *BOGR* PO21 ...... 261 J3
Vivienne Cl *CRAWW* RH11 ...... 31 H2
Vowels La *EGRIN* RH19 ...... 59 F1
Vulcan Cl *CRAWW* RH11 ...... 55 G1
Vulcan Rd *EMRTH* PO10 ...... 239 H2

W

Waddington Cl *CRAWW* RH11 ...... 30 E8
Wade End *SELS* PO20 ...... 264 D3
The Wadeys *SELS* PO20 ...... 264 D3
The Wadeys *BIL* RH14 ...... 102 A3
Wadham Cl *BOGR* PO21 ...... 32 C2
Wadhurst Cl *BOGR* PO21 ...... 12 A4
Wadhurst Dr *FERR* BN12 ...... 253 F1
Wadlands Brook Rd *EGRIN* RH19 ...... 22 B6
The Wad *SELS* PO20 ...... 256 E2
Wagg Cl *EGRIN* RH19 ...... 36 F2
Waggoners Wells Rd *GSHT* GU26 ...... 39 G1
Wagtail Cl *HORS* RH12 ...... 51 J4
Wain End *HORS* RH12 ...... 4 C2
Wainwrights *CRAWW* RH11 ...... 2 C6
Wakefields Rd *ROTT* BN2 ...... 11 D2
Wakefield Wy *BOGR* PO21 ...... 245 G7
Wakehams Green Dr *CRAWE* RH10 ...... 32 D2
Wakehurst Cl *CRAWE* RH10 ...... 2 E1
Wakehurst La *RHWH* RH17 ...... 84 C3
Wakehurst Ms *HORS* RH12 ...... 77 F2
Wakehurst Pl *ANG/EP* BN16 ...... 250 E1
Wakestone La *PUL/STOR* RH20 ...... 127 G2
Walberton Cl *MIDOS* PO22 ...... 13 F3
Waldegrave Rd *BRI* BN1 ...... 237 F1
Walders Rd *ANG/EP* BN16 ...... 250 C1
Waldron Av *BRI* BN1 ...... 213 K5
Walesbeech *CRAWE* RH10 ...... 3 F4 ⬛
Waley's La *RDKG* RH5 ...... 26 D2
Walker Rd *CRAWE* RH10 ...... 32 B7
Wallace Av *WTHG* BN11 ...... 253 H3
Wallace Rd *ANG/EP* BN16 ...... 250 C1
Wallage La *CRAWE* RH10 ...... 33 K5
The Walled Gdn *BIL* RH14 ...... 46 B4
Wallfield *BOGR* PO21 ...... 262 C1 ⬛
Wall Hill Rd *FROW* RH18 ...... 37 H6
Wallis Wy *BURH* RH15 ...... 138 C7 ⬛
Walmer Crs *MIDOS* PO22 ...... 247 C6
Walmer Rd *SWTR* RH13 ...... 105 C1
Walmsleys Wy *SELS* PO20 ...... 258 B7
Walnut Av *ANG/EP* BN16 ...... 250 D1
Walnut Cl *BRI* BN1 ...... 212 A8
Walnut Cl *CRAWW* RH11 ...... 31 F2
Walnut Pk *HWH* RH16 ...... 112 D7 ⬛
Walnut Tree Dr *EMRTH* PO10 ...... 191 J8
Walnut Tree Wy *SALV* BN13 ...... 229 F6 ⬛
Walpole Av *FERR* BN12 ...... 253 H1
Walpole Rd *ROTT* BN2 ...... 11 E6
Walpole Ter *ROTT* BN2 ...... 11 F5
Walsham Cl *MIDOS* PO22 ...... 13 E2
Walsingham Rd *HOVE* BN3 ...... 235 H5
Waltham Park Rd *PUL/STOR* RH20 ...... 153 H5
Walton Av *BOGR* PO21 ...... 225 K5
Walton Cl *SALV* BN13 ...... 229 G5
Walton Dr *SWTR* RH13 ...... 52 E7
Walton Heath *CRAWE* RH10 ...... 32 D3 ⬛
Walton La *RCCH* PO18 ...... 217 C6
Walton Ldg *SALV* BN13 ...... 229 K5 ⬛
Walton Rd *BOGR* PO21 ...... 12 C5
Wandle Cl *CRAWE* RH10 ...... 32 C6 ⬛
Wandleys Cl *SELS* PO20 ...... 222 D2
Wandleys Dr *SELS* PO20 ...... 222 D2
Wandleys La *SELS* PO20 ...... 222 E2
Wansford Wy *MIDOS* PO22 ...... 247 C2
Wantage Cl *CRAWE* RH10 ...... 32 C8
Wantley Hill Est *HFD* BN5 ...... 161 H5
Wantley La *PUL/STOR* RH20 ...... 180 C1
Wantley Rd *FIN/BW* BN14 ...... 230 A2
Warble Heath Cl *RCCH* PO18 ...... 195 F5
Warblers *CRAWW* RH11 ...... 12 A1
Warblington Rd *EMRTH* PO10 ...... 214 C4
Warburton Rd *EGRIN* RH19 ...... 36 E2 ⬛
Ward Crs *EMRTH* PO10 ...... 190 F8
Warden Cl *RHWH* RH17 ...... 111 F5
Warelands *BURH* RH15 ...... 165 F2
Warenne Rd *HOVE* BN3 ...... 211 G8
Warleigh Rd *BRI* BN1 ...... 10 C2
Warltersville Wy *HORL* RH6 ...... 18 C2
Warmdene Av *BRI* BN1 ...... 213 F5 ⬛
Warmdene Cl *BRI* BN1 ...... 213 F6 ⬛
Warmdene Rd *BRI* BN1 ...... 213 F5
Warmdene Wy *BRI* BN1 ...... 213 F5
Warminghurst Cl *PUL/STOR* RH20 ...... 157 K6 ⬛
Warner Cl *CRAWE* RH10 ...... 56 C1
Warner Rd *FIN/BW* BN14 ...... 9 F2
 SELS PO20 ...... 264 D5
Warner's La *SELS* PO20 ...... 264 D3
Warnham Cl *FERR* BN12 ...... 253 H2 ⬛
 HORS RH12 ...... 4 A2
Warnham Ri *BRI* BN1 ...... 213 G6
Warnham Rd *CRAWE* RH10 ...... 3 F5
 FERR BN12 ...... 253 H1
 HORS RH12 ...... 4 A2

HORS RH12 ...... 4 A6
HORS RH12 ...... 50 D7
Warninglid La *SWTR* RH13 ...... 80 A7
Warren Cl *EGRIN* RH19 ...... 21 G8
Warren Crs *ANG/EP* BN16 ...... 251 H1
Warren Cft *PUL/STOR* RH20 ...... 179 K2
Warren Dr *CRAWW* RH11 ...... 30 E4
 SWTR RH13 ...... 77 G8
Warren Farm La *CCH* PO19 ...... 219 F1
Warren Gdns *FIN/BW* BN14 ...... 230 B4
Warren Rd *FIN/BW* BN14 ...... 230 B4
 LISS GU33 ...... 62 A4
 LISS GU33 ...... 62 D1
Warren Side *EPSF* GU31 ...... 118 B6
The Warren *BURH* RH15 ...... 165 J2
 FERR BN12 ...... 252 D3
Warrington Cl *CRAWW* RH11 ...... 54 C1
Warrior Cl *PTSD* BN41 ...... 235 F1
Warwick Cl *WTHG* BN11 ...... 9 E4
Warwick Pl *MIDOS* PO22 ...... 247 H6
 WTHG BN11 ...... 9 E4 ⬛
Warwick Rd *WTHG* BN11 ...... 9 E4
Warwick St *WTHG* BN11 ...... 9 D4
Washington Bostal
 PUL/STOR RH20 ...... 181 J6
Washington Rd *CRAWW* RH11 ...... 30 C8
 EMRTH PO10 ...... 214 D2
 HWH RH16 ...... 112 B6
 PUL/STOR RH20 ...... 180 E3
 STEY/UB BN44 ...... 182 D4
Washington St *CCH* PO19 ...... 6 B2 ⬛
 ROTT BN2 ...... 11 D4
Wassand Cl *CRAWE* RH10 ...... 3 F5
Waterbury Rd *RHWH* RH17 ...... 85 K5
Waterdyke Av *STHW* BN42 ...... 234 C4 ⬛
Waterfield Cl *SWTR* RH13 ...... 5 D4 ⬛
Waterfield Gdns *CRAWW* RH11 ...... 30 C7
Waterhall Rd *BRI* BN1 ...... 212 C5
Waterlands La *HORS* RH12 ...... 49 J3
Water La *ANG/EP* BN16 ...... 227 J5
 LHPTN BN17 ...... 249 K1
 PUL/STOR RH20 ...... 156 C3
 PUL/STOR RH20 ...... 180 D1
 STEY/UB BN44 ...... 182 D1
Water Lea *CRAWE* RH10 ...... 3 F4
Waterloo Rd *MIDOS* PO22 ...... 13 F4
Waterloo Sq *BOGR* PO21 ...... 12 B6 ⬛
Waterloo St *HOVE* BN3 ...... 236 D6
The Waterplat *CCH* PO19 ...... 7 E1 ⬛
Waters Edge *BOGR* PO21 ...... 262 B2
 PUL/STOR RH20 ...... 154 C2 ⬛
Waters Edge Gdns *EMRTH* PO10 ...... 214 D3
Watersedge Gdns *SELS* PO20 ...... 257 H5
Watersfield Rd *FIN/BW* BN14 ...... 8 B1
Waterside *EGRIN* RH19 ...... 37 F2
Waterside Cl *CRAWW* RH11 ...... 30 C7
Waterside Dr *CCH* PO19 ...... 6 B6
Waterstone Cl *SELS* PO20 ...... 240 E4 ⬛
Watling Cl *STHW* BN42 ...... 234 C4 ⬛
Watson Cl *CRAWE* RH10 ...... 32 C8
Watson Wy *SELS* PO20 ...... 222 B4
Waverley Crs *BRI* BN1 ...... 11 D1
Waverley Rd *ANG/EP* BN16 ...... 250 E1
 BOGR PO21 ...... 245 J7
Wavertree Rd *FERR* BN12 ...... 229 H8
Wayfarer's Wk *EMRTH* PO10 ...... 214 C4
Wayfield Av *HOVE* BN3 ...... 235 J2
Wayfield Cl *HOVE* BN3 ...... 235 K2 ⬛
Wayland Av *BRI* BN1 ...... 212 C7
Wayland Hts *BRI* BN1 ...... 212 C7
Wayside *BRI* BN1 ...... 212 D5
 CRAWW RH11 ...... 30 C7
Wayside Av *SALV* BN13 ...... 229 H4
The Way *ANG/EP* BN16 ...... 251 J4
Weald Av *HOVE* BN3 ...... 235 K2
Weald Cl *HPPT/KEY* BN6 ...... 163 K5
Weald Dr *CRAWE* RH10 ...... 3 F6
Weald Dyke *SHOR* BN43 ...... 233 H5
Wealden Wy *HWH* RH16 ...... 111 K7
Wealdon Cl *SWTR* RH13 ...... 105 F3
Weald Ri *HWH* RH16 ...... 111 K6
Weald Rd *BURH* RH15 ...... 138 E8 ⬛
The Weald *EGRIN* RH19 ...... 22 D8
Wear Cl *SALV* BN13 ...... 229 G4
Weare St *RDKG* RH5 ...... 26 C4
Wear Rd *SALV* BN13 ...... 229 G4
Weaver Cl *CRAWW* RH11 ...... 30 C6 ⬛
Weavers Cl *BURH* RH15 ...... 165 K2
 MIDH GU29 ...... 122 D1
Weavers Gn *HAV* PO9 ...... 190 A8
Weavers Hl *ANG/EP* BN16 ...... 227 J5
Weavers Ring *ANG/EP* BN16 ...... 227 J6
Webb Cl *BOGR* PO21 ...... 261 H4
 CRAWW RH11 ...... 55 F2
Weddell Rd *CRAWE* RH10 ...... 3 E6
The Wedges *SWTR* RH13 ...... 75 H6
Wedgwood Rd *MIDOS* PO22 ...... 13 F4
Weirbrook *CRAWE* RH10 ...... 3 F6
Welbeck Av *HOVE* BN3 ...... 235 J5
Welbeck Cl *BURH* RH15 ...... 139 K7
Welbeck Dr *BURH* RH15 ...... 139 K7

The Welkin *HWH* RH16 ...... 1?
Welland Cl *SALV* BN13 ...... 22?
Welland Rd *SALV* BN13 ...... 22?
Wellcroft Cottages
 HPPT/KEY BN6 ...... 1?
Weller Cl *CRAWE* RH10 ...... ?
Wellesley Av *FERR* BN12 ...... 2?
Wellfield *EGRIN* RH19 ...... ?
Wellhouse La *BURH* RH15 ...... 16?
Wellingham La *SALV* BN13 ...... 2?
Wellington Cl *CRAWE* RH10 ...... 32?
Wellington Gdns *SELS* PO20 2
Wellington Rd *BOGR* PO21 2
 CCH PO19 2
 HORS RH12 2
 PTSD BN41 ...... 2?
 ROTT BN2 2
Wellington St *ROTT* BN2 2
Wellington Town Rd *EGRIN* RH19 ...... ?
Well La *HASM* GU27 ...... ?
Well Rd *BOGR* PO21 ...... 2?
Wells Cl *HORS* RH12 ...... ?
Wells Crs *BOGR* PO21 2
 CCH PO19 2
Wellsfield *SELS* PO20 2
Wells Lea *EGRIN* RH19 ...... ?
Wells Meadow *EGRIN* RH19 ...... 2?
Wells Rd *CRAWE* RH10 ...... 5?
Wellswood Gdns *HAV* PO9 ...... 1?
Wellsworth La *HAV* PO9 ...... 1?
Wellwood Cl *SWTR* RH13 ...... 52?
Welwyn Cl *CRAWW* RH11 ...... ?
Wembley Av *LAN/SOMP* BN15 2
Wembley Gdns
 LAN/SOMP BN15 ...... 23?
Wembury Pk *LING* RH7 ...... ?
Wenban Rd *WTHG* BN11 ...... 9?
Wenceling Cottages
 LAN/SOMP BN15 ...... 23?
Wendy Rdg *ANG/EP* BN16 2
Wenlock Cl *CRAWW* RH11 ...... ?
Wensleydale *CRAWW* RH11 ...... ?
Wensley Gdns *EMRTH* PO10 ...... 1?
Wentworth Cl *MIDOS* PO22 ...... 2?
 SALV BN13 ...... 2?
Wentworth Dr *CRAWE* RH10 ...... ?
Wentworth St *ROTT* BN2 ...... 11?
Wesley Cl *CRAWW* RH11 ...... ?
Wessex Av *BOGR* PO21 ...... 26?
 SELS PO20 2
West Ashling Rd *RCCH* PO18 2
West Av *BOGR* PO21 2
 CRAWE RH10 2
 LAN/SOMP BN15 2
 MIDOS PO22 2
 WTHG BN11 2
West Beach Rd *LAN/SOMP* BN15 2
Westbourne Av *EMRTH* PO10 2
 FIN/BW BN14 ...... ?
Westbourne Cl *EMRTH* PO10 ...... 21?
Westbourne Gdns *HOVE* BN3 2
Westbourne Pl *HOVE* BN3 ...... ?
Westbourne Rd *EMRTH* PO10 ...... ?
Westbourne St *HOVE* BN3 ...... ?
Westbourne Vls *HOVE* BN3 ...... ?
West Bracklesham Dr *SELS* PO20 ...... ?
West Brook Cl *RCCH* PO18 ...... ?
Westbrooke *WTHG* BN11 ...... ?
Westbrook Fld *RCCH* PO18 ...... ?
Westbrook Wy *STHW* BN42 ...... ?
West Broyle Dr *CCH* PO19 ...... ?
West Buildings *WTHG* BN11 ...... ?
West Burton La *PUL/STOR* RH20 ...... ?
West Chiltington La *BIL* RH14 ...... ?
 BIL RH14 ...... ?
 BIL RH14 ...... ?
 SWTR RH13 ...... ?
West Chiltington Rd
 PUL/STOR RH20 ...... ?
 PUL/STOR RH20 ...... ?
 PUL/STOR RH20 ...... ?
West Cl *HASM* GU27 ...... ?
 MIDOS PO22 ...... ?
West Common *HWH* RH16 ...... ?
West Common Dr *HWH* RH16 ...... ?
Westcott Cl *CRAWW* RH11 ...... 5?
Westcourt Pl *FIN/BW* BN14 ...... ?
Westcourt Rd *FIN/BW* BN14 ...... ?
Westdean Rd *FIN/BW* BN14 ...... ?
Westdene Dr *BRI* BN1 ...... ?
West Dr *ANG/EP* BN16 ...... ?
 BOGR PO21 ...... ?
 FERR BN12 ...... ?
 MIDOS PO22 ...... ?
 ROTT BN2 ...... ?
West End La *HASM* GU27 ...... ?
 HFD BN5 ...... ?
West End Wy *LAN/SOMP* BN15 ...... ?
Westergate Cl *FERR* BN12 ...... ?
Westergate Ms *SELS* PO20 ...... ?
Westergate St *SELS* PO20 ...... ?
Western Av *EMRTH* PO10 ...... ?
Western Cl *LAN/SOMP* BN15 ...... ?
Western Pde *EMRTH* PO10 ...... ?
Western Pl *WTHG* BN11 ...... ?

Windlesham Gdns
ANG/EP BN16 .... 251 J1 2
BRI BN1 .... 10 A4
SHOR BN43 .... 233 H3
Windlesham Rd *BRI* BN1 .... 10 A4
SHOR BN43 .... 233 H3
Windmill *SELS* PO20 .... 221 F2
Windmill Av *HPPT/KEY* BN6 .... 165 F8
Windmill Cl *BOGR* PO21 .... 261 J2
HOVE BN3 .... 235 K1
PUL/STOR RH20 .... 158 A6
STEY/UB BN44 .... 208 D1
SWTR RH13 .... 5 F4
Windmill Copse *PUL/STOR* RH20 ... 180 B1
Windmill Ct *CRAWW* RH11 .... 2 C1
SELS PO20 .... 257 J4
Windmill Dr *ANG/EP* BN16 .... 251 F1
BRI BN1 .... 212 C5
BURH RH15 .... 139 G7
Windmill Fld *RCCH* PO18 .... 216 E6
Windmill La *EGRIN* RH19 .... 22 B8
EGRIN RH19 .... 37 G4
HFD BN5 .... 161 F8
Windmill Platt *RHWH* RH17 .... 81 G3
Windmill Rd *LHPTN* BN17 .... 249 K4
STHW BN42 .... 234 C2
Windmill St *ROTT* BN2 .... 11 D5
Windmill Ter *ROTT* BN2 .... 11 D4 8
Windmill Vw *BRI* BN1 .... 213 G5
Windrush Cl *CRAWW* RH11 .... 30 D7
SALV BN13 .... 229 G3 1
Windsor Cl *ANG/EP* BN16 .... 226 D8 10
BOGR PO21 .... 245 G7
CRAWW RH11 .... 55 G3
HOVE BN3 .... 212 A4
HWH RH16 .... 140 A1
SWTR RH13 .... 105 G2
Windsor Dr *ANG/EP* BN16 .... 226 D8
SELS PO20 .... 257 H4
Windsor Pl *EGRIN* RH19 .... 36 E3 1
Windsor Rd *CCH* PO19 .... 7 E5
PSF GU32 .... 88 D8
SELS PO20 .... 265 F5
WTHG BN11 .... 9 F3
Windsor St *BRI* BN1 .... 10 B5 13
Windsor Wy *LAN/SOMP* BN15 ... 232 D5
Windward Cl *LHPTN* BN17 .... 250 C2
Windyridge *CRAWW* RH11 .... 30 E6 3
Wineham La *HFD* BN5 .... 136 B8
Winfield Av *BRI* BN1 .... 213 F5
Winfield Cl *BRI* BN1 .... 213 F6 4
PTSD BN41 .... 270 E7
Winfield Wy *EMRTH* PO10 .... 190 D7 1
Wingle Tye Rd *BURH* RH15 .... 165 G5
Winguard Wy *CCH* PO19 .... 6 C4 2
Winkhurst Wy *BURH* RH15 .... 165 K2
Winnet Wy *SWTR* RH13 .... 105 G1
Winston Cl *BOGR* PO21 .... 245 H4
Winston Crs *BOGR* PO21 .... 245 H5
Winston Rd *LAN/SOMP* BN15 ... 231 J8
Winterbourne *HORS* RH12 .... 52 B4
Winterbourne Cl *SALV* BN13 ... 229 F6 13
Winterbourne Rd *CCH* PO19 .... 219 G1
Winterbourne Wy *SALV* BN13 ... 229 F6
Winterfold *CRAWE* RH10 .... 3 F6 8
The Winter Knoll *LHPTN* BN17 ... 250 B2
Winterpit Cl *SWTR* RH13 .... 79 F5
Winterpit La *SWTR* RH13 .... 79 F5
Winters La *MIDH* GU29 .... 94 C8
Winterton Ct *SWTR* RH13 .... 4 C5 1
Winterton Wy *SHOR* BN43 .... 233 K5
Winton Rd *PSF* GU32 .... 88 D8
Wire Mill La *LING* RH7 .... 21 G3
Wisborough Ct *CRAWW* RH11 ... 30 D8 3
Wisborough Gdns *BIL* RH14 .... 101 F3
Wisborough La *PUL/STOR* RH20 ... 180 C2 2
Wisden Av *BURH* RH15 .... 138 E6
Wish Rd *HOVE* BN3 .... 235 J5
Wiston Av *CCH* PO19 .... 6 A5
FIN/BW BN14 .... 8 B1
Wiston Cl *FIN/BW* BN14 .... 8 B1
Wiston Cl *CRAWW* RH11 .... 30 D8 3
FERR BN12 .... 253 F3
Withdean Av *BRI* BN1 .... 236 D1
Withdean Court Av *BRI* BN1 .... 212 D8
Withdean Crs *BRI* BN1 .... 212 E8
Withdean Ri *BRI* BN1 .... 212 D8
Withdean Rd *BRI* BN1 .... 236 D1
Withey Brook Rd *RHWH* RH6 ... 17 H2 1
Withey Mdw *HORL* RH6 .... 17 H2
Withy Bush *BURH* RH15 .... 138 E7 8
BURH RH15 .... 138 E6
Withypitts *CRAWE* RH10 .... 34 C8
Withypitts East *CRAWE* RH10 .... 34 C8
Wivelsfield Rd *HWH* RH16 .... 140 A1
Woburn Cl *CRAWW* RH11 .... 30 E7
Wold Cl *CRAWW* RH11 .... 30 D7
Woldhurstlea Cl *CRAWW* RH11 ... 30 E7
Wolfmere La *LISS* GU33 .... 62 A1
Wolseley Rd *BRI* BN1 .... 213 K5
PTSD BN41 .... 234 E3
Wolsey Cl *BOGR* PO21 .... 261 J2
Wolstenbury Rd *ANG/EP* BN16... 226 E8

Wolstonbury Cl *CRAWW* RH11 .... 2 B5
Wolstonbury Rd *HOVE* BN3 .... 10 A3 6
Wolstonbury Wy *BURH* RH15 ... 165 C1 2
Wolverstone Dr *BRI* BN1 .... 237 J1
Wolverton Cl *HORL* RH6 .... 17 K2
Wolverton Gdns *HORL* RH6 .... 17 K1
Woodard Rd *LAN/SOMP* BN15 ... 232 B4
Woodards Vw *SHOR* BN43 .... 233 F6
Woodberry La *EMRTH* PO10 .... 190 D4
HAV PO9 .... 190 B2
Woodborough Cl *SELS* PO20 .... 258 B5
Woodbourne Av *BRI* BN1 .... 213 F7
Woodbourne Cl *LISS* GU33 .... 62 A7 1
Woodbridge Pk *ANG/EP* BN16 ... 251 J2
Woodbury Av *EGRIN* RH19 .... 37 F3
PSF GU32 .... 88 C6
Woodbury Cl *EGRIN* RH19 .... 37 F3
Woodcock Hl *LING* RH7 .... 21 H5
Woodcote La *LHPTN* BN17 .... 225 K6
PUL/STOR RH20 .... 127 K6
Woodcote Rd *FROW* RH18 .... 61 J1
Woodcourt *CRAWW* RH11 .... 55 C2 8
Woodcroft Rd *BURH* RH15 .... 165 F2
Woodcroft *BURH* RH15 .... 139 F6 4
Woodcroft Rd *CRAWW* RH11 ... 30 B7 8
Wooddale La *BIL* RH14 .... 102 E2
Wood End *HORS* RH12 .... 52 E6
Woodend Cl *CRAWE* RH10 .... 3 F1 8
Woodfield *SWTR* RH13 .... 104 E2
Woodfield Cl *BOGR* PO21 .... 261 H4
CRAWE RH10 .... 3 D2
SELS PO20 .... 221 F2
Woodfield Park Rd *EMRTH* PO10 ... 215 F2
Woodfield Rd *CRAWE* RH10 .... 3 E1
HORS RH12 .... 48 B4
Woodgason La *HISD* PO11 .... 238 A2
Woodgate Cl *SELS* PO20 .... 222 B6
Woodgate Pk *SELS* PO20 .... 222 B6
Woodgate Rd *SELS* PO20 .... 222 B6
Woodgates Cl *SWTR* RH13 .... 5 E4
Woodhall Cl *RHWH* RH17 .... 111 F4
Woodhatch *SWTR* RH13 .... 105 F1
Woodhorn La *SELS* PO20 .... 221 F4
Woodhouse La *HAV* PO9 .... 166 A7
Woodhouse Rd *HOVE* BN3 .... 235 J4
Wooding Gv *CRAWW* RH11 .... 55 F2 3
Woodland Av *BURH* RH15 .... 139 J7
HOVE BN3 .... 212 B7
SALV BN13 .... 229 J2
Woodland Cl *BIL* RH14 .... 74 C5
BURH RH15 .... 139 J7 8
HOVE BN3 .... 236 B1
SWTR RH13 .... 52 D7
Woodland Dr *CRAWE* RH10 .... 34 D3
HOVE BN3 .... 212 B8
Woodland La *SWTR* RH13 .... 53 K8
Woodland Rd *SELS* PO20 .... 264 E6
Woodlands *CRAWE* RH10 .... 32 D3
HOVE BN3 .... 236 C1
Woodlands Av *ANG/EP* BN16 .... 250 E2
EMRTH PO10 .... 190 C8
Woodlands Cl *ANG/EP* BN16 .... 227 J4
CRAWE RH10 .... 34 D4
HPPT/KEY BN6 .... 165 F7 1
SALV BN13 .... 228 D2 2
Woodlands La *CCH* PO19 .... 6 B1
HASM GU27 .... 40 D4
LISS GU33 .... 90 B1
RCCH PO18 .... 191 J1
Woodlands Rd *EGRIN* RH19 .... 22 E7
HPPT/KEY BN6 .... 165 F7
HWH RH16 .... 112 B7
LHPTN BN17 .... 250 A3
MIDOS PO22 .... 12 A2
The Woodlands *BRI* BN1 .... 212 E6
Woodlands Wk *SWTR* RH13 .... 78 E6
Woodland Wy *BIL* RH14 .... 102 C5
SWTR RH13 .... 104 E3
Woodland Wy *BRI* BN1 .... 213 F7
SWTR RH13 .... 5 F3
Wood La *HFD* BN5 .... 185 H5
Woodlark Gdns *EPSF* GU31 .... 89 G8
Woodlea Rd *SALV* BN13 .... 8 A2
Woodleigh Cl *HAV* PO9 .... 190 A1
Woodleigh Rd *BURH* RH15 .... 139 J7
Woodmancote La *EMRTH* PO10 ... 191 J7
Woodmancote Rd *FIN/BW* BN14 ... 8 B2
Woodmans Hl *CRAWW* RH11 .... 55 G2
Woodpecker Crs *HPPT/KEY* BN6 ... 138 D8
Woodpecker Rd *RDKG* RH5 .... 14 E1
PUL/STOR RH20 .... 180 C2
Woodpecker Rd *PETW* GU28 ... 125 K4 8
Woodpecker Wy *SALV* BN13 .... 229 G6
Wood Ride *HWH* RH16 .... 111 K8
Woodridge Cl *HWH* RH16 .... 112 C8 2
Woodroyd Av *HORL* RH6 .... 17 K1
Woodroyd Gdns *HORL* RH6 .... 17 K2
Woodruff Av *HOVE* BN3 .... 236 C1
Woods Hill Cl *EGRIN* RH19 .... 37 H5
Woods Hill La *EGRIN* RH19 .... 37 H5
Woodside *MIDOS* PO22 .... 223 F5
SWTR RH13 .... 52 D7
Woodside Av *BRI* BN1 .... 236 D1
Woodside Cl *PUL/STOR* RH20 ... 180 C1
SWTR RH13 .... 135 F7

Woodside Rd *CRAWE* RH10 .... [cut]
FIN/BW BN14 .... [cut]
Woodstock *EGRIN* RH19 .... [cut]
Woodstock Cl *HORS* RH12 .... [cut]
Woodstock Gdns *BOGR* PO21 ... 262
Wood St *BOGR* PO21 12
EGRIN RH19 .... [cut]
Woods Wy *FERR* BN12 .... 2[cut]
Wood Vw *ARUN* BN18 .... 2[cut]
Woodview *SHOR* BN43 .... 23[cut]
Woodview Cl *BRI* BN1 .... 2[cut]
Woodwards *CRAWW* RH11 .... [cut]
Woodwards Cl *BURH* RH15 ... 165[cut]
Woolbeding La *MIDH* GU29 .... [cut]
Woolborough Cl *CRAWE* RH10 3
Woolborough La *CRAWE* RH10 3
CRAWE RH10 .... [cut]
Woolborough Rd *CRAWE* RH10 .... [cut]
Wool La *MIDH* GU29 1
Woolmer Hill Rd *HASM* GU27 .... [cut]
Woolmer La *LIPH* GU30 .... [cut]
Woolmer St *EMRTH* PO10 1
Woolner Av *PSF* GU32 .... [cut]
The Woolstaplers *CCH* PO19 .... [cut]
Woolven Cl *BURH* RH15 1
Wophams La *SELS* PO20 .... [cut]
Worcester Rd *CRAWE* RH10 .... [cut]
Worcester Vls *HOVE* BN3 2
Wordsworth Cl *CRAWE* RH10 .... 3[cut]
Wordsworth Gdns *MIDOS* PO22 ... 2
Wordsworth Pl *HORS* RH12 52
Wordsworth Ri *EGRIN* RH19 .... 36[cut]
Wordsworth Rd *WTHG* BN11 2
Wordsworth St *HOVE* BN3 2
Worms La *MIDOS* PO22 2
Worsted La *EGRIN* RH19 2
Worthing Rd *ANG/EP* BN16 2
HORS RH12 2
LHPTN BN17 .... 22[cut]
SWTR RH13 1
SWTR RH13 1
Worthing Road Picts Hl
HORS RH12 1
Worth Park Av *CRAWE* RH10 1
Worth Rd *CRAWE* RH10 1
Worth Wy *CRAWE* RH10 32
Wray Cl *EGRIN* RH19 1
Wraysbury Park Dr *EMRTH* PO10... 1
Wren Cl *HORS* RH12 1
Wren Crs *MIDOS* PO22 1
Wright Cl *CRAWE* RH10 .... 5[cut]
Wroxham Wy *MIDOS* PO22 1
Wyatt Cl *BIL* RH14 1
Wyatts La *RHWH* RH17 1
Wyberlye Rd *BURH* RH15 1
Wychperry Rd *HWH* RH16 1
Wychwood *BIL* RH14 1
Wychwood Cl *BOGR* PO21 1
Wychwood Gdns *WTHG* BN11 ... 23[cut]
Wychwood Wk *BOGR* PO21 1
Wyde Feld *BOGR* PO21 1
Wye Cl *CRAWW* RH11 1
Wyke Av *WTHG* BN11 1
Wykeham Cl *STEY/UB* BN44 1
Wykeham Rd *WTHG* BN11 1
Wykeham Wy *BURH* RH15 .... 16[cut]
Wyke La North *MIDOS* PO22 1
Wykwood *LIPH* GU30 3
Wylde Green La *LISS* GU33 1
Wylds La *PSF* GU32 1
Wyncombe Cl *PUL/STOR* RH20 1
Wyndham Lea *PUL/STOR* RH20 1
Wyndham Rd *PETW* GU28 1
Wyndham St *ROTT* BN2 11
Wynlea Cl *CRAWE* RH10 1
Wynnes Ms *HOVE* BN3 .... 23[cut]
The Wyshe *POY/PYE* BN45 1
Wythering Cl *BOGR* PO21 1
Wythwood *HWH* RH16 1
Wyvern Cl *SELS* PO20 1

Y

Yapton La *ARUN* BN18 .... [cut]
Yapton Rd *MIDOS* PO22 .... [cut]
Yardley St *BRI* BN1 .... [cut]
Yarmouth Cl *CRAWE* RH10 .... [cut]
Yarrow Cl *HORS* RH12 .... [cut]
Yeoman Rd *SALV* BN13 .... [cut]
Yeomans Acre *BOGR* PO21 .... [cut]
Yeomans Fld *RCCH* PO18 .... [cut]
Yeomans La *LIPH* GU30 .... [cut]
Yeoman Wy *SALV* BN13 .... [cut]
Yew La *EGRIN* RH19 .... [cut]
Yew Tree Cl *MIDOS* PO22 .... [cut]
Yewtree Cl *SWTR* RH13 .... [cut]
Yew Tree Pl *LISS* GU33 .... [cut]
Yew Tree Rd *HORL* RH6 .... [cut]
York Av *EGRIN* RH19 .... [cut]
HOVE BN3 .... [cut]
York Cha *CCH* PO19 .... [cut]
York Cl *PSF* GU32 .... [cut]

Index - featured places

Broadwater C of E School
FIN/BW BN14 .... **8** C1
Broadwater Manor School
FIN/BW BN14 .... **9** D1
Brookers Road Industrial Estate
BIL RH14 .... **102** C4
Brookham School
LIPH GU30 .... **64** E1
Brooklands Trading Estate
FIN/BW BN14 .... **8** C3
Buckingham Middle School
SHOR BN43 .... **233** J3
Burgess Hill Clinic
BURH RH15 .... **165** F1
Burgess Hill School
BURH RH15 .... **165** H1
Burgess Hill Town Football Club
BURH RH15 .... **139** H6
Buriton Business Park
EPSF GU31 .... **116** A4
Buriton CP School
EPSF GU31 .... **116** B6
Bury School
PUL/STOR RH20 .... **177** F4
Business Centre
ANG/EP BN16 .... **250** E2
Camelsdale County First School
HASM GU27 .... **40** B6
Canon Gallery
PETW GU28 .... **125** K3
Cardinal Newman School
HOVE BN3 .... **236** D3
Carlton Hill CP School
ROTT BN2 .... **11** D5
The Car Surgery
LHPTN BN17 .... **225** K8
Castledean School
BRI BN1 .... **237** H1
Catherington School
CRAWW RH11 .... **31** H1
Centenary Industrial Estate
BRI BN1 .... **11** D1
Central C of E Junior School
CCH PO19 .... **6** B2
The Central Hove Surgery
HOVE BN3 .... **236** B5
Chanctonbury Leisure Centre
PUL/STOR RH20 .... **179** K1
Charlwoods Industrial Estate
EGRIN RH19 .... **22** C8
Charlwood Village School
HORL RH6 .... **16** D4
Charter Medical Centre
HOVE BN3 .... **236** D4
Chartham Park Golf Club
EGRIN RH19 .... **22** A5
Chelsea College
SHOR BN43 .... **233** F4
Chesswood Middle School
WTHG BN11 .... **9** E2
Chesworth Junior School
SWTR RH13 .... **5** D4
Chichester Cathedral
CCH PO19 .... **6** B3
Chichester College of Arts
  Science & Technology
BOGR PO21 .... **12** C5
Chichester College of Arts
  Science & Technology
CCH PO19 .... **6** C3
Chichester College of Arts
  Science & Technology
CCH PO19 .... **6** A3
Chichester College of Technology
CCH PO19 .... **6** A3
Chichester District Council
MIDH GU29 .... **122** B3
Chichester District Museum
CCH PO19 .... **6** C3
Chichester District Museum
CCH PO19 .... **7** F2
Chichester Festival Theatre
CCH PO19 .... **6** C1
Chichester Gallery
CCH PO19 .... **6** C3
Chichester Health Authority
CCH PO19 .... **219** C2
Chichester High School for Boys
CCH PO19 .... **6** C4
Chichester High School for Girls
CCH PO19 .... **6** B4
Chichester Lawn Tennis &
  Squash Club
CCH PO19 .... **6** C2

Chichester Priory Park
  Cricket & Hockey Club
CCH PO19 .... **6** C2
Chichester Rugby Club
CCH PO19 .... **6** C1
Chichester School of English
CCH PO19 .... **6** C3
Chichester Yacht Club
SELS PO20 .... **241** K4
Chiddingford Golf Club
MFD/CHID GU8 .... **43** F2
Chidham Parochial Primary School
RCCH PO18 .... **216** C5
Child Clinic
BRI BN1 .... **10** C5
Christchurch Medical Centre
HAV PO9 .... **190** A8
Christs Hospital Infirmary
SWTR RH13 .... **76** E5
Christ's Hospital (school)
SWTR RH13 .... **76** D6
The Christs Hospital Sports Centre
SWTR RH13 .... **76** D5
Churchers College
EPSF GU31 .... **88** E7
Churchers College Junior School
PSF GU32 .... **88** C8
Churchill Square Shopping Centre
BRI BN1 .... **10** B5
Church of England School
RHWH RH17 .... **87** F7
Church Surgery
ROTT BN2 .... **11** E1
City Business Centre
CCH PO19 .... **6** C4
City Business Centre
SWTR RH13 .... **4** C6
The City Business Centre
CRAWW RH11 .... **31** H1
City Fields Business Park
SELS PO20 .... **221** F1
Civic Centre
LHPTN BN17 .... **250** A2
Civic Centre
SHOR BN43 .... **233** H4
Clapham & Patching C of E
  Primary School
SALV BN13 .... **228** C2
Clarence Road School
SWTR RH13 .... **4** C6
Clermont C P U School
BRI BN1 .... **236** E1
The Clockhouse Business Centre
MIDH GU29 .... **122** B3
Club House
FIN/BW BN14 .... **230** B2
The Club House
LISS GU33 .... **62** E7
Coldean Junior & Infant School
BRI BN1 .... **213** K5
Colgate School
SWTR RH13 .... **54** A5
The College of St Barnabas
LING RH7 .... **22** D3
Collyers Sixth Form College
HORS RH12 .... **4** C3
Coln Gallery
CCH PO19 .... **6** C2
Community Mental Health Centre
BURH RH15 .... **139** G7
Compton & Upmarden C of E
  Primary School
RCCH PO18 .... **167** K1
Connaught Theatre
WTHG BN11 .... **9** D4
The Constable Gallery Artshop
WTHG BN11 .... **8** B5
Contour Gallery
LIPH GU30 .... **38** B7
Conway Court Clinic
HOVE BN3 .... **236** B3
Coombe Road County
  Primary School
ROTT BN2 .... **11** F1
The Coppice Surgery
ANG/EP BN16 .... **251** F1
The Copthorne Business Centre
CRAWE RH10 .... **19** H8
Copthorne Fairway Infant School
CRAWE RH10 .... **19** H8
Copthorne Golf Club
CRAWE RH10 .... **19** J8
Copthorne Junior School
CRAWE RH10 .... **19** H8

Copthorne Squash Club
CRAWE RH10 .... **33**
The Corner Gallery
HWH RH16 .... **112**
Cornerstones Independent School
HOVE BN3 .... **236**
Corn Exchange Theatre
BRI BN1 .... **10**
Cornfield School
LHPTN BN17 .... **226**
Cottesmore Golf & Country Club
CRAWW RH11 .... **54**
Cottesmore St Marys RC
  Primary School
HOVE BN3 .... **236**
Cottesmore School
CRAWW RH11 .... **54**
Council Offices
EPSF GU31 .... **89**
Count Primary School
BURH RH15 .... **16**
County First School
SALV BN13 .... **226**
County Middle School
STHW BN42 .... **23**
County Oak Retail Park
CRAWW RH11 .... **3**
County Primary School
BRI BN1 .... **23**
Court Meadow School
RHWH RH17 .... **11**
The Courtyard Surgery
HORS RH12 .... **4**
Cowdray Park Golf Club
MIDH GU29 .... **12**
The Craftsman Gallery
HPPT/KEY BN6 .... **16**
Craftwork Gallery
CCH PO19 .... **6**
Crawley College
CRAWE RH10 .... **3**
Crawley College
HORS RH12 .... **4**
Crawley College Annexe
CRAWW RH11 .... **3**
Crawley Down C of E Infant School
CRAWE RH10 .... **3**
Crawley Down C of E School
CRAWE RH10 .... **3**
Crawley Down Health Centre
CRAWE RH10 .... **3**
Crawley Health Clinic
CRAWE RH10 .... **3**
Crawley Hospital
CRAWW RH11 .... **3**
The Crawley Lawn Tennis Club
CRAWE RH10 .... **3**
Crawley Leisure Centre
CRAWE RH10 .... **3**
Crawley Rugby Club
CRAWW RH11 .... **3**
Crawley Town Football Club
CRAWW RH11 .... **5**
The Croft Surgery
SELS PO20 .... **22**
Crosspost Industrial Estate
RHWH RH17 .... **13**
Crown Court
HOVE BN3 .... **23**
Crow Place Doctors Surgery
CRAWW RH11 .... **3**
Cuckfield Medical Practice
RHWH RH17 .... **11**
Cumnor House School
RHWH RH17 .... **8**
The Cyril Richings Business
  Centre 202-210
SHOR BN43 .... **23**
Davigdor County Infants School
HOVE BN3 .... **23**
Davison C of E Secondary
  School for Girls
WTHG BN11 .... **8**
Deerswood School
CRAWW RH11 .... **3**
Dell Quay Sailing Club
SELS PO20 .... **24**
Desmond Anderson School
CRAWE RH10 .... **5**
Ditcham Park Sch
EPSF GU31 .... **14**
Ditchling Gallery
HPPT/KEY BN6 .... **16**

...ling Health Centre
PPT/KEY BN6 .... **165** K8

...ling Museum
PPT/KEY BN6 .... **165** J8

...ling Primary School
PPT/KEY BN6 .... **165** K8

...n Place (School)
HWH RH17 .... **82** A3

...House Museum
ETW GU28 .... **125** K4

...nin Leisure Centre
WH RH16 .... **111** K5

...et House School
UL/STOR RH20 .... **177** H4

...nlands School
PPT/KEY BN6 .... **165** F8

...nlands School
ETW GU28 .... **149** K5

...nsbrook CP School
V/BW BN14 .... **9** E1

...nsbrook Middle School
V/BW BN14 .... **9** E1

...nsbrook Trading Estate
V/BW BN14 .... **230** E5

...ns County First School
RI BN1 .... **10** C2

...ns Junior School
2I BN1 .... **10** C1

...ss Park School
SD BN41 .... **235** F1

...rview County Primary School
DOS PO22 .... **13** E2

...*TT* BN2 .... **11** D5

...ton C of E First School
TW GU28 .... **151** F4

...urst School
F GU32 .... **88** C5

...ings Squash Club
RIN RH19 .... **36** C5

...ngton First & Middle School
LV BN13 .... **229** J4

...ngton Health Centre
LV BN13 .... **229** H5

...ngton High School
LV BN13 .... **229** J6

...Estate
RH14 .... **102** B4

...ourne Primary School
DH GU29 .... **94** D8

...ourt
RIN RH19 .... **36** D1

...rgate C of E Primary School
LS PO20 .... **222** C4

...ate Gallery
H PO19 .... **6** C3

...rinstead Health Clinic
RIN RH19 .... **36** C1

...rinstead Sports Club
RIN RH19 .... **36** A6

...ants District Council
F GU32 .... **88** B8

...ead Industrial Estate
CH PO18 .... **194** E4

...reston CP School
G/EP BN16 .... **251** J1

...reet Medical Centre
PTN BN17 .... **249** K2

...ussex County Council
VE BN3 .... **211** J8

...ittering County
...mary School
S PO20 .... **257** J4

...rd Bryant County
...mary School
GR PO21 .... **12** C4

...ham Park Golf Club
AWE RH10 .... **20** B7

...ove County First School
HG BN11 .... **229** K8

...ove County Infants School
PTN BN17 .... **250** A1

...ove CP School
IT BN2 .... **11** E3

...orth Museum
RTH PO10 .... **214** D2

...orth Primary School
RTH PO10 .... **214** C2

...orth Surgery
RTH PO10 .... **214** D3

...h Gallery
Y PO9 .... **190** A1

...n Martyrs RC School
PR BN12 .... **229** H6

Escotts County Primary School
FERR RH19 .... **36** E2

Evolution Health Centre
BRI BN1 .... **10** A4

Fairfield Medical Centre
PETW GU28 .... **125** K4

Fairlight County Primary School
ROTT BN2 .... **11** E2

Far Horizons Gallery
PSF GU32 .... **88** D8

Faringdon Gallery
ARUN BN18 .... **201** H8

Farlington School
HORS RH12 .... **50** B5

Faygate Business Centre
HORS RH12 .... **53** H2

Felbridge CP School
EGRIN RH19................................. **21** H7

Felpham Community College
MIDOS PO22 .... **13** E3

Felpham & Middleton Health
Centre
MIDOS PO22 .... **247** H6

Felpham Sailing Club
MIDOS PO22 .... **13** F5

Ferring C of E Primary School
FERR BN12 .... **252** D1

Ferring Football Club
FERR BN12 .... **252** C1

Fireside Gallery
BOGR PO21 .... **244** E8

Firsland Park Estate
HFD BN5 .... **162** D2

Fishbourne C of E Primary School
CCH PO19 .... **218** B4

Fishersgate First School
PTSD BN41 .... **234** E4

Fittleworth C of E First School
PUL/STOR RH20 .... **127** G8

Flansham Business Centre
MIDOS PO22 .... **247** F4

Fletching C of E School
UCK TN22.................................. **115** K8

Flora Mcdonald County
Junior School
LHPTN BN17 .... **249** J1

The Fold School
HOVE BN3 .... **235** H4

Fonthill Lodge School
EGRIN RH19................................. **36** A5

Fontwell Medical Centre
ARUN BN18 .... **198** E8

Fontwell Park Race Course
ARUN BN18 .... **198** D8

Fordwater School
CCH PO19 .... **219** G2

Forest Community School
SWTR RH13 .... **5** E6

Forest Row Business Park
FROW RH18................................. **37** K8

Forest Row C of E Infant School
FROW RH18................................. **61** K1

Forge Wood Industrial Estate
CRAWE RH10 .... **32** B1

Forum House Business Centre
CCH PO19 .... **6** C3

Fowlers Business Centre
SWTR RH13 .... **135** G2

Foxbridge Golf Club
BIL RH14 .... **71** J2

The Framing Studio & Gallery
LAN/SOMP BN15 .... **232** A6

Freshbrook County First School
LAN/SOMP BN15 .... **232** A5

Freshbrook School
LAN/SOMP BN15 .... **232** A5

Friends of Arundel Castle
Cricket Club
ARUN BN18 .... **201** G7

Funtington County Primary
School
RCCH PO18 .... **193** F8

Furnace Green Surgery
CRAWE RH10 .... **3** E5

Gallery
ROTT BN2 .... **11** E6

The Gallery
BRI BN1 .... **10** A5

The Gallery
HOVE BN3 .... **236** A4

The Gallery
PETW GU28 .... **125** K3

The Gallery
WTHG BN11............................... **8** B5

Gattons Cp School
BURH RH15 .... **138** E8

Gatwick Medical Centre
HORL RH6 .... **18** B4

Gatwick Park Hospital
HORL RH6 .... **17** J4

Gemini Business Centre
HOVE BN3 .... **236** A3

Genesis Business Centre
SWTR RH13 .... **5** E4

George & Dragon Surgery
EMRTH PO10 .... **191** F8

George House Gallery
PETW GU28 .... **125** K3

George Pringle School
FERR BN12 .... **229** H6

Georgian Gardens CP School
ANG/EP BN16 .... **251** G1

Gerald Daniel Sailing Club
RCCH PO18 .... **240** C1

Gerrard House Business Centre
ANG/EP BN16 .... **251** H1

Gerston Business Park
PUL/STOR RH20 .... **180** A3

Ghyll House Farm Estate
SWTR RH13 .... **105** K2

Gillets Surgery
RHWH RH17 .... **83** G2

Glade County Infant School
BOGR PO21 .... **245** J6

Glebe CP School
STHW BN42 .... **234** B4

The Glebe Surgery
PUL/STOR RH20 .... **180** A2

Glenwood School
EMRTH PO10 .... **214** C2

Goldstone Junior School
HOVE BN3 .... **235** J2

Golf Club Bungalow
MIDH GU29 .... **122** D2

The Good Start School
POY/PYE BN45 .... **187** G6

Goodwood Golf Club
RCCH PO18 .... **196** A4

Goring C of E School
FERR BN12 .... **253** G1

Goring Cricket Club
FERR BN12 .... **252** E1

Gossops Green Clinic
CRAWW RH11 .... **30** D7

Gossops Green First &
Middle School
CRAWW RH11 .... **30** E6

Graham Whitehouse Practice
BURH RH15 .... **138** E7

The Grange Leisure Centre
MIDH GU29 .... **122** A4

Graylingwell Hospital
CCH PO19 .... **219** H2

Grayswood C of E School
HASM GU27 .... **41** H1

Great Ballard School
RCCH PO18 .... **198** B4

Great Walstead School
HWH RH16................................. **113** H5

Greenfield School
FROW RH18................................. **61** G2

Greenway School
HORS RH12 .... **4** A4

Grove House Surgery
BOGR PO21 .... **261** K1

Halsford Park Primary School
EGRIN RH19................................. **35** K1

Ham Bridge Trading Estate
FIN/BW BN14 .... **231** G7

Hambrook Business Centre
RCCH PO18 .... **192** B7

Ham Business Centre
SHOR BN43 .... **233** J4

Hamilton Lodge School
ROTT BN2 .... **11** F5

Ham Manor Golf Club
ANG/EP BN16 .... **227** F7

Ham Manor Golf Course
ANG/EP BN16 .... **226** E6

Handcross Park School
RHWH RH17 .... **81** H1

Handcross Primary School
RHWH RH17 .... **81** G2

Hangleton County Junior &
Infant School
HOVE BN3 .... **235** J1

Hapstead Business Centre
RHWH RH17 .... **84** D3

...s Farm Estate
VTR RH13 .... **76** A1
...ey Industrial Estate
D BN5 .... **185** H5
...son Gallery
TW GU28 .... **125** J3
...enbower First School
RAWE RH10 .... **32** C7
...Manhood Community
...llege
LS PO20 .... **264** E3
...ings Heath Golf Club
VTR RH13 .... **79** G4
...r Farm Business Centre
Y/PYE BN45 .... **187** H6
...r Field CP School
RH RH15 .... **139** J7
...r House Hospital
VE BN3 .... **236** A4
...r Sports Ground Pavilion
/BW BN11 .... **9** D1
...C of E Primary School
CH PO19 .... **219** K2
...swell Industrial Estate
H PO19 .... **219** H2
...et Place
RH RH15 .... **165** G1
...orough Business Centre
V/SOMP BN15 .... **231** K7
...ins Museum
OR BN43 .... **233** G5
...ott Goodwood Park Hotel &
...untry Club
CH PO18 .... **196** C6
...ott Goodwood Park Hotel &
...untry Club
CH PO18 .... **196** B5
...ood Surgery
GR PO21 .... **12** A4
...eadows Surgery
RH RH15 .... **138** D7
...s School
RIN RH19 .... **36** C4
...erry County Primary School
LS PO20 .... **264** E4
...el Ayres County Junior
...hool
GR PO21 .... **245** J6
...el Hall School
OW RH18 .... **61** H2
...e Street Primary School
BN1 .... **10** B5
...eton Business Park
OOS PO22 .... **247** J5
...eton Medical Centre
OOS PO22 .... **247** J6
...rst C of E Primary School
H GU29 .... **122** A4
...rst Gallery
H GU29 .... **122** B4
...rst Grammar School
H GU29 .... **122** A3
...rst Intermediate School
H GU29 .... **122** C1
...ak Clinic
D BN41 .... **210** D8
...ak Junior School
D BN41 .... **210** D8
... School
TR RH13 .... **5** E5
...een Industrial Estate
H RH16 .... **112** A5
...ew Hospital
VE BN3 .... **235** J2
...Mount School
WE RH10 .... **32** C3
...ield Surgery
RIN RH19 .... **36** C1
...rn Mould Business Centre
PTN BN17 .... **249** H1
...rn Moulds Business Centre
HG BN15 .... **231** J7
...on House School
*GU32 .... **88** C8
...y Street Health Centre
TT BN2 .... **11** D4
...en School
VE BN3 .... **236** D2
...am House School
TR RH13 .... **75** J7
...im
GR PO21 .... **12** C6
...im
OR BN43 .... **233** F4

The Museum
STEY/UB BN44 .... **183** K8
Natural Health Centre
CCH PO19 .... **6** B4
Newdigate School
RDKG RH5 .... **14** D2
Newhouse Farm Business Centre
HORS RH12 .... **52** E4
Newick House Special School
BURH RH15 .... **165** J2
Newlands Health Clinic
HWH RH16 .... **112** A7
New Life School
EGRIN RH19 .... **36** B1
Newmans Loner School
HOVE BN3 .... **236** D3
New Pond Row Surgery
LAN/SOMP BN15 .... **232** A6
Newtown Surgery
LIPH GU30 .... **64** B1
New Venture Theatre
BRI BN1 .... **10** A5
The Nicholas Rowe Practice
RHWH RH17 .... **110** E5
Norfolk Square Surgery
BOGR PO21 .... **12** A6
Northbourne Medical Centre
SHOR BN43 .... **233** J3
Northbrook College
FIN/BW BN14 .... **8** C1
Northbrook College
SALV BN13 .... **229** F7
Northbrook Trading Estate
FIN/BW BN14 .... **230** E5
Northchapel Primary School
PETW GU28 .... **68** E4
Northdale Vet Surgery
WTHG BN11 .... **8** C3
Northgate First & Middle School
CRAWE RH10 .... **3** D1
Northgate House School
CCH PO19 .... **6** B2
Northgate Surgery
CRAWE RH10 .... **3** D1
North Heath CP School
HORS RH12 .... **4** C2
Northlands Business Park
HORS RH12 .... **26** C7
Northlands Wood CP School
HWH RH16 .... **112** D7
Northlands Wood Surgery
HWH RH16 .... **112** D7
North Mundham County
Primary School
SELS PO20 .... **243** K1
Northolmes County Junior School
HORS RH12 .... **5** F2
Nuffield Hospital
SELS PO20 .... **220** B6
Nyewood C of E Junior &
Infant School
BOGR PO21 .... **245** J7
Oakendene Industrial Estate
SWTR RH13 .... **135** K2
Oakley Surgery
SWTR RH13 .... **134** C8
Oakmeads Community School
BURH RH15 .... **165** G1
The Oaks First & Middle School
CRAWE RH10 .... **3** E6
Oakwood Industrial Park
CRAWE RH10 .... **32** A2
Oakwood Preparatory School
RCCH PO18 .... **217** K1
Oathall Community College
HWH RH16 .... **112** B5
Odeon Cinema
BRI BN1 .... **10** B5
Old Barn Theatre
CRAWW RH11 .... **30** D3
Old Club House
CRAWE RH10 .... **34** B7
Old Club House
RHWH RH17 .... **81** G2
Old Darlington Mushroom Farm
Industrial Estate
ANG/EP BN16 .... **227** J6
The Old Town Hall Gallery
MIDH GU29 .... **122** B4
The Open University
EGRIN RH19 .... **36** C2
Orchards Middle School
FERR BN12 .... **229** H7

Our Lady of Sion Junior School
WTHG BN11 .... **9** D4
Our Lady of Sion School
WTHG BN11 .... **8** C4
Pagham Cricket Club
BOGR PO21 .... **261** H2
Pagham Football Club
BOGR PO21 .... **261** H2
Pagham Yacht Club
BOGR PO21 .... **261** H4
Parham Historic House
PUL/STOR RH20 .... **179** F2
Park Ho (Hotel)
MIDH GU29 .... **147** G1
Parkland Business Centre
LAN/SOMP BN15 .... **231** K7
Parklands County Primary
School
CCH PO19 .... **6** A2
Parklands Surgery
CCH PO19 .... **6** A3
Park Surgery
HORS RH12 .... **4** B5
The Park Surgery
LHPTN BN17 .... **250** B2
Park View Leisure Centre
HOVE BN3 .... **235** J4
Patcham CP School
BRI BN1 .... **213** F5
Patcham First School
BRI BN1 .... **212** E5
Patcham High School
BRI BN1 .... **213** F5
Patcham House School
BRI BN1 .... **212** E5
Paul Cooper Galleries
ANG/EP BN16 .... **250** E2
The Pavilion Clinic
BRI BN1 .... **10** A5
Pavilion Theatre
WTHG BN11 .... **9** E5
Paxton Business Centre
HOVE BN3 .... **235** H3
Peacock Industrial Estate
HOVE BN3 .... **236** D4
Pennthorpe School
HORS RH12 .... **48** A4
Peregrine Gallery
FERR BN12 .... **252** C3
Peter Gladwin School
PTSD BN41 .... **234** E1
Petersfield Business Park
PSF GU32 .... **88** B8
Petersfield Community Hospital
PSF GU32 .... **88** C8
Petersfield County Infant School
EPSF GU31 .... **88** D8
Petersfield Golf Club
PSF GU32 .... **89** G3
Petersfield Rugby Football Club
EPSF GU31 .... **89** H7
Petersfield School
PSF GU32 .... **116** C1
Petersfield Swimming Pool
EPSF GU31 .... **88** D8
Petersfield Town Council
EPSF GU31 .... **88** E8
Petersfield Town Football
Club Ltd
EPSF GU31 .... **88** E7
Petworth C of E Primary School
PETW GU28 .... **125** K4
Petworth Cottage Museum
PETW GU28 .... **125** K3
Petworth House
PETW GU28 .... **125** K3
Phillips Business Centre
CCH PO19 .... **218** D6
Philpots Manor School
EGRIN RH19 .... **58** E6
Pier
BOGR PO21 .... **12** B6
Plaistow Primary School
BIL RH14 .... **45** F8
Platform Theatre
RHWH RH17 .... **110** A5
Portfield Football Club
CCH PO19 .... **7** E2
Portland Business Park
HOVE BN3 .... **235** H4
Portland Industrial Estate
HOVE BN3 .... **235** J3
Portland Road Industrial Estate
HOVE BN3 .... **235** H3

Portland Surgery
HOVE BN3 .... **235** K4

Portslade Community College
STHW BN41 .... **234** D1

Portslade Health Centre
PTSD BN41 .... **235** F4

Pound Hill First & Middle School
CRAWE RH10 .... **32** C4

Pound Hill Surgery
CRAWE RH10 .... **32** C4

Prebendal School
CCH PO19 .... **6** B3

Preston Furniture Gallery
BRI BN1 .... **237** F1

Preston Park Clinic
BRI BN1 .... **10** C1

Preston Park Surgery
BRI BN1 .... **10** C2

Priest House
EGRIN RH19 .... **59** G5

Primary School
STEY/UB BN44 .... **208** C1

Prince Regent Swimming Complex
BRI BN1 .... **10** C5

The Princes Royal Hospital
HWH RH16 .... **140** B1

Queen Alexandra Hospital Home
WTHG BN11 .... **8** B4

Queen Elizabeth Ii Silver Jubilee School
SWTR RH13 .... **5** E6

Queensdown School
BRI BN1 .... **213** J8

Queens Park County Primary School
ROTT BN2 .... **11** E5

Queen Victoria Hospital N H S Trust
EGRIN RH19 .... **22** D8

Quell Farm Industrial Estate
PUL/STOR RH20 .... **154** A7

Rake C of E Controlled First School
LISS GU33 .... **63** F6

Rapha House Surgery
RHWH RH17 .... **83** F2

Regent Business Centre
BURH RH15 .... **164** E1

Richards Osteopathic Clinic & Natural Health Centre
CRAWE RH10 .... **3** D3

Rikkyo Sch
BIL RH14 .... **47** F3

Riverbank Business Centre
SHOR BN43 .... **233** F4

River Gallery
ARUN BN18 .... **225** H1

Riverside Business Centre
SHOR BN43 .... **233** H5

Riverside Gallery
PETW GU28 .... **125** K3

Riverside Industrial Estate
LHPTN BN17 .... **249** H2

Rock & Bowl Bowling Alley
EGRIN RH19 .... **36** C2

Roffey Social & Sports Club
HORS RH12 .... **5** F2

Rogate C of E Controlled School
EPSF GU31 .... **91** F7

Rose Green County Infant School
BOGR PO21 .... **261** K1

Rose Green County Junior School
BOGR PO21 .... **244** E8

The Rotherfield Sports Ground
MIDH GU29 .... **122** B2

Rowfant Business Centre
CRAWE RH10 .... **34** A5

Royal Alexandra Hospital
BRI BN1 .... **10** B4

Royal George Clinic
BURH RH15 .... **138** E8

The Royal School
HASM GU27 .... **40** C1

Royal & Sunalliance Sports Club
HORS RH12 .... **5** D1

Royal Sussex County Hospital NHS Trust
ROTT BN2 .... **11** F6

Rudford Industrial Estate
ARUN BN18 .... **248** E2

Rudgwick Medical Centre
HORS RH12 .... **48** A4

Rudgwick School
HORS RH12 .... **48** B4

Rugby Club
EGRIN RH19 .... **36** A6

Rugby Football Club
RHWH RH17 .... **110** D3

Rumboldswyke C of E Infant School
CCH PO19 .... **7** E4

Rusper School
HORS RH12 .... **28** E4

Rustington Primary School
ANG/EP BN16 .... **250** D1

Rustington Retail Park
ANG/EP BN16 .... **227** F8

The Rydon Community School
PUL/STOR RH20 .... **180** D1

Sackville Road First School
FIN/BW BN14 .... **9** E2

Sackville School
EGRIN RH19 .... **36** E2

St Andrews C of E (aided) School
SWTR RH13 .... **106** B2

St Andrews C of E High School for Boys
FIN/BW BN14 .... **9** E2

St Andrews C of E School
HOVE BN3 .... **236** B5

St Andrews Primary School
CRAWE RH10 .... **3** F5

St Anthonys School
CCH PO19 .... **6** B1

St Bartholomews C of E Primary School
BRI BN1 .... **10** C3

St Bartholomews C of E School
HASM GU27 .... **40** E3

St Bartholomews Middle School
HASM GU27 .... **40** E4

St Bernadettes First Middle Va School
BRI BN1 .... **236** E1

St Catherines RC Primary School
LHPTN BN17 .... **249** K1

St Christophers School
HOVE BN3 .... **236** A4

St Cuthmans School
MIDH GU29 .... **93** G5

St Dominics Gallery
HPPT/KEY BN6 .... **165** J8

St Francis Middle School
CRAWE RH10 .... **3** D4

St James C of E Primary School
EMRTH PO10 .... **214** D1

St James C of E School
PUL/STOR RH20 .... **153** J5

St James County Primary School
CCH PO19 .... **7** E2

St James Industrial Estate
CCH PO19 .... **7** E2

St John Baptist Primary School
FIN/BW BN14 .... **205** H5

St Johns RC Primary School
HORS RH12 .... **77** G1

St Johns Residential School
ROTT BN2 .... **11** F5

St John the Baptist RC Primary School
ROTT BN2 .... **11** F5

St Josephs R C Primary School
HWH RH16 .... **112** A7

St Lawrence Surgery
FIN/BW BN14 .... **8** A2

St Leonards County Infants School
SWTR RH13 .... **4** C5

St Lukes Junior & Infant School
ROTT BN2 .... **11** E4

St Lukes Swimming Pool
ROTT BN2 .... **11** E4

St Margarets C of E Primary School
CRAWW RH11 .... **2** A2

St Margarets C of E School
ANG/EP BN16 .... **227** H4

St Marks School
RHWH RH17 .... **81** K6

St Martins C of E Primary School
ROTT BN2 .... **11** E2

St Mary Magdalene School
BRI BN1 .... **10** A5

St Marys C of E (aided) Primary School
PUL/STOR RH20 .... **128** E8

St Marys C of E First School
PUL/STOR RH20 .... **181** H5

St Marys C of E Primary School
LHPTN BN17 .... **248** E3

St Marys C of E School
EGRIN RH19 .... **3**

St Marys Hall School for Girls
ROTT BN2 .... **1**

St Marys Hospital
CCH PO19 ....

St Marys Primary School
HORS RH12 ....

St Marys RC Primary School
BOGR PO21 .... **1**

St Marys RC Primary School
WTHG BN11 ....

St Marys RC School
PTSD BN41 .... **23**

St Nicholas & St. Mary School
SHOR BN43 .... **23**

St Pauls C of E School
BRI BN1 .... **1**

St Pauls RC Comprehensive School
HWH RH16 .... **11**

St Peters C of E Primary School
SWTR RH13 .... **13**

St Peters C of E School
RHWH RH17 .... **8**

St Peters County Infant School
PTSD BN41 .... **23**

St Peters RC School
EGRIN RH19 .... **3**

St Peters R C School
SHOR BN43 .... **23**

The St Philip Howard High School
MIDOS PO22 .... **22**

St Philips RC Primary School
ARUN BN18 .... **20**

St Richards Hospital
CCH PO19 ....

St Richards RC Primary School
CCH PO19 ....

St Robert Southwell RC First School
HORS RH12 ....

St Wilfrids C of E School
HWH RH16 .... **11**

St Wilfrids R C Primary School
ANG/EP BN16 .... **22**

St Wilfrids RC School
BURH RH15 .... **16**

St Wilfrids RC School
CRAWW RH11 ....

Sandhurst School
WTHG BN11 ....

The Scott Gallery
HORL RH6 ....

Seaford College
PETW GU28 .... **15**

Seal County Primary School
SELS PO20 .... **20**

Sea Life Centre
ROTT BN2 ....

Selsey Business Centre
SELS PO20 .... **20**

Selsey Country Club Ltd
SELS PO20 .... **20**

Selsey Cricket Club
SELS PO20 .... **20**

Selsey Golf Club
SELS PO20 .... **20**

Selsey Health Centre
SELS PO20 .... **20**

Selsey Indoor Market
SELS PO20 .... **20**

The Seven Dials Medical Centre
BRI BN1 ....

Seymour First & Middle School
CRAWW RH11 ....

Sheddindean Business Centre
BURH RH15 .... **1**

Sheddingdean First School
BURH RH15 .... **13**

Sheet CP School
PSF GU32 ....

Sheila Cashin Gallery
BRI BN1 ....

Shelley Surgery
WTHG BN11 ....

Shelly Primary School
HORS RH12 ....

The Sherburne Hospital
CCH PO19 .... **2**

Shillinglee Park Golf Club
MFD/CHID GU8 ....

The Ship House Surgery
LIPH GU30 .... **3**

hip Street Surgery
RIN RH19 .... 36 C3
whyke Industrial Centre
LS PO20 .... 7 F2
ham Beach County First
ool
OR BN43 .... 233 J5
ham College
OR BN43 .... 234 B4
ham County First School
OR BN43 .... 233 G3
ham Football Club
D BN41 .... 235 F4
ham Health Centre
OR BN43 .... 233 G4
ermill County Middle School
SM GU27 .... 40 B4
nam County Primary School
S PO20 .... 259 J3
ham Football Club
S PO20 .... 260 A3
ton C of E Primary School
CH PO18 .... 171 K4
n C of E School
JN BN18 .... 199 H7
n College
JN BN18 .... 199 F6
d C of E Primary School
TR RH13 .... 49 H7
d Park Golf & Country Club
TR RH13 .... 49 F8
hill Business Centre
AWE RH10 .... 20 C7
hill County Junior School
VE BN3 .... 236 D5
rset Hospital
W GU28 .... 125 K2
Bersted C of E
nary School
OOS PO22 .... 12 B3
bourne County Junior
nfant School
RTH PO10 .... 215 J3
bourne Surgery
RTH PO10 .... 215 J3
Downs Health Clinic
BN1 .... 10 B4
ields Industrial Estate
CH PO18 .... 217 F5
gate First School
AWE RH10 .... 2 C6
gate Middle School
AWE RH10 .... 2 C5
gate School
AWW RH11 .... 2 B5
water Business Park
TR RH13 .... 105 F2
water County Junior &
nt School
TR RH13 .... 105 F1
way County Junior School
PT/KEY BN6 .... 138 D8
wick Business Centre
D BN41 .... 234 C5
wick Manor Hall County
t School
W BN42 .... 234 D4
field Industrial Estate
VH RH17 .... 140 B6
herham Business Centre
RS RH12 .... 28 A4
rd Junior School
BN1 .... 10 B2
ead House
PO9 .... 191 G2
oad Trading Estate
TR RH13 .... 134 C8
m CP School
H GU29 .... 121 F2
School
GU32 .... 88 C4
ng Athletic Club
Y/UB BN44 .... 183 J8
ng Grammar School
Y/UB BN44 .... 183 K8
ng Health Centre
Y/UB BN44 .... 183 K8
ng St Andrews C of E
nary School
Y/UB BN44 .... 183 J7
ng Sports Centre
Y/UB BN44 .... 183 J7
ng Town Football Club
Y/UB BN44 .... 183 K7

Stonelands School of Ballet &
Theatre
HOVE BN3 .... 236 B5
Storrington Cp School
PUL/STOR RH20 .... 180 A1
Storrington Gallery
PUL/STOR RH20 .... 180 B2
Storrington Lawn Tennis Club
PUL/STOR RH20 .... 180 A2
The Strand Surgery
FERR BN12 .... 229 H7
Summerlea County Primary
School
ANG/EP BN16 .... 226 D8
Sussex Clinic Ltd
WTHG BN11 .... 8 C4
Sussex County Cricket Club
HOVE BN3 .... 236 C4
Sussex Eye Hospital
ROTT BN2 .... 11 F6
Sussex House Industrial Estate
HOVE BN3 .... 235 K3
Sussex Manor Business Park
CRAWE RH10 .... 32 A1
Sussex Nuffield Hospital
HOVE BN3 .... 235 K5
The Sussex Toy & Model Museum
BRI BN1 .... 10 C4
Swandean Hospital
SALV BN13 .... 229 H3
Swan Street Surgery
PSF GU32 .... 88 C8
Swedish School
CRAWE RH10 .... 3 E5
Sydney West Sports Centre
BURH RH15 .... 139 G7
Synogogue
BRI BN1 .... 10 B6
Tadds Cottage Gallery
SELS PO20 .... 264 E4
Tanbridge House School
HORS RH12 .... 4 A6
Tanbridge Retail Park
HORS RH12 .... 4 A6
Tangmere County Primary School
SELS PO20 .... 221 F1
Tangmere Military Aviation
Museum Trust Co
SELS PO20 .... 221 F2
Tavistock & Summerhill School
HWH RH16 .... 112 B4
Templars County Infants School
LAN/SOMP BN15 .... 231 H5
Thakeham C P School
PUL/STOR RH20 .... 157 F4
Thomas A Becket First School
SALV BN13 .... 8 A1
Thomas A Becket Middle School
FIN/BW BN14 .... 8 B1
Thomas Bennett
Community College
CRAWW RH11 .... 2 C6
Thornberry Middle School
LAN/SOMP BN15 .... 232 B6
Thorney County Primary School
EMRTH PO10 .... 214 E8
Three Bridge County
Middle School
CRAWE RH10 .... 3 E3
Three Bridges Cricket Club
CRAWE RH10 .... 3 F3
Three Bridges First School
CRAWE RH10 .... 3 F2
Three Bridges Football Club
CRAWE RH10 .... 3 F3
Ticehurst Clinic
HOVE BN3 .... 236 A5
Tilgate Forest Business Centre
CRAWW RH11 .... 55 H2
Tilgate Forest Golf Club
CRAWE RH10 .... 56 A1
Tobias School of Art
EGRIN RH19 .... 36 C5
Touch for Health Centre
BOGR PO21 .... 12 A5
Trafalgar County Infant School
HORS RH12 .... 4 A3
Tristar Business Centre
SWTR RH13 .... 160 C1
Turners Hill C of E School
CRAWE RH10 .... 34 C8
Turnpike Gallery
EPSF GU31 .... 88 D8

Unicorn Trading Estate
HASM GU27 .... 40 D5
University of Brighton
ROTT BN2 .... 237 J1
Uplands School
BRI BN1 .... 237 J1
Upper Beeding Surgery
STEY/UB BN44 .... 208 C1
Vale CP School
SALV BN13 .... 229 K1
Varndean College
BRI BN1 .... 213 F8
Varndean High School
BRI BN1 .... 213 G8
Vicarage Lane Clinic
HASM GU27 .... 40 B5
Victoria Cottage Hospital
EMRTH PO10 .... 214 D3
Victoria Road Surgery
WTHG BN11 .... 8 C3
Vinnetrow Farm Business Centre
SELS PO20 .... 220 A8
Virgin Multiplex Cinema
CRAWW RH11 .... 2 C2
Walberton & Binstead C of E
Primary
ARUN BN18 .... 223 J2
Warden Park School
RHWH RH17 .... 111 G6
Warnham C of E School
HORS RH12 .... 51 F3
Warnham Court School
HORS RH12 .... 51 F5
Warninglid Primary School
RHWH RH17 .... 108 E1
Waterfield School
CRAWW RH11 .... 30 C7
Waterhall Golf Course
BRI BN1 .... 212 B4
Watershed Theatre
BOGR PO21 .... 12 C6
Waytefield Clinic
BRI BN1 .... 236 E1
Weald & Downland Open Air
Museum
RCCH PO18 .... 171 K5
Weald School
BIL RH14 .... 102 A4
Welfare Clinic
HOVE BN3 .... 235 J1
Westbourne County Primary
School
EMRTH PO10 .... 191 F7
Westbourne House School
SELS PO20 .... 220 B4
Westbourne Surgery
EMRTH PO10 .... 191 F8
West Chiltington Golf Club
PUL/STOR RH20 .... 156 B1
West Chiltington School
PUL/STOR RH20 .... 156 C2
West Dean C of E Primary School
RCCH PO18 .... 170 E6
West Dean College
RCCH PO18 .... 171 G5
Westdene Primary School
BRI BN1 .... 212 C6
Westergate Community College
SELS PO20 .... 222 C4
Westgate Leisure Centre
CCH PO19 .... 6 B3
Westgate Surgery
CCH PO19 .... 6 B3
West Green County First School
CRAWW RH11 .... 2 B2
West Hoathly School
EGRIN RH19 .... 59 G5
Westholme Clinic Ltd
FERR BN12 .... 253 H1
West Hove Middle School
HOVE BN3 .... 235 J4
West Lavington C of E School
MIDH GU29 .... 122 C6
West Park C of E Controlled
First & Middle School
FERR BN12 .... 253 H1
West Pier (Under Repair)
BRI BN1 .... 10 A6
West Sands Leisure Centre
SELS PO20 .... 264 C4
West Sussex Area Health Authority
WTHG BN11 .... 9 F4
West Sussex County Council
ANG/EP BN16 .... 251 F1

e 2

n Cl
rs
r Rw
Cl
ights

e 3

ey Ms
old Rd
etye Rd
sh Rd
am Cl
eld Cl
 Cl
eech

e 10

d Rd
d Sq
on St
estern St
K Buildings
K Ms
sbury Ms
d Pl
d Rd
St
n St
n Ter

ham St
 Rd
ard St

Zion Pl
 Rd
y St
 St
us St
loucester Rd

n Pl
St
rough Ms
rough St
 St
d St
 Rw
 Pl
 Rd
aret's Pl

orth St
r St

t St
ury Rd
ury St
lls Rw
gland St
 Ct
 Pl
s Pl

omews
e
n Pl
 St

 St
arade Ms

ood St
St
ugh Pl
 House La

l
t
ne
 Rw
l
Buildings
Pde
St
lbert St
a Pl
s St
 St
e's St
dns
a
ne St
t
St

11

en Rd
an Rd
gh Rd
ill Rd
ill St
Magdalene St

Cl

F6
1 Belgrave Pl
2 Chapel Ter
3 Chesham Pl
4 Chichester Pl
5 Clarendon Ter
6 Eastern Ter
7 Eastern Terrace Ms
8 Kemp Town Pl
9 Millfield Cottages
10 Percival Ter
11 St Mary's Sq
12 Seymour Sq
13 Seymour St
14 Sudeley Ter
15 Upper Sudeley St

Page 30

B7
1 Coniston Cl
2 Kittiwake Cl
3 Langdale Rd
4 Sandpiper Cl
5 Woodcroft Rd

C6
1 Arnfield Cl
2 Beaumont Cl
3 Behenna Cl
4 Bitmead Cl
5 Compassion Cl
6 Dewar Cl
7 Dobbins Pl
8 Excalibur Cl
9 Garton Cl
10 Gorling Cl
11 Grier Cl
12 Strickland Cl
13 Talman Cl
14 Tunnmeade
15 Weaver Cl

C7
1 Comper Cl
2 Harmony Cl
3 Hyperion Ct
4 Lutyens Cl
5 Neptune Cl
6 Peacemaker Cl
7 Samaritan Cl
8 Saturn Cl
9 Soane Cl

C8
1 Brettingham Cl
2 Ivory Wk
3 Milne Cl
4 Oberon Wy
5 Vanbrugh Cl

D8
1 Donnington Ct
2 Hassocks Cl
3 Madehurst Ct
4 Petworth Ct
5 Pyecombe Ct
6 Slaugham Ct
7 Telham Ct
8 Wisborough Ct
9 Wiston Ct

E6
1 Almond Cl
2 Dairyfields
3 Rickfield
4 Ryelands
5 Windyridge

Page 31

F3
1 Binstead Cl
2 Birdham Cl
3 Colgate Cl
4 Mole Cl

F2
1 Hawthorn Cl
2 Langley Pl
3 Martyrs Av

G6
1 Hill Pl

G8
1 Swaledale Cl

H2
1 Adelaide Cl
2 Auckland Cl
3 Brisbane Cl
4 Canberra Cl
5 Friends Cl
6 Old Martyrs
7 Penn Cl
8 St Edmund Cl
9 Stephen Cl

H5
1 High St
2 The Square

H7
1 Falmer Cl
2 Kithurst Cl
3 Oakhaven
4 Sullington Hl
5 Sunningdale Ct

H8
1 Caxton Cl
2 Loriners
3 Saddler Rw
4 Smith Cl
5 Wainwrights

J4
1 Covert Cl
2 Northgate Pl
3 The Parade
4 Vanners
5 Woolborough Cl

J6
1 Beechside
2 Friary Wy
3 Richmond Ct

K5
1 Haversham Cl
2 Ridgeside
3 Rowan Cl

Page 54

E1
1 Borage Cl
2 Burdock Cl
3 Celandine Cl
4 Charlock Cl
5 Crowberry Cl
6 Herm Cl
7 St Helier Cl
8 Sark Cl
9 Sundew Cl

Page 165

K8
1 Boddingtons La
2 The Dymock's

Page 226

C8
1 Bailey Pl
2 Buttermere Wy
3 Coniston Wy
4 Foxglove Wy
5 Grassmere Cl
6 Hollyhock Wy
7 Honeysuckle Cl
8 Jasmine Cl
9 Jib Cl
10 Kendal Cl
11 Pebble Wk
12 Rockall Cl
13 Solent Cl

D8
1 Blenheim Cl
2 Brookenbee Cl
3 Chatsworth Cl
4 Chatsworth Dr
5 Cowdray Cl
6 Hamilton Cl
7 Harebell Cl
8 Snowdrop Cl
9 Wilton Cl
10 Windsor Cl

Page 229

F6
1 Ashburnham Cl
2 Batemans Cl
3 Beckworth Cl
4 Deerswood Cl
5 Gatcombe Cl
6 Highclere Wy
7 Lilac Cl
8 Magnolia Cl
9 Orkney Ct
10 Rochester Cl
11 Scotney Cl
12 Shetland Ct
13 Summerdown Cl
14 Walnut Tree Wy
15 Winterbourne Cl

F8
1 Denton Cl
2 Galsworthy Cl
3 Southwater Cl
4 Steyning Cl

H4
1 Kennet Cl
2 Kingsbridge Ms
3 Medway Cl
4 Salvington Cl
5 Sandringham Ms
6 Treharne Cl

H8
1 Avondale Cl
2 Grenville Av

J2
1 Cherry Gdns

K4
1 Blackdown Rd
2 Plantation Cl
3 Roxburgh Cl

K6
1 Leeward Cl
2 Lindum Wy

K8
1 Canterbury Ct
2 Chancton View Rd

Page 230

D5
1 Bramley Cl

D8
1 Gordon Rd
2 Hertford Rd
3 Newland St
4 Railway Ap
5 Stanhope Rd
6 Wenban Rd

Page 236

D6
1 Brunswick Ms
2 Brunswick St West
3 Chapel Ms
4 Donkey Ms
5 Ivy Pl
6 Lansdowne Sq
7 Lower Market St
8 Upper Market St

E4
1 Belmont
2 Caburn Rd
3 Chanctonbury Rd
4 Wolstonbury Rd

E6
1 Bedford Pl
2 Bedford Sq
3 Hampton St
4 Little Western St
5 Norfolk Buildings
6 Norfolk Ms
7 Queensbury Ms
8 Sillwood St
9 Sillwood Rd
10 Spring St
11 Western St
12 Western Ter

Page 237

F5
1 Buckingham St
2 Clifton Rd
3 Guildford St
4 Kew St
5 Mount Zion Pl
6 North Rd
7 Railway St
8 Surrey St
9 Terminus St
10 Upper Gloucester Rd

F6
1 Cannon Pl
2 Crown St
3 Marlborough Ms
4 Marlborough St
5 Middle St
6 Portland St
7 Regent Rw
8 Russell Pl
9 Russell Rd
10 St Margaret's Pl
11 Ship St
12 Upper North St
13 Windsor St

G1
1 Hollingbury Ter

G4
1 Belmont
2 Kingsbury Rd
3 Kingsbury St
4 Marshalls Rw
5 New England St
6 Oxford Cl
7 Oxford Pl
8 Queen's Pl

G5
1 Blackman St
2 Cheltenham Pl
3 Gloucester Pl
4 Kensington Gdns
5 Kensington St
6 Pelham Sq
7 Robert St
8 St George's La
9 St George's Pl
10 Station St
11 Trafalgar St
12 Trafalgar Pl
13 Upper Gardner St
14 Vine St
15 Whitecross St

G6
1 Bartholomews
2 Bond St
3 Brighton Pl
4 Dorset St
5 East St
6 Gardner St
7 Grand Parade Ms
8 Jew St
9 King Pl
10 King St
11 Kingswood St
12 Market St
13 Marlborough Pl
14 Meeting House La
15 New Rd
16 Nile St
17 North Pl
18 North St
19 Old Steine
20 Orange Rw
21 Palace Pl
22 Pavilion Buildings
23 Pavilion Pde
24 Pavilion St
25 Prince Albert St
26 Prince's Pl
27 Prince's St
28 Regent St
29 St James's St
30 Steine Gdns
31 Steine La
32 Tichborne St
33 Union St
34 William St

H4
1 Hanover Crs
2 Newport St
3 St Martin's St

H6
1 Carlton Pl
2 Cavendish St
3 Dorset Pl
4 Egremont Pl
5 George St
6 Grosvenor St
7 Mighell St
8 Mount Pleasant
9 Nelson Rw
10 St James's Street Ms
11 St John's Cl
12 Tilbury Pl
13 Upper Park Pl
14 White St

J4
1 Bernard Pl
2 Coronation St
3 Cromwell St
4 Normanton St

J7
1 Bloomsbury Pl
2 Bloomsbury St
3 Marine Terrace Ms
4 Royal Crescent Ms
5 Telegraph St

K7
1 Belgrave Pl
2 Chapel Ter
3 Chesham Pl
4 Chichester Pl
5 Clarendon Ter
6 Eastern Ter
7 Eastern Terrace Ms
8 Kemp Town Pl
9 Millfield Cottages
10 Percival Ter
11 St Mary's Sq
12 Seymour St
13 Seymour St
14 Sudeley St
15 Upper Sudeley St

Notes

Notes

Notes

Notes

Notes

Notes